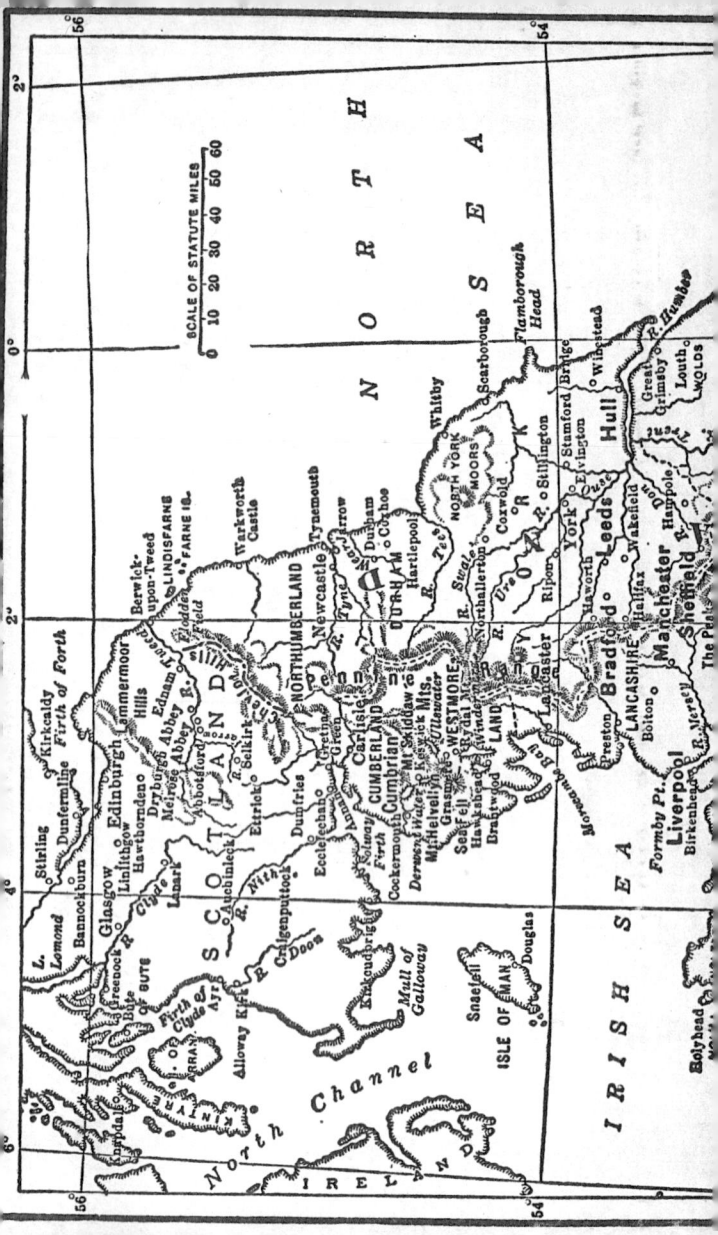

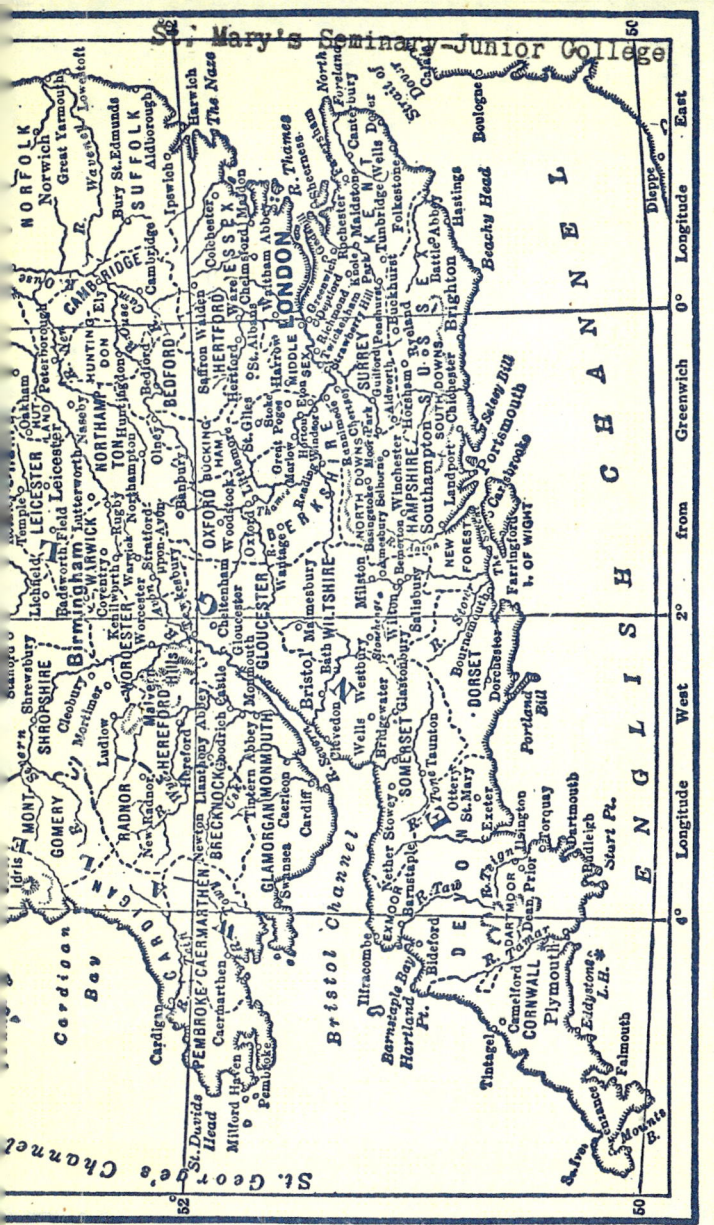

ENGLISH LITERATURE

THE ROMANTIC PERIOD

EDITED BY

ALBERT GRANBERRY REED

Professor of English and Comparative Literature
Louisiana State University

CHARLES SCRIBNER'S SONS

NEW YORK　　　CHICAGO　　　ATLANTA
SAN FRANCISCO　　　DALLAS

COPYRIGHT, 1929, BY
CHARLES SCRIBNER'S SONS

Printed in the United States of America

All rights reserved. No part of this book may be reproduced in any form without the permission of Charles Scribner's Sons

K

CONTENTS

	PAGE
INTRODUCTION—ALBERT GRANBERRY REED	xiii

WILLIAM COWPER (1731–1800)
Oh! for a Closer Walk with God (1772 1779)	1
God Moves in a Mysterious Way (1773 1779)	2
On the Loss of the Royal George (1782 1803)	3
The Task (1785), Book IV	4
On the Receipt of My Mother's Picture (1790 1798)	27
Sonnet to Mrs. Unwin (1793 1803)	31
The Castaway (1799 1803)	31

GEORGE CRABBE (1754–1832)
The Village (1783), Book I	34

ROBERT BURNS (1759–1796)
Mary Morison (1781 1800)	44
Green Grow the Rashes (1783 1786)	45
Epistle to John Lapraik (1785 1786)	46
To a Mouse (1785 1786)	51
The Cotter's Saturday Night (1785 1786)	53
Address to the Unco Guid (1786 1787)	60
To a Mountain Daisy (1786)	62
Of A' the Airts (1788 1790)	64
My Heart's in the Highlands (1788 1790)	65
A Red, Red Rose (1788 1796)	65
Auld Lang Syne (1788 1793)	66
John Anderson My Jo (1789 1790)	67
Tam o' Shanter (1790 1791)	68
Ye Flowery Banks (1791 1792)	75
Sweet Afton (1791 1796)	76
Ae Fond Kiss (1791 1792)	77
Highland Mary (1792)	78
Duncan Gray (1792)	79

v

CONTENTS

	PAGE
Scots, Wha Hae (1793 1794)	81
A Man's a Man for A' That (1795)	82

WILLIAM BLAKE (1757–1827)
Poetical Sketches (1783)
  Song: How Sweet I Roamed 83
  Song: My Silks and Fine Array 84
  Mad Song 85
  To the Muses 85
Songs of Innocence (1789)
  Introduction: Piping Down the Valleys 86
  The Shepherd 87
  The Lamb 87
  The Blossom 88
  The Divine Image 88
  Night 89
  Infant Joy 91
  A Dream 91
  On Another's Sorrow 92
Songs of Experience (1794)
  The Clod and the Pebble 94
  A Poison Tree 94
  A Cradle Song: Sleep, Beauty Bright 95
  The Tiger 95
From the Prophetic Book "Milton" (1804) 96

WILLIAM WORDSWORTH (1770–1850)
We Are Seven (1798 1800) 97
Lines Written in Early Spring (1798) 99
Expostulation and Reply (1798) 100
The Tables Turned (1798) 102
Lines Composed a Few Miles above Tintern Abbey (1798) 103
The Lucy Poems (1799 1800)
  Strange Fits of Passion 108
  She Dwelt among the Untrodden Ways 109
  I Travelled among Unknown Men 109

CONTENTS

	PAGE
Three Years She Grew	110
A Slumber Did My Spirit Seal	112
Michael (1800)	112
To the Cuckoo (1802 1807)	126
My Heart Leaps Up (1802 1807)	127
Resolution and Independence (1802 1807)	128
To the Daisy: With Little Here to Do (1802 1807)	132
Composed Upon Westminster Bridge (1802 1807)	134
It is a Beauteous Evening (1802 1807)	135
On the Extinction of the Venetian Republic (1802 1807)	135
Written in London, September, 1802 (1802 1807)	136
London, 1802 (1802 1807)	136
It is Not To Be Thought Of (1803)	137
She Was a Phantom of Delight (1804 1807)	137
The Solitary Reaper (1804 1807)	138
I Wandered Lonely as a Cloud (1804 1807)	139
The Prelude (1800–1805 1850)	
From Book I. Introduction—Childhood and School-time	140
From Book III.—Residence at Cambridge	142
From Book XI.—France (Concluded)	145
Elegiac Stanzas (1805 1807)	147
Ode to Duty (1805 1807)	149
Character of the Happy Warrior (1805 1807)	151
Ode: Intimations of Immortality from Recollections of Early Childhood (1803–1806 1807)	154
The World is Too Much with Us (1807)	161
After-Thought (1820)	161
Scorn Not the Sonnet (1827)	162
Preface to Lyrical Ballads (1800)	162

SAMUEL TAYLOR COLERIDGE (1772–1834)

This Lime-Tree Bower my Prison (1797 1800)	191
Kubla Khan (1797 1816)	193
The Rime of the Ancient Mariner (1798)	196
Frost at Midnight (1798)	221
France: an Ode (1798)	223

CONTENTS

	PAGE
Christabel (1797–1800 1816)	227
Dejection: an Ode (1802)	250
Hymn Before Sunrise (1802)	255
Work without Hope (1825 1828)	257
Epitaph (1833 1834)	258
Biographia Literaria (1817)	258

ROBERT SOUTHEY (1774–1843)
- The Battle of Blenheim (1798) ... 267
- Bishop Bruno (1798 1799) ... 269
- My Days Among the Dead Are Past (1818 1823) ... 272

SIR WALTER SCOTT (1771–1832)
- Caledonia: From *The Lay of the Last Minstrel* (1802–1804 1805) ... 273
- Lochinvar (Lady Heron's Song): From *Marmion* (1806–1808 1808) *Canto V* ... 274
- Hunting Song (1808 1814) ... 276
- Soldier Rest (Ellen's Song): From *The Lady of the Lake* (1809–1810 1810) *Canto I* ... 277
- Coronach: From *The Lady of the Lake* (1809–1810 1810) *Canto III* ... 279
- Brignall Banks (Edmund's Song): From *Rokeby* (1811–1813 1813) *Canto III* ... 280
- The Cavalier (Edmund's Song): From *Rokeby*, (1811–1813 1813) *Canto V*, ... 282
- Jock of Hazeldean (1816) ... 283
- Pibroch of Donuil Dhu (1816) ... 284
- Proud Maisie: From *The Heart of Midlothian* (1818), *Chapter XI* ... 286
- County Guy: From *Quentin Durward* (1823), *Chapter IV* ... 286
- Here's a Health to King Charles: From *Woodstock* (1826), *Chapter XX* ... 287

THOMAS CAMPBELL (1777–1844)
- Ye Mariners of England (1799–1800 1801) ... 288
- Hohenlinden (1802) ... 289
- Lord Ullin's Daughter (1805 1809) ... 291

CONTENTS

THOMAS MOORE (1779–1852)
The Harp that Once through Tara's Hall (1808) 293
'Tis the Last Rose of Summer (1808) 293
Oft in the Stilly Night (1816)...................... 294

GEORGE GORDON, LORD BYRON (1788–1824)
Oh! Snatch'd away in Beauty's Bloom (1814 1815)... 295
She Walks in Beauty (1814 1815).................. 296
The Destruction of Sennacherib (1814 1815)....... 297
Stanzas for Music (1815 1816): There be None of
    Beauty's Daughters............................ 298
Sonnet on Chillon (1816).......................... 298
The Prisoner of Chillon (1816)..................... 299
Childe Harold's Pilgrimage: Canto III (1816)........ 312
To Thomas Moore (1817 1821): My Boat is on the
    Shore.. 355
Don Juan (1819–1821 1821): From Canto III...... 356
Stanzas Written on the Road between Florence and
    Pisa (1821).................................. 369
On this Day I Complete my Thirty-Sixth Year (1824) 369

PERCY BYSSHE SHELLEY (1792–1822)
Hymn to Intellectual Beauty (1816 1817).......... 371
Ozymandias (1817 1818).......................... 374
Stanzas Written in Dejection, Near Naples (1818
    1824)....................................... 375
Prometheus Unbound (1818–1819 1820): Act II,
    Scene 5 (The Transformation of Asia).......... 376
Ode to the West Wind (1819 1820).............. 380
The Indian Serenade (1819 1822)................. 383
The Cloud (1820).................................. 384
To a Skylark (1820)............................... 387
To Night (1821 1824)............................ 391
Time (1821 1824)................................ 392
Song: Rarely, Rarely, Comest Thou (1821 1824)... 393
Mutability (1821 1824)........................... 395
A Lament (1821 1824)........................... 396
Adonais (1821).................................... 396

CONTENTS

	PAGE
The Final Chorus from Hellas (1821 1823)	418
To—: One Word is too often Profaned (1821 1824)	420
Lines: When the Lamp is Shattered (1822 1824)	420
A Dirge (1822 1824)	422

JOHN KEATS (1795–1821)
Keen, Fitful Gusts (1815 1817)	422
On First Looking into Chapman's Homer (1816 1817)	423
To One Who Has Been Long in City Pent (1816 1817)	423
Proem to Endymion (1817 1818): From Book I	424
When I have Fears that I may Cease to Be (1818 1848)	426
Lines on the Mermaid Tavern (1818 1820)	426
Robin Hood (1818 1820)	427
The Eve of St. Agnes (1819 1820)	429
La Belle Dame Sans Merci (1819 1820)	444
Ode: Bards of Passion and of Mirth (1819 1820)	446
Ode to a Nightingale (1819 1820)	447
Ode on a Grecian Urn (1819 1820)	450
Ode to Psyche (1819 1820)	452
Ode on Melancholy (1819 1820)	454
To Autumn (1819 1820)	456
Bright Star (1820 1846)	457

WALTER SAVAGE LANDOR (1775–1864)
Rose Aylmer (1806)	457
Lyrics to Ianthe (1831)	
Mild is the Parting Year	458
Past Ruined Ilion	458
The Death of Artemidora (1836)	459
To Robert Browning (1846)	459
Imaginary Conversations	
Admiral Blake and Humphrey Blake (1853)	460
On His Seventy-Fifth Birthday (1853)	464
To My Ninth Decade (1863)	464

THOMAS HOOD (1799–1845)
The Bridge of Sighs (1843)	464
The Song of the Shirt (1843)	468

CONTENTS

CHARLES LAMB (1775–1834)
Dream-Children (1822) 471
The Superannuated Man (1825) 476

WILLIAM HAZLITT (1778–1830)
On Poetry in General (1818) 485
On Familiar Style (1821) 488

LEIGH HUNT (1784–1859)
Abou Ben Adhem (1834) 497
Getting Up on Cold Mornings (1820) 498

THOMAS DE QUINCEY (1785–1859)
Suspiria de Profundis: Levana and our Ladies of Sorrow (1845) 504

NOTES 513
INDEX OF AUTHORS 559
INDEX OF TITLES 561
INDEX OF FIRST LINES OF POETRY 567

INTRODUCTION

I

The great literary upheaval which took place in England during the latter part of the eighteenth and the early part of the nineteenth century is known in English literary history as the Romantic Movement and the epoch is referred to as the Romantic Period. To fix definite dates for this period, or for any other notable epoch in literature, is impossible. The thoughts which dominate a literary era and determine its character often have their origin in the preceding age; and having found expression in the literature of a particular period, they become the heritage of subsequent ages. Thus many of the characteristics of the Romantic Period are found both in the preceding and in the succeeding periods of English literature. The Romantic Movement may therefore seem to have its roots in the classical age and its branches in the Victorian era. But as Professor Neilson and others have pointed out, Romanticism is not limited to any age, but is a permanent tendency which is found in some degree in every period of English literature. It is notably present in the Middle Ages, in the Renaissance, and even in the Age of Pope. It is true, nevertheless, that the so-called Romantic Period produced a group of writers whose works show certain romantic characteristics which appear with greater persistency and vigor than in any other period of English literary history. For all practical purposes we may say this period began about the time of the publication of

Cowper's *Task* in 1785 and came to a formal close with the publication of Tennyson's notable volume of *Poems Chiefly Lyrical* in 1830, when a new age was ushered in.

II

The first of these dates is almost coincident with the outbreak of the French Revolution in 1789, and the second with the passage of the English Reform Bill of 1832. The period is one of the most remarkable in the history of Modern Europe. The Renaissance quickened men's minds, brought great advancement in commerce and colonization, and gave, through its great literature, a broader conception of life. The Reformation attacked a religion that had existed for hundreds of years, established new faiths, and opened the way for greater intellectual freedom. The Age of Rationalism in the eighteenth century made tremendous advancement in philosophy and science. While each of these movements contributed somewhat to the advancement of conditions in Europe, none of them had a far-reaching effect upon the social and political conditions of the masses. The French Revolution, which involved the whole of Europe in the most bloody and disastrous wars the world had ever witnessed, brought enormous changes in social and political affairs, sweeping aside the traditions of a thousand years and preparing the way for democracy, which has become the form of government in most of the civilized nations. During the same period a change equally important, but less noticed at the time, began in England in what is known as the Industrial Revolution, which through a series of mechanical inventions and the application of power to machinery revolutionized the industrial world.

To appreciate the changes effected by these two revo-

INTRODUCTION

lutions one must understand the social, religious, and political conditions that prevailed in Europe during the latter part of the eighteenth century prior to the French Revolution. In many respects these conditions had existed for hundreds of years and could not be changed until the minds of the people had been stirred by the upheaval of the Revolutionary period.

Europe at this time was predominantly agricultural. Probably nine-tenths of the inhabitants on the continent, and almost as large a proportion in England, were peasants or serfs. These people were simple, rude, and uneducated. They were grouped in small villages that nestled among the hills or dotted the plains. They lived in small huts with thatched roofs, usually without any means of heating during the cold winter months. Their farming utensils were the most primitive and their crops were small; in most cases they lived in the direst poverty. Their condition was made more unbearable by the seigniorial burdens which rested upon all of them; for although many peasants owned their own land they had not purchased free-holds exempt from feudal dues. Moreover, each peasant was required to grind his corn in his lord's mill, to bake his bread in his lord's oven, and to crush his grapes in his lord's winepress—for all of which he paid exorbitant fees. The game laws restricted hunting to the nobility, so that the peasant was not allowed to eat the deer or the rabbit that fattened on his own crops. In addition to these burdens he was required to pay a tenth of the gross produce of his land to the established church and heavy taxes to the king. With all this he had no voice in the making of laws, and he was subject to a heavy fine or imprisonment for violating them. Of course the condition of the peasant was not equally bad in every country or in every case in the same country; but in general, ignorance, poverty, and oppression prevailed. Crabbe's *Village* is a true picture of the English peasant of this period; Burns's *Cotter's Saturday Night*, also a realistic picture of the times, represents the home-life of the typical, pious old cotter in Scotland at the end of a week of toil and drudgery.

This large body of ignorant and oppressed peasants, together with the small number of day laborers in the urban communities, constituted the lowest rank in Europe. Above this group was the middle class (called the *bourgeoisie* in France) who lived in the boroughs and cities. This class was made up of business and professional men, including merchants, bankers, manufacturers, lawyers, physicians, and men of letters. It contained among its numbers some of the ablest and most substantial men of Europe. Many of them were well educated, and some of them possessed great wealth. They had the intelligence and the capacity for leadership; and in England and France they held important public offices. But their low birth denied them the highest social position; the regulations of the army excluded them from military rank; and custom kept them out of high office in the church. Such discriminations, together with the teachings of the French philosophers of the last half of the eighteenth century, made the middle class, especially in France, greatly discontented. The *bourgeoisie* were to become the principal leaders in the French Revolution which was rapidly approaching.

Above the middle class in rank and privileges were the nobility, who constituted the highest class in the social life of Europe at this time. Their number was comparatively small. In France, where the proportion was somewhat larger than in England, it is estimated that out of a population of 25,000,000 there were 150,000 nobles—that is, about six to every thousand inhabitants. Usually they lived in splendor on large estates, and owned considerable land from which they collected exorbitant fees from the poor peasants. Everywhere they were proud and arrogant: they thought their blood was better than that of other people; they must be addressed in terms of respect; and they considered it beneath their dignity to marry below their rank. Their noble birth admitted them to the polite society of the court and gave them preferment in the higher positions of the army and navy. Usually they held important offices in the state, and in England they often directed the council of the nation. In some countries they possessed much of the wealth, but were generally exempt from taxation. Professor Edward R. Turner sums up the position of the nobility as follows: "In Europe of this old régime, the nobles, whether great lords or petty knights of the empire, were the splendid top of a society which rested upon the toil and the support of the immense multitude of the people."

One of the most important and powerful institutions of this time was the church. The Roman Catholic Church, which dominated the middle ages, was still the state religion in most of the countries of Europe. The Anglican Church, whose independence from Papal authority was established during the reign of Henry VIII, was the state church of England, Ireland, and Wales, and had followers in Scotland and the British colonies. Everywhere the established church of the nation possessed great wealth. Professor Carlton Hayes reminds us that "one-third of the land of Europe, one-half the revenue, and two-thirds of the capital, were in the hands of the Christian churches." As in the social life, there was a sharp contrast between the higher and the lower clergy. Like the nobles, the higher clergy lived in great pomp and splendor. They looked upon their office as a source of revenue, and often abandoned their dioceses for most of the year to live at court. Many of them were worldly and dissipated, and consequently rendered very little spiritual service to their adherents. The lower clergy lived hard, laborious lives like the peasants whom they served, and were much loved by the great body of the people. In France during the earlier stages of the French Revolution the lower clergy rendered the *bourgeoisie* valuable assistance in their movement against oppression.

But the church was most objectionable for the power and authority it assumed in social and civil life. In France, education was largely under the control of the Catholic Church; marriages were illegal unless performed by the Catholic clergy; and children born out of Christian wedlock could not inherit property. In England, the Anglican Church, like the Catholic Church on the continent, had supreme authority. It collected tithes from communicants and non-communicants alike. Toward the Protestant dissenters its attitude was very bigoted. To be sure, these dissenters had been granted the right of worship by the Toleration Act of 1689; but baptism and marriages performed by their clergy were illegal, and they could not hold political office without special permission from parliament. The Catholic dissenters suffered even more from the hands of the Anglican Church. Besides having no political rights they were forbidden to practice their religion openly, and were required by law to attend the services of the Church of England.

The political conditions were no better. The governments of most of the European countries were absolute monarchies; Great Britain was the notable exception. In France, the most powerful nation on the continent, the king was supreme in all matters of state. Louis XV

INTRODUCTION

(1715-1774) could truthfully say: "The Sovereign authority is vested in my person. . . . My people are one only with me; national rights and national interests are necessarily combined with my own and rest only in my hands." But as a matter of fact this pleasure-loving despot spent most of his time in hunting and gambling, and entrusted the government to officials, composed of the royal council, the governors of the provinces, the intendants, the mayors, and the town councils. The overlapping powers of these officials and the consequent lack of responsibility produced a state of bewilderment in the minds of the common people. Moreover, there was confusion in the numerous bodies of law, unequally enforced in various parts of France, and in the various courts of law—royal, feudal, church, financial, and military—before which an offender might be tried. These conditions, together with the burden of an unjust taxation, brought about a state of oppression which the French people could no longer endure.

The government of England was a limited constitutional monarchy. During the Renaissance the English ruler had almost supreme authority in political affairs. But by the end of the eighteenth century the king of England had lost most of his power. Under the law he still appointed officials, presided over the administration of affairs, and executed the laws; but he could no longer make laws or levy taxes. This authority had passed into the hands of Parliament, which, with a cabinet presided over by the prime minister, had become solely responsible for the administration of political affairs. But the English Parliament at this time was the weak spot in the British government, because it did not in any modern sense represent the will of the people. Both in the counties and in the boroughs the franchise was restricted to property owners and to those who had inherited the right of suffrage. Consequently less than one-tenth of the people could vote. Many towns and districts were therefore not represented. This condition enabled the House of Lords, composed of wealthy nobles and bishops, to buy up the "rotten" or "pocket" boroughs and control the House of Commons. Although the English people suffered less oppression than their neighbors across the channel, they had no political or civil rights; and, like the French, they were heavily taxed for the support of a government in which they had little part.

A strong influence against the political and social oppression of the times appeared in a new manner of thought which was largely the achievement of eighteenth century philosophers and social reformers.

The greatest political reformer of this time was Montesquieu (1689-1775). His *Spirit of the Laws* (1748) represents the concentrated effort of twenty years. In this monumental treatise, which contains thirty-one books, he discusses the political, economic, and religious conditions of various countries and analyzes the whole system of Roman, French, and feudal laws. But the real significance of the work lies not in the systematic treatment of conditions and laws, but rather in the singular views, illustrated by examples, which the author sets forth on legal and political subjects. Montesquieu preferred a republic, but believed the English form of government, properly administered, was best suited to France. Many of his ideas are embodied in the Constitution of the United States. The influence of his work upon political and legal thought was immense.

But the greatest single influence of the time was Jean Jacques Rousseau (1712-1778). He was neither a rational deist nor an orthodox Christian; he believed

INTRODUCTION

that "to love God above all things, and your neighbor as yourself, is the sum of the law." He sympathized with the poor, for he had felt their bitter sufferings and had seen the cynical indifference of the rich. In his *Discourse Concerning Inequality of Conditions* (1754) he shows how inequality originated from the greed and selfishness of men who fenced off plots of land and forced the weak to acknowledge the right of private property, and how this condition had reduced the human race to servitude and misery. In his *Julia or New Heloise,* a sentimental novel in the form of letters, he emphasizes external nature and simple living. Concerning nature he says: "It is on the summit of the mountains, in the depths of forests, on deserted islands that nature reveals her most potent charms." This doctrine suggests Wordsworth and Shelley, upon whom Rousseau had a tremendous influence. In his best-known work, *The Social Contract* (1761), he points out that in the beginning of society men entered into a civil contract by which they surrendered certain rights in return for services rendered by their ruler, and that if the ruler failed to render these services the contract could be rescinded. This idea, which exploded the theory of the divine right of kings, spread rapidly among the revolutionists, by whom Rousseau was held almost in idolatry. The famous panegyric in *Childe Harold* (Canto III, Stanzas 79 ff.) shows the esteem in which he was held by the Revolutionists long after his death.

A reaction against the religious conditions prevailing in the Church of England is seen in the great religious awakening under the preaching of John Wesley (1703-1791). After his graduation from Oxford he was ordained a minister of the Anglican Church, and preached for several years in small churches near Oxford. Then followed a deep spiritual change in his life and "the first rise of Methodism" among a small group of Oxford students. In 1735, on the death of his father, he came to Georgia; in the next year he formed a little society of the serious members of his flock, and thus began, in Savannah, Georgia, "the second rise of Methodism." But it was not until 1738, when he returned to England and came under the influences of Peter Böhler, a Moravian preacher, that he received what he termed his real conversion, and that the great Methodist Movement began, which spread throughout the British Empire. Through his great oratorical power and religious fervor Wesley appealed to the emotions of the laboring class, often moving them to tears. Much of his preaching was in the open air, where as many as 30,000 people would gather and wait patiently until the great evangelist appeared on horseback. It is estimated that during the fifty years of his ministry he travelled 250,000 miles and preached 40,000 sermons. The Methodist Movement did more than establish a religious sect which has been a tremendous force in the world. In an age of reason it brought people to a fuller realization of the value of inspiration and emotion; it placed greater emphasis on the individual man and helped to develop the spirit of human brotherhood; and most of all it gave greater impulse to the reading of the Bible, which more than anything else kept the English people, during the tumult of the Revolution, comparatively undisturbed.

In this survey of European conditions at the outbreak of the French Revolution we have seen the poverty-stricken peasants groaning under the burden of taxation, the more prosperous middle class demanding greater power and recognition, the two dominant churches manifesting a spirit of intolerance toward the non-conformists, and the French and English governments disregarding the rights of the lower classes. Aroused by the teachings of the French philosophers, the *bourgeoisie* began the revolutionary cry of "Liberty, Equality, Fraternity," which in the throats of the masses sent terror to the hearts of kings and nobles. Revolutionary wars convulsed the whole of Europe. As a result of the conservative nature of the English people and the powerful influence of Burke, England remained for a while unmolested. But when Napoleon tried to force Europe into a tariff union which affected British trade, England became involved in the crisis, and was saved from invasion only by the supremacy of her navy and the victories of Nelson and Wellington. In France the Revolution abolished feudalism, guaranteed personal liberty in constitutional documents, made the peasants full owners of their lands, introduced a more just system of taxation, and established religious freedom. These reforms came to England gradually, and were effected through the quieter process of legislation. Her Industrial Revolution resulted in the rapid expansion of industry, in the rapid growth of cities, and in a larger increase of wealth. The change strengthened and enriched the middle class, but threw thousands of laborers out of work, and, as a result of long hours and poor working conditions, entailed great hardship upon the poor. But the evils of the factory system were offset by the passage of the Reform Bill, which gave greater freedom of speech and equal opportunity to all.

III

The literature of the Romantic Period is closely related to the spirit of the times. For while Romanticism makes itself principally felt in literature, it has its roots in the social conditions of man, in the political status of the nation, and in the religious pulse of the people. The Romantic Movement, therefore, is primarily a revolt against institutions, against authorities, and against government.

In England this spirit of radicalism appears everywhere in the literature of the Romantic Period. The revolt against social oppression is seen particularly in the literature of the early poets. Cowper, Crabbe, Burns, and Wordsworth all express sympathy and admiration for the poverty-stricken peasant; Burns proclaims the doctrine of universal brotherhood; and Byron, an aristocrat by birth, shows sympathy for the people at large. The deep religious fervor of the Methodist Movement finds expression in the poetry of Cowper, and is emphasized in the general religious tone of most of the poets of the period. The revolt against political oppression appears in Wordsworth, Byron, and Shelley. Wordsworth in his early years was an ardent sympathizer with the French cause; Byron said, "I have simplified my politics into a detestation of all existing governments;" and Shelley, under the influence of Godwin, a radical reformer, goes still further in opposing all social institutions and customs.

But the Romantic Movement is also a reaction against the literary tendencies of the eighteenth century. Pseudo-classical literature is largely didactic in purpose, and appeals primarily to the intellect. It represents the life of the city and the aristocracy of the court. Satire and social criticism are the favorite subjects, and prose predominates as the form of literary expression. Poetry is restricted almost entirely to the heroic couplet, which is characterized by balance, clarity, and technical excellence. The revolt against literary tendencies will perhaps be clearer after giving further characteristics of the Romantic Period.

INTRODUCTION

What is Romanticism? Numerous attempts have been made to define the term. Heine, with the Romantic Movement of Germany in mind, defines it as "the reproduction in modern art or literature of the life and thought of the middle ages." Brunetière says: "Romanticism is a social phenomenon, characterized by a tendency toward individualism, whose poetic expression could be only lyricism." Walter Pater tells us that "the essential elements of the Romantic spirit are curiosity and the love of beauty." Theodore Watts-Dunton in a finely chosen phrase defines the term as "the Renascence of Wonder." Professor Irving Babbitt, emphasizing the same idea, says: "A thing is Romantic when it is strange, unexpected, intense, superlative, extreme, unique." Professor Herford thinks of Romanticism as "an extraordinary development of imaginative sensibility." Professor William Allan Neilson defines it as "the tendency characterized by the predominance of imagination over reason and the sense of fact." Professor Cazamian says: "The Romantic spirit can be defined as an accentuated predominance of emotional life, provoked or directed by the exercise of imaginative vision."

The keynote of the Romantic Movement is found in the three words—individualism, emotion, and imagination. The spirit of individual freedom manifests itself in the work of every writer of the period. Each is a law unto himself. But however much these writers may differ, due to individual temperaments, all are dominated by a vivid and powerful imagination growing out of a deep and powerful emotion.

This deep feeling, accompanied by imaginative vision, asserts itself in various ways in the literature of the period. In the first place there is a profound sense of the worth and dignity of the individual man. The glorification of humble life is the central theme of many of the poems of the early Romanticists. Never before had the life of the lowly been set forth in such splendor and beauty. Even Crabbe's realism is not without sympathy for the poor.

This intense emotion, transfused by creative imagination, is found even to a greater extent in the enthusiasm for nature. Each of the poets, unlike in many ways, shows the influence of external nature. There is not merely an unusual appreciation of its forms and colors, but a deep feeling of the power of nature to transform men's minds and to reveal hidden truths of the mysteries of life. To Wordsworth it was almost a religion. To Byron it was an escape, which meant solitude and a time for meditation. And Shelley longs to be one with the West Wind. Nor was this reverence for the hills and the seas, for the flowers and birds, felt by the poets only: it was cherished by the prose writers as well.

Finally this imaginative insight, permeated with emotion, is shown in the fondness of the Romanticists for the remote past. Sometimes this asserts itself in a return to the literature of the Greeks for models and inspiration, as in the poetry of Shelley, Keats, and Landor; sometimes it appears in the emphasis on Mediævalism, as in the novels of Scott; sometimes it is manifested in the interest in Orientalism, as in the poetry of Southey and Byron. Even the elements of terror and wonder, so dear to the German Romanticists, are reflected in the novels of "Monk" Lewis and Ann Radcliffe. From the English poets of the sixteenth and seventeenth centuries they drew special inspiration. Spenser became a power to Byron, Shelley, and Keats; the Elizabethan lyrists influenced Blake and Landor; Shakespeare was worshiped by Coleridge, Lamb, and Keats; and Milton was the chief inspiration of Cowper. As the late Professor Lewis E. Gates well puts it: "The Romanticists sought to enrich life with new emotions, to conquer new fields of experience, to come into imaginative touch with far distant times, to give its due to the encompassing world of darkness and mystery, and even to pierce through the darkness in the hope of finding, at the heart of the mystery, a transcendental world of infinite beauty and eternal truth."

This literature of emotion and imagination is transfused with a strong current of intellectualism which carries on the rational thought of the eighteenth century, and connects the Romantic Period with the Victorian Era into which England enters after 1830. The eighteenth century philosophy of Hobbes and Locke, and their French disciples, Voltaire, Holbach, and Helvetius, had a profound influence on the writers of the Romantic Period. Rousseau's influence on Wordsworth and Shelley has already been pointed out. The influence of Godwin's *Political Justice* is felt throughout the poetry of Shelley. And the transcendental movement of Germany from Kant to Hegel inspired much of the philosophy of Coleridge. In short, as Professor Herford points out, "Romanticism, beyond all other literary movements, is impregnated with speculative elements; its poets are teachers and prophets, ardent reformers, philosophic reactionaries, innovators in religion, or in criticism, or in history."

Though the Age of Romanticism was primarily an age of poetry, it also produced a considerable body of prose, many of the poets themselves being equally at home in either form. The prose represents literary criticism, the essay, and the novel. In the various prefaces to his poems, Wordsworth attempts to justify his own theory of poetry, based on humble life and simplicity of diction. In his discussion of æsthetic values, Coleridge shows greater mental depth than Wordsworth; his

Biographia Literaria stamps him as one of the first great philosophical critics. Hazlitt, a man of enormous reading and always in perfect touch with the spirit of his age, ranks high among impressionistic critics. Although his mind was not always free from emotional bias, he could at all times detect genius when he encountered it, and his enthusiasm is frequently contagious. Charles Lamb, the London representative of the Lake School poets, is one of the best personal essayists in our language. He could write sanely and intelligently about the Elizabethan dramatists, but he could also give us subjective essays that are humorous, touching, and charming. Leigh Hunt, a journalist of more than average ability, was never a very brilliant or profound critic, but could make others enjoy with him the finer subtleties of great literature. Like Byron, Shelley, and Keats, De Quincey shows the spirit of unrest, and his essays are fused with imaginative idealism. Walter Savage Landor is famous for his psychological dialogues, and brings back to life the figures of the past. Outclassed in poetry by Byron, Scott is best known as a novelist; in the field of prose romance and in the revival of the historic past he has no equal.

ALBERT GRANBERRY REED.

WILLIAM COWPER (1731-1800)

OLNEY HYMNS

WALKING WITH GOD

Gen. V, 24

Oh! for a closer walk with God,
A calm and heavenly frame;
A light to shine upon the road
That leads me to the Lamb!

Where is the blessedness I knew
When first I saw the Lord?
Where is the soul-refreshing view
Of Jesus and his word?

What peaceful hours I once enjoyed!
How sweet their memory still!   10
But they have left an aching void
The world can never fill.

Return, O holy Dove, return,
Sweet messenger of rest!
I hate the sins that made thee mourn
And drove thee from my breast.

The dearest idol I have known,
Whate'er that idol be,
Help me to tear it from thy throne,
And worship only thee.   20

So shall my walk be close with God,
  Calm and serene my frame;
So purer light shall mark the road
  That leads me to the Lamb.

1772   1779

LIGHT SHINING OUT OF DARKNESS

GOD moves in a mysterious way
  His wonders to perform;
He plants his footsteps in the sea,
  And rides upon the storm.

Deep in unfathomable mines
  Of never-failing skill,
He treasures up his bright designs,
  And works his sovereign will.

Ye fearful saints, fresh courage take,
  The clouds ye so much dread   10
Are big with mercy, and shall break
  In blessings on your head.

Judge not the Lord by feeble sense,
  But trust him for his grace:
Behind a frowning providence
  He hides a smiling face.

His purposes will ripen fast,
  Unfolding every hour;
The bud may have a bitter taste,
  But sweet will be the flower.   20

Blind unbelief is sure to err,
  And scan his work in vain:

God is his own interpreter,
  And He will make it plain.

1773   1779

ON THE LOSS OF THE ROYAL GEORGE

Toll for the brave!
  The brave that are no more!
All sunk beneath the wave,
  Fast by their native shore!

Eight hundred of the brave,
  Whose courage well was tried,
Had made the vessel heel,
  And laid her on her side.

A land-breeze shook the shrouds,
  And she was overset;   10
Down went the Royal George,
  With all her crew complete.

Toll for the brave!
  Brave Kempenfelt is gone;
His last sea-fight is fought;
  His work of glory done.

It was not in the battle;
  No tempest gave the shock;
She sprang no fatal leak;
  She ran upon no rock.   20

His sword was in the sheath;
  His fingers held the pen,
When Kempenfelt went down
  With twice four hundred men.

>   Weigh the vessel up,
>   Once dreaded by our foes,
>   And mingle with our cup
>   The tears that England owes.
>
>   Her timbers yet are sound,
>   And she may float again,   30
>   Full charged with England's thunder,
>   And plough the distant main.
>
>   But Kempenfelt is gone,
>   His victories are o'er;
>   And he and his eight hundred
>   Shall plough the wave no more.

1782   1803

THE TASK, BOOK IV

THE WINTER EVENING

Hark! 't is the twanging horn! O'er yonder bridge
That with its wearisome but needful length
Bestrides the wintry flood, in which the moon
Sees her unwrinkled face reflected bright,
He comes, the herald of a noisy world,
With spattered boots, strapped waist, and frozen locks,
News from all nations lumbering at his back.
True to his charge, the close-packed load behind,
Yet careless what he brings, his one concern
Is to conduct it to the destined inn,   10
And, having dropped the expected bag, pass on.
He whistles as he goes, light-hearted wretch,
Cold and yet cheerful; messenger of grief
Perhaps to thousands, and of joy to some;
To him indifferent whether grief or joy.

THE TASK, BOOK IV

Houses in ashes, and the fall of stocks,
Births, deaths, and marriages, epistles wet
With tears that trickled down the writer's cheeks
Fast as the periods from his fluent quill,
Or charged with amorous sighs of absent swains,   20
Or nymphs responsive, equally affect
His horse and him, unconscious of them all.
But oh the important budget! ushered in
With such heart-shaking music, who can say
What are its tidings? have our troops awaked?
Or do they still, as if with opium drugged,
Snore to the murmurs of the Atlantic wave?
Is India free? and does she wear her plumed
And jewelled turban with a smile of peace?
Or do we grind her still? The grand debate,   30
The popular harangue, the tart reply,
The logic, and the wisdom, and the wit,
And the loud laugh—I long to know them all;
I burn to set the imprisoned wranglers free,
And give them voice and utterance once again.

Now stir the fire, and close the shutters fast,
Let fall the curtains, wheel the sofa round,
And while the bubbling and loud-hissing urn
Throws up a steamy column, and the cups
That cheer but not inebriate, wait on each,   40
So let us welcome peaceful evening in.
Not such his evening, who with shining face
Sweats in the crowded theatre, and squeezed
And bored with elbow-points through both his sides,
Outscolds the ranting actor on the stage:
Nor his, who patient stands till his feet throb,
And his head thumps, to feed upon the breath
Of patriots bursting with heroic rage,
Or placemen all tranquillity and smiles.
This folio of four pages, happy work!   50

Which not even critics criticise; that holds
Inquisitive attention while I read,
Fast bound in chains of silence, which the fair,
Though eloquent themselves, yet fear to break;
What is it but a map of busy life,
Its fluctuations and its vast concerns?
Here runs the mountainous and craggy ridge
That tempts Ambition. On the summit, see
The seals of office glitter in his eyes;
He climbs, he pants, he grasps them! At his heels,   60
Close at his heels, a demagogue ascends,
And with a dextrous jerk soon twists him down
And wins them, but to lose them in his turn.
Here rills of oily eloquence in soft
Meanders lubricate the course they take;
The modest speaker is ashamed and grieved
To engross a moment's notice, and yet begs,
Begs a propitious ear for his poor thoughts,
However trivial all that he conceives.
Sweet bashfulness! it claims at least this praise;   70
The dearth of information and good sense
That it foretells us, always comes to pass.
Cataracts of declamation thunder here,
There forests of no meaning spread the page,
In which all comprehension wanders lost;
While fields of pleasantry amuse us there
With merry descants on a nation's woes.
The rest appears a wilderness of strange
But gay confusion; roses for the cheeks
And lilies for the brows of faded age,   80
Teeth for the toothless, ringlets for the bald,
Heaven, earth, and ocean, plundered of their sweets,
Nectareous essences, Olympian dews,
Sermons, and city feasts, and favorite airs,
Ethereal journeys, submarine exploits,

THE TASK, BOOK IV

And Katterfelto, with his hair on end
At his own wonders, wondering for his bread.
   'T is pleasant through the loopholes of retreat
To peep at such a world; to see the stir
Of the great Babel, and not feel the crowd;
To hear the roar she sends through all her gates
At a safe distance, where the dying sound
Falls a soft murmur on the uninjured ear.
Thus sitting, and surveying thus at ease
The globe and its concerns, I seem advanced
To some secure and more than mortal height,
That liberates and exempts me from them all.
It turns submitted to my view, turns round
With all its generations; I behold
The tumult, and am still. The sound of war
Has lost its terrors ere it reaches me;
Grieves, but alarms me not. I mourn the pride
And avarice that make man a wolf to man;
Hear the faint echo of those brazen throats
By which he speaks the language of his heart,
And sigh, but never tremble at the sound.
He travels and expatiates, as the bee
From flower to flower, so he from land to land;
The manners, customs, policy of all
Pay contribution to the store he gleans;
He sucks intelligence in every clime,
And spreads the honey of his deep research
At his return, a rich repast for me.
He travels, and I too. I tread his deck,
Ascend his topmast, through his peering eyes
Discover countries, with a kindred heart
Suffer his woes and share in his escapes;
While fancy, like the finger of a clock,
Runs the great circuit, and is still at home.
   Oh Winter, ruler of the inverted year,

Thy scattered hair with sleet like ashes filled,
Thy breath congealed upon thy lips, thy cheeks
Fringed with a beard made white with other snows
Than those of age, thy forehead wrapped in clouds,
A leafless branch thy sceptre, and thy throne
A sliding car indebted to no wheels,
But urged by storms along its slippery way,
I love thee, all unlovely as thou seemest,
And dreaded as thou art! Thou holdest the sun
A prisoner in the yet undawning east,   130
Shortening his journey between morn and noon,
And hurrying him, impatient of his stay,
Down to the rosy west; but kindly still
Compensating his loss with added hours
Of social converse and instructive ease,
And gathering, at short notice, in one group
The family dispersed, and fixing thought,
Not less dispersed by daylight and its cares.
I crown thee king of intimate delights,
Fireside enjoyments, homeborn happiness,   140
And all the comforts that the lowly roof
Of undisturbed Retirement, and the hours
Of long uninterrupted evening know.
No rattling wheels stop short before these gates;
No powdered pert, proficient in the art
Of sounding an alarm, assaults these doors
Till the street rings; no stationary steeds
Cough their own knell, while, heedless of the sound,
The silent circle fan themselves, and quake:
But here the needle plies its busy task,   150
The pattern grows, the well-depicted flower,
Wrought patiently into the snowy lawn,
Unfolds its bosom; buds, and leaves, and sprigs,
And curly tendrils, gracefully disposed,
Follow the nimble finger of the fair;

THE TASK, BOOK IV

A wreath that cannot fade, of flowers that blow
With most success when all besides decay.
The poet's or historian's page, by one
Made vocal for the amusement of the rest;
The sprightly lyre, whose treasure of sweet sounds   160
The touch from many a trembling chord shakes out;
And the clear voice, symphonious yet distinct,
And in the charming strife triumphant still,
Beguile the night, and set a keener edge
On female industry; the threaded steel
Flies swiftly, and unfelt the task proceeds.
The volume closed, the customary rites
Of the last meal commence: a Roman meal,
Such as the mistress of the world once found
Delicious, when her patriots of high note,   170
Perhaps by moonlight, at their humble doors,
And under an old oak's domestic shade,
Enjoyed, spare feast! a radish and an egg.
Discourse ensues, not trivial, yet not dull,
Nor such as with a frown forbids the play
Of fancy, or proscribes the sound of mirth:
Nor do we madly, like an impious world,
Who deem religion frenzy, and the God
That made them an intruder on their joys,
Start at his awful name, or deem his praise   180
A jarring note. Themes of a graver tone,
Exciting oft our gratitude and love,
While we retrace with Memory's pointing wand,
That calls the past to our exact review,
The dangers we have 'scaped, the broken snare,
The disappointed foe, deliverance found
Unlooked for, life preserved, and peace restored,
Fruits of omnipotent eternal love.
"Oh evenings worthy of the gods!" exclaimed
The Sabine bard. Oh evenings, I reply,   190

More to be prized and coveted than yours,
As more illumined and with nobler truths,
That I, and mine, and those we love, enjoy.
   Is winter hideous in a garb like this?
Needs he the tragic fur, the smoke of lamps,
The pent-up breath of an unsavoury throng,
To thaw him into feeling, or the smart
And snappish dialogue, that flippant wits
Call comedy, to prompt him with a smile?
The self-complacent actor, when he views   200
(Stealing a sidelong glance at a full house)
The slope of faces from the floor to the roof,
(As if one master-spring controlled them all)
Relaxed into an universal grin,
Sees not a countenance there that speaks of joy
Half so refined or so sincere as ours.
Cards were superfluous here, with all the tricks
That idleness has ever yet contrived
To fill the void of an unfurnished brain,
To palliate dulness and give time a shove.   210
Time, as he passes us, has a dove's wing,
Unsoiled, and swift, and of a silken sound;
But the World's Time is Time in masquerade.
Theirs, should I paint him, has his pinions fledged
With motley plumes, and, where the peacock shows
His azure eyes, is tinctured black and red,
With spots quadrangular of diamond form,
Ensanguined hearts, clubs typical of strife,
And spades, the emblem of untimely graves.
What should be and what was an hourglass once, 220
Becomes a dicebox, and a billiard mace
Well does the work of his destructive scythe.
Thus decked, he charms a world whom Fashion blinds
To his true worth, most pleased when idle most;
Whose only happy are their wasted hours.

THE TASK, BOOK IV

Even misses, at whose age their mothers wore
The backstring and the bib, assume the dress
Of womanhood, sit pupils in the school
Of card-devoted Time, and night by night
Placed at some vacant corner of the board,   230
Learn every trick, and soon play all the game.
But truce with censure. Roving as I rove,
Where shall I find an end, or how proceed?
As he that travels far oft turns aside
To view some rugged rock or mouldering tower,
Which, seen, delights him not; then, coming home,
Describes and prints it, that the world may know
How far he went for what was nothing worth;
So I, with brush in hand and pallet spread,
With colours mixed for a far different use,   240
Paint cards and dolls, and every idle thing
That Fancy finds in her excursive flights.

  Come, Evening, once again, season of peace;
Return, sweet Evening, and continue long!
Methinks I see thee in the streaky west,
With matron step slow moving, while the Night
Treads on thy sweeping train; one hand employed
In letting fall the curtain of repose
On bird and beast, the other charged for man
With sweet oblivion of the cares of day;   250
Not sumptuously adorned, nor needing aid,
Like homely-featured Night, of clustering gems;
A star or two, just twinkling on thy brow,
Suffices thee; save that the moon is thine
No less than hers, not worn indeed on high
With ostentatious pageantry, but set
With modest grandeur in thy purple zone,
Resplendent less, but of an ampler round.
Come, then, and thou shalt find thy votary calm,
Or make me so. Composure is thy gift: **260**

And whether I devote thy gentle hours
To books, to music, or the poet's toil;
To weaving nets for bird-alluring fruit;
Or twining silken threads round ivory reels,
When they command whom man was born to please;
I slight thee not, but make thee welcome still.

    Just when our drawing-rooms begin to blaze
With lights, by clear reflection multiplied
From many a mirror, in which he of Gath,
Goliath, might have seen his giant bulk   270
Whole without stooping, towering crest and all,
My pleasures too begin. But me, perhaps,
The glowing hearth may satisfy a while
With faint illumination, that uplifts
The shadow to the ceiling, there by fits
Dancing uncouthly to the quivering flame.
Not undelightful is an hour to me
So spent in parlour twilight; such a gloom
Suits well the thoughtful or unthinking mind,
The mind contemplative, with some new theme   280
Pregnant, or indisposed alike to all.
Laugh ye, who boast your more mercurial powers,
That never feel a stupor, know no pause,
Nor need one; I am conscious and confess,
Fearless, a soul that does not always think.
Me oft has fancy, ludicrous and wild,
Soothed with a waking dream of houses, towers,
Trees, churches, and strange visages expressed
In the red cinders, while with poring eye
I gazed, myself creating what I saw.   290
Nor less amused have I quiescent watched
The sooty films that play upon the bars,
Pendulous, and foreboding, in the view
Of superstition, prophesying still
Though still deceived, some stranger's near approach.

THE TASK, BOOK IV

'T is thus the understanding takes repose
In indolent vacuity of thought,
And sleeps and is refreshed. Meanwhile the face
Conceals the mood lethargic with a mask
Of deep deliberation, as the man   300
Were tasked to his full strength, absorbed and lost.
Thus oft, reclined at ease, I lose an hour
At evening, till at length the freezing blast,
That sweeps the bolted shutter, summons home
The recollected powers, and snapping short
The glassy threads with which the fancy weaves
Her brittle toys, restores me to myself.
How calm is my recess, and how the frost,
Raging abroad, and the rough wind, endear
The silence and the warmth enjoyed within!   310
I saw the woods and fields at close of day
A variegated show; the meadows green
Though faded; and the lands where lately waved
The golden harvest, of a mellow brown,
Upturned so lately by the forceful share.
I saw far off the weedy fallows smile
With verdure not unprofitable, grazed
By flocks, fast feeding and selecting each
His favourite herb; while all the leafless groves
That skirt the horizon, wore a sable hue,   320
Scarce noticed in the kindred dusk of eve.
To-morrow brings a change, a total change!
Which even now, though silently performed
And slowly, and by most unfelt, the face
Of universal nature undergoes.
Fast falls a fleecy shower; the downy flakes
Descending, and with never-ceasing lapse
Softly alighting upon all below,
Assimilate all objects. Earth receives
Gladly the thickening mantle, and the green   330

And tender blade, that feared the chilling blast,
Escapes unhurt beneath so warm a veil.
  In such a world, so thorny, and where none
Finds happiness unblighted, or, if found,
Without some thistly sorrow at its side,
It seems the part of wisdom, and no sin
Against the law of love, to measure lots
With less distinguished than ourselves, that thus
We may with patience bear our moderate ills,
And sympathise with others suffering more.   340
Ill fares the traveller now, and he that stalks
In ponderous boots beside his reeking team.
The wain goes heavily, impeded sore
By congregating loads adhering close
To the clogged wheels; and in its sluggish pace,
Noiseless, appears a moving hill of snow.
The toiling steeds expand the nostril wide,
While every breath, by respiration strong
Forced downward, is consolidated soon
Upon their jutting chests. He, formed to bear   350
The pelting brunt of the tempestuous night,
With half-shut eyes, and puckered cheeks, and teeth
Presented bare against the storm, plods on.
One hand secures his hat, save when with both
He brandishes his pliant length of whip,
Resounding oft, and never heard in vain.
Oh happy! and, in my account, denied
That sensibility of pain with which
Refinement is endued, thrice happy thou!
Thy frame, robust and hardy, feels indeed   360
The piercing cold, but feels it unimpaired.
The learnèd finger never need explore
Thy vigorous pulse, and the unhealthful East,
That breathes the spleen, and searches every bone
Of the infirm, is wholesome air to thee.

THE TASK, BOOK IV

Thy days roll on exempt from household care:
The waggon is thy wife; and the poor beasts,
That drag the dull companion to and fro,
Thine helpless charge, dependent on thy care.
Ah, treat them kindly! rude as thou appearest,   370
Yet show that thou hast mercy, which the great,
With needless hurry whirled from place to place,
Humane as they would seem, not always show.

    Poor, yet industrious, modest, quiet, neat,
Such claim compassion in a night like this,
And have a friend in every feeling heart.
Warmed, while it lasts, by labour, all day long
They brave the season, and yet find at eve,
Ill-clad and fed but sparely, time to cool.
The frugal housewife trembles when she lights   380
Her scanty stock of brushwood, blazing clear,
But dying soon, like all terrestrial joys.
The few small embers left she nurses well;
And while her infant race, with outspread hands
And crowded knees, sit cowering o'er the sparks,
Retires, content to quake, so they be warmed.
The man feels least, as more inured than she
To winter, and the current in his veins
More briskly moved by his severer toil;
Yet he too finds his own distress in theirs.   390
The taper soon extinguished, which I saw
Dangled along at the cold finger's end
Just when the day declined, and the brown loaf
Lodged on the shelf, half eaten, without sauce
Of savoury cheese, or butter costlier still,
Sleep seems their only refuge: for, alas!
Where penury is felt the thought is chained,
And sweet colloquial pleasures are but few.
With all this thrift they thrive not. All the care
Ingenious parsimony takes but just   400

Saves the small inventory, bed and stool,
Skillet and old carved chest, from public sale.
They live, and live without extorted alms
From grudging hands, but other boast have none
To soothe their honest pride, that scorns to beg;
Nor comfort else, but in their mutual love.
I praise you much, ye meek and patient pair,
For ye are worthy; choosing rather far
A dry but independent crust, hard earned,
And eaten with a sigh, than to endure 410
The rugged frowns and insolent rebuffs
Of knaves in office, partial in their work
Of distribution; liberal of their aid
To clamorous importunity in rags,
But oft-times deaf to suppliants who would blush
To wear a tattered garb however coarse,
Whom famine cannot reconcile to filth;
These ask with painful shyness, and, refused
Because deserving, silently retire.
But be ye of good courage. Time itself 420
Shall much befriend you. Time shall give increase,
And all your numerous progeny, well trained,
But helpless, in few years shall find their hands,
And labour too. Meanwhile ye shall not want
What, conscious of your virtues, we can spare,
Nor what a wealthier than ourselves may send.
I mean the man who, when the distant poor
Need help, denies them nothing but his name.

   But poverty with most, who whimper forth
Their long complaints, is self-inflicted woe, 430
The effect of laziness or sottish waste.
Now goes the nightly thief prowling abroad
For plunder, much solicitous how best
He may compensate for a day of sloth
By works of darkness and nocturnal wrong.

THE TASK, BOOK IV

Woe to the gardener's pale, the farmer's hedge
Plashed neatly, and secured with driven stakes
Deep in the loamy bank. Uptorn by strength,
Resistless in so bad a cause, but lame
To better deeds, he bundles up the spoil,   440
An ass's burden, and, when laden most
And heaviest, light of foot steals fast away.
Nor does the boarded hovel better guard
The well-stacked pile of riven logs and roots
From his pernicious force. Nor will he leave
Unwrenched the door, however well secured,
Where chanticleer amidst his harem sleeps
In unsuspecting pomp. Twitched from the perch,
He gives the princely bird, with all his wives,
To his voracious bag, struggling in vain,   450
And loudly wondering at the sudden change.
Nor this to feed his own! 'T were some excuse,
Did pity of their sufferings warp aside
His principle, and tempt him into sin
For their support, so destitute. But they
Neglected pine at home, themselves, as more
Exposed than others, with less scruple made
His victims, robbed of their defenceless all.
Cruel is all he does. 'T is quenchless thirst
Of ruinous ebriety that prompts   460
His every action, and imbrutes the man.
Oh for a law to noose the villain's neck
Who starves his own, who persecutes the blood
He gave them in his children's veins, and hates
And wrongs the woman he has sworn to love.

   Pass where we may, through city or through town,
Village or hamlet, of this merry land,
Though lean and beggared, every twentieth pace
Conducts the unguarded nose to such a whiff
Of stale debauch, forth-issuing from the styes   470

That law has licensed, as makes Temperance reel.
There sit, involved and lost in curling clouds
Of Indian fume, and guzzling deep, the boor,
The lackey, and the groom; the craftsman there
Takes a Lethean leave of all his toil;
Smith, cobbler, joiner, he that plies the shears,
And he that kneads the dough; all loud alike,
All learnèd, and all drunk. The fiddle screams
Plaintive and piteous, as it wept and wailed
Its wasted tones, and harmony unheard: 480
Fierce the dispute, whate'er the theme; while she,
Fell Discord, arbitress of such debate,
Perched on the signpost, holds with even hand
Her undecisive scales. In this she lays
A weight of ignorance; in that, of pride:
And smiles delighted with the eternal poise.
Dire is the frequent curse, and its twin sound
The cheek-distending oath, not to be praised
As ornamental, musical, polite,
Like those which modern senators employ, 490
Whose oath is rhetoric, and who swear for fame.
Behold the schools in which plebeian minds,
Once simple, are initiated in arts,
Which some may practise with politer grace,
But none with readier skill!—'T is here they learn
The road that leads from competence and peace
To indigence and rapine; till at last
Society, grown weary of the load,
Shakes her encumbered lap, and casts them out.
But censure profits little: vain the attempt 500
To advertise in verse a public pest,
That like the filth with which the peasant feeds
His hungry acres, stinks, and is of use.
The excise is fattened with the rich result
Of all this riot; and ten thousand casks,

THE TASK, BOOK IV

For ever dribbling out their base contents,
Touched by the Midas finger of the state,
Bleed gold for ministers to sport away.
Drink and be mad then; 't is your country bids!
Gloriously drunk, obey the important call!   510
Her cause demands the assistance of your throats;
Ye all can swallow and she asks no more.
   Would I had fallen upon those happier days
That poets celebrate; those golden times
And those Arcadian scenes that Maro sings,
And Sidney, warbler of poetic prose.
Nymphs were Dianas then, and swains had hearts
That felt their virtues; Innocence, it seems,
From courts dismissed, found shelter in the groves;
The footsteps of simplicity, impressed   520
Upon the yielding herbage (so they sing),
Then were not all effaced; then speech profane,
And manners profligate, were rarely found,
Observed as prodigies, and soon reclaimed.
Vain wish; those days were never: airy dreams
Sat for the picture; and the poet's hand,
Imparting substance to an empty shade,
Imposed a gay delirium for a truth.
Grant it:—I still must envy them an age
That favoured such a dream, in days like these   530
Impossible, when Virtue is so scarce,
That to suppose a scene where she presides
Is tramontane, and stumbles all belief.
No: we are polished now! The rural lass,
Whom once her virgin modesty and grace,
Her artless manners, and her neat attire,
So dignified, that she was hardly less
Than the fair shepherdess of old romance,
Is seen no more. The character is lost!
Her head, adorned with lappets pinned aloft,   540

And ribbons streaming gay, superbly raised,
And magnified beyond all human size,
Indebted to some smart wig-weaver's hand
For more than half the tresses it sustains;
Her elbows ruffled, and her tottering form
Ill propped upon French heels; she might be deemed
(But that the basket dangling on her arm
Interprets her more truly) of a rank
Too proud for dairy work, or sale of eggs.
Expect her soon with footboy at her heels,   550
No longer blushing for her awkward load,
Her train and her umbrella all her care.

   The town has tinged the country; and the stain
Appears a spot upon a vestal's robe,
The worse for what it soils. The fashion runs
Down into scenes still rural; but, alas,
Scenes rarely graced with rural manners now!
Time was when in the pastoral retreat
The unguarded door was safe; men did not watch
To invade another's right, or guard their own.   560
Then sleep was undisturbed by fear, unscared
By drunken howlings; and the chilling tale
Of midnight murder was a wonder heard
With doubtful credit, told to frighten babes.
But farewell now to unsuspicious nights,
And slumbers unalarmed! Now, ere you sleep,
See that your polished arms be primed with care,
And drop the night-bolt;—ruffians are abroad;
And the first larum of the cock's shrill throat
May prove a trumpet, summoning your ear   570
To horrid sounds of hostile feet within.
Even daylight has its dangers; and the walk
Through pathless wastes and woods, unconscious once
Of other tenants than melodious birds
Or harmless flocks, is hazardous and bold.

THE TASK, BOOK IV

Lamented change! to which full many a cause
Inveterate, hopeless of a cure, conspires.
The course of human things from good to ill,
From ill to worse, is fatal, never fails.
Increase of power begets increase of wealth; 580
Wealth luxury and luxury excess;
Excess, the scrofulous and itchy plague
That seizes first the opulent, descends
To the next rank contagious, and in time
Taints downward all the graduated scale
Of order, from the chariot to the plough.
The rich, and they that have an arm to check
The licence of the lowest in degree,
Desert their office; and themselves intent
On pleasure, haunt the capital, and thus 590
To all the violence of lawless hands
Resign the scenes their presence might protect.
Authority herself not seldom sleeps,
Though resident, and witness of the wrong.
The plump convivial parson often bears
The magisterial sword in vain, and lays
His reverence and his worship both to rest
On the same cushion of habitual sloth.
Perhaps timidity restrains his arm;
When he should strike he trembles, and sets free, 600
Himself enslaved by terror of the band,
The audacious convict, whom he dares not bind.
Perhaps, though by profession ghostly pure,
He too may have his vice, and sometimes prove
Less dainty than becomes his grave outside
In lucrative concerns. Examine well
His milkwhite hand; the palm is hardly clean—
But here and there an ugly smutch appears.
Foh! 't was a bribe that left it: he has touched
Corruption! Whoso seeks an audit here 610

Propitious, pays his tribute, game or fish,
Wildfowl or venison, and his errand speeds.

  But faster far, and more than all the rest,
A noble cause, which none who bears a spark
Of public virtue ever wished removed,
Works the deplored and mischievous effect.
'T is universal soldiership has stabbed
The heart of merit in the meaner class.
Arms, through the vanity and brainless rage
Of those that bear them, in whatever cause,   620
Seem most at variance with all moral good,
And incompatible with serious thought.
The clown, the child of nature, without guile,
Blest with an infant's ignorance of all
But his own simple pleasures, now and then
A wrestling match, a footrace, or a fair,
Is balloted, and trembles at the news:
Sheepish he doffs his hat, and mumbling swears
A Bible-oath to be whate'er they please,
To do he knows not what. The task performed,   630
That instant he becomes the serjeant's care,
His pupil, and his torment, and his jest.
His awkward gait, his introverted toes,
Bent knees, round shoulders, and dejected looks,
Procure him many a curse. By slow degrees,
Unapt to learn, and formed of stubborn stuff,
He yet by slow degrees puts off himself,
Grows conscious of a change, and likes it well:
He stands erect, his slouch becomes a walk;
He steps right onward, martial in his air,   640
His form and movement; is as smart above
As meal and larded locks can make him; wears
His hat or his plumed helmet with a grace;
And, his three years of heroship expired,
Returns indignant to the slighted plough.

THE TASK, BOOK IV

He hates the field in which no fife or drum
Attends him, drives his cattle to a march,
And sighs for the smart comrades he has left.
'T were well if his exterior change were all,
But with his clumsy port the wretch has lost   650
His ignorance and harmless manners too.
To swear, to game, to drink; to show at home
By lewdness, idleness, and sabbath-breach,
The great proficiency he made abroad;
To astonish and to grieve his gazing friends;
To break some maiden's and his mother's heart;
To be a pest where he was useful once;
Are his sole aim, and all his glory now.
   Man in society is like a flower
Blown in its native bed; 't is there alone   660
His faculties, expanded in full bloom,
Shine out; there only reach their proper use.
But man associated and leagued with man
By regal warrant, or self-joined by bond
For interest sake, or swarming into clans
Beneath one head for purposes of war,
Like flowers selected from the rest, and bound
And bundled close to fill some crowded vase,
Fades rapidly, and by compression marred,
Contracts defilement not to be endured.   670
Hence chartered boroughs are such public plagues;
And burghers, men immaculate perhaps
In all their private functions, once combined,
Become a loathsome body, only fit
For dissolution, hurtful to the main.
Hence merchants, unimpeachable of sin
Against the charities of domestic life,
Incorporated, seem at once to lose
Their nature, and, disclaiming all regard
For mercy and the common rights of man,   680

Build factories with blood, conducting trade
At the sword's point, and dyeing the white robe
Of innocent commercial justice red.
Hence, too, the field of glory, as the world
Misdeems it, dazzled by its bright array,
With all its majesty of thundering pomp,
Enchanting music, and immortal wreaths,
Is but a school where thoughtlessness is taught
On principle, where foppery atones
For folly, gallantry for every vice. 690

  But slighted as it is, and by the great
Abandoned, and, which still I more regret,
Infected with the manners and the modes
It knew not once, the country wins me still.
I never framed a wish, or formed a plan,
That flattered me with hopes of earthly bliss,
But there I laid the scene. There early strayed
My Fancy, ere yet liberty of choice
Had found me, or the hope of being free.
My very dreams were rural; rural too 700
The firstborn efforts of my youthful Muse,
Sportive, and jingling her poetic bells,
Ere yet her ear was mistress of their powers.
No bard could please me but whose lyre was tuned
To Nature's praises. Heroes and their feats
Fatigued me, never weary of the pipe
Of Tityrus, assembling, as he sang,
The rustic throng beneath his favourite beech.
Then Milton had indeed a poet's charms:
New to my taste his Paradise surpassed 710
The struggling efforts of my boyish tongue
To speak its excellence; I danced for joy;
I marvelled much that, at so ripe an age
As twice seven years, his beauties had then first
Engaged my wonder, and admiring still.

THE TASK, BOOK IV

And still admiring, with regret supposed
The joy half lost because not sooner found.
Thee too enamoured of the life I loved,
Pathetic in its praise, in its pursuit
Determined, and possessing it at last					720
With transports such as favoured lovers feel,
I studied, prized, and wished that I had known,
Ingenious Cowley! and though now reclaimed
By modern lights from an erroneous taste,
I cannot but lament thy splendid wit
Entangled in the cobwebs of the schools.
I still revere thee, courtly though retired;
Though stretched at ease in Chertsey's silent bowers,
Not unemployed, and finding rich amends
For a lost world in solitude and verse.					730
'T is born with all: the love of Nature's works
Is an ingredient in the compound, man,
Infused at the creation of the kind.
And though the Almighty Maker has throughout
Discriminated each from each, by strokes
And touches of his hand, with so much art
Diversified, that two were never found
Twins at all points—yet this obtains in all,
That all discern a beauty in his works,
And all can taste them: minds that have been formed	740
And tutored with a relish more exact,
But none without some relish, none unmoved.
It is a flame that dies not even there
Where nothing feeds it. Neither business, crowds,
Nor habits of luxurious city-life,
Whatever else they smother of true worth
In human bosoms, quench it or abate.
The villas with which London stands begirt,
Like a swarth Indian with his belt of beads,
Prove it. A breath of unadulterate air,					750

The glimpse of a green pasture, how they cheer
The citizen, and brace his languid frame!
Even in the stifling bosom of the town,
A garden in which nothing thrives, has charms
That soothe the rich possessor; much consoled
That here and there some sprigs of mournful mint,
Of nightshade, or valerian, grace the well
He cultivates. These serve him with a hint
That Nature lives; that sight-refreshing green
Is still the livery she delights to wear, 760
Though sickly samples of the exuberant whole.
What are the casements lined with creeping herbs,
The prouder sashes fronted with a range
Of orange, myrtle, or the fragrant weed,
The Frenchman's darling? are they not all proofs
That man immured in cities, still retains
His inborn inextinguishable thirst
Of rural scenes, compensating his loss
By supplemental shifts, the best he may?
The most unfurnished with the means of life, 770
And they that never pass their brick-wall bounds
To range the fields and treat their lungs with air,
Yet feel the burning instinct: over-head
Suspend their crazy boxes, planted thick,
And watered duly. There the pitcher stands
A fragment, and the spoutless teapot there;
Sad witnesses how close-pent man regrets
The country, with what ardour he contrives
A peep at Nature, when he can no more.

   Hail, therefore, patroness of health and ease 780
And contemplation, heart-consoling joys
And harmless pleasures, in the thronged abode
Of multitudes unknown! hail, rural life!
Address himself who will to the pursuit
Of honours, or emolument, or fame,

I shall not add myself to such a chase,
Thwart his attempts, or envy his success.
Some must be great. Great offices will have
Great talents: and God gives to every man
The virtue, temper, understanding, taste,   790
That lifts him into life, and lets him fall
Just in the niche he was ordained to fill.
To the deliverer of an injured land
He gives a tongue to enlarge upon, a heart
To feel, and courage to redress her wrongs;
To monarchs dignity; to judges sense;
To artists ingenuity and skill;
To me an unambitious mind, content
In the low vale of life, that early felt
A wish for ease and leisure, and ere long   800
Found here that leisure and that ease I wished.
                                    1785

ON THE RECEIPT OF MY MOTHER'S PICTURE

OH that those lips had language! Life has passed
With me but roughly since I heard thee last.
Those lips are thine—thy own sweet smile I see,
The same that oft in childhood solaced me;
Voice only fails, else how distinct they say,
"Grieve not, my child, chase all thy fears away!"
The meek intelligence of those dear eyes
(Blessed be the art that can immortalize,
The art that baffles Time's tyrannic claim
To quench it) here shines on me still the same.   10
    Faithful remembrancer of one so dear,
O welcome guest, though unexpected, here!
Who bidst me honor with an artless song,
Affectionate, a mother lost so long,

I will obey, not willingly alone,
But gladly, as the precept were her own:
And while that face renews my filial grief,
Fancy shall weave a charm for my relief—
Shall steep me in Elysian reverie,
A momentary dream, that thou art she.

My mother! when I learned that thou wast dead,
Say, wast thou conscious of the tears I shed?
Hovered thy spirit o'er thy sorrowing son,
Wretch even then, life's journey just begun?
Perhaps thou gavest me, thought unfelt, a kiss;
Perhaps a tear, if souls can weep in bliss—
Ah, that maternal smile! It answers—Yes.
I heard the bell tolled on thy burial day,
I saw the hearse that bore thee slow away,
And, turning from my nursery window, drew
A long, long sigh, and wept a last adieu!
But was it such?—It was.—Where thou art gone
Adieus and farewells are a sound unknown.
May I but meet thee on that peaceful shore,
The parting word shall pass my lips no more!
Thy maidens grieved themselves at my concern,
Oft gave me promise of thy quick return.
What ardently I wished, I long believed,
And, disappointed still, was still deceived;
By expectation every day beguiled,
Dupe of to-morrow even from a child.
Thus many a sad to-morrow came and went,
Till, all my stock of infant sorrow spent,
I learned at last submission to my lot;
But, though I less deplored thee, ne'er forgot.

Where once we dwelt our name is heard no more,
Children not thine have trod my nursery floor;
And where the gardener Robin, day by day,

MY MOTHER'S PICTURE

Drew me to school along the public way,
Delighted with my bauble coach, and wrapped   50
In scarlet mantle warm, and velvet capped,
'T is now become a history little known,
That once we called the pastoral house our own.
Shortlived possession! but the record fair,
That memory keeps of all thy kindness there,
Still outlives many a storm that has effaced
A thousand other themes less deeply traced.
Thy nightly visits to my chamber made,
That thou mightest know me safe and warmly laid;
Thy morning bounties ere I left my home,   60
The biscuit, or confectionary plum;
The fragrant waters on my cheeks bestowed
By thy own hand, till fresh they shone and glowed:
All this, and more endearing still than all,
Thy constant flow of love, that knew no fall,
Ne'er roughened by those cataracts and brakes,
That humor interposed too often makes;
All this still legible in memory's page,
And still to be so to my latest age,
Adds joy to duty, makes me glad to pay   70
Such honors to thee as my numbers may;
Perhaps a frail memorial, but sincere,
Not scorned in Heaven, though little noticed here.

   Could Time, his flight reversed, restore the hours
When, playing with thy vesture's tissued flowers,
The violet, the pink, and jassamine,
I pricked them into paper with a pin
(And thou wast happier than myself the while,
Wouldst softly speak, and stroke my head and smile),
Could those few pleasant days again appear,   80
Might one wish bring them, would I wish them here?
I would not trust my heart—the dear delight

Seems so to be desired, perhaps I might.—
But no—what here we call our life is such,
So little to be loved, and thou so much,
That I should ill requite thee to constrain
Thy unbound spirit into bonds again.

    Thou, as a gallant bark from Albion's coast
(The storms all weathered and the ocean crossed)
Shoots into port at some well-havened isle,   90
Where spices breathe, and brighter seasons smile,
There sits quiescent on the floods that show
Her beauteous form reflected clear below,
While airs impregnated with incense play
Around her, fanning light her streamers gay—
So thou, with sails how swift! hast reached the shore,
"Where tempests never beat nor billows roar,"
And thy loved consort on the dangerous tide
Of life, long since has anchored by thy side.
But me, scarce hoping to attain that rest,   100
Always from port withheld, always distressed—
Me howling blasts drive devious, tempest-tost,
Sails ripped, seams opening wide, and compass lost,
And day by day some current's thwarting force
Sets me more distant from a prosperous course.
Yet, oh the thought, that thou art safe, and he!
That thought is joy, arrive what may to me.
My boast is not, that I deduce my birth
From loins enthroned, and rulers of the earth;
But higher far my proud pretensions rise—   110
The son of parents passed into the skies.
And now, farewell.—Time unrevoked has run
His wonted course, yet what I wished is done.
By contemplation's help, not sought in vain,
I seem to have lived my childhood o'er again;
To have renewed the joys that once were mine,

THE CASTAWAY

Without the sin of violating thine;
And while the wings of Fancy still are free,
And I can view this mimic show of thee,
Time has but half succeeded in his theft—　　　120
Thyself removed, thy power to soothe me left.
　1790　　　　　　　　　　　　　　　　　　1798

SONNET TO MRS. UNWIN

Mary! I want a lyre with other strings,
Such aid from heaven as some have feigned they drew,
An eloquence scarce given to mortals, new,
And undebased by praise of meaner things,
That, ere through age or woe I shed my wings,
I may record thy worth with honor due,
In verse as musical as thou art true,
Verse that immortalizes whom it sings!
But thou hast little need. There is a book
By seraphs writ with beams of heavenly light,　　10
On which the eyes of God not rarely look,
A chronicle of actions just and bright:
There all thy deeds, my faithful Mary, shine,
And, since thou ownest that praise, I spare thee mine.
　1793　　　　　　　　　　　　　　　　　　1803

THE CASTAWAY

Obscurest night involved the sky,
　　The Atlantic billows roared,
When such a destined wretch as I,
　　Washed headlong from on board,
Of friends, of hope, of all bereft,
His floating home forever left.

No braver chief could Albion boast
   Than he with whom he went,
Nor ever ship left Albion's coast
   With warmer wishes sent.
He loved them both, but both in vain,
Nor him beheld, nor her again.

Not long beneath the whelming brine,
   Expert to swim, he lay;
Nor soon he felt his strength decline,
   Or courage die away:
But waged with Death a lasting strife,
Supported by despair of life.

He shouted: nor his friends had failed
   To check the vessel's course,
But so the furious blast prevailed,
   That, pitiless perforce,
They left their outcast mate behind,
And scudded still before the wind.

Some succor yet they could afford;
   And, such as storms allow,
The cask, the coop, the floated cord,
   Delayed not to bestow:
But he, they knew, nor ship nor shore,
Whate'er they gave, should visit more.

Nor, cruel as it seemed, could he
   Their haste himself condemn,
Aware that flight, in such a sea,
   Alone could rescue them:
Yet bitter felt it still to die
Deserted, and his friends so nigh.

THE CASTAWAY

He long survives, who lives an hour
   In ocean, self-upheld:
And so long he, with unspent power,
   His destiny repelled;
And ever, as the minutes flew,
Entreated help, or cried "Adieu!"

At length, his transient respite past,
   His comrades, who before
Had heard his voice in every blast,
   Could catch the sound no more:
For then, by toil subdued, he drank
The stifling wave, and then he sank.

No poet wept him; but the page
   Of narrative sincere,
That tells his name, his worth, his age,
   Is wet with Anson's tear:
And tears by bards or heroes shed
Alike immortalize the dead.

I therefore purpose not, or dream,
   Descanting on his fate,
To give the melancholy theme
   A more enduring date:
But misery still delights to trace
Its semblance in another's case.

No voice divine the storm allayed,
   No light propitious shone,
When, snatched from all effectual aid,
   We perished, each alone:
But I beneath a rougher sea,
And whelmed in deeper gulfs than he.

1799   1803

GEORGE CRABBE (1754-1832)

THE VILLAGE

BOOK I

The Village Life, and every care that reigns
O'er youthful peasants and declining swains;
What labor yields, and what, that labor past,
Age, in its hour of languor, finds at last;
What form the real Picture of the Poor,
Demand a song—the Muse can give no more.

   Fled are those times, when, in harmonious strains,
The rustic poet praised his native plains:
No shepherds now, in smooth alternate verse,
Their country's beauty or their nymphs' rehearse;   10
Yet still for these we frame the tender strain,
Still in our lays fond Corydons complain,
And shepherds' boys their amorous pains reveal,
The only pains, alas! they never feel.

   On Mincio's banks, in Cæsar's bounteous reign,
If Tityrus found the Golden Age again,
Must sleepy bards the flattering dream prolong,
Mechanic echoes of the Mantuan song?
From Truth and Nature shall we widely stray,
Where Virgil, not where Fancy, leads the way?   20

   Yes, thus the Muses sing of happy swains,
Because the Muses never knew their pains:
They boast their peasant's pipes; but peasants now
Resign their pipes and plod behind the plough;
And few, amid the rural-tribe, have time
To number syllables, and play with rime.
Save honest Duck, what son of verse could share
The poet's rapture, and the peasant's care?

THE VILLAGE

Or the great labors of the field degrade,
With the new peril of a poorer trade? 30
   From this chief cause these idle praises spring,
That themes so easy few forbear to sing;
For no deep thought the trifling subjects ask;
To sing of shepherds is an easy task:
The happy youth assumes the common strain,
A nymph his mistress, and himself a swain;
With no sad scenes he clouds his tuneful prayer,
But all, to look like her, is painted fair.
   I grant indeed that fields and flocks have charms
For him that grazes or for him that farms; 40
But when amid such pleasing scenes I trace
The poor laborious natives of the place,
And see the mid-day sun, with fervid ray,
On their bare heads and dewy temples play,
While some, with feebler heads, and fainter hearts
Deplore their fortune, yet sustain their parts—
Then shall I dare these real ills to hide
In tinsel trappings of poetic pride?
   No; cast by Fortune on a frowning coast,
Which neither groves nor happy valleys boast; 50
Where other cares than those the Muse relates,
And other shepherds dwell with other mates;
By such examples taught, I paint the Cot,
As Truth will paint it, and as Bards will not.
Nor you, ye poor, of lettered scorn complain:
To you the smoothest song is smooth in vain;
O'ercome by labor, and bowed down by time,
Feel you the barren flattery of a rime?
Can poets soothe you, when you pine for bread,
By winding myrtles round your ruined shed? 60
Can their light tales your weighty griefs o'erpower,
Or glad with airy mirth the toilsome hour?

Lo! where the heath, with withering brake grown o'er,
Lends the light turf that warms the neighboring poor;
From thence a length of burning sand appears,
Where the thin harvest waves its withered ears;
Rank weeds, that every art and care defy,
Reign o'er the land, and rob the blighted rye:
There thistles stretch their prickly arms afar,
And to the ragged infant threaten war;   70
There poppies nodding, mock the hope of toil;
There the blue bugloss paints the sterile soil;
Hardy and high, above the slender sheaf,
The slimy mallow waves her silky leaf;
O'er the young shoot the charlock throws a shade,
And clasping tares cling round the sickly blade;
With mingled tints the rocky coasts abound,
And a sad splendor vainly shines around.
So looks the nymph whom wretched arts adorn,
Betrayed by man, then left for man to scorn;   80
Whose cheek in vain assumes the mimic rose,
While her sad eyes the troubled breast disclose;
Whose outward splendor is but folly's dress,
Exposing most when most it gilds distress.

  Here joyless roam a wild amphibious race,
With sullen woe displayed in every face;
Who, far from civil arts and social fly,
And scowl at strangers with suspicious eye.

  Here too the lawless merchant of the main
Draws from his plough the intoxicated swain;   90
Want only claimed the labor of the day,
But vice now steals his nightly rest away.

  Where are the swains, who, daily labor done,
With rural games played down the setting sun;
Who struck with matchless force the bounding ball,
Or made the pond'rous quoit obliquely fall;

THE VILLAGE

While some huge Ajax, terrible and strong,
Engaged some artful stripling of the throng,
And fell beneath him, foiled, while far around
Hoarse triumph rose, and rocks returned the sound? 100
Where now are these?—Beneath yon cliff they stand,
To show the freighted pinnace where to land;
To load the ready steed with guilty haste,
To fly in terror o'er the pathless waste,
Or, when detected, in their straggling course,
To foil their foes by cunning or by force;
Or, yielding part (which equal knaves demand),
To gain a lawless passport through the land.

Here, wand'ring long, amid these frowning fields,
I sought the simple life that Nature yields; 110
Rapine and Wrong and Fear usurped her place,
And a bold, artful, surly, savage race;
Who, only skilled to take the finny tribe,
The yearly dinner, or septennial bribe,
Wait on the shore, and, as the waves run high,
On the tossed vessel bend their eager eye,
Which to their coast directs its vent'rous way;
Theirs or the ocean's miserable prey.

As on their neighbouring beach yon swallows stand,
And wait for favoring winds to leave the land, 120
While still for flight the ready wing is spread:
So waited I the favoring hour, and fled;
Fled from these shores where guilt and famine reign,
And cried, Ah! hapless they who still remain;
Who still remain to hear the ocean roar,
Whose greedy waves devour the lessening shore;
Till some fierce tide, with more imperious sway
Sweeps the low hut and all it holds away;
When the sad tenant weeps from door to door,
And begs a poor protection from the poor! 130

But these are scenes where Nature's niggard hand
Gave a spare portion to the famished land;
Hers is the fault, if here mankind complain
Of fruitless toil and labor spent in vain;
But yet in other scenes more fair in view,
When Plenty smiles—alas! she smiles for few—
And those who taste not, yet behold her store,
Are as the slaves that dig the golden ore—
The wealth around them makes them doubly poor.
Or will you deem them amply paid in health,   140
Labor's fair child, that languishes with wealth?
Go then! and see them rising with the sun,
Through a long course of daily toil to run;
See them beneath the Dog-star's raging heat,
When the knees tremble and the temples beat;
Behold them, leaning on their scythes, look o'er
The labor past, and toils to come explore;
See them alternate suns and showers engage,
And hoard up aches and anguish for their age;
Through fens and marshy moors their steps pursue, 150
When their warm pores imbibe the evening dew;
Then own that labor may as fatal be
To these thy slaves, as thine excess to thee.

   Amid this tribe too oft a manly pride
Strives in strong toil the fainting heart to hide;
There may you see the youth of slender frame
Contend with weakness, weariness, and shame;
Yet, urged along, and proudly loth to yield,
He strives to join his fellows of the field.
Till long-contending nature droops at last,   160
Declining health rejects his poor repast,
His cheerless spouse the coming danger sees,
And mutual murmurs urge the slow disease.

   Yet grant them health, 't is not for us to tell,
Though the head droops not, that the heart is well;

THE VILLAGE

Or will you praise that homely, healthy fare,
Plenteous and plain, that happy peasants share!
Oh! trifle not with wants you cannot feel,
Nor mock the misery of a stinted meal;
Homely, not wholesome, plain, not plenteous, such   170
As you who praise, would never deign to touch.

   Ye gentle souls, who dream of rural ease,
Whom the smooth stream and smoother sonnet please;
Go! if the peaceful cot your praises share,
Go look within, and ask if peace be there;
If peace be his—that drooping weary sire,
Or theirs, that offspring round their feeble fire;
Or hers, that matron pale, whose trembling hand
Turns on the wretched hearth the expiring brand!

   Nor yet can Time itself obtain for these   180
Life's latest comforts, due respect and ease;
For yonder see that hoary swain, whose age
Can with no cares except its own engage;
Who, propped on that rude staff, looks up to see
The bare arms broken from the withering tree,
On which, a boy, he climbed the loftiest bough,
Then his first joy, but his sad emblem now.

   He once was chief in all the rustic trade;
His steady hand the straightest furrow made;
Full many a prize he won, and still is proud   190
To find the triumphs of his youth allowed;
A transient pleasure sparkles in his eyes,
He hears and smiles, then thinks again and sighs.
For now he journeys to his grave in pain;
The rich disdain him; nay, the poor disdain:
Alternate masters now their slave command,
Urge the weak efforts of his feeble hand,
And, when his age attempts its task in vain,
With ruthless taunts, of lazy poor complain.

Oft may you see him, when he tends the sheep,   200
His winter charge, beneath the hillock weep;
Oft hear him murmur to the winds that blow
O'er his white locks and bury them in snow,
When, roused by rage and muttering in the morn,
He mends the broken hedge with icy thorn:—

"Why do I live, when I desire to be
At once from life and life's long labour free?
Like leaves in spring, the young are blown away,
Without the sorrows of a slow decay;
I, like yon withered leaf, remain behind,   210
Nipped by the frost, and shivering in the wind;
There it abides till younger buds come on,
As I, now all my fellow-swains are gone;
Then, from the rising generation thrust,
It falls, like me, unnoticed to the dust.

"These fruitful fields, these numerous flocks I see,
Are others' gain, but killing cares to me;
To me the children of my youth are lords,
Cool in their looks, but hasty in their words:
Wants of their own demand their care; and who   220
Feels his own want and succours others too?
A lonely, wretched man, in pain I go,
None need my help, and none relieve my woe;
Then let my bones beneath the turf be laid,
And men forget the wretch they would not aid."

Thus groan the old, till, by disease oppressed,
They taste a final woe, and then they rest.

Theirs is yon house that holds the parish-poor,
Whose walls of mud scarce bear the broken door;
There, where the putrid vapours, flagging, play,   230
And the dull wheel hums doleful through the day;—
There children dwell who know no parents' care;
Parents, who know no children's love, dwell there!

THE VILLAGE

Heartbroken matrons on their joyless bed,
Forsaken wives, and mothers never wed;
Dejected widows with unheeded tears,
And crippled age with more than childhood fears;
The lame, the blind, and, far the happiest they!
The moping idiot and the madman gay.

 Here too the sick their final doom receive,   240
Here brought, amid the scenes of grief, to grieve,
Where the loud groans from some sad chamber flow,
Mixed with the clamours of the crowd below;
Here, sorrowing, they each kindred sorrow scan,
And the cold charities of man to man:
Whose laws indeed for ruined age provide,
And strong compulsion plucks the scrap from pride;
But still that scrap is bought with many a sigh,
And pride embitters what it can't deny.

 Say, ye, oppressed by some fantastic woes,   250
Some jarring nerve that baffles your repose;
Who press the downy couch, while slaves advance
With timid eye, to read the distant glance;
Who with sad prayers the weary doctor tease,
To name the nameless ever-new disease;
Who with mock patience dire complaints endure,
Which real pain and that alone can cure;
How would ye bear in real pain to lie,
Despised, neglected, left alone to die?
How would ye bear to draw your latest breath,   260
Where all that's wretched paves the way for death?

 Such is that room which one rude beam divides,
And naked rafters form the sloping sides;
Where the vile bands that bind the thatch are seen,
And lath and mud are all that lie between,
Save one dull pane, that, coarsely patched, gives way
To the rude tempest, yet excludes the day:

Here, on a matted flock, with dust o'er-spread,
The drooping wretch reclines his languid head;
For him no hand the cordial cup applies,   270
Or wipes the tear that stagnates in his eyes;
No friends with soft discourse his pain beguile,
Or promise hope till sickness wears a smile.

But soon a loud and hasty summons calls,
Shakes the thin roof, and echoes round the walls;
Anon, a figure enters, quaintly neat,
All pride and business, bustle and conceit;
With looks unaltered by these scenes of woe,
With speed that, entering, speaks his haste to go,
He bids the gazing throng around him fly,   280
And carries fate and physic in his eye:
A potent quack, long versed in human ills,
Who first insults the victim whom he kills;
Whose murd'rous hand a drowsy Bench protect,
And whose most tender mercy is neglect.

Paid by the parish for attendance here,
He wears contempt upon his sapient sneer;
In haste he seeks the bed where Misery lies,
Impatience marked in his averted eyes;
And, some habitual queries hurried o'er,   290
Without reply, he rushes on the door:
His drooping patient, long inured to pain,
And long unheeded, knows remonstrance vain;
He ceases now the feeble help to crave
Of man; and silent sinks into the grave.

But ere his death some pious doubts arise,
Some simple fears, which 'bold bad' men despise;
Fain would he ask the parish-priest to prove
His title certain to the joys above:
For this he sends the murmuring nurse, who calls   300
The holy stranger to these dismal walls:

THE VILLAGE

And doth not he, the pious man, appear,
He, "passing rich with forty pounds a year?"
Ah! no; a shepherd of a different stock,
And far unlike him, feeds this little flock:
A jovial youth, who thinks his Sunday's task
As much as God or man can fairly ask;
The rest he gives to loves and labors light,
To fields the morning, and to feasts the night;
None better skilled the noisy pack to guide,   310
To urge their chase, to cheer them or to chide;
A sportsman keen, he shoots through half the day,
And, skilled at whist, devotes the night to play:
Then, while such honors bloom around his head,
Shall he sit sadly by the sick man's bed,
To raise the hope he feels not, or with zeal
To combat fears that e'en the pious feel?

  Now once again the gloomy scene explore,
Less gloomy now; the bitter hour is o'er,
The man of many sorrows sighs no more.—   320
Up yonder hill, behold how sadly slow
The bier moves winding from the vale below:
There lie the happy dead, from trouble free,
And the glad parish pays the frugal fee:
No more, O Death! thy victim starts to hear
Churchwarden stern, or kingly overseer;
No more the farmer claims his humble bow,
Thou art his lord, the best of tyrants thou!

  Now to the church behold the mourners come,
Sedately torpid and devoutly dumb;   330
The village children now their games suspend,
To see the bier that bears their ancient friend:
For he was one in all their idle sport,
And like a monarch ruled their little court;
The pliant bow he formed, the flying ball,
The bat, the wicket, were his labours all;

Him now they follow to his grave, and stand
Silent and sad, and gazing, hand in hand;
While bending low, their eager eyes explore
The mingled relics of the parish poor.   340
The bell tolls late, the moping owl flies round,
Fear marks the flight and magnifies the sound;
The busy priest, detained by weightier care,
Defers his duty till the day of prayer;
And, waiting long, the crowd retire distressed,
To think a poor man's bones should lie unblessed.

1783

ROBERT BURNS (1759-1796)

MARY MORISON

O Mary, at thy window be,
    It is the wish'd, the trysted hour!
Those smiles and glances let me see,
    That make the miser's treasure poor:
How blythely wad I bide the stoure,[1]
    A weary slave frae sun to sun,
Could I the rich reward secure,
    The lovely Mary Morison.

Yestreen[2] when to the trembling string
    The dance gaed[3] thro' the lighted ha'   10
To thee my fancy took its wing,
    I sat, but neither heard nor saw:
Tho' this was fair, and that was braw,[4]
    And yon the toast of a' the town,
I sigh'd, and said amang them a',
    "Ye are na Mary Morison."

[1] struggle
[2] last night
[3] went
[4] fine-looking

GREEN GROW THE RASHES

O Mary, canst thou wreck his peace,
  Wha for thy sake wad gladly die?
Or canst thou break that heart of his,
  Whase only faut[1] is loving thee?
If love for love thou wilt na gie
  At least be pity to me shown:
A thought ungentle canna be
  The thought o' Mary Morison.

1781   1800

GREEN GROW THE RASHES

CHORUS.—Green grow the rashes,[2] O!
  Green grow the rashes, O!
    The sweetest hours that e'er I spend
    Are spent amang the lasses, O.

There's nought but care on ev'ry han',
  In every hour that passes, O:
What signifies the life o' man,
  An 't were na for the lasses, O?

The war'ly race may riches chase,
  An' riches still may fly them, O;
An' tho' at last they catch them fast,
  Their hearts can ne'er enjoy them, O.

But gie me a cannie[3] hour at e'en,
  My arms about my dearie, O;
An' war'ly cares, an' war'ly men,
  May a' gae tapsalteerie,[4] O.

For you sae douce,[5] ye sneer at this;
  Ye're nought but senseless asses, O:

[1] fault   [2] rushes   [3] quiet   [4] topsy-turvy   [5] solemn

> The wisest man the warl' e'er saw,
>   He dearly lov'd the lasses, O.

> Auld Nature swears, the lovely dears
>   Her noblest work she classes, O:
> Her prentice han' she try'd on man,
>   An' then she made the lasses, O.

1783   1786

EPISTLE TO JOHN LAPRAIK, AN OLD SCOTTISH BARD

> While briers, an' woodbines budding green,
> And paitricks[1] scraichin[2] loud at e'en,
> An' morning poussie[3] whiddin[4] seen,
>   Inspire my Muse,
> This freedom, in an unknown frien'
>   I pray excuse.

> On Fasten-e'en[5] we had a rockin,[6]
> To ca' the crack[7] and weave our stockin;
> And there was muckle fun and jokin,
>   Ye need na doubt;
> At length we had a hearty yokin,[8]
>   At "sang about."

> There was ae sang, amang the rest,
> Aboon them a' it pleased me best,
> That some kind husband had addrest
>   To some sweet wife:

---

[1] partridges   [2] screeching   [3] hare
[4] running   [5] evening before lent
[6] a social gathering (the women spinning on the rock or distaff)   [7] to have a chat   [8] set-to

EPISTLE TO JOHN LAPRAIK

It thirled [1] the heart-strings thro' the breast,
  A' to the life.

I've scarce heard ought described sae weel,
What gen'rous, manly bosoms feel;
Thought I, "Can this be Pope or Steele,
  Or Beattie's wark?"
They tauld me 't was an odd kind chiel [2]
  About Muirkirk.

It pat me fidgin-fain [3] to hear 't,
An' sae about him there I spier 't; [4]
Then a' that kent him round declared
  He had ingine; [5]
That nane excelled it, few came near 't,
  It was sae fine:

That, set him to a pint of ale,
An' either douce [6] or merry tale,
Or rhymes an' sangs he'd made himsel,
  Or witty catches,
'Tween Inverness an' Teviotdale,
  He had few matches.

Then up I gat, an' swoor an aith,
Tho' I should pawn my pleugh an' graith, [7]
Or die a cadger pownie's [8] death,
  At some dyke-back, [9]
A pint an' gill I'd gie them baith,
  To hear your crack.[10]

[1] thrilled   [2] young fellow   [3] fidgeting-glad
[4] asked   [5] genius   [6] serious   [7] harness accouterments
[8] peddler's pony's   [9] back of a fence   [10] talk

But, first an' foremost, I should tell,
Amaist as soon as I could spell,
I to the crambo-pingle [1] fell;
    Tho' rude an' rough—
Yet crooning to a body's sel,
    Does weel eneugh.

I am nae poet, in a sense;
But just a rhymer like by chance,   50
An' hae to learning nae pretence;
    Yet, what the matter?
Whene'er my Muse does on me glance,
    I jingle at her.

Your critic-folk may cock their nose,
And say, "How can you e'er propose,
You wha ken hardly verse frae prose,
    To mak a sang?"
But, by your leaves, my learnèd foes,
    Ye 're maybe wrang.   60

What's a' your jargon o' your Schools,
Your Latin names for horns an' stools?
If honest Nature made you fools,
    What sairs [2] your grammars?
Ye'd better taen up spades and shools,
    Or knappin-hammers.[3]

A set o' dull, conceited hashes [4]
Confuse their brains in college-classes,
They gang in stirks,[5] and come out asses,
    Plain truth to speak;   70

---

[1] rhyming   [2] serves   [3] stone-breakers' hammers
[4] fools   [5] young steers

EPISTLE TO JOHN LAPRAIK

An' syne [1] they think to climb Parnassus
    By dint o' Greek!

Gie me ae spark o' Nature's fire,
That's a' the learning I desire;
Then, tho' I drudge thro' dub [2] an' mire
    At pleugh or cart,
My Muse, tho' hamely in attire,
    May touch the heart.

O for a spunk [3] o' Allan's glee,
Or Fergusson's, the bauld an' slee,[4]
Or bright Lapraik's, my friend to be,
    If I can hit it!
That would be lear [5] eneugh for me,
    If I could get it.

Now, sir, if ye hae friends enow,
Tho' real friends I b'lieve are few,
Yet, if your catalogue be fou,[6]
    I 'se no insist:
But, gif ye want ae friend that's true,
    I'm on your list.

I winna blaw about mysel,
As ill I like my fauts to tell;
But friends, an' folks that wish me well,
    They sometimes roose [7] me;
Tho', I maun own, as monie still
    As far abuse me.

---

[1] then   [2] puddle   [3] spark   [4] sly (cunning)
[5] learning   [6] full   [7] praise

There's ae wee faut they whyles lay to me,
I like the lasses—Gude forgie me!
For monie a plack [1] they wheedle frae me
    At dance or fair;
Maybe some ither thing they gie me,
    They weel can spare.

But Mauchline Race or Mauchline Fair,
I should be proud to meet you there;
We 'se gie ae night's discharge to care,
    If we forgather;
And hae a swap o' rhymin-ware [2]
    Wi' ane anither.

The four-gill chap,[3] we 'se gar [4] him clatter,
An' kirsen [5] him wi' reekin' [6] water;
Syne we 'll sit down an' tak our whitter,[7]
    To cheer our heart;
An' faith, we 'se be acquainted better
    Before we part.

Awa ye selfish warly race,
Wha think that havins,[8] sense, an' grace,
Ev'n love an' friendship should give place
    To Catch-the-Plack! [9]
I dinna like to see your face,
    Nor hear your crack.[10]

But ye whom social pleasure charms,
Whose hearts the tide of kindness warms,

---

[1] Coin   [2] rhyming verses   [3] i.e. the light-drinking chap
[4] make   [5] christen   [6] steaming
[7] hearty draught of liquor   [8] good manners
[9] hunt the coin   [10] talk

Who hold your being on the terms,
    "Each aid the others,"
Come to my bowl, come to my arms,
    My friends, my brothers!
But, to conclude my lang epistle,
As my auld pen 's worn to the grissle,
Twa lines frae you wad gar me fissle,[1]
    Who am most fervent,   130
While I can either sing or whistle,
    Your friend and servant.

1785   1786

TO A MOUSE

Wee, sleekit,[2] cowrin, tim'rous beastie,
O, what a panic 's in thy breastie!
Thou need na start awa sae hasty
    Wi' bickering brattle![3]
I wad be laith to rin an' chase thee,
    Wi' murdering pattle![4]

I'm truly sorry man's dominion
Has broken Nature's social union,
An' justifies that ill opinion
    Which makes thee startle   10
At me, thy poor, earth-born companion
    An' fellow-mortal!

I doubt na, whyles,[5] but thou may thieve;
What then? poor beastie, thou maun live:
A daimen icker in a thrave[6]
    'S a sma' request;

---

[1] make me tingle with delight   [2] sleek
[3] hurrying scamper   [4] plow-spade   [5] sometimes
[6] occasional ear in twenty-four sheaves of corn

I'll get a blessin' wi' the lave,[1]
    An' never miss 't!

Thy wee-bit housie, too, in ruin!
Its silly wa's the win's are strewin!
An' naething, now, to big[2] a new ane,
    O' foggage green!
An' bleak December's win's ensuin,
    Baith snell[3] an' keen!

Thou saw the fields laid bare an' waste,
An' weary winter comin fast,
An' cozie here, beneath the blast,
    Thou thought to dwell,
Till crash! the cruel coulter passed
    Out through thy cell.

That wee bit heap o' leaves an' stibble,
Has cost thee monie a weary nibble!
Now thou 's turned out, for a' thy trouble,
    But house or hald,[4]
To thole[5] the winter's sleety dribble,
    An' cranreuch[6] cauld!

But Mousie, thou art no thy lane,
In proving foresight may be vain:
The best-laid schemes o' mice an' men
    Gang aft agley,[7]
An' lea'e us naught but grief an' pain,
    For promised joy!

---

[1] remainder   [2] build   [3] biting
[4] without house or holding   [5] endure   [6] hoar-frost
[7] amiss

THE COTTER'S SATURDAY NIGHT

    Still thou art blest, compared wi' me!
    The present only toucheth thee:
    But och! I backward cast my e'e,
        On prospects drear!
    An' forward, tho' I canna see,
        I guess an' fear!

1785   1786

THE COTTER'S SATURDAY NIGHT

My loved, my honoured, much respected friend!
    No mercenary bard his homage pays;
With honest pride, I scorn each selfish end,
    My dearest meed, a friend's esteem and praise:
    To you I sing, in simple Scottish lays,
The lowly train in life's sequestered scene;
    The native feelings strong, the guileless ways;
What Aiken in a cottage would have been;
Ah, tho' his worth unknown, far happier there I ween!

November chill blaws loud wi' angry sugh;[1]   10
    The short'ning winter-day is near a close;
The miry beasts retreating frae the pleugh;
    The black'ning trains o' craws to their repose:
    The toil-worn Cotter frae his labour goes—
This night his weekly moil[2] is at an end,
    Collects his spades, his mattocks, and his hoes,
Hoping the morn in ease and rest to spend,
And weary, o'er the moor, his course does hameward bend.

At length his lonely cot appears in view,
    Beneath the shelter of an agèd tree;   20

[1] moan   [2] toil

Th' expectant wee-things, toddlin, stacher [1] through
   To meet their dad, wi' flichterin' [2] noise and glee.
His wee bit ingle,[3] blinkin bonilie,
His clean hearth-stane, his thrifty wifie's smile,
   The lisping infant, prattling on his knee,
Does a' his weary kiaugh [4] and care beguile,
And makes him quite forget his labour and his toil.

Belyve,[5] the elder bairns come drapping in,
   At service out, amang the farmers roun';
Some ca [6] the pleugh, some herd, some tentie [7] rin
   A cannie [8] errand to a neebor town:
   Their eldest hope, their Jenny, woman-grown,
In youthfu' bloom, love sparkling in her e'e,
   Comes hame; perhaps, to shew a braw [9] new gown,
Or deposite her sair-worn [10] penny-fee,
To help her parents dear, if they in hardship be.

With joy unfeigned, brothers and sisters meet,
   And each for other's weelfare kindly spiers:[11]
The social hours, swift-winged, unnoticed fleet;
   Each tells the uncos [12] that he sees or hears.
   The parents partial eye their hopeful years;
Anticipation forward points the view;
   The mother, wi' her needle and her sheers,
Gars [13] auld claes look amaist as weel 's the new;
The father mixes a' wi' admonition due.

Their master's and their mistress's command
   The younkers a' are warnèd to obey;
And mind their labours wi' an eydent [14] hand,

[1] stagger   [2] fluttering   [3] fire   [4] anxiety
[5] presently   [6] drive   [7] heedful   [8] careful
[9] fine   [10] hard-won   [11] inquires
[12] news   [13] makes   [14] busy

THE COTTER'S SATURDAY NIGHT

And ne'er, though out o' sight, to jauk [1] or play:
"And O! be sure to fear the Lord alway, 50
And mind your duty, duly, morn and night;
Lest in temptation's path ye gang astray,
Implore His counsel and assisting might:
They never sought in vain that sought the Lord aright."

But hark! a rap comes gently to the door;
Jenny, wha kens the meaning o' the same,
Tells how a neebor lad came o'er the moor,
To do some errands, and convoy her hame.
The wily mother sees the conscious flame
Sparkle in Jenny's e'e, and flush her cheek; 60
With heart-struck anxious care, enquires his name,
While Jenny hafflins [2] is afraid to speak;
Weel-pleased the mother hears, it 's nae wild, worthless rake.

With kindly welcome, Jenny brings him ben; [3]
A strappin' youth, he takes the mother's eye;
Blythe Jenny sees the visit 's no ill taen;
The father cracks [4] of horses, pleughs, and kye.
The youngster's artless heart o'erflows wi' joy,
But blate and laithfu', [5] scarce can weel behave;
The mother, wi' a woman's wiles, can spy 70
What makes the youth sae bashfu' and sae grave;
Weel-pleased to think her bairn's respected like the lave. [6]

O happy love! where love like this is found:
O heart-felt raptures! bliss beyond compare!

---

[1] trifle   [2] half   [3] in   [4] talks
[5] bashful and sheepish   [6] rest

I've pacèd much this weary, mortal round,
  And sage experience bids me this declare:—
"If Heaven a draught of heavenly pleasure spare,
One cordial in this melancholy vale,
  'T is when a youthful, loving, modest pair,
In other's arms, breathe out the tender tale   80
Beneath the milk-white thorn that scents the evening gale."

Is there, in human form, that bears a heart,
  A wretch! a villain! lost to love and truth!
That can, with studied, sly, ensnaring art,
  Betray sweet Jenny's unsuspecting youth?
  Curse on his perjured arts! dissembling, smooth
Are honour, virtue, conscience, all exiled?
  Is there no pity, no relenting ruth,
Points to the parents fondling o'er their child?
Then paints the ruined maid, and their distraction wild?   90

But now the supper crowns their simple board,
  The healsome parrich,[1] chief o' Scotia's food;
The soupe[2] their only hawkie[3] does afford,
  That 'yont the hallan[4] snugly chows her cood;
  The dame brings forth, in complimental mood,
To grace the lad, her weel-hained kebbuck, fell;[5]
  And aft[6] he's prest, and aft he ca's it guid;
The frugal wifie, garrulous, will tell,
How 't was a towmond[7] auld, sin' lint was i' the bell.

The chearfu' supper done, wi' serious face,   100
  They, round the ingle, form a circle wide;

[1] wholesome porridge   [2] milk   [3] cow
[4] beyond the partition wall   [5] well-saved, strong cheese
[6] often   [7] twelve-month

THE COTTER'S SATURDAY NIGHT

The sire turns o'er, wi' patriarchal grace,
   The big ha'-Bible, ance his father's pride.
   His bonnet rev'rently is laid aside,
His lyart haffets [1] wearing thin and bare;
   Those strains that once did sweet in Zion glide,
He wales [2] a portion with judicious care,
And "Let us worship God!" he says, with solemn air.

They chant their artless notes in simple guise,
   They tune their hearts, by far the noblest aim;   110
Perhaps *Dundee's* wild-warbling measures rise,
   Or plaintive *Martyrs,* worthy of the name;
   Or noble *Elgin* beets [3] the heaven-ward flame,
The sweetest far of Scotia's holy lays:
   Compared with these, Italian trills are tame;
The tickled ears no heart-felt raptures raise;
Nae unison hae they, with our Creator's praise.

The priest-like father reads the sacred page,
   How Abram was the friend of God on high;
Or Moses bade eternal warfare wage   120
   With Amalek's ungracious progeny;
   Or, how the royal Bard did groaning lie
Beneath the stroke of Heaven's avenging ire;
   Or Job's pathetic plaint, and wailing cry;
Or rapt Isaiah's wild, seraphic fire;
Or other holy Seers that tune the sacred lyre.

Perhaps the Christian volume is the theme:
   How guiltless blood for guilty man was shed;
How He, who bore in Heaven the second name,
   Had not on earth whereon to lay His head;   130
   How His first followers and servants sped;

[1] gray side-locks   [2] selects   [3] kindles

The precepts sage they wrote to many a land:
　　How he, who lone in Patmos banishèd,
Saw in the sun a mighty angel stand,
And heard great Bab'lon's doom pronounced by Heaven's command.

Then kneeling down to Heaven's Eternal King,
　　The saint, the father, and the husband prays:
Hope "springs exulting on triumphant wing,"
　　That thus they all shall meet in future days,
　　There, ever bask in uncreated rays, 140
No more to sigh or shed the bitter tear,
　　Together hymning their Creator's praise,
In such society, yet still more dear;
While circling Time moves round in an eternal sphere.

Compared with this, how poor Religion's pride,
　　In all the pomp of method, and of art;
When men display to congregations wide
　　Devotion's ev'ry grace, except the heart,
　　The Power, incensed, the pageant will desert,
The pompous strain, the sacerdotal stole; 150
　　But haply, in some cottage far apart,
May hear, well-pleased, the language of the soul,
And in His Book of Life the inmates poor enroll.

Then homeward all take off their sev'ral way;
　　The youngling cottagers retire to rest:
The parent-pair their secret homage pay,
　　And proffer up to Heaven the warm request,
　　That He who stills the raven's clam'rous nest,
And decks the lily fair in flow'ry pride,
　　Would, in the way His wisdom sees the best, 160
For them and for their little ones provide;
But chiefly in their hearts with Grace Divine preside.

THE COTTER'S SATURDAY NIGHT

From scenes like these, old Scotia's grandeur springs,
   That makes her loved at home, revered abroad:
Princes and lords are but the breath of kings,
   "An honest man's the noblest work of God;"
   And certes, in fair Virtue's heavenly road,
The cottage leaves the palace far behind;
   What is a lordling's pomp? a cumbrous load,
Disguising oft the wretch of human kind,   170
Studied in arts of Hell, in wickedness refined!

O Scotia! my dear, my native soil!
   For whom my warmest wish to Heaven is sent!
Long may thy hardy sons of rustic toil
   Be blest with health, and peace, and sweet content!
   And O may Heaven their simple lives prevent
From Luxury's contagion, weak and vile!
   Then, howe'er crowns and coronets be rent,
A virtuous populace may rise the while,
And stand a wall of fire around their much-loved
   Isle.   180

O Thou, who poured the patriotic tide,
   That streamed through Wallace's undaunted heart,
Who dared to, nobly, stem tyrannic pride,
   Or nobly die, the second glorious part:
   (The patriot's God, peculiarly Thou art,
His friend, inspirer, guardian, and reward!)
   O never, never Scotia's realm desert;
But still the patriot, and the patriot-bard
In bright succession raise, her ornament and guard!
1785   1786

ADDRESS TO THE UNCO GUID OR THE RIGIDLY RIGHTEOUS

O ye wha are sae guid yoursel,
    Sae pious and sae holy,
Ye've nought to do but mark and tell
    Your neebour's fauts and folly!
Whase life is like a weel-gaun [1] mill,
    Supplied wi' store o' water,
The heapet happer's [2] ebbing still,
    And still the clap [3] plays clatter,—

Hear me, ye venerable core,[4]
    As counsel for poor mortals   10
That frequent pass douce [5] Wisdom's door
    For glaikit [6] Folly's portals:
I, for their thoughtless, careless sakes,
    Would here propone defences—
Their donsie [7] tricks, their black mistakes,
    Their failings and mischances.

Ye see your state wi' theirs compar'd,
    And shudder at the niffer;[8]
But cast a moment's fair regard,
    What makes the mighty differ? [9]   20
Discount what scant occasion gave,
    That purity ye pride in,
And (what's aft mair than a' the lave [10])
    Your better art o' hidin.

---

[1] well-going   [2] heaped hopper (of a mill)
[3] clapper   [4] company   [5] staid
[6] giddy   [7] reckless   [8] exchange
[9] difference   [10] rest

ADDRESS TO THE UNCO GUID

Think, when your castigated pulse
   Gies now and then a wallop,
What ragings must his veins convulse
   That still eternal gallop!
Wi' wind and tide, fair i' your tail,
   Right on ye scud your sea-way;
But in the teeth o' baith to sail,
   It makes an unco [1] leeway.

See Social Life and Glee sit down,
   All joyous and unthinking,
Till, quite transmugrify'd,[2] they're grown
   Debauchery and Drinking:
O would they stay to calculate
   Th' eternal consequences,
Or—your more dreaded hell to state—
   Damnation of expenses!

Ye high, exalted, virtuous dames,
   Tied up in godly laces,
Before ye gie poor Frailty names,
   Suppose a change o' cases:
A dear-lov'd lad, convenience snug,
   A treach'rous inclination—
But, let me whisper i' your lug,[3]
   Ye're aiblins [4] nae temptation.

Then gently scan your brother man,
   Still gentler sister woman;
Tho' they may gang a kennin [5] wrang,
   To step aside is human:

---

[1] uncommon   [2] metamorphosed   [3] ear
[4] perhaps   [5] a trifle

One point must still be greatly dark,
  The moving *why* they do it;
And just as lamely can ye mark
  How far perhaps they rue it.

Who made the heart, 'tis He alone
  Decidedly can try us;
He knows each chord, its various tone,
  Each spring, its various bias: 60
Then at the balance let's be mute,
  We never can adjust it;
What's done we partly may compute,
  But know not what's resisted.

1786   1787

TO A MOUNTAIN DAISY

Wee, modest, crimson-tippèd flow'r,
Thou's met me in an evil hour;
For I maun crush amang the stoure[1]
    Thy slender stem:
To spare thee now is past my pow'r,
    Thou bonie gem.

Alas! it's no thy neebor sweet,
  The bonie lark, companion meet,
Bending thee 'mang the dewy weet,
    Wi' spreckled breast! 10
When upward-springing, blythe, to greet
    The purpling east.

Cauld blew the bitter-biting north
Upon thy early, humble birth;

[1] dust

TO A MOUNTAIN DAISY

Yet cheerfully thou glinted forth
    Amid the storm,
Scarce reared above the parent-earth
    Thy tender form.

The flaunting flow'rs our gardens yield,
High shelt'ring woods and wa's maun shield;   20
But thou, beneath the random bield [1]
    O' clod or stane,
Adorns the histie [2] stibble-field,[3]
    Unseen, alane.

There, in thy scanty mantle clad,
Thy snawie bosom sunward spread,
Thou lifts thy unassuming head
    In humble guise;
But now the share uptears thy bed,
    And low thou lies!   30

Such is the fate of artless maid,
Sweet flow'ret of the rural shade!
By love's simplicity betrayed,
    And guileless trust;
Till she, like thee, all soiled, is laid
    Low i' the dust.

Such is the fate of simple Bard,
On Life's rough ocean luckless starred!
Unskilful he to note the card
    Of prudent lore,   40
Till billows rage, and gales blow hard,
    And whelm him o'er!

---

[1] shelter   [2] bare   [3] stubble-field

Such fate to suffering Worth is giv'n,
Who long with wants and woes has striv'n,
By human pride or cunning driv'n
    To mis'ry's brink;
Till, wrenched of ev'ry stay but Heav'n,
    He, ruined, sink!

Ev'n thou who mourn'st the Daisy's fate,
That fate is thine—no distant date;   50
Stern Ruin's plough-share drives elate,
    Full on thy bloom,
Till crushed beneath the furrow's weight
    Shall be thy doom!

                1786

OF A' THE AIRTS

Of a' the airts [1] the wind can blaw
    I dearly like the west,
For there the bonie lassie lives,
    The lassie I lo'e best.
There wild woods grow, and rivers row,[2]
    And monie a hill between,
But day and night my fancy's flight
    Is ever wi' my Jean.

I see her in the dewy flowers—
    I see her sweet and fair.   10
I hear her in the tunefu' birds—
    I hear her charm the air:
There's not a bonie flower that springs
    By fountain, shaw,[3] or green,

---

[1] directions   [2] roll   [3] wood

There's not a bonie bird that sings,
  But minds me o' my Jean.

1788   1790

MY HEART'S IN THE HIGHLANDS

My heart's in the Highlands, my heart is not here,
My heart's in the Highlands a-chasing the deer,
A-chasing the wild deer and following the roe—
My heart's in the Highlands, wherever I go!

Farewell to the Highlands, farewell to the North,
The birthplace of valour, the country of worth!
Wherever I wander, wherever I rove,
The hills of the Highlands for ever I love.

Farewell to the mountains high covered with snow,
Farewell to the straths [1] and green valleys below,   10
Farewell to the forests and wild-hanging woods,
Farewell to the torrents and loud-pouring floods!

My heart's in the Highlands, my heart is not here,
My heart's in the Highlands a-chasing the deer,
A-chasing the wild deer and following the roe—
My heart's in the Highlands, wherever I go!

1788   1790

A RED, RED ROSE

My luve is like a red, red rose,
  That's newly sprung in June.
My luve is like the melodie,
  That's sweetly played in tune.

[1] river valleys

As fair art thou, my bonie lass,
  So deep in luve am I;
And I will luve thee still, my dear,
  Till a' the seas gang dry.

Till a' the seas gang dry, my dear,
  And the rocks melt wi' the sun!   10
And I will luve thee still, my dear,
  While the sands o' life shall run.

And fare thee weel, my only luve,
  And fare thee weel awhile!
And I will come again, my luve,
  Tho' it were ten thousand mile!

1788   1796

AULD LANG SYNE

Should auld acquaintance be forgot,
  And never brought to mind?
Should auld acquaintance be forgot,
  And auld lang syne!

Chorus.—For auld lang syne, my dear,
  For auld lang syne,
We'll tak a cup o' kindness yet,
  For auld lang syne!

And surely ye'll be your pint-stowp,[1]
  And surely I'll be mine,   10
And we'll tak a cup o' kindness yet
  For auld lang syne!

[1] pint-cup

AULD LANG SYNE

We twa ae run about the braes,[1]
    And pou'd [2] the gowans [3] fine,
But we've wandered monie a weary fit [4]
    Sin' auld lang syne.

We twa hae paidled in the burn [5]
    Frae morning sun til dine,[6]
But seas between us braid hae roared
    Sin' auld lang syne.   20

And there's a hand, my trusty fiere,[7]
    And gie's a hand o' thine,
And we'll tak a right guid-willie waught [8]
    For auld lang syne.

1788   1793

JOHN ANDERSON MY JO

JOHN ANDERSON my jo,[9] John,
    When we were first acquent,
Your locks were like the raven,
    Your bonie brow was brent; [10]
But now your brow is beld,[11] John,
    Your locks are like the snaw,
But blessings on your frosty pow,[12]
    John Anderson my jo!

John Anderson my jo, John,
    We clamb the hill thegither,   10
And monie a cantie [13] day, John,
    We've had wi' ane anither;

---

[1] hills   [2] plucked   [3] daisies   [4] foot   [5] brook
[6] noon   [7] comrade   [8] hearty draught   [9] sweetheart
[10] steep (not sloping from baldness)   [11] bald
[12] head   [13] jolly

Now we maun totter down, John,
And hand in hand we'll go,
And sleep thegither at the foot,
John Anderson my jo!

1789   **1790**

TAM O' SHANTER

When chapman billies [1] leave the street,
And drouthy [2] neebors neebors meet;
As market-days are wearing late,
An' folk begin to tak the gate;[3]
While we sit bousing at the nappy,[4]
An' getting fou and unco [5] happy,
We think na on the lang Scots miles,
The mosses, waters, slaps,[6] and styles,
That lie between us and our hame,
Whare sits our sulky, sullen dame,   10
Gathering her brows like gathering storm,
Nursing her wrath to keep it warm.

This truth fand honest Tam o' Shanter,
As he frae Ayr ae night did canter:
(Auld Ayr, wham ne'er a town surpasses,
For honest men and bonie lasses).

O Tam, had'st thou but been sae wise,
As taen thy ain wife Kate's advice!
She tauld thee weel thou was a skellum,[7]
A blethering,[8] blustering, drunken blellum;[9]   20
That frae November till October,
Ae market-day thou was nae sober;
That ilka [10] melder [11] wi' the miller,

---

[1] fellow-peddlers   [2] thirsty   [3] take the road (home)
[4] ale   [5] uncommonly   [6] gaps (in a fence)
[7] scamp   [8] gabbling   [9] babbler
[10] every   [11] grinding (of grain)

TAM O' SHANTER

Thou sat as lang as thou had siller;
That ev'ry naig was ca'd a shoe on,[1]
The smith and thee gat roaring fou on;
That at the Lord's house, even on Sunday,
Thou drank wi' Kirkton Jean till Monday.
She prophesied, that, late or soon,
Thou would be found deep drowned in Doon,
Or catched wi' warlocks[2] in the mirk[3]
By Alloway's auld, haunted kirk.

Ah! gentle dames, it gars me greet,[4]
To think how monie counsels sweet,
How monie lengthened, sage advices
The husband frae the wife despises!

But to our tale: Ae market-night,
Tam had got planted unco right,
Fast by an ingle,[5] bleezing finely,
Wi' reaming swats,[6] that drank divinely;
And at his elbow, Souter[7] Johnie,
His ancient, trusty, drouthy cronie:
Tam lo'ed him like a very brither;
They had been fou for weeks thegither.
The night drave on wi' sangs and clatter;
And ay the ale was growing better:
The landlady and Tam grew gracious
Wi' secret favours, sweet and precious:
The Souter tauld his queerest stories;
The landlord's laugh was ready chorus:
The storm without might rair and rustle,
Tam did na mind the storm a whistle.

Care, mad to see a man sae happy,
E'en drowned himself amang the nappy.
As bees flee hame wi' lades o' treasure,
The minutes winged their way wi' pleasure:

[1] driven a shoe on (i.e., shod)   [2] wizards   [3] dark
[4] makes me weep   [5] fireplace   [6] foaming ale   [7] cobbler

Kings may be blest but Tam was glorious,
O'er a' the ills o' life victorious!
  But pleasures are like poppies spread:
You seize the flow'r, its bloom is shed;   60
Or like the snow falls in the river,
A moment white—then melts forever;
Or like the borealis race,
That flit ere you can point their place;
Or like the rainbow's lovely form
Evanishing amid the storm.
Nae man can tether time or tide;
The hour approaches Tam maun ride:
That hour, o' night's black arch the key-stane,
That dreary hour Tam mounts his beast in;   70
And sic a night he taks the road in,
As ne'er poor sinner was abroad in.

  The wind blew as 't wad blawn its last;
The rattling showers rose on the blast;
The speedy gleams the darkness swallowed;
Loud, deep, and lang the thunder bellowed:
That night, a child might understand,
The Deil had business on his hand.
  Weel mounted on his gray mare Meg,
A better never lifted leg,   80
Tam skelpit on [1] through dub [2] and mire,
Despising wind, and rain, and fire;
Whiles holding fast his guid blue bonnet,
Whiles crooning o'er some auld Scots sonnet,
Whiles glow'ring round wi' prudent cares,
Lest bogles [3] catch him unawares:
Kirk-Alloway was drawing nigh,
Whare ghaists and houlets [4] nightly cry.

---

[1] hurried on   [2] puddle
[3] bogies   [4] owls

TAM O' SHANTER

By this time he was cross the ford,
Whare in the snaw the chapman smoored;[1]
And past the birks[2] and meikle stane,
Whare drunken Charlie brak's neck-bane;
And thro' the whins,[3] and by the cairn,[4]
Whare hunters fand the murdered bairn;
And near the thorn, aboon the well,
Whare Mungo's mither hanged hersel.
Before him Doon pours all his floods;
The doubling storm roars through the woods;
The lightnings flash from pole to pole;
Near and more near the thunders roll:
When, glimmering thro' the groaning trees,
Kirk-Alloway seemed in a bleeze,
Through ilka bore[5] the beams were glancing,
And loud resounded mirth and dancing.

Inspiring bold John Barleycorn,
What dangers thou canst make us scorn!
Wi' tippenny,[6] we fear nae evil;
Wi' usquebae,[7] we'll face the Devil!
The swats[8] sae reamed in Tammie's noddle,
Fair play, he cared na deils a boddle.[9]
But Maggie stood, right sair astonished,
Till, by the heel and hand admonished,
She ventured forward on the light;
And, vow! Tam saw an unco sight!

Warlocks and witches in a dance:
Nae cotillion, brent new[10] frae France,
But hornpipes, jigs, strathspeys, and reels,
Put life and mettle in their heels.
A winnock-bunker[11] in the east,
There sat Auld Nick, in shape o' beast;

[1] smothered   [2] birches   [3] furze   [4] pile of stones
[5] crevice   [6] two-penny ale   [7] whiskey   [8] new ale
[9] he cared not for devils a farthing   [10] brand new
[11] window-seat

A tousie tyke,[1] black, grim, and large,
To gie them music was his charge:
He screwed the pipes and gart them skirl,[2]
Till roof and rafters a' did dirl.[3]
Coffins stood round, like open presses,
That shawed the dead in their last dresses;
And, by some devilish cantraip [4] sleight,
Each in its cauld hand held a light:
By which heroic Tam was able
To note upon the haly table,   130
A murderer's banes, in gibbet-airns;[5]
Twa span-lang, wee, unchristened bairns;
A thief, new-cutted frae a rape—
Wi' his last gasp his gab [6] did gape;
Five tomahawks wi' bluid red-rusted;
Five scymitars wi' murder crusted;
A garter which a babe had strangled;
A knife a father's throat had mangled—
Whom his ain son o' life bereft—
The grey-hairs yet stack to the heft;   140
Wi' mair of horrible and awefu',
Which even to name wad be unlawfu'.

   As Tammie glowered, amazed, and curious,
The mirth and fun grew fast and furious;
The piper loud and louder blew,
The dancers quick and quicker flew,
They reeled, they set, they crossed, they cleekit,[7]
Till ilka carlin swat and reekit,[8]
And coost her duddies to the wark,[9]
And linket [10] at it in her sark! [11]   150

---

[1] shaggy dog   [2] made them shriek   [3] vibrate
[4] magic   [5] gibbet-irons   [6] mouth   [7] clinched
[8] till every hag did sweat and steam
[9] cast off her clothes for the work (orgy)
[10] danced actively   [11] chemise

TAM O' SHANTER

Now Tam, O Tam! had thae been queans,[1]
A' plump and strapping in their teens!
Their sarks, instead o' creeshie[2] flannen,
Been snaw-white seventeen-hunder linen!—
Thir breeks[3] o' mine, my only pair,
That ance were plush, o' guid blue hair,
I wad hae gi'en them off my hurdies[4]
For ae blink o' the bonie burdies!
But withered beldams, auld and droll,
Rigwoodie[5] hags wad spean[6] a foal, 160
Louping[7] and flinging on a crummock,[8]
I wonder didna turn thy stomach!
But Tam kend what was what fu' brawlie:[9]
There was ae winsome wench and wawlie,[10]
That night enlisted in the core,[11]
Lang after kend on Carrick shore
(For monie a beast to dead she shot,
An' perished monie a bonie boat,
And shook baith meikle corn and bear,[12]
And kept the country-side in fear). 170
Her cutty sark,[13] o' Paisley harn,[14]
That while a lassie she had worn,
In longitude tho' sorely scanty,
It was her best, and she was vauntie.[15]. . .
Ah! little kend thy reverend grannie,
That sark she coft[16] for her wee Nannie,
Wi' twa pund Scots ('t was a' her riches),
Wad ever graced a dance o' witches!
But here my Muse her wing maun cour,
Sic flights are far beyond her power: 180

[1] young women   [2] greasy   [3] these breeches
[4] hips   [5] old   [6] wean (by disgust)   [7] leaping
[8] crooked staff   [9] well   [10] well-formed   [11] company
[12] barley   [13] short undergarment
[14] coarse cloth   [15] proud   [16] bought

To sing how Nannie lap and flang
(A souple jad[1] she was and strang),
And how Tam stood like ane bewitched,
And thought his very een enriched;
Even Satan glowered, and fidged fu' fain,
And hotched[2] and blew wi' might and main;
Till first ae caper, syne[3] anither,
Tam tint[4] his reason a' thegither,
And roars out: "Weel done, Cutty-sark!"
And in an instant all was dark;   190
And scarcely had he Maggie rallied,
When out the hellish legion sallied.

    As bees bizz out wi' angry fyke,[5]
When plundering herds assail their byke;[6]
As open pussie's[7] mortal foes,
When, pop! she starts before their nose;
As eager runs the market-crowd,
When "Catch the thief!" resounds aloud:
So Maggie runs, the witches follow,
Wi' monie an eldritch[8] skriech and hollo   200
    Ah, Tam! ah, Tam! thou'll get thy fairin![9]
In hell they'll roast thee like a herrin!
In vain thy Kate awaits thy comin!
Kate soon will be a woefu' woman!
Now, do thy speedy utmost, Meg,
And win the key-stane of the brig[10]
There, at them thou thy tail may toss,
A running stream they dare na cross!
But ere the key-stane she could make,
The fient a tail[11] she had to shake;   210

---

[1] lass   [2] jerked with his arm like a bagpiper
[3] then   [4] lost   [5] fuss
[6] hive   [7] hare's   [8] unearthly
[9] reward (present given at a fair)   [10] bridge
[11] devil a tail

For Nannie, far before the rest,
Hard upon noble Maggie prest,
And flew at Tam wi' furious ettle;[1]
But little wist she Maggie's mettle!
Ae[2] spring brought off her master hale,[3]
But left behind her ain grey tail:
The carlin[4] claught[5] her by the rump,
And left poor Maggie scarce a stump.

   Now, wha this tale o' truth shall read,
Ilk man, and mother's son, take heed: 220
Whene'er to drink you are inclined,
Or cutty sarks run in your mind,
Think! ye may buy the joys o'er dear:
Remember Tam o' Shanter's mare.
1790   1791

YE FLOWERY BANKS

  Ye flowery banks o' bonie Doon,
    How can ye blume sae fair?
  How can ye chant, ye little birds,
    And I sae fu' o' care?

  Thou'll break my heart, thou bonie bird,
    That sings upon the bough:
  Thou minds me o' the happy days
    When my fause Luve was true!

  Thou'll break my heart, thou bonie bird,
    That sings beside thy mate: 10
  For sae I sat, and sae I sang,
    And wist na o' my fate!

[1] aim   [2] one   [3] whole
[4] witch   [5] seized

> Aft hae I roved by bonie Doon
>   To see the woodbine twine,
> And ilka[1] bird sang o' its luve,
>   And sae did I o' mine.
>
> Wi' lightsome heart I pu'd[2] a rose
>   Frae aff its thorny tree,
> And my fause luver staw[3] my rose,
>   But left the thorn wi' me.   20

1791   1792

SWEET AFTON

Flow gently, sweet Afton, among thy green braes![4]
Flow gently, I'll sing thee a song in thy praise!
My Mary's asleep by thy murmuring stream—
Flow gently, sweet Afton, disturb not her dream!

Thou stock-dove whose echo resounds through the glen,
Ye wild whistling blackbirds in yon thorny den,
Thou green-crested lapwing, thy screaming forbear—
I charge you disturb not my slumbering fair!

How lofty, sweet Afton, thy neighbouring hills,
Far marked with the courses of clear, winding rills!   10
There daily I wander, as noon rises high,
My flocks and my Mary's sweet cot in my eye.

How pleasant thy banks and green valleys below,
Where wild in the woodlands the primroses blow!
There oft, as mild Evening weeps over the lea,
The sweet-scented birk[5] shades my Mary and me.

[1] every [2] plucked [3] stole
[4] hillsides [5] birch

Thy crystal stream, Afton, how lovely it glides,
And winds by the cot where my Mary resides!
How wanton thy waters her snowy feet lave,
As, gathering sweet flowerets, she stems thy clear
    wave!   20

Flow gently, sweet Afton, among thy green braes!
Flow gently, sweet river, the theme of my lays!
My Mary's asleep by thy murmuring stream—
Flow gently, sweet Afton disturb not her dream!
  1791   1792

AE FOND KISS

Ae fond kiss, and then we sever!
Ae farewell, and then forever!
Deep in heart-wrung tears I'll pledge thee,
Warring sighs and groans I'll wage thee.
Who shall say that Fortune grieves him,
While the star of hope she leaves him?
Me, nae cheerfu' twinkle lights me,
Dark despair around benights me.

I'll ne'er blame my partial fancy:
Naething could resist my Nancy!   **10**
But to see her was to love her,
Love but her, and love forever.
Had we never loved sae kindly,
Had we never loved sae blindly,
Never met—or never parted—
We had ne'er been broken-hearted.

Fare-thee-weel, thou first and fairest!
Fare-thee-weel, thou best and dearest!

Thine be ilka[1] joy and treasure,
Peace, Enjoyment, Love, and Pleasure!   20
Ae fond kiss, and then we sever!
Ae farewell, alas, for ever!
Deep in heart-wrung tears I'll pledge thee,
Warring sighs and groans I'll wage thee.
1791   1792

HIGHLAND MARY

Ye banks, and braes,[2] and streams around
  The castle o' Montgomery,
Green be your woods and fair your flowers,
  Your waters never drumlie![3]
There simmer first unfauld her robes,
  And there the langest tarry;
For there I took the last fareweel,
  O' my sweet Highland Mary.

How sweetly bloomed the gay green birk,[4]
  How rich the hawthorn's blossom,   10
As underneath their fragrant shade
  I clasped her to my bosom!
The golden hours, on angel wings,
  Flew o'er me and my dearie;
For dear to me as light and life,
  Was my sweet Highland Mary.

Wi' monie a vow and locked embrace
  Our parting was fu' tender;
And, pledging aft to meet again,
  We tore oursels asunder;   20

[1] every   [2] hillsides
[3] muddy   [4] birch

DUNCAN GRAY

But O! fell death's untimely frost,
    That nipt my flower sae early!
Now green's the sod, and cauld's the clay,
    That wraps my Highland Mary!

O pale, pale now, those rosy lips,
    I aft hae kissed sae fondly!
And closed for aye the sparkling glance,
    That dwelt on me sae kindly!
And mould'ring now in silent dust,
    That heart that lo'ed me dearly!   30
But still within my bosom's core
    Shall live my Highland Mary.

                                    1792

DUNCAN GRAY

Duncan Gray came here to woo,
    Ha, ha, the wooin o't![1]
On blythe Yule night when we were fou,
    Ha, ha, the wooin o't!
Maggie coost her head fu high,
Look'd asklent,[2] and unco skeigh,[3]
Gart[4] poor Duncan stand abeigh;[5]
    Ha, ha, the wooin o't!

Duncan fleech'd,[6] and Duncan pray'd;
    Ha, ha, the wooin o't!   10
Meg was deaf as Ailsa Craig,
    Ha, ha, the wooin o't!
Duncan sigh'd baith out and in,

---

[1] of it
[2] askance
[3] very skittish
[4] made
[5] aloof
[6] flattered

Grat[1] his een baith bleer't and blin',
Spak o' lowpin[2] owre a linn;[3]
   Ha, ha, the wooin o't!

Time and chance are but a tide,
   Ha, ha, the wooin o't!
Slighted love is sair[4] to bide,[5]
   Ha, ha, the wooin o't!
"Shall I, like a fool," quoth he,
"For a haughty hizzie die?
She may gae to—France for me!"
   Ha, ha, the wooin o't!

How it comes let doctors tell,
   Ha, ha, the wooin o't!
Meg grew sick as he grew hale,
   Ha, ha, the wooin o't!
Something in her bosom wrings,
For relief a sigh she brings;
And O! her een, they spak sic things!
   Ha, ha, the wooin o't!

Duncan was a lad o' grace,
   Ha, ha, the wooin o't!
Maggie's was a piteous case,
   Ha, ha, the wooin o't!
Duncan could na be her death,
Swelling pity smoor'd[6] his wrath;
Now they're crouse[7] and cantie[8] baith;
   Ha, ha, the wooin o't!

1792

[1] wept
[2] leaping
[3] waterfall
[4] hard
[5] endure
[6] smothered
[7] bright
[8] happy

SCOTS, WHA HAE

Scots, wha hae wi' Wallace bled,
Scots, wham Bruce has aften led,
Welcome to your gory bed,
    Or to victorie!

Now's the day, and now's the hour:
See the front o' battle lour,
See approach proud Edward's power—
    Chains and slaverie!

Wha will be a traitor knave?
Wha can fill a coward's grave?
Wha sae base as be a slave?—
    Let him turn, and flee!

Wha for Scotland's King and Law
Freedom's sword will strongly draw,
Freeman stand or freeman fa',
    Let him follow me!

By Oppression's woes and pains,
By your sons in servile chains,
We will drain our dearest veins
    But they shall be free!

Lay the proud usurpers low!
Tyrants fall in every foe!
Liberty's in every blow!
    Let us do, or die!

1793   1794

A MAN'S A MAN FOR A' THAT

Is there for honest poverty
  That hings his head, an' a' that?
The coward slave, we pass him by—
  We dare be poor for a' that!
For a' that, an' a' that,
  Our toils obscure, an' a' that,
The rank is but the guinea's stamp,
  The man's the gowd [1] for a' that.

What though on hamely fare we dine,
  Wear hoddin [2] grey, an' a' that?   10
Gie fools their silks, and knaves their wine—
  A man's a man for a' that.
For a' that, an' a' that,
  Their tinsel show, an' a' that,
The honest man, though e'er sae poor,
  Is king o' men for a' that.

Ye see yon birkie [3] ca'd a lord,
  Wha struts, an' stares, an' a' that?
Though hundreds worship at his word,
  He's but a cuif [4] for a' that.   20
For a' that, an' a' that,
  His ribband, star, an' a' that,
The man o' independent mind,
  He looks an' laughs at a' that.

A prince can mak a belted knight,
  A marquis, duke, an' a' that!

---

[1] gold   [2] coarse grey cloth of undyed wool
[3] conceited fellow   [4] ninny

But an honest man's aboon his might—
   Guid faith, he mauna fa'[1] that!
For a' that, an' a' that,
   Their dignities, an' a' that,   30
The pith o' sense an' pride o' worth
   Are higher rank than a' that.

Then let us pray that come it may
   (As come it will for a' that)
That Sense and Worth o'er a' the earth
   Shall bear the gree[2] an' a' that!
For a' that, an' a' that,
   It's comin yet for a' that,
That man to man the world o'er
   Shall brithers be for a' that.   40

1795

WILLIAM BLAKE (1757-1827)

POETICAL SKETCHES (1783)

SONG

How sweet I roamed from field to field,
   And tasted all the summer's pride,
Till I the Prince of Love beheld
   Who in the sunny beams did glide.

He showed me lilies for my hair,
   And blushing roses for my brow;
He led me through his gardens fair,
   Where all his golden pleasures grow.

---

[1] claim   [2] have the first place

With sweet May-dews my wings were wet,
   And Phœbus fired my vocal rage;   10
He caught me in his silken net,
   And shut me in his golden cage.

He loves to sit and hear me sing,
   Then, laughing, sports and plays with me;
Then stretches out my golden wing,
   And mocks my loss of liberty.

SONG

My silks and fine array,
   My smiles and languished air,
By love are driven away;
   And mournful lean Despair
Brings me yew to deck my grave:
Such end true lovers have.

His face is fair as heaven
   When springing buds unfold;
Oh why to him was't given,
   Whose heart is wintry cold?   10
His breast is love's all worshiped tomb,
Where all love's pilgrims come.

Bring me an axe and spade,
   Bring me a winding-sheet;
When I my grave have made,
   Let winds and tempests beat:
Then down I'll lie, as cold as clay.
True love doth pass away!

MAD SONG

The wild winds weep,
And the night is a-cold;
Come hither, Sleep;
And my griefs enfold! . . .
But lo! the morning peeps
Over the eastern steeps,
And the rustling [birds] of dawn
The earth do scorn.

Lo! to the vault
Of paved heaven,
With sorrow fraught,
My notes are driven:
They strike the ear of night,
Make weep the eyes of day;
They make mad the roaring winds,
And with tempests play.

Like a fiend in a cloud,
With howling woe
After night I do crowd
And with night will go;
I turn my back to the east
From whence comforts have increased;
For light doth seize my brain
With frantic pain.

TO THE MUSES

Whether on Ida's shady brow,
  Or in the chambers of the East,

The chambers of the sun, that now
  From ancient melody have ceased;

Whether in Heaven ye wander fair,
  Or the green corners of the earth,
Or the blue regions of the air
  Where the melodious winds have birth;

Whether on crystal rocks ye rove,
  Beneath the bosom of the sea,   10
Wandering in many a coral grove,
  Fair Nine, forsaking Poetry!

How have you left the ancient love
  That bards of old enjoyed in you!
The languid strings do scarcely move!
  The sound is forced, the notes are few!

Songs of Innocence (1789)

PIPING DOWN THE VALLEYS WILD

Piping down the valleys wild,
  Piping songs of pleasant glee,
On a cloud I saw a child,
  And he laughing said to me:

"Pipe a song about a Lamb!"
  So I piped with merry cheer.
"Piper, pipe that song again;"
  So I piped: he wept to hear.

"Drop thy pipe, thy happy pipe;
  Sing thy songs of happy cheer!"   10

THE LAMB

So I sang the same again,
    While he wept with joy to hear.

"Piper, sit thee down and write
    In a book, that all may read."
So he vanished from my sight;
    And I plucked a hollow reed,

And I made a rural pen,
    And I stained the water clear,
And I wrote my happy songs
    Every child may joy to hear.

THE SHEPHERD

How sweet is the shepherd's sweet lot!
    From the morn to the evening he strays;
He shall follow his sheep all the day,
    And his tongue shall be filled with praise.

For he hears the lamb's innocent call,
    And he hears the ewe's tender reply;
He is watchful while they are in peace,
    For they know when their shepherd is nigh.

THE LAMB

Little Lamb, who made thee?
    Dost thou know who made thee?
Gave thee life, and bid thee feed
By the stream and o'er the mead;
Gave thee clothing of delight,
Softest clothing, woolly, bright;
Gave thee such a tender voice,

Farewell, green fields and happy grove,
Where flocks have ta'en delight;
Where lambs have nibbled, silent move
The feet of angels bright;
   Unseen, they pour blessing,
   And joy without ceasing,
   On each bud and blossom,
   And each sleeping bosom.

They look in every thoughtless nest,
Where birds are covered warm;
They visit caves of every beast,
To keep them all from harm.
   If they see any weeping
   That should have been sleeping,
   They pour sleep on their head,
   And sit down by their bed.

When wolves and tigers howl for prey,
They pitying stand and weep,
Seeking to drive their thirst away,
And keep them from the sheep.
   But if they rush dreadful,
   The angels, most heedful,
   Receive each mild spirit,
   New worlds to inherit.

And there the lion's ruddy eyes
Shall flow with tears of gold:
And pitying the tender cries,
And walking round the fold:
   Saying "Wrath by His meekness,
   And by His health, sickness,
   Are driven away
   From our immortal day.

"And now beside thee, bleating lamb,
I can lie down and sleep,
Or think on Him who bore thy name,
Graze after thee, and weep.
  For wash'd in life's river,
  My bright mane forever
  Shall shine like the gold,
  As I guard o'er the fold."

INFANT JOY

"I have no name;
I am but two days old."
  What shall I call thee?
"I happy am,
Joy is my name."
  Sweet joy befall thee!

Pretty joy!
Sweet joy, but two days old.
  Sweet joy I call thee:
Thou dost smile,
I sing the while;
  Sweet joy befall thee!

A DREAM

Once a dream did weave a shade
O'er my angel-guarded bed,
That an emmet lost its way
Where on grass methought I lay.

Troubled, wildered, and forlorn,
Dark, benighted, travel-worn,

Over many a tangled spray,
All heart-broke, I heard her say:

"Oh my children! do they cry,
Do they hear their father sigh?   10
Now they look abroad to see,
Now return and weep for me."

Pitying, I dropped a tear;
But I saw a glow-worm near,
Who replied, "What wailing wight
Calls the watchman of the night?

"I am set to light the ground,
While the beetle goes his round:
Follow now the beetle's hum;
Little wanderer, hie thee home!"   20

ON ANOTHER'S SORROW

CAN I see another's woe,
And not be in sorrow too?
Can I see another's grief,
And not seek for kind relief?

Can I see a falling tear,
And not feel my sorrow's share?
Can a father see his child
Weep, nor be with sorrow fill'd?

Can a mother sit and hear
An infant groan, an infant fear?   10
No, no! never can it be!
Never, never can it be!

ON ANOTHER'S SORROW

And can He, who smiles on all,
Hear the wren, with sorrow small,
Hear the small bird's grief and care,
Hear the woes that infants bear?

And not sit beside the nest,
Pouring Pity in their breast,
And not sit the cradle near,
Weeping tear on infant's tear?   20

And not sit both night and day,
Wiping all our tears away?
Oh, no! never can it be!
Never, never can it be!

He doth give His joy to all:
He becomes an infant small,
He becomes a man of woe,
He doth feel the sorrow too.

Think not thou canst sigh a sigh,
And thy Maker is not by: 30
Think not thou canst weep a tear,
And thy Maker is not near.

Oh! He gives to us His joy,
That our griefs He may destroy.
Till our grief is fled and gone
He doth sit by us and moan.

WILLIAM BLAKE

Songs of Experience (1794)

THE CLOD AND THE PEBBLE

"Love seeketh not itself to please,
   Nor for itself hath any care,
But for another gives its ease,
   And builds a Heaven in Hell's despair."

So sung a little clod of clay,
   Trodden with the cattle's feet,
But a pebble of the brook
   Warbled out these meters meet:

"Love seeketh only self to please,
   To bind another to its delight,   10
Joys in another's loss of ease,
   And builds a Hell in Heaven's despite."

A POISON TREE

I was angry with my friend:
I told my wrath, my wrath did end.
I was angry with my foe:
I told it not, my wrath did grow.

And I watered it in fears
Night and morning with my tears,
And I sunnèd it with smiles
And with soft deceitful wiles.

And it grew both day and night
Till it bore an apple bright,   10
And my foe beheld it shine,
And he knew that it was mine,—

And into my garden stole
When the night had veiled the pole;
In the morning, glad, I see
My foe outstretched beneath the tree.

A CRADLE SONG

Sleep, sleep, beauty bright,
Dreaming in the joys of night;
Sleep, sleep; in thy sleep
Little sorrows sit and weep.

Sweet babe, in thy face
Soft desires I can trace,
Secret joys and secret smiles,
Little pretty infant wiles.

As thy softest limbs I feel,
Smiles as of the morning steal   10
O'er thy cheek, and o'er thy breast
Where thy little heart does rest.

Oh the cunning wiles that creep
In thy little heart asleep!
When thy little heart does wake,
Then the dreadful light shall break.

THE TIGER

Tiger, Tiger, burning bright
In the forest of the night,
What immortal hand or eye
Framed thy fearful symmetry?

In what distant deeps or skies
Burned that fire within thine eyes?
On what wings dared he aspire?
What the hand dared seize the fire?

And what shoulder, and what art,
Could twist the sinews of thy heart? 10
When thy heart began to beat,
What dread hand formed thy dread feet?

What the hammer, what the chain,
Knit thy strength and forged thy brain?
What the anvil? What dread grasp
Dared thy deadly terrors clasp?

When the stars threw down their spears,
And watered heaven with their tears,
Did he smile his work to see?
Did he who made the lamb make thee? 20

FROM THE PROPHETIC BOOK "MILTON"

AND did those feet in ancient time
   Walk upon England's mountains green?
And was the holy Lamb of God
   On England's pleasant pastures seen?

And did the Countenance Divine
   Shine forth upon our clouded hills?
And was Jerusalem builded here
   Among these dark Satanic Mills?

Bring me my bow of burning gold!
   Bring me my arrows of desire!

Bring me my spear! O clouds, unfold!
   Bring me my chariot of fire!

I will not cease from mental fight,
   Nor shall my sword sleep in my hand,
Till we have built Jerusalem
   In England's green and pleasant land.

1804

WILLIAM WORDSWORTH (1770-1850)

WE ARE SEVEN

————A SIMPLE Child,
That lightly draws its breath,
And feels its life in every limb,
What should it know of death?

I met a little cottage Girl:
She was eight years old, she said;
Her hair was thick with many a curl
That clustered round her head.

She had a rustic, woodland air,
And she was wildly clad: 10
Her eyes were fair, and very fair;
—Her beauty made me glad.

"Sisters and brothers, little Maid,
How many may you be?"
"How many? Seven in all," she said,
And wondering looked at me.

"And where are they? I pray you tell."
She answered, "Seven are we;

And two of us at Conway dwell,
And two are gone to sea.   20

"Two of us in the church-yard lie,
My sister and my brother;
And, in the church-yard cottage, I
Dwell near them with my mother."

"You say that two at Conway dwell,
And two are gone to sea,
Yet ye are seven!—I pray you tell,
Sweet maid, how this may be."

Then did the little Maid reply,
"Seven boys and girls are we;   30
Two of us in the church-yard lie,
Beneath the church-yard tree."

"You run about, my little Maid,
Your limbs they are alive;
If two are in the church-yard laid,
Then ye are only five."

"Their graves are green, they may be seen,"
The little maid replied,
"Twelve steps or more from my mother's door,
And they are side by side.   40

"My stockings there I often knit,
My kerchief there I hem;
And there upon the ground I sit,
And sing a song to them.

"And often after sunset, sir,
When it is light and fair,

LINES WRITTEN IN EARLY SPRING

I take my little porringer,
And eat my supper there.

"The first that died was sister Jane;
In bed she moaning lay,
Till God released her of her pain;
And then she went away.

"So in the church-yard she was laid;
And, when the grass was dry,
Together round her grave we played,
My brother John and I.

"And when the ground was white with snow,
And I could run and slide,
My brother John was forced to go,
And he lies by her side."

"How many are you, then," said I,
"If they two are in heaven?"
Quick was the little Maid's reply,
"O master! we are seven."

"But they are dead; those two are dead!
Their spirits are in heaven!"
'T was throwing words away; for still
The little Maid would have her will,
And said, "Nay, we are seven!"

1798   1800

LINES WRITTEN IN EARLY SPRING

I HEARD a thousand blended notes,
While in a grove I sate reclined,

In that sweet mood when pleasant thoughts
Bring sad thoughts to the mind.

To her fair works did Nature link
The human soul that through me ran;
And much it grieved my heart to think
What man has made of man.

Through primrose tufts, in that green bower,
The periwinkle trailed its wreaths;   10
And 't is my faith that every flower
Enjoys the air it breathes.

The birds around me hopped and played,
Their thoughts I cannot measure:—
But the least motion which they made,
It seemed a thrill of pleasure.

The budding twigs spread out their fan,
To catch the breezy air;
And I must think, do all I can,
That there was pleasure there.   20

If this belief from heaven be sent,
If such be Nature's holy plan,
Have I not reason to lament
What man has made of man?

1798   1798

EXPOSTULATION AND REPLY

"Why, William, on that old grey stone,
Thus for the length of half a day,
Why, William, sit you thus alone,
And dream your time away?

EXPOSTULATION AND REPLY

"Where are your books?—that light bequeathed
To Beings else forlorn and blind!
Up! up! and drink the spirit breathed
From dead men to their kind.

"You look round on your Mother Earth,
As if she for no purpose bore you;
As if you were her first-born birth,
And none had lived before you!"

One morning thus, by Esthwaite lake,
When life was sweet, I knew not why,
To me my good friend Matthew spake,
And thus I made reply:

"The eye—it cannot choose but see;
We cannot bid the ear be still;
Our bodies feel, where'er they be,
Against or with our will.

"Nor less I deem that there are Powers
Which of themselves our minds impress;
That we can feed this mind of ours
In a wise passiveness.

"Think you, 'mid all this mighty sum
Of things for ever speaking,
That nothing of itself will come,
But we must still be seeking?

"—Then ask not wherefore, here, alone,
Conversing as I may,
I sit upon this old grey stone,
And dream my time away."

1798   1798

THE TABLES TURNED

Up! up! my Friend, and quit your books;
Or surely you'll grow double:
Up! up! my Friend, and clear your looks;
Why all this toil and trouble?

The sun, above the mountain's head,
A freshening lustre mellow
Through all the long green fields has spread,
His first sweet evening yellow.

Books! 't is a dull and endless strife:
Come, hear the woodland linnet,　　　　　　10
How sweet his music! on my life,
There's more of wisdom in it.

And hark! how blithe the throstle sings!
He, too, is no mean preacher:
Come forth into the light of things,
Let Nature be your Teacher.

She has a world of ready wealth,
Our minds and hearts to bless—
Spontaneous wisdom breathed by health,
Truth breathed by cheerfulness.　　　　　　20

One impulse from a vernal wood
May teach you more of man,
Of moral evil and of good,
Than all the sages can.

Sweet is the lore which Nature brings;
Our meddling intellect

Misshapes the beauteous forms of things :—
We murder to dissect.

Enough of Science and of Art;
Close up those barren leaves;   30
Come forth, and bring with you a heart
That watches and receives.

1798   1798

LINES

COMPOSED A FEW MILES ABOVE TINTERN ABBEY, ON
REVISITING THE BANKS OF THE WYE DURING A TOUR.
JULY 13, 1798.

FIVE years have past; five summers, with the length
Of five long winters! and again I hear
These waters, rolling from their mountain-springs
With a soft inland murmur.—Once again
Do I behold these steep and lofty cliffs,
That on a wild secluded scene impress
Thoughts of more deep seclusion; and connect
The landscape with the quiet of the sky.
The day is come when I again repose
Here, under this dark sycamore, and view   10
These plots of cottage-ground, these orchard-tufts,
Which at this season, with their unripe fruits,
Are clad in one green hue, and lose themselves
'Mid groves and copses. Once again I see
These hedge-rows, hardly hedge-rows, little lines
Of sportive wood run wild: these pastoral farms,
Green to the very door; and wreaths of smoke
Sent up, in silence, from among the trees!
With some uncertain notice, as might seem
Of vagrant dwellers in the houseless woods,   20

Or of some Hermit's cave, where by his fire
The Hermit sits alone.

                     These beauteous forms,
Through a long absence, have not been to me
As is a landscape to a blind man's eye:
But oft, in lonely rooms, and 'mid the din
Of towns and cities, I have owed to them,
In hours of weariness, sensations sweet,
Felt in the blood, and felt along the heart;
And passing even into my purer mind,
With tranquil restoration:—feelings too
Of unremembered pleasure: such, perhaps,
As have no slight or trivial influence
On that best portion of a good man's life,
His little, nameless, unremembered, acts
Of kindness and of love. Nor less, I trust,
To them I may have owed another gift,
Of aspect more sublime; that blessèd mood,
In which the burthen of the mystery,
In which the heavy and the weary weight
Of all this unintelligible world,
Is lightened:—that serene and blessèd mood,
In which the affections gently lead us on,—
Until, the breath of this corporeal frame
And even the motion of our human blood
Almost suspended, we are laid asleep
In body, and become a living soul:
While with an eye made quiet by the power
Of harmony, and the deep power of joy,
We see into the life of things.

                            If this
Be but a vain belief, yet, oh! how oft—
In darkness and amid the many shapes
Of joyless daylight; when the fretful stir
Unprofitable, and the fever of the world,

Have hung upon the beatings of my heart—
How oft, in spirit, have I turned to thee,
O sylvan Wye! thou wanderer through the woods,
How often has my spirit turned to thee!

And now, with gleams of half-extinguished thought,
With many recognitions dim and faint,
And somewhat of a sad perplexity, 60
The picture of the mind revives again:
While here I stand, not only with the sense
Of present pleasure, but with pleasing thoughts
That in this moment there is life and food
For future years. And so I dare to hope,
Though changed, no doubt, from what I was when first
I came among these hills; when like a roe
I bounded o'er the mountains, by the sides
Of the deep rivers, and the lonely streams,
Wherever nature led: more like a man 70
Flying from something that he dreads than one
Who sought the thing he loved. For nature then
(The coarser pleasures of my boyish days,
And their glad animal movements all gone by)
To me was all in all.—I cannot paint
What then I was. The sounding cataract
Haunted me like a passion: the tall rock,
The mountain, and the deep and gloomy wood,
Their colours and their forms, were then to me
An appetite; a feeling and a love, 80
That had no need of a remoter charm,
By thought supplied, nor any interest
Unborrowed from the eye.—That time is past,
And all its aching joys are now no more,
And all its dizzy raptures. Not for this
Faint I, nor mourn nor murmur; other gifts
Have followed; for such loss, I would believe,
Abundant recompense. For I have learned

To look on nature, not as in the hour
Of thoughtless youth; but hearing oftentimes 90
The still, sad music of humanity,
Nor harsh nor grating, though of ample power
To chasten and subdue. And I have felt
A presence that disturbs me with the joy
Of elevated thoughts; a sense sublime
Of something far more deeply interfused,
Whose dwelling is the light of setting suns,
And the round ocean and the living air,
And the blue sky, and in the mind of man:
A motion and a spirit, that impels 100
All thinking things, all objects of all thought,
And rolls through all things. Therefore am I still
A lover of the meadows and the woods,
And mountains; and of all that we behold
From this green earth; of all the mighty world
Of eye, and ear,—both what they half create,
And what perceive; well pleased to recognise
In nature and the language of the sense
The anchor of my purest thoughts, the nurse,
The guide, the guardian of my heart, and soul 110
Of all my moral being.
                  Nor perchance,
If I were not thus taught, should I the more
Suffer my genial spirits to decay:
For thou art with me here upon the banks
Of this fair river; thou my dearest Friend,
My dear, dear Friend; and in thy voice I catch
The language of my former heart, and read
My former pleasures in the shooting lights
Of thy wild eyes. Oh! yet a little while
May I behold in thee what I was once, 120
My dear, dear Sister! and this prayer I make,
Knowing that Nature never did betray

ABOVE TINTERN ABBEY

The heart that loved her; 't is her privilege,
Through all the years of this our life, to lead
From joy to joy: for she can so inform
The mind that is within us, so impress
With quietness and beauty, and so feed
With lofty thoughts, that neither evil tongues,
Rash judgments, nor the sneers of selfish men,
Nor greetings where no kindness is, nor all   130
The dreary intercourse of daily life,
Shall e'er prevail against us, or disturb
Our cheerful faith, that all which we behold
Is full of blessings. Therefore let the moon
Shine on thee in thy solitary walk;
And let the misty mountain-winds be free
To blow against thee; and, in after years,
When these wild ecstasies shall be matured
Into a sober pleasure; when thy mind
Shall be a mansion for all lovely forms,   140
Thy memory be as a dwelling-place
For all sweet sounds and harmonies; oh! then,
If solitude, or fear, or pain, or grief,
Should be thy portion, with what healing thoughts
Of tender joy wilt thou remember me,
And these my exhortations! Nor, perchance—
If I should be where I no more can hear
Thy voice, nor catch from thy wild eyes these gleams
Of past existence—wilt thou then forget
That on the banks of this delightful stream   150
We stood together; and that I, so long
A worshipper of Nature, hither came
Unwearied in that service: rather say
With warmer love—oh! with far deeper zeal
Of holier love. Nor wilt thou then forget
That after many wanderings, many years
Of absence, these steep woods and lofty cliffs,

And this green pastoral landscape, were to me
More dear, both for themselves and for thy sake!
   1798   1798

LUCY POEMS

STRANGE FITS OF PASSION HAVE I KNOWN

STRANGE fits of passion have I known:
And I will dare to tell,
But in the Lover's ear alone,
What once to me befell.

When she I loved looked every day
Fresh as a rose in June,
I to her cottage bent my way,
Beneath an evening-moon.

Upon the moon I fixed my eye,
All over the wide lea;   10
With quickening pace my horse drew nigh
Those paths so dear to me.

And now we reached the orchard-plot;
And, as we climbed the hill,
The sinking moon to Lucy's cot
Came near, and nearer still.

In one of those sweet dreams I slept,
Kind Nature's gentlest boon!
And all the while my eyes I kept
On the descending moon.   20

My horse moved on; hoof after hoof
He raised, and never stopped:

When down behind the cottage roof,
At once, the bright moon dropped.

What fond and wayward thoughts will slide
Into a Lover's head!
"O mercy!" to myself I cried,
"If Lucy should be dead!"

1799 1800

- J.M.
2013

maggie discovered a shell that sang
sweetly she couldn't remember her troubles

"People tend to find books when they are
ready for them"

WAYS

ways

praise

know

1800

I TRAVELLED AMONG UNKNOWN MEN

I TRAVELLED among unknown men,
In lands beyond the sea;
Nor, England! did I know till then
What love I bore to thee.

'T is past, that melancholy dream!
  Nor will I quit thy shore
A second time; for still I seem
  To love thee more and more.

Among thy mountains did I feel
  The joy of my desire;
And she I cherished turned her wheel
  Beside an English fire.

Thy mornings showed, thy nights concealed
  The bowers where Lucy played;
And thine too is the last green field
  That Lucy's eyes surveyed.

1799   1800

THREE YEARS SHE GREW

THREE years she grew in sun and shower;
Then Nature said, "A lovelier flower
On earth was never sown;
This Child I to myself will take;
She shall be mine, and I will make
A Lady of my own.

"Myself will to my darling be
Both law and impulse: and with me
The Girl, in rock and plain,
In earth and heaven, in glade and bower,
Shall feel an overseeing power
To kindle or restrain.

"She shall be sportive as the fawn
That wild with glee across the lawn

LUCY POEMS

Or up the mountain springs;
And hers shall be the breathing balm,
And hers the silence and the calm
Of mute insensate things.

"The floating clouds their state shall lend
To her; for her the willow bend;
Nor shall she fail to see
Even in the motions of the Storm
Grace that shall mould the Maiden's form
By silent sympathy.

"The stars of midnight shall be dear
To her; and she shall lean her ear
In many a secret place
Where rivulets dance their wayward round,
And beauty born of murmuring sound
Shall pass into her face.

"And vital feelings of delight
Shall rear her form to stately height,
Her virgin bosom swell;
Such thoughts to Lucy I will give
While she and I together live
Here in this happy dell."

Thus Nature spake—The work was done—
How soon my Lucy's race was run!
She died, and left to me
This heath, this calm, and quiet scene;
The memory of what has been,
And never more will be.

1799   1800

A SLUMBER DID MY SPIRIT SEAL

A slumber did my spirit seal;
  I had no human fears:
She seemed a thing that could not feel
  The touch of earthly years.

No motion has she now, no force;
  She neither hears nor sees;
Rolled round in earth's diurnal course,
  With rocks, and stones, and trees.

1799   1800

MICHAEL

A PASTORAL POEM

If from the public way you turn your steps
Up the tumultuous brook of Greenhead Ghyll,
You will suppose that with an upright path
Your feet must struggle; in such bold ascent
The pastoral mountains front you, face to face.
But, courage! for around that boisterous brook
The mountains have all opened out themselves
And made a hidden valley of their own.
No habitation can be seen; but they
Who journey thither find themselves alone   10
With a few sheep, with rocks and stones, and kites
That overhead are sailing in the sky.
It is in truth an utter solitude;
Nor should I have made mention of this Dell
But for one object which you might pass by,
Might see and notice not. Beside the brook
Appears a straggling heap of unhewn stones!

MICHAEL

And to that simple object appertains
A story—unenriched with strange events,
Yet not unfit, I deem, for the fireside,   20
Or for the summer shade. It was the first
Of those domestic tales that spake to me
Of Shepherds, dwellers in the valleys, men
Whom I already loved;—not verily
For their own sakes, but for the fields and hills
Where was their occupation and abode.
And hence this Tale, while I was yet a Boy
Careless of books, yet having felt the power
Of Nature, by the gentle agency
Of natural objects, led me on to feel   30
For passions that were not my own, and think
(At random and imperfectly indeed)
On man, the heart of man, and human life.
Therefore, although it be a history
Homely and rude, I will relate the same
For the delight of a few natural hearts;
And, with yet fonder feeling, for the sake
Of youthful Poets, who among these hills
Will be my second self when I am gone.

   Upon the forest-side in Grasmere Vale   40
There dwelt a Shepherd, Michael was his name;
An old man, stout of heart, and strong of limb.
His bodily frame had been from youth to age
Of an unusual strength: his mind was keen,
Intense, and frugal, apt for all affairs,
And in his shepherd's calling he was prompt
And watchful more than ordinary men.
Hence had he learned the meaning of all winds,
Of blasts of every tone; and oftentimes,
When others heeded not, He heard the South   50
Make subterraneous music, like the noise
Of bagpipers on distant Highland hills.

The Shepherd, at such warning, of his flock
Bethought him, and he to himself would say,
"The winds are now devising work for me!"
And, truly, at all times, the storm, that drives
The traveller to a shelter, summoned him
Up to the mountains: he had been alone
Amid the heart of many thousand mists,
That came to him, and left him, on the heights. 60
So lived he till his eightieth year was past.
And grossly that man errs, who should suppose
That the green valleys, and the streams and rocks,
Were things indifferent to the Shepherd's thoughts.
Fields, where with cheerful spirits he had breathed
The common air; hills, which with vigorous step
He had so often climbed; which had impressed
So many incidents upon his mind
Of hardship, skill or courage, joy or fear;
Which, like a book, preserved the memory 70
Of the dumb animals, whom he had saved,
Had fed or sheltered, linking to such acts
The certainty of honourable gain;
Those fields, those hills—what could they less? had laid
Strong hold on his affections, were to him
A pleasurable feeling of blind love,
The pleasure which there is in life itself.

  His days had not been passed in singleness.
His Helpmate was a comely matron, old—
Though younger than himself full twenty years. 80
She was a woman of a stirring life,
Whose heart was in her house: two wheels she had
Of antique form; this large, for spinning wool;
That small, for flax; and, if one wheel had rest,
It was because the other was at work.
The Pair had but one inmate in their house,
An only Child, who had been born to them

MICHAEL

When Michael, telling o'er his years, began
To deem that he was old,—in shepherd's phrase,
With one foot in the grave. This only Son,   90
With two brave sheep-dogs tried in many a storm,
The one of an inestimable worth,
Made all their household. I may truly say,
That they were as a proverb in the vale
For endless industry. When day was gone,
And from their occupations out of doors
The Son and Father were come home, even then,
Their labour did not cease; unless when all
Turned to the cleanly supper-board, and there,
Each with a mess of pottage and skimmed milk,   100
Sat round the basket piled with oaten cakes,
And their plain home-made cheese. Yet when the meal
Was ended, Luke (for so the Son was named)
And his old Father both betook themselves
To such convenient work as might employ
Their hands by the fireside; perhaps to card
Wool for the Housewife's spindle, or repair
Some injury done to sickle, flail, or scythe,
Or other implement of house or field.

  Down from the ceiling, by the chimney's edge,   110
That in our ancient uncouth country style
With huge and black projection overbrowed
Large space beneath, as duly as the light
Of day grew dim the Housewife hung a lamp;
An aged utensil, which had performed
Service beyond all others of its kind.
Early at evening did it burn—and late,
Surviving comrade of uncounted hours,
Which, going by from year to year, had found,
And left, the couple neither gay perhaps   **120**
Nor cheerful, yet with objects and with hopes,
Living a life of eager industry.

And now, when Luke had reached his eighteenth year,
There by the light of this old lamp they sate,
Father and Son, while far into the night
The Housewife plied her own peculiar work,
Making the cottage through the silent hours
Murmur as with the sound of summer flies.
This light was famous in its neighbourhood,
And was a public symbol of the life   130
That thrifty Pair had lived. For, as it chanced,
Their cottage on a plot of rising ground
Stood single, with large prospect, north and south,
High into Easedale, up to Dunmail-Raise,
And westward to the village near the lake;
And from this constant light, so regular,
And so far seen, the House itself, by all
Who dwelt within the limits of the vale,
Both old and young, was named THE EVENING STAR.

   Thus living on through such a length of years,   140
The Shepherd, if he loved himself, must needs
Have loved his Helpmate; but to Michael's heart
This son of his old age was yet more dear—
Less from instinctive tenderness, the same
Fond spirit that blindly works in the blood of all—
Than that a child, more than all other gifts
That earth can offer to declining man,
Brings hope with it, and forward-looking thoughts,
And stirrings of inquietude, when they
By tendency of nature needs must fail.   150
Exceeding was the love he bare to him,
His heart and his heart's joy! For oftentimes
Old Michael, while he was a babe in arms,
Had done him female service, not alone
For pastime and delight, as is the use
Of fathers, but with patient mind enforced

MICHAEL

To acts of tenderness; and he had rocked
His cradle, as with a woman's gentle hand.
    And in a later time, ere yet the Boy
Had put on boy's attire, did Michael love,   160
Albeit of a stern unbending mind,
To have the Young-one in his sight, when he
Wrought in the field, or on his shepherd's stool
Sate with a fettered sheep before him stretched
Under the large old oak, that near his door
Stood single, and, from matchless depth of shade,
Chosen for the Shearer's covert from the sun,
Thence in our rustic dialect was called
The CLIPPING TREE, a name which yet it bears.
There, while they two were sitting in the shade,   170
With others round them, earnest all and blithe,
Would Michael exercise his heart with looks
Of fond correction and reproof bestowed
Upon the Child, if he disturbed the sheep
By catching at their legs, or with his shouts
Scared them, while they lay still beneath the shears.
    And when by Heaven's good grace the boy grew up
A healthy Lad, and carried in his cheek
Two steady roses that were five years old;
Then Michael from a winter coppice cut   180
With his own hand a sapling, which he hooped
With iron, making it throughout in all
Due requisites a perfect shepherd's staff,
And gave it to the Boy; wherewith equipt
He as a watchman oftentimes was placed
At gate or gap, to stem or turn the flock;
And, to his office prematurely called,
There stood the urchin, as you will divine,
Something between a hindrance and a help;
And for this cause not always, I believe,   190
Receiving from his Father hire of praise;

Though nought was left undone which staff, or voice,
Or looks, or threatening gestures, could perform.

   But soon as Luke, full ten years old, could stand
Against the mountain blasts; and to the heights,
Not fearing toil, nor length of weary ways,
He with his Father daily went, and they
Were as companions, why should I relate
That objects which the Shepherd loved before
Were dearer now? that from the Boy there came   200
Feelings and emanations—things which were
Light to the sun and music to the wind;
And that the old Man's heart seemed born again?

   Thus in his Father's sight the Boy grew up:
And now, when he had reached his eighteenth year,
He was his comfort and his daily hope.

   While in this sort the simple household lived
From day to day, to Michael's ear there came
Distressful tidings. Long before the time
Of which I speak, the Shepherd had been bound   210
In surety for his brother's son, a man
Of an industrious life, and ample means;
But unforeseen misfortunes suddenly
Had prest upon him; and old Michael now
Was summoned to discharge the forfeiture,
A grievous penalty, but little less
Than half his substance. This unlooked-for claim,
At the first hearing, for a moment took
More hope out of his life than he supposed
That any old man ever could have lost.   220
As soon as he had armed himself with strength
To look his trouble in the face, it seemed
The Shepherd's sole resource to sell at once
A portion of his patrimonial fields.
Such was his first resolve; he thought again,
And his heart failed him. "Isabel," said he,

MICHAEL

Two evenings after he had heard the news,
"I have been toiling more than seventy years,
And in the open sunshine of God's love
Have we all lived; yet, if these fields of ours   230
Should pass into a stranger's hand, I think
That I could not lie quiet in my grave.
Our lot is a hard lot; the sun himself
Has scarcely been more diligent than I;
And I have lived to be a fool at last
To my own family. An evil man
That was, and made an evil choice, if he
Were false to us; and, if he were not false,
There are ten thousand to whom loss like this
Had been no sorrow. I forgive him;—but   240
'T were better to be dumb than to talk thus.

  "When I began, my purpose was to speak
Of remedies and of a cheerful hope.
Our Luke shall leave us, Isabel; the land
Shall not go from us, and it shall be free;
He shall possess it, free as is the wind
That passes over it. We have, thou know'st,
Another kinsman—he will be our friend
In this distress. He is a prosperous man,
Thriving in trade—and Luke to him shall go,   250
And with his kinsman's help and his own thrift
He quickly will repair this loss, and then
He may return to us. If here he stay,
What can be done? Where every one is poor,
What can be gained?"
                 At this the old Man paused,
And Isabel sat silent, for her mind
Was busy, looking back into past times.
There's Richard Bateman, thought she to herself,
He was a parish-boy—at the church-door
They made a gathering for him, shillings, pence,   260

And halfpennies, wherewith the neighbours bought
A basket, which they filled with pedlar's wares;
And, with this basket on his arm, the lad
Went up to London, found a master there,
Who, out of many, chose the trusty boy
To go and overlook his merchandise
Beyond the seas; where he grew wondrous rich,
And left estates and monies to the poor,
And, at his birth-place, built a chapel floored
With marble, which he sent from foreign lands.   270
These thoughts, and many others of like sort,
Passed quickly through the mind of Isabel,
And her face brightened. The old Man was glad,
And thus resumed:—"Well, Isabel! this scheme
These two days has been meat and drink to me.
Far more than we have lost is left us yet.

"We have enough—I wish indeed that I
Were younger;—but this hope is a good hope.
Make ready Luke's best garments, of the best
Buy for him more, and let us send him forth   280
To-morrow, or the next day, or to-night:
If he *could* go, the Boy should go to-night."

Here Michael ceased, and to the fields went forth
With a light heart. The Housewife for five days
Was restless morn and night, and all day long
Wrought on with her best fingers to prepare
Things needful for the journey of her son.
But Isabel was glad when Sunday came
To stop her in her work: for, when she lay
By Michael's side, she through the last two nights   290
Heard him, how he was troubled in his sleep:
And when they rose at morning she could see
That all his hopes were gone. That day at noon
She said to Luke, while they two by themselves
Were sitting at the door, "Thou must not go:

MICHAEL

We have no other Child but thee to lose,
None to remember—do not go away,
For if thou leave thy Father he will die."
The Youth made answer with a jocund voice;
And Isabel, when she had told her fears, 300
Recovered heart. That evening her best fare
Did she bring forth, and all together sat
Like happy people round a Christmas fire.

   With daylight Isabel resumed her work;
And all the ensuing week the house appeared
As cheerful as a grove in Spring: at length
The expected letter from their kinsman came,
With kind assurances that he would do
His utmost for the welfare of the Boy;
To which, requests were added, that forthwith 310
He might be sent to him. Ten times or more
The letter was read over; Isabel
Went forth to show it to the neighbours round;
Nor was there at that time on English land
A prouder heart than Luke's. When Isabel
Had to her house returned, the old Man said,
"He shall depart to-morrow." To this word
The Housewife answered, talking much of things
Which, if at such short notice he should go,
Would surely be forgotten. But at length 320
She gave consent, and Michael was at ease.

   Near the tumultuous brook of Greenhead Ghyll,
In that deep valley, Michael had designed
To build a Sheep-fold; and, before he heard
The tidings of his melancholy loss,
For this same purpose he had gathered up
A heap of stones, which by the streamlet's edge
Lay thrown together, ready for the work.
With Luke that evening thitherward he walked:
And soon as they had reached the place he stopped, 330

And thus the old Man spake to him:—"My son,
To-morrow thou wilt leave me: with full heart
I look upon thee, for thou art the same
That wert a promise to me ere thy birth,
And all thy life hast been my daily joy.
I will relate to thee some little part
Of our two histories; 't will do thee good
When thou art from me, even if I should touch
On things thou canst not know of.—After thou
First cam'st into the world—as oft befalls   340
To new-born infants—thou didst sleep away
Two days, and blessings from thy Father's tongue
Then fell upon thee. Day by day passed on,
And still I loved thee with increasing love.
Never to living ear came sweeter sounds
Than when I heard thee by our own fireside
First uttering, without words, a natural tune;
While thou, a feeding babe, didst in thy joy
Sing at thy Mother's breast. Month followed month,
And in the open fields my life was passed   350
And on the mountains; else I think that thou
Hadst been brought up upon thy Father's knees.
But we were playmates, Luke: among these hills,
As well thou knowest, in us the old and young
Have played together, nor with me didst thou
Lack any pleasure which a boy can know."
Luke had a manly heart; but at these words
He sobbed aloud. The old Man grasped his hand,
And said, "Nay, do not take it so—I see
That these are things of which I need not speak.   360
—Even to the utmost I have been to thee
A kind and a good Father: and herein
I but repay a gift which I myself
Received at others' hands; for, though now old
Beyond the common life of man, I still

MICHAEL

Remember them who loved me in my youth.
Both of them sleep together: here they lived,
As all their Forefathers had done; and, when
At length their time was come, they were not loth
To give their bodies to the family mould.　　　370
I wished that thou shouldst live the life they lived,
But 't is a long time to look back, my Son,
And see so little gain from threescore years.
These fields were burthened when they came to me;
Till I was forty years of age, not more
Than half of my inheritance was mine.
I toiled and toiled; God blessed me in my work,
And till these three weeks past the land was free.
—It looks as if it never could endure
Another Master. Heaven forgive me, Luke,　　　380
If I judge ill for thee, but it seems good
That thou shouldst go."
　　　　　　　At this the old Man paused;
Then, pointing to the stones near which they stood,
Thus, after a short silence, he resumed:
"This was a work for us; and now, my Son,
It is a work for me. But, lay one stone—
Here, lay it for me, Luke, with thine own hands.
Nay, Boy, be of good hope;—we both may live
To see a better day. At eighty-four
I still am strong and hale;—do thou thy part;　　　390
I will do mine.—I will begin again
With many tasks that were resigned to thee:
Up to the heights, and in among the storms,
Will I without thee go again, and do
All works which I was wont to do alone,
Before I knew thy face.—Heaven bless thee, Boy!
Thy heart these two weeks has been beating fast
With many hopes; it should be so—yes—yes—
I knew that thou couldst never have a wish

To leave me, Luke: thou hast been bound to me 400
Only by links of love: when thou art gone,
What will be left to us!—But I forget
My purposes. Lay now the corner-stone,
As I requested; and hereafter, Luke,
When thou art gone away, should evil men
Be thy companions, think of me, my Son,
And of this moment; hither turn thy thoughts,
And God will strengthen thee: amid all fear
And all temptation, Luke, I pray that thou
May'st bear in mind the life thy Fathers lived, 410
Who, being innocent, did for that cause
Bestir them in good deeds. Now, fare thee well—
When thou return'st, thou in this place wilt see
A work which is not here: a covenant
'T will be between us; but, whatever fate
Befall thee, I shall love thee to the last,
And bear thy memory with me to the grave."

The Shepherd ended here; and Luke stooped down,
And, as his Father had requested, laid
The first stone of the Sheep-fold. At the sight 420
The old Man's grief broke from him; to his heart
He pressed his Son, he kissèd him and wept;
And to the house together they returned.
—Hushed was that House in peace, or seeming peace,
Ere the night fell:—with morrow's dawn the Boy
Began his journey, and, when he had reached
The public way, he put on a bold face;
And all the neighbours, as he passed their doors,
Came forth with wishes and with farewell prayers,
That followed him till he was out of sight. 430

A good report did from their Kinsman come,
Of Luke and his well-doing: and the Boy
Wrote loving letters, full of wondrous news,
Which, as the Housewife phrased it, were throughout

"The prettiest letters that were ever seen."
Both parents read them with rejoicing hearts.
So, many months passed on: and once again
The Shepherd went about his daily work
With confident and cheerful thoughts; and now
Sometimes when he could find a leisure hour   440
He to that valley took his way, and there
Wrought at the Sheep-fold. Meantime Luke began
To slacken in his duty; and, at length,
He in the dissolute city gave himself
To evil courses: ignominy and shame
Fell on him, so that he was driven at last
To seek a hiding-place beyond the seas.

There is a comfort in the strength of love;
'T will make a thing endurable, which else
Would overset the brain, or break the heart: 450
I have conversed with more than one who well
Remember the old Man, and what he was
Years after he had heard this heavy news.
His bodily frame had been from youth to age
Of an unusual strength. Among the rocks
He went, and still looked up to sun and cloud,
And listened to the wind; and, as before,
Performed all kinds of labour for his sheep,
And for the land, his small inheritance.
And to that hollow dell from time to time   460
Did he repair, to build the Fold of which
His flock had need. 'T is not forgotten yet
The pity which was then in every heart
For the old Man—and 't is believed by all
That many and many a day he thither went,
And never lifted up a single stone.

There, by the Sheep-fold, sometimes was he seen
Sitting alone, or with his faithful Dog,

Then old, beside him, lying at his feet.
The length of full seven years, from time to time, 470
He at the building of this Sheep-fold wrought,
And left the work unfinished when he died.
Three years, or little more, did Isabel
Survive her Husband: at her death the estate
Was sold, and went into a stranger's hand.
The Cottage which was named the EVENING STAR
Is gone—the ploughshare has been through the ground
On which it stood; great changes have been wrought
In all the neighbourhood:—yet the oak is left
That grew beside their door; and the remains 480
Of the unfinished Sheep-fold may be seen
Beside the boisterous brook of Greenhead Ghyll.
  1800   1800

TO THE CUCKOO

O BLITHE New-comer! I have heard,
  I hear thee and rejoice.
O Cuckoo! shall I call thee Bird,
  Or but a wandering Voice?

While I am lying on the grass
  Thy twofold shout I hear;
From hill to hill it seems to pass
  At once far off, and near.

Though babbling only to the Vale,
  Of sunshine and of flowers, 10
Thou bringest unto me a tale
  Of visionary hours.

Thrice welcome, darling of the Spring!
  Even yet thou art to me

MY HEART LEAPS UP

No bird, but an invisible thing,
A voice, a mystery;

The same whom in my schoolboy days
I listened to; that cry
Which made me look a thousand ways
In bush, and tree, and sky.   20

To seek thee did I often rove
Through woods and on the green;
And thou wert still a hope, a love;
Still longed for, never seen.

And I can listen to thee yet;
Can lie upon the plain
And listen, till I do beget
That golden time again.

O blessèd Bird! the earth we pace
Again appears to be   30
An unsubstantial, faery place;
That is fit home for Thee!

1802   1807

MY HEART LEAPS UP

My heart leaps up when I behold
  A rainbow in the sky:
So was it when my life began;
So is it now I am a man;
So be it when I shall grow old,
  Or let me die!
The Child is father of the Man;

And I could wish my days to be
Bound each to each by natural piety.

1802   1807

RESOLUTION AND INDEPENDENCE

There was a roaring in the wind all night;
The rain came heavily and fell in floods;
But now the sun is rising calm and bright;
The birds are singing in the distant woods;
Over his own sweet voice the Stock-dove broods;
The Jay makes answer as the Magpie chatters;
And all the air is filled with pleasant noise of waters.

All things that love the sun are out of doors;
The sky rejoices in the morning's birth;
The grass is bright with rain-drops;—on the moors   10
The hare is running races in her mirth;
And with her feet she from the plashy earth
Raises a mist; that, glittering in the sun,
Runs with her all the way, wherever she doth run.

I was a Traveller then upon the moor;
I saw the hare that raced about with joy;
I heard the woods and distant waters roar;
Or heard them not, as happy as a boy:
The pleasant season did my heart employ:
My old remembrances went from me wholly;   20
And all the ways of men, so vain and melancholy.

But, as it sometimes chanceth, from the might
Of joy in minds that can no further go,
As high as we have mounted in delight
In our dejection do we sink as low;
To me that morning did it happen so;

RESOLUTION AND INDEPENDENCE

And fears and fancies thick upon me came;
Dim sadness—and blind thoughts, I knew not, nor could
   name.

I heard the sky-lark warbling in the sky;
And I bethought me of the playful hare:
Even such a happy Child of earth am I;
Even as these blissful creatures do I fare;
Far from the world I walk, and from all care;
But there may come another day to me—
Solitude, pain of heart, distress, and poverty.

My whole life I have lived in pleasant thought,
As if life's business were a summer mood;
As if all needful things would come unsought
To genial faith, still rich in genial good;
But how can He expect that others should
Build for him, sow for him, and at his call
Love him, who for himself will take no heed at all?

I thought of Chatterton, the marvellous Boy,
The sleepless Soul that perished in his pride;
Of Him who walked in glory and in joy
Following his plough, along the mountainside:
By our own spirits are we deified:
We Poets in our youth begin in gladness;
But thereof come in the end despondency and madness.

Now, whether it were by peculiar grace,
A leading from above, a something given,
Yet it befell that, in this lonely place,
When I with these untoward thoughts had striven,
Beside a pool bare to the eye of heaven
I saw a Man before me unawares:
The oldest man he seemed that ever wore grey hairs.

As a huge stone is sometimes seen to lie
Couched on the bald top of an eminence;
Wonder to all who do the same espy,
By what means it could thither come, and whence;   60
So that it seems a thing endued with sense:
Like a sea-beast crawled forth, that on a shelf
Of rock or sand reposeth, there to sun itself;

Such seemed this Man, not all alive nor dead,
Nor all asleep—in his extreme old age:
His body was bent double, feet and head
Coming together in life's pilgrimage;
As if some dire constraint of pain, or rage
Of sickness felt by him in times long past,
A more than human weight upon his frame had cast.   70

Himself he propped, limbs, body, and pale face,
Upon a long grey staff of shaven wood:
And, still as I drew near with gentle pace,
Upon the margin of that moorish flood
Motionless as a cloud the old Man stood,
That heareth not the loud winds when they call;
And moveth all together, if it move at all.

At length, himself unsettling, he the pond
Stirred with his staff, and fixedly did look
Upon the muddy water, which he conned,   80
As if he had been reading in a book:
And now a stranger's privilege I took;
And, drawing to his side, to him did say,
"This morning gives us promise of a glorious day."

A gentle answer did the old Man make,
In courteous speech which forth he slowly drew:
And him with further words I thus bespake,

RESOLUTION AND INDEPENDENCE

"What occupation do you there pursue?
This is a lonesome place for one like you."
Ere he replied, a flash of mild surprise 90
Broke from the sable orbs of his yet-vivid eyes.

His words came feebly, from a feeble chest,
But each in solemn order followed each,
With something of a lofty utterance drest—
Choice word and measured phrase, above the reach
Of ordinary men; a stately speech;
Such as grave Livers do in Scotland use,
Religious men, who give to God and man their dues.

He told, that to these waters he had come
To gather leeches, being old and poor: 100
Employment hazardous and wearisome!
And he had many hardships to endure:
From pond to pond he roamed, from moor to moor;
Housing, with God's good help, by choice or chance;
And in this way be gained an honest maintenance.

The old Man still stood talking by my side;
But now his voice to me was like a stream
Scarce heard; nor word from word could I divide;
And the whole body of the Man did seem
Like one whom I had met with in a dream; 110
Or like a man from some far region sent,
To give me human strength, by apt admonishment.

My former thoughts returned: the fear that kills;
And hope that is unwilling to be fed;
Cold, pain, and labour, and all fleshly ills;
And mighty Poets in their misery dead.
—Perplexed, and longing to be comforted,

My question eagerly did I renew,
"How is it that you live, and what is it you do?"

He with a smile did then his words repeat; 120
And said that, gathering leeches, far and wide
He travelled; stirring thus about his feet
The waters of the pools where they abide.
"Once I could meet with them on every side;
But they have dwindled long by slow decay;
Yet still I persevere, and find them where I may."

While he was talking thus, the lonely place,
The old Man's shape, and speech—all troubled me:
In my mind's eye I seemed to see him pace
About the weary moors continually, 130
Wandering about alone and silently.
While I these thoughts within myself pursued,
He, having made a pause, the same discourse renewed.

And soon with this he other matter blended,
Cheerfully uttered, with demeanour kind,
But stately in the main; and, when he ended,
I could have laughed myself to scorn to find
In that decrepit Man so firm a mind.
"God," said I, "be my help and stay secure;
I'll think of the Leech-gatherer on the lonely moor!" 140
  1802   1807

TO THE DAISY

WITH little here to do or see
Of things that in the great world be,
Daisy! again I talk to thee,
   For thou art worthy,
Thou unassuming Common-place

TO THE DAISY

Of Nature, with that homely face,
And yet with something of a grace
  Which love makes for thee!

Oft on the dappled turf at ease
I sit, and play with similes,
Loose types of things through all degrees,
  Thoughts of thy raising:
And many a fond and idle name
I give to thee, for praise or blame,
As is the humour of the game,
  While I am gazing.

A nun demure of lowly port;
Or sprightly maiden, of Love's court,
In thy simplicity the sport
  Of all temptations;
A queen in crown of rubies drest;
A starveling in a scanty vest;
Are all, as seems to suit thee best,
  Thy appellations.

A little Cyclops with one eye
Staring to threaten and defy,
That thought comes next—and instantly
  The freak is over,
The shape will vanish—and behold
A silver shield with boss of gold,
That spreads itself, some faery bold
  In fight to cover!

I see thee glittering from afar—
And then thou art a pretty star;
Not quite so fair as many are
  In heaven above thee!

WILLIAM WORTHSWORTH

    Yet like a star, with glittering crest,
    Self-poised in air thou seem'st to rest;—
    May peace come never to his nest,
        Who shall reprove thee!   40

    Bright *Flower!* for by that name at last,
    When all my reveries are past,
    I call thee, and to that cleave fast,
        Sweet silent creature!
    That breath'st with me in sun and air,
    Do thou, as thou art wont, repair
    My heart with gladness, and a share
        Of thy meek nature!

1802   1807

COMPOSED UPON WESTMINSTER BRIDGE, SEPTEMBER 3, 1802

  EARTH has not anything to show more fair.
Dull would he be of soul who could pass by
A sight so touching in its majesty:
This City now doth, like a garment, wear
The beauty of the morning; silent, bare,
Ships, towers, domes, theatres, and temples lie
Open unto the fields, and to the sky;
All bright and glittering in the smokeless air.
Never did sun more beautifully steep
In his first splendour, valley, rock, or hill;   10
Ne'er saw I, never felt, a calm so deep!
The river glideth at his own sweet will:
Dear God! the very houses seem asleep;
And all that mighty heart is lying still!

1802   1807

IT IS A BEAUTEOUS EVENING

It is a beauteous evening, calm and free,
The holy time is quiet as a Nun
Breathless with adoration; the broad sun
Is sinking down in its tranquillity;
The gentleness of heaven broods o'er the Sea:
Listen! the mighty Being is awake,
And doth with his eternal motion make
A sound like thunder—everlastingly.
Dear Child! dear Girl! that walkest with me here,
If thou appear untouched by solemn thought,   10
Thy nature is not therefore less divine:
Thou liest in Abraham's bosom all the year;
And worshipp'st at the Temple's inner shrine,
God being with thee when we know it not.

1802   1807

ON THE EXTINCTION OF THE VENETIAN REPUBLIC

Once did She hold the gorgeous East in fee;
And was the safeguard of the West: the worth
Of Venice did not fall below her birth,
Venice, the eldest Child of Liberty.
She was a maiden City, bright and free;
No guile seduced, no force could violate;
And, when she took unto herself a Mate,
She must espouse the everlasting Sea.
And what if she had seen those glories fade,
Those titles vanish, and that strength decay;   10
Yet shall some tribute of regret be paid
When her long life hath reached its final day:

Men are we, and must grieve when even the Shade
Of that which once was great is passed away.
   1802   1807

WRITTEN IN LONDON, SEPTEMBER, 1802

O Friend! I know not which way I must look
For comfort, being, as I am, opprest,
To think that now our life is only drest
For show; mean handy-work of craftsman, cook,
Or groom!—We must run glittering like a brook
In the open sunshine, or we are unblest:
The wealthiest man among us is the best:
No grandeur now in nature or in book
Delights us. Rapine, avarice, expense,
This is idolatry; and these we adore: 10
Plain living and high thinking are no more:
The homely beauty of the good old cause
Is gone; our peace, our fearful innocence,
And pure religion breathing household laws.
   1802   1807

LONDON, 1802

Milton! thou shouldst be living at this hour:
England hath need of thee: she is a fen
Of stagnant waters: altar, sword, and pen,
Fireside, the heroic wealth of hall and bower,
Have forfeited their ancient English dower
Of inward happiness. We are selfish men;
Oh! raise us up, return to us again;
And give us manners, virtue, freedom, power.
Thy soul was like a Star, and dwelt apart;
Thou hadst a voice whose sound was like the sea: 10
Pure as the naked heavens, majestic, free,

So didst thou travel on life's common way,
In cheerful godliness; and yet thy heart
The lowliest duties on herself did lay.

1802   1807

IT IS NOT TO BE THOUGHT OF THAT THE FLOOD

It is not to be thought of that the Flood
Of British freedom, which, to the open sea
Of the world's praise, from dark antiquity
Hath flowed, "with pomp of waters, unwithstood,"
Roused though it be full often to a mood
Which spurns the check of salutary bands,
That this most famous Stream in bogs and sands
Should perish; and to evil and to good
Be lost for ever. In our halls is hung
Armory of the invincible Knights of old: 10
We must be free or die, who speak the tongue
That Shakspere spake: the faith and morals hold
Which Milton held. In everything we are sprung
Of Earth's first blood, have titles manifold.

1802 or 1803   1803   1807

SHE WAS A PHANTOM OF DELIGHT

She was a Phantom of delight
When first she gleamed upon my sight;
A lovely Apparition, sent
To be a moment's ornament;
Her eyes as stars of Twilight fair;
Like Twilight's, too, her dusky hair;
But all things else about her drawn
From May-time and the cheerful Dawn;

A dancing Shape, an Image gay,
To haunt, to startle, and waylay.   10

I saw her upon nearer view,
A Spirit, yet a Woman too!
Her household motions light and free,
And steps of virgin-liberty;
A countenance in which did meet
Sweet records, promises as sweet;
A Creature not too bright or good
For human nature's daily food;
For transient sorrows, simple wiles,
Praise, blame, love, kisses, tears, and smiles.   20

And now I see with eye serene
The very pulse of the machine;
A Being breathing thoughtful breath,
A Traveller between life and death;
The reason firm, the temperate will,
Endurance, foresight, strength, and skill;
A perfect Woman, nobly planned,
To warn, to comfort, and command;
And yet a Spirit still, and bright
With something of angelic light.   30

1804   1807

THE SOLITARY REAPER

Behold her, single in the field,
Yon solitary Highland Lass!
Reaping and singing by herself;
Stop here, or gently pass!
Alone she cuts and binds the grain,
And sings a melancholy strain;
O listen! for the Vale profound
Is overflowing with the sound.

I WANDERED LONELY AS A CLOUD

    No Nightingale did ever chaunt
    More welcome notes to weary bands   10
    Of travellers in some shady haunt,
    Among Arabian sands:
    A voice so thrilling ne'er was heard
    In spring-time from the Cuckoo-bird,
    Breaking the silence of the seas
    Among the farthest Hebrides.

    Will no one tell me what she sings?—
    Perhaps the plaintive numbers flow
    For old, unhappy, far-off things,
    And battles long ago: 20
    Or is it some more humble lay,
    Familiar matter of to-day?
    Some natural sorrow, loss, or pain,
    That has been, and may be again?

    Whate'er the theme, the Maiden sang
    As if her song could have no ending;
    I saw her singing at her work,
    And o'er the sickle bending;—
    I listened, motionless and still;
    And, as I mounted up the hill,   30
    The music in my heart I bore,
    Long after it was heard no more.

1804   1807

I WANDERED LONELY AS A CLOUD

    I WANDERED lonely as a cloud
    That floats on high o'er vales and hills,
    When all at once I saw a crowd,
    A host, of golden daffodils;

Beside the lake, beneath the trees,
Fluttering and dancing in the breeze.

Continuous as the stars that shine
And twinkle on the milky way,
They stretched in never-ending line
Along the margin of a bay: 10
Ten thousand saw I at a glance,
Tossing their heads in sprightly dance.

The waves beside them danced; but they
Out-did the sparkling waves in glee:
A poet could not but be gay,
In such a jocund company:
I gazed—and gazed—but little thought
What wealth the show to me had brought:

For oft, when on my couch I lie
In vacant or in pensive mood,   20
They flash upon that inward eye
Which is the bliss of solitude;
And then my heart with pleasure fills,
And dances with the daffodils.

1804   1807

THE PRELUDE

Selections

BOOK FIRST

CHILDHOOD AND SCHOOL-TIME
(*Lines* 425-478)

AND in the frosty season, when the sun
Was set, and visible for many a mile

THE PRELUDE 141

The cottage windows blazed through twilight gloom,
I heeded not their summons: happy time
It was indeed for all of us—for me
It was a time of rapture! Clear and loud 430
The village clock tolled six,—I wheeled about,
Proud and exulting like an untired horse
That cares not for his home. All shod with steel,
We hissed along the polished ice in games
Confederate, imitative of the chase
And woodland pleasures,—the resounding horn,
The pack loud chiming, and the hunted hare.
So through the darkness and the cold we flew,
And not a voice was idle; with the din
Smitten, the precipices rang aloud; 440
The leafless trees and every icy crag
Tinkled like iron; while far distant hills
Into the tumult sent an alien sound
Of melancholy not unnoticed, while the stars
Eastward were sparkling clear, and in the west
The orange sky of evening died away.
Not seldom from the uproar I retired
Into a silent bay, or sportively
Glanced sideway, leaving the tumultuous throng,
To cut across the reflex of a star 450
That fled, and, flying still before me, gleamed
Upon the glassy plain; and oftentimes,
When we had given our bodies to the wind,
And all the shadowy banks on either side
Came sweeping through the darkness, spinning still
The rapid line of motion, then at once
Have I, reclining back upon my heels,
Stopped short; yet still the solitary cliffs
Wheeled by me—even as if the earth had rolled
With visible motion her diurnal round! 460
Behind me did they stretch in solemn train,

Feebler and feebler, and I stood and watched
Till all was tranquil as a dreamless sleep.

  Ye Presences of Nature in the sky
And on the earth! Ye Visions of the hills!
And Souls of lonely places! can I think
A vulgar hope was yours when ye employed
Such ministry, when ye through many a year
Haunting me thus among my boyish sports,
On caves and trees, upon the woods and hills,   470
Impressed upon all forms the characters
Of danger or desire; and thus did make
The surface of the universal earth
With triumph and delight, with hope and fear,
Work like a sea?

                      Not uselessly employed,
Might I pursue this theme through every change
Of exercise and play, to which the year
Did summon us in his delightful round.
  1800   1850

BOOK THIRD

RESIDENCE AT CAMBRIDGE
(*Lines* 1-82)

It was a dreary morning when the wheels
Rolled over a wide plain o'erhung with clouds,
And nothing cheered our way till first we saw
The long-roofed chapel of King's College lift
Turrets and pinnacles in answering files,
Extended high above a dusky grove.
  Advancing, we espied upon the road
A student clothed in gown and tasselled cap,
Striding along as if o'ertasked by Time,

THE PRELUDE

Or covetous of exercise and air; 10
He passed—nor was I master of my eyes
Till he was left an arrow's flight behind.
As near and nearer to the spot we drew,
It seemed to suck us in with an eddy's force.
Onward we drove beneath the Castle; caught,
While crossing Magdalene Bridge, a glimpse of Cam;
And at the *Hoop* alighted, famous Inn.

My spirit was up, my thoughts were full of hope;
Some friends I had, acquaintances who there
Seemed friends, poor simple schoolboys, now hung round 20
With honour and importance; in a world
Of welcome faces up and down I roved;
Questions, directions, warnings and advice,
Flowed in upon me, from all sides; fresh day
Of pride and pleasure! to myself I seemed
A man of business and expense, and went
From shop to shop about my own affairs,
To Tutor or to Tailor, as befell,
From street to street with loose and careless mind.

I was the Dreamer, they the Dream; I roamed 30
Delighted through the motley spectacle;
Gowns grave, or gaudy, doctors, students, streets,
Courts, cloisters, flocks of churches, gateways, towers:
Migration strange for a stripling of the hills,
A northern villager.

                As if the change
Had waited on some Fairy's wand, at once
Behold me rich in monies, and attired
In splendid garb, with hose of silk, and hair
Powdered like rimy trees, when frost is keen.
My lordly dressing-gown, I pass it by, 40
With other signs of manhood that supplied
The lack of beard.—The weeks went roundly on,

With invitations, suppers, wine and fruit,
Smooth housekeeping within, and all without
Liberal, and suiting gentleman's array.

   The Evangelist St. John my patron was:
Three Gothic courts are his, and in the first
Was my abiding-place, a nook obscure;
Right underneath, the College kitchens made
A humming sound, less tuneable than bees,   50
But hardly less industrious; with shrill notes
Of sharp command and scolding intermixed.
Near me hung Trinity's loquacious clock,
Who never let the quarters, night or day,
Slip by him unproclaimed, and told the hours
Twice over with a male and female voice.
Her pealing organ was my neighbour too;
And from my pillow, looking forth by light
Of moon or favoring stars, I could behold
The antechapel where the statue stood   60
Of Newton with his prism and silent face,
The marble index of a mind for ever
Voyaging through strange seas of Thought, alone.

   Of College labours, of the Lecturer's room
All studded round, as thick as chairs could stand,
With loyal students faithful to their books,
Half-and-half idlers, hardy recusants,
And honest dunces—of important days,
Examinations, when the man was weighed
As in a balance! of excessive hopes,   70
Tremblings withal and commendable fears,
Small jealousies, and triumphs good or bad—
Let others that know more speak as they know.
Such glory was but little sought by me,
And little won. Yet from the first crude days
Of settling time in this untried abode,
I was disturbed at times by prudent thoughts,

Wishing to hope without a hope, some fears
About my future worldly maintenance,
And, more than all, a strangeness in the mind, 80
A feeling that I was not for that hour,
Nor for that place.
　1804　　　　　　　　　　　　　　　　　　1850

BOOK ELEVENTH

FRANCE—(Concluded)

(Lines 1-17, 105-144)

From that time forth, Authority in France
Put on a milder face; Terror had ceased,
Yet everything was wanting that might give
Courage to them who looked for good by light
Of rational Experience, for the shoots
And hopeful blossoms of a second spring:
Yet, in me, confidence was unimpaired;
The Senate's language, and the public acts
And measures of the Government, though both
Weak, and of heartless omen, had not power 10
To daunt me; in the People was my trust,
And in the virtues which mine eyes had seen.
I knew that wound external could not take
Life from the young Republic; that new foes
Would only follow, in the path of shame,
Their brethren, and her triumphs be in the end
Great, universal, irresistible.

　　. . . . .

　O pleasant exercise of hope and joy!
For mighty were the auxiliars which then stood
Upon our side, us who were strong in love!
Bliss was it in that dawn to be alive,

But to be young was very Heaven! O times,
In which the meagre, stale, forbidding ways   110
Of custom, law, and statute, took at once
The attraction of a country in romance!
When Reason seemed the most to assert her rights
When most intent on making of herself
A prime enchantress—to assist the work,
Which then was going forward in her name!
Not favoured spots alone, but the whole Earth,
The beauty wore of promise—that which sets
(As at some moments might not be unfelt
Among the bowers of Paradise itself)   120
The budding rose above the rose full blown.
What temper at the prospect did not wake
To happiness unthought of? The inert
Were roused, and lively natures rapt away!
They who had fed their childhood upon dreams,
The play-fellows of fancy, who had made
All powers of swiftness, subtilty, and strength
Their ministers,—who in lordly wise had stirred
Among the grandest objects of the sense,
And dealt with whatsoever they found there   130
As if they had within some lurking right
To wield it;—they, too, who of gentle mood
Had watched all gentle motions, and to these
Had fitted their own thoughts, schemers more mild,
And in the region of their peaceful selves;—
Now was it that *both* found, the meek and lofty
Did both find, helpers to their hearts' desire,
And stuff at hand, plastic as they could wish,—
Were called upon to exercise their skill,
Not in Utopia,—subterranean fields,—   140
Or some secreted island, Heaven knows where!
But in the very world, which is the world

Of all of us,—the place where, in the end,
We find our happiness, or not at all!
    1804   1850

ELEGIAC STANZAS

SUGGESTED BY A PICTURE OF PEELE CASTLE, IN A STORM,
PAINTED BY SIR GEORGE BEAUMONT

I was thy neighbour once, thou rugged Pile!
Four summer weeks I dwelt in sight of thee:
I saw thee every day; and all the while
Thy Form was sleeping on a glassy sea.

So pure the sky, so quiet was the air!
So like, so very like, was day to day!
Whene'er I looked, thy Image still was there;
It trembled, but it never passed away.

How perfect was the calm! it seemed no sleep;
No mood, which season takes away, or brings: 10
I could have fancied that the mighty Deep
Was even the gentlest of all gentle Things.

Ah! then, if mine had been the Painter's hand,
To express what then I saw; and add the gleam,
The light that never was, on sea or land,
The consecration, and the Poet's dream;

I would have planted thee, thou hoary Pile
Amid a world how different from this!
Beside a sea that could not cease to smile;
On tranquil land, beneath a sky of bliss.   20

Thou shouldst have seemed a treasure-house divine
Of peaceful years; a chronicle of heaven;—
Of all the sunbeams that did ever shine
The very sweetest had to thee been given.

A Picture had it been of lasting ease,
Elysian quiet, without toil or strife;
No motion but the moving tide, a breeze,
Or merely silent Nature's breathing life.

Such, in the fond illusion of my heart,
Such Picture would I at that time have made: 30
And seen the soul of truth in every part,
A steadfast peace that might not be betrayed.

So once it would have been,—'t is so no more;
I have submitted to a new control:
A power is gone, which nothing can restore;
A deep distress hath humanised my Soul.

Not for a moment could I now behold
A smiling sea, and be what I have been:
The feeling of my loss will ne'er be old;
This, which I know, I speak with mind serene.   40

Then, Beaumont, Friend! who would have been the Friend,
If he had lived, of Him whom I deplore,
This work of thine I blame not, but commend;
This sea in anger, and that dismal shore.

O 't is a passionate Work!—yet wise and well,
Well chosen is the spirit that is here;
That Hulk which labours in the deadly swell,
This rueful sky, this pageantry of fear!

And this huge Castle, standing here sublime,
I love to see the look with which it braves, 50
Cased in the unfeeling armour of old time,
The lightning, the fierce wind, and trampling waves.

Farewell, farewell the heart that lives alone,
Housed in a dream, at distance from the Kind!
Such happiness, wherever it be known,
Is to be pitied; for 't is surely blind.

But welcome fortitude, and patient cheer,
And frequent sights of what is to be borne!
Such sights, or worse, as are before me here.—
Not without hope we suffer and we mourn. 60
  1805   1807

ODE TO DUTY

"Jam non consil'o bonus sed more eo perductus, ut non tantum recte facere possim, sed nisi recte facere non possim."

STERN Daughter of the Voice of God!
O Duty! if that name thou love
Who art a light to guide, a rod
To check the erring, and reprove;
Thou, who art victory and law
When empty terrors overawe;
From vain temptations dost set free;
And calm'st the weary strife of frail humanity!

There are who ask not if thine eye
Be on them; who, in love and truth, **10**
Where no misgiv'ng is, rely
Upon the genial sense of youth:
Glad Hearts! without reproach or blot;
Who do thy work, and know it not:

Oh! if through confidence misplaced
They fail, thy saving arms, dread Power! around them cast.

Serene will be our days and bright,
And happy will our nature be,
When love is an unerring light,
And joy its own security. 20
And they a blissful course may hold
Even now, who, not unwisely bold,
Live in the spirit of this creed;
Yet seek thy firm support, according to their need.

I, loving freedom, and untried;
No sport of every random gust,
Yet being to myself a guide,
Too blindly have reposed my trust:
And oft, when in my heart was heard
Thy timely **mandate**, I deferred 30
The task, in **smoother** walks to stray;
But thee I **now would** serve more strictly, if I may.

Through no disturbance of my soul,
Or strong compunction in me wrought,
I supplicate for thy control;
But in the quietness of thought:
Me this unchartered freedom tires;
I feel the weight of chance-desires:
My hopes no more must change their name,
I long for a repose that ever is the same. 40

Stern Lawgiver! yet thou dost wear
The Godhead's most benignant grace;
Nor know we anything so fair
As is the smile upon thy face:

Flowers laugh before thee on their beds
And fragrance in thy footing treads;
Thou dost preserve the stars from wrong;
And the most ancient heavens, through Thee, are fresh
    and strong.

To humbler functions, awful Power!
I call thee: I myself commend   50
Unto thy guidance from this hour;
Oh, let my weakness have an end!
Give unto me, made lowly wise,
The spirit of self-sacrifice;
The confidence of reason give;
And in the light of truth thy Bondman let me live!
  1805   1807

CHARACTER OF THE HAPPY WARRIOR

Who is the happy Warrior? Who is he
That every man in arms should wish to be?
—It is the generous Spirit, who, when brought
Among the tasks of real life, hath wrought
Upon the plan that pleased his boyish thought:
Whose high endeavors are an inward light
That makes the path before him always bright:
Who, with a natural instinct to discern
What knowledge can perform, is diligent to learn;
Abides by this resolve, and stops not there,   10
But makes his moral being his prime care;
Who, doomed to go in company with Pain,
And Fear, and Bloodshed, miserable train!
Turns his necessity to glorious gain;
In face of these doth exercise a power
Which is our human nature's highest dower;
Controls them and subdues, transmutes, bereaves

Of their bad influence, and their good receives:
By objects, which might force the soul to abate
Her feeling, rendered more compassionate;   20
Is placable—because occasions rise
So often that demand such sacrifice;
More skilful in self-knowledge, even more pure,
As tempted more; more able to endure,
As more exposed to suffering and distress;
Thence, also, more alive to tenderness.
—'Tis he whose law is reason; who depends
Upon that law as on the best of friends;
Whence, in a state where men are tempted still
To evil for a guard against worse ill,   30
And what in quality or act is best
Doth seldom on a right foundation rest,
He labours good on good to fix, and owes
To virtue every triumph that he knows:
—Who, if he rise to station of command,
Rises by open means; and there will stand
On honourable terms, or else retire,
And in himself possess his own desire;
Who comprehends his trust, and to the same
Keeps faithful with a singleness of aim;   40
And therefore does not stoop, nor lie in wait
For wealth, or honours, or for worldly state;
Whom they must follow; on whose head must fall,
Like showers of manna, if they come at all:
Whose powers shed round him in the common strife,
Or mild concerns of ordinary life,
A constant influence, a peculiar grace;
But who, if he be called upon to face
Some awful moment to which Heaven has joined
Great issues, good or bad for human kind,   50
Is happy as a Lover; and attired
With sudden brightness, like a Man inspired;

THE HAPPY WARRIOR

And, through the heat of conflict, keeps the law
In calmness made, and sees what he foresaw;
Or if an unexpected call succeed,
Come when it will, is equal to the need:
—He who, though thus endued as with a sense
And faculty for storm and turbulence,
Is yet a Soul whose master-bias leans
To homefelt pleasures and to gentle scenes; 60
Sweet images! which, wheresoe'er he be,
Are at his heart; and such fidelity
It is his darling passion to approve;
More brave for this, that he hath much to love:—
'Tis, finally, the Man, who, lifted high,
Conspicuous object in a Nation's eye,
Or left unthought-of in obscurity,—
Who, with a toward or untoward lot,
Prosperous or adverse, to his wish or not—
Plays, in the many games of life, that one 70
Where what he most doth value must be won:
Whom neither shape of danger can dismay,
Nor thought of tender happiness betray;
Who, not content that former worth stand fast,
Looks forward, persevering to the last,
From well to better, daily self-surpast:
Who, whether praise of him must walk the earth
For ever, and to noble deeds give birth,
Or he must fall to sleep without his fame,
And leave a dead unprofitable name, 80
Finds comfort in himself and in his cause;
And, while the mortal mist is gathering, draws
His breath in confidence of Heaven's applause:
This is the happy Warrior; this is He
Whom every Man in arms should wish to be.

1805   1807

ODE

INTIMATIONS OF IMMORTALITY FROM RECOLLECTIONS OF EARLY CHILDHOOD

I

There was a time when meadow, grove, and stream,
The earth, and every common sight,
    To me did seem
    Apparelled in celestial light,
The glory and the freshness of a dream.
It is not now as it hath been of yore;—
    Turn wheresoe'er I may,
    By night or day,
The things which I have seen I now can see no more.

II

    The Rainbow comes and goes,   10
    And lovely is the Rose,
    The Moon doth with delight
Look round her when the heavens are bare,
    Waters on a starry night
    Are beautiful and fair;
The sunshine is a glorious birth;
But yet I know, where'er I go,
That there hath past away a glory from the earth.

III

Now, while the birds thus sing a joyous song,
    And while the young lambs bound   20
    As to the tabor's sound,

ODE ON IMMORTALITY

To me alone there came a thought of grief:
A timely utterance gave that thought relief,
    And I again am strong:
The cataracts blow their trumpets from the steep;
No more shall grief of mine the season wrong;
I hear the Echoes through the mountains throng,
The Winds come to me from the fields of sleep,
    And all the earth is gay;
        Land and sea   30
  Give themselves up to jollity,
    And with the heart of May
Doth every Beast keep holiday;—
    Thou Child of Joy,
Shout round me, let me hear thy shouts, thou happy Shepherd-boy!

IV

Ye blessèd Creatures, I have heard the call
  Ye to each other make; I see
The heavens laugh with you in your jubilee;
    My heart is at your festival,
    My head hath its coronal,   40
The fulness of your bliss, I feel—I feel it all.
      Oh evil day! if I were sullen
      While Earth herself is adorning,
        This sweet May-morning,
      And the Children are culling
        On every side,
    In a thousand valleys far and wide,
    Fresh flowers; while the sun shines warm,
And the Babe leaps up on his Mother's arm:—
      I hear, I hear, with joy I hear!   50
    —But there's a Tree, of many, one,
A single Field which I have looked upon,

Both of them speak of something that is **gone**:
> The Pansy at my feet
> Doth the same tale repeat:
Whither is fled the visionary gleam?
Where is it now, the glory and the dream?

V

Our birth is but a sleep and a forgetting.
The Soul that rises with us, our life's Star,
> Hath had elsewhere its setting,
> And cometh from afar:
> Not in entire forgetfulness,
> And not in utter nakedness,
But trailing clouds of glory do we come
> From God, who is our home:
Heaven lies about us in our infancy!
Shades of the prison-house begin to close
> Upon the growing Boy,
But He beholds the light, and whence it flows,
> He sees it in his joy;
The Youth, who daily farther from the east
> Must travel, still is Nature's Priest,
> And by the vision splendid
> Is on his way attended;
At length the Man perceives it die away,
And fade into the light of common day.

VI

Earth fills her lap with pleasures of her own;
Yearnings she hath in her own natural kind,
And, even with something of a Mother's mind,
> And no unworthy aim,
> The homely Nurse doth all she can

ODE ON IMMORTALITY

To make her Foster-child, her Inmate Man,
    Forget the glories he hath known,
And that imperial palace whence he came.

VII

Behold the Child among his new-born blisses,
A six years' Darling of a pigmy size!
See, where 'mid work of his own hand he lies,
Fretted by sallies of his mother's kisses,
With light upon him from his father's eyes!
See, at his feet, some little plan or chart,
Some fragment from his dream of human life,
Shaped by himself with newly-learned art;
    A wedding or a festival,
    A mourning or a funeral;
      And this hath now his heart,
    And unto this he frames his song:
      Then will he fit his tongue
To dialogues of business, love, or strife;
    But it will not be long
    Ere this be thrown aside,
    And with new joy and pride
The little Actor cons another part;
Filling from time to time his "humorous stage"
With all the Persons, down to palsied Age,
That Life brings with her in her equipage;
    As if his whole vocation
    Were endless imitation.

VIII

Thou, whose exterior semblance doth belie
    Thy Soul's immensity;
Thou best Philosopher, who yet dost keep

158   WILLIAM WORDSWORTH

Thy heritage, thou Eye among the blind,
That, deaf and silent, read'st the eternal deep,
Haunted for ever by the eternal mind,—
    Mighty Prophet! Seer blest!
    On whom those truths do rest,
Which we are toiling all our lives to find,
In darkness lost, the darkness of the grave;
Thou, over whom thy Immortality
Broods like the Day, a Master o'er a Slave,
A Presence which is not to be put by;   120
Thou little Child, yet glorious in the might
Of heaven-born freedom on thy being's height,
Why with such earnest pains dost thou provoke
The years to bring the inevitable yoke,
Thus blindly with thy blessedness at strife?
Full soon thy Soul shall have her earthly freight,
And custom lie upon thee with a weight,
Heavy as frost, and deep almost as life!

IX

    O joy! that in our embers
    Is something that doth live,   130
    That nature yet remembers
    What was so fugitive!
The thought of our past years in me doth breed
Perpetual benediction: not indeed
For that which is most worthy to be blest;
Delight and liberty, the simple creed
Of Childhood, whether busy or at rest,
With new-fledged hope still fluttering in his breast:—
    Not for these I raise
    The song of thanks and praise;   140
    But for those obstinate questionings
    Of sense and outward things,

ODE ON IMMORTALITY

    Fallings from us, vanishings;
    Blank misgivings of a Creature
Moving about in worlds not realised,
High instincts before which our mortal Nature
Did tremble like a guilty Thing surprised:
    But for those first affections,
    Those shadowy recollections,
  Which, be they what they may,
Are yet the fountain-light of all our day,
Are yet a master-light of all our seeing;
  Uphold us, cherish, and have power to make
Our noisy years seem moments in the being
Of the eternal Silence: truths that wake,
    To perish never:
Which neither listlessness, nor mad endeavour,
    Nor Man nor Boy,
Nor all that is at enmity with joy,
Can utterly abolish or destroy!
  Hence in a season of calm weather
    Though inland far we be,
Our Souls have sight of that immortal sea
    Which brought us hither,
  Can in a moment travel thither,
And see the Children sport upon the shore,
And hear the mighty waters rolling evermore.

X

Then sing, ye Birds, sing, sing a joyous song!
    And let the young Lambs bound
    As to the tabor's sound!
We in thought will join your throng,
    Ye that pipe and ye that play,
    Ye that through your hearts to-day

  Feel the gladness of the May!
What though the radiance which was once so bright
Be now for ever taken from my sight,
 Though nothing can bring back the hour
Of splendour in the grass, of glory in the flower;
  We will grieve not, rather find
  Strength in what remains behind;   180
  In the primal sympathy
  Which having been must ever be;
  In the soothing thoughts that spring
  Out of human suffering;
  In the faith that looks through death,
In years that bring the philosophic mind.

XI

And O, ye Fountains, Meadows, Hills, and Groves,
Forebode not any severing of our loves!
Yet in my heart of hearts I feel your might;
I only have relinquished one delight   190
To live beneath your more habitual sway.
I love the Brooks which down their channels fret,
Even more than when I tripped lightly as they;
The innocent brightness of a new-born Day
   Is lovely yet;
The Clouds that gather round the setting sun
Do take a sober colouring from an eye
That hath kept watch o'er man's mortality;
Another race hath been, and other palms are won.
Thanks to the human heart by which we live, 200
 Thanks to its tenderness, its joys, and fears,
 To me the meanest flower that blows can give
 Thoughts that do often lie too deep for tears.
1803-1806   1807

THE WORLD IS TOO MUCH WITH US

The world is too much with us; late and soon,
Getting and spending, we lay waste our powers:
Little we see in Nature that is ours;
We have given our hearts away, a sordid boon!
This Sea that bares her bosom to the moon;
The winds that will be howling at all hours,
And are up-gathered now like sleeping flowers;
For this, for everything, we are out of tune;
It moves us not.—Great God! I'd rather be
A Pagan suckled in a creed outworn;   10
So might I, standing on this pleasant lea,
Have glimpses that would make me less forlorn;
Have sight of Proteus rising from the sea;
Or hear old Triton blow his wreathèd horn.
1807   1807

AFTER-THOUGHT

I thought of Thee, my partner and my guide,
As being past away.—Vain sympathies!
For, backward, Duddon! as I cast my eyes,
I see what was, and is, and will abide;
Still glides the Stream, and shall forever glide;
The Form remains, the Function never dies;
While we, the brave, the mighty, and the wise,
We Men, who in our morn of youth defied
The elements, must vanish;—be it so!
Enough, if something from our hands have power   10
To live, and act, and serve the future hour;
And if, as toward the silent tomb we go,

Through love, through hope, and faith's transcendent dower,
We feel that we are greater than we know.
1820   1820

SCORN NOT THE SONNET

Scorn not the Sonnet; Critic, you have frowned,
Mindless of its just honours; with this key
Shakspeare unlocked his heart; the melody
Of this small lute gave ease to Petrarch's wound;
A thousand times this pipe did Tasso sound;
With it Camöens soothed an exile's grief;
The Sonnet glittered a gay myrtle leaf
Amid the cypress with which Dante crowned
His visionary brow: a glow-worm lamp,
It cheered mild Spenser, called from Faeryland   10
To struggle through dark ways; and when a damp
Fell round the path of Milton, in his hand
The Thing became a trumpet; whence he blew
Soul-animating strains—alas, too few!
1827   1827

PREFACE TO *LYRICAL BALLADS*

The first Volume of these Poems has already been submitted to general perusal. It was published as an experiment, which, I hoped, might be of some use to ascertain how far, by fitting to metrical arrangement a selection of the real language of men in a state of vivid sensation, that sort of pleasure and that quantity of pleasure may be imparted, which a Poet may rationally endeavour to impart.

I had formed no very inaccurate estimate of the probable effect of those Poems: I flattered myself that they who should be pleased with them would read them with more than common pleasure: and, on the other hand, I was well aware that by those who should dislike them they would be read with more than common dislike. The result has differed from my expectation in this only, that a greater number have been pleased than I ventured to hope I should please.

Several of my Friends are anxious for the success of these Poems, from a belief, that, if the views with which they were composed were indeed realised, a class of Poetry would be produced, well adapted to interest mankind permanently, and not unimportant in the quality, and in the multiplicity of its moral relations: and on this account they have advised me to prefix a systematic defence of the theory upon which the Poems were written. But I was unwilling to undertake the task, knowing that on this occasion the Reader would look coldly upon my arguments, since I might be suspected of having been principally influenced by the selfish and foolish hope of *reasoning* him into an approbation of these particular Poems: and I was still more unwilling to undertake the task, because, adequately to display the opinions, and fully to enforce the arguments, would require a space wholly disproportionate to a preface. For, to treat the subject with the clearness and coherence of which it is susceptible, it would be necessary to give a full account of the present state of the public taste in this country, and to determine how far this taste is healthy or depraved; which, again, could not be determined without pointing out in what manner language and the human mind act and re-act on each other, and without retracing the revolutions, not of literature alone, but likewise of society itself. I have therefore altogether declined to enter regularly upon this defence; yet I am sensible that there would be something like impropriety in abruptly obtruding upon the Public, without a few words of introduction, Poems so materially different from those upon which general approbation is at present bestowed.

It is supposed that by the act of writing in verse an Author makes a formal engagement that he will gratify certain known habits of association; that he not only thus apprises the Reader that certain classes of ideas and expressions will be found in his book, but that others will be carefully excluded. This exponent or symbol held forth by metrical language must in different eras of literature have excited very different expectations: for example, in the age of Catullus, Terence, and Lucretius, and that of Statius or Claudian; and in our own country, in the age of Shakspeare and Beaumont and Fletcher, and that of Donne and Cowley, or Dryden, or Pope. I will not take upon me to determine the exact import of the promise which, by the act of writing in verse, an Author in the present day makes to his reader: but it will undoubtedly appear to many persons that I have not fulfilled the terms of an engagement thus voluntarily contracted. They who have been accustomed to the gaudiness and inane phraseology of many modern writers, if they persist in reading this book to its conclusion, will, no doubt, frequently have to struggle with feelings of strangeness and awkwardness: they will look round for poetry, and will be induced to inquire by what species of courtesy these attempts can be permitted to assume that title. I hope therefore the Reader will not censure me for attempting to state what I have proposed to myself to perform; and also (as far as the limits of a preface will permit) to explain some of the chief reasons which have determined me in the choice of my purpose: that at least he may be spared any unpleasant feeling of disappointment, and that I myself

PREFACE TO LYRICAL BALLADS

may be protected from one of the most dishonourable accusations which can be brought against an Author; namely, that of an indolence which prevents him from endeavouring to ascertain what is his duty, or, when his duty is ascertained, prevents him from performing it.

The principal object, then, proposed in these Poems was to choose incidents and situations from common life, and to relate or describe them throughout, as far as was possible, in a selection of language really used by men, and, at the same time, to throw over them a certain colouring of imagination, whereby ordinary things should be presented to the mind in an unusual aspect; and further, and above all, to make these incidents and situations interesting by tracing in them, truly though not ostentatiously, the primary laws of our nature: chiefly, as far as regards the manner in which we associate ideas in a state of excitement. Humble and rustic life was generally chosen, because in that condition the essential passions of the heart find a better soil in which they can attain their maturity, are less under restraint, and speak a plainer and more emphatic language; because in that condition of life our elementary feelings coexist in a state of greater simplicity, and, consequently, may be more accurately contemplated, and more forcibly communicated; because the manners of rural life germinate from those elementary feelings, and, from the necessary character of rural occupations, are more easily comprehended, and are more durable; and, lastly, because in that condition the passions of men are incorporated with the beautiful and permanent forms of nature. The language, too, of these men has been adopted (purified indeed from what appear to be its real defects, from all lasting and rational causes of dislike or disgust) because such men hourly communicate with the best objects from which the best part of language is originally derived; and because, from their rank in society and the sameness and narrow circle of their intercourse, being less under the influence of social vanity, they convey their feelings and notions in simple and unelaborated expressions. Accordingly, such a language, arising out of repeated experience and regular feelings, is a more permanent, and a far more philosophical language, than that which is frequently substituted for it by Poets, who think that they are conferring honour upon themselves and their art, in proportion as they separate themselves from the sympathies of men, and indulge in arbitrary and capricious habits of expression, in order to furnish food for fickle tastes and fickle appetites of their own creation.

I cannot, however, be insensible to the present outcry against the triviality and meanness, both of thought and language, which some of my contemporaries have occasionally introduced into their metrical compositions; and I acknowledge that this defect, where it exists, is more dishonourable to the Writer's own character than false refinement or arbitrary innovation, though I should contend at the same time that it is far less pernicious in the sum of its consequences. From such verses the Poems in these volumes will be found distinguished at least by one mark of difference, that each of them has a worthy *purpose*. Not that I always began to write with a distinct purpose formally conceived; but habits of meditation have, I trust, so prompted and regulated my feelings, that my descriptions of such objects as strongly excite those feelings, will be found to carry along with them a *purpose*. If this opinion be erroneous, I can have little right to the name of a Poet. For all good poetry is the spontaneous overflow of powerful feelings: and though this be true, Poems to which any value can be attached were never produced on any

PREFACE TO LYRICAL BALLADS

variety of subjects but by a man who, being possessed of more than usual organic sensibility, had also thought long and deeply. For our continued influxes of feeling are modified and directed by our thoughts, which are indeed the representatives of all our past feelings; and, as by contemplating the relation of these general representatives to each other, we discover what is really important to men, so, by the repetition and continuance of this act, our feelings will be connected with important subjects, till at length, if we be originally possessed of much sensibility, such habits of mind will be produced that, by obeying blindly and mechanically the impulses of those habits, we shall describe objects, and utter sentiments, of such a nature, and in such connection with each other, that the understanding of the Reader must necessarily be in some degree enlightened, and his affections strengthened and purified.

It has been said that each of these Poems has a purpose. Another circumstance must be mentioned which distinguishes these Poems from the popular Poetry of the day; it is this, that the feeling therein developed gives importance to the action and situation, and not the action and situation to the feeling.

A sense of false modesty shall not prevent me from asserting that the Reader's attention is pointed to this mark of distinction, far less for the sake of these particular Poems than from the general importance of the subject. The subject is indeed important! For the human mind is capable of being excited without the application of gross and violent stimulants; and he must have a very faint perception of its beauty and dignity who does not know this, and who does not further know, that one being is elevated above another, in proportion as he possesses this capability. It has therefore appeared to me, that to endeavour to produce or enlarge this capability is one of the best services in which, at any period, a Writer can be engaged; but this service, excellent at all times, is especially so at the present day. For a multitude of causes, unknown to former times, are now acting with a combined force to blunt the discriminating powers of the mind, and, unfitting it for all voluntary exertion, to reduce it to a state of almost savage torpor. The most effective of these causes are the great national events which are daily taking place, and the increasing accumulation of men in cities, where the uniformity of their occupations produces a craving for extraordinary incident which the rapid communication of intelligence hourly gratifies. To this tendency of life and manners the literature and theatrical exhibitions of the country have conformed themselves. The invaluable works of our elder writers, I had almost said the works of Shakspeare and Milton, are driven into neglect by frantic novels, sickly and stupid German Tragedies, and deluges of idle and extravagant stories in verse.—When I think upon this degrading thirst after outrageous stimulation, I am almost ashamed to have spoken of the feeble endeavour made in these volumes to counteract it; and, reflecting upon the magnitude of the general evil, I should be oppressed with no dishonourable melancholy, had I not a deep impression of certain inherent and indestructible qualities of the human mind, and likewise of certain powers in the great and permanent objects that act upon it, which are equally inherent and indestructible; and were there not added to this impression a belief that the time is approaching when the evil will be systematically opposed by men of greater powers, and with far more distinguished success.

Having dwelt thus long on the subjects and aim of these Poems, I shall request the Reader's permission to apprise him of a few circumstances relating to their

PREFACE TO LYRICAL BALLADS

style, in order, among other reasons, that he may not censure me for not having performed what I never attempted. The Reader will find that personifications of abstract ideas rarely occur in these volumes, and are utterly rejected as an ordinary device to elevate the style and raise it above prose. My purpose was to imitate, and, as far as possible, to adopt the very language of men; and assuredly such personifications do not make any natural or regular part of that language. They are, indeed, a figure of speech occasionally prompted by passion, and I have made use of them as such; but have endeavoured utterly to reject them as a mechanical device of style, or as a family language which Writers in metre seem to lay claim to by prescription. I have wished to keep the Reader in the company of flesh and blood, persuaded that by so doing I shall interest him. Others who pursue a different track will interest him likewise; I do not interfere with their claim, but wish to prefer a claim of my own. There will also be found in these volumes little of what is usually called poetic diction; as much pains has been taken to avoid it as is ordinarily taken to produce it; this has been done for the reason already alleged, to bring my language near to the language of men; and further, because the pleasure which I have proposed to myself to impart, is of a kind very different from that which is supposed by many persons to be the proper object of poetry. Without being culpably particular, I do not know how to give my Reader a more exact notion of the style in which it was my wish and intention to write, than by informing him that I have at all times endeavoured to look steadily at my subject; consequently there is, I hope, in these Poems little falsehood of description, and my ideas are expressed in language fitted to their respective importance. Something must have been gained by this practice, as it is friendly to one property of all good poetry, namely, good sense: but it has necessarily cut me off from a large portion of phrases and figures of speech which from father to son have long been regarded as the common inheritance of Poets. I have also thought it expedient to restrict myself still further, having abstained from the use of many expressions, in themselves proper and beautiful, but which have been foolishly repeated by bad Poets, till such feelings of disgust are connected with them as it is scarcely possible by any art of association to overpower.

If in a poem there should be found a series of lines, or even a single line, in which the language, though naturally arranged, and according to the strict laws of metre, does not differ from that of prose, there is a numerous class of critics, who, when they stumble upon these prosaisms, as they call them, imagine that they have made a notable discovery, and exult over the Poet as over a man ignorant of his own profession. Now these men would establish a canon of criticism which the Reader will conclude he must utterly reject, if he wishes to be pleased with these volumes. And it would be a most easy task to prove to him, that not only the language of a large portion of every good poem, even of the most elevated character, must necessarily, except with reference to the metre, in no respect differ from that of good prose, but likewise that some of the most interesting parts of the best poems will be found to be strictly the language of prose when prose is well written. The truth of this assertion might be demonstrated by innumerable passages from almost all the poetical writings, even of Milton himself. To illustrate the subject in a general manner, I will here adduce a short composition of Gray, who was at the head of those who, by their reasonings, have attempted to widen the space

PREFACE TO LYRICAL BALLADS

of separation betwixt Prose and Metrical composition, and was more than any other man curiously elaborate in the structure of his own poetic diction.

> 'In vain to me the smiling mornings shine,
> And reddening Phœbus lifts his golden fire:
> The birds in vain their amorous descant join,
> Or cheerful fields resume their green attire.
> These ears, alas! for other notes repine;
> *A different object do these eyes require;*
> *My lonely anguish melts no heart but mine;*
> *And in my breast the imperfect joys expire;*
> Yet morning smiles the busy race to cheer,
> And new-born pleasure brings to happier men;
> The fields to all their wonted tribute bear;
> To warm their little loves the birds complain.
> *I fruitless mourn to him that cannot hear,*
> *And weep the more because I weep in vain."*

It will easily be perceived, that the only part of this Sonnet which is of any value is the lines printed in Italics; it is equally obvious that, except in the rhyme, and in the use of the single word "fruitless" for fruitlessly, which is so far a defect, the language of these lines does in no respect differ from that of prose.

By the foregoing quotation it has been shown that the language of Prose may yet be well adapted to Poetry; and it was previously asserted, that a large portion of the language of every good poem can in no respect differ from that of good Prose. We will go further. It may be safely affirmed, that there neither is, nor can be, any *essential* difference between the language of prose and metrical composition. We are fond of tracing the resemblance between Poetry and Painting, and, accordingly, we call them Sisters: but where shall we find bonds of connection sufficiently strict to typify the affinity betwixt metrical and prose composition? They both speak by and to the same organs; the bodies in which both of them are clothed may be said to be of the same substance, their affections are kindred, and almost identical, not necessarily differing even in degree; Poetry sheds no tears "such as Angels weep," but natural and human tears; she can boast of no celestial ichor that distinguishes her vital juices from those of prose; the same human blood circulates through the veins of them both.

If it be affirmed that rhyme and metrical arrangement of themselves constitute a distinction which overturns what has just been said on the strict affinity of metrical language with that of prose, and paves the way for other artificial distinctions which the mind voluntarily admits, I answer that the language of such Poetry as is here recommended is, as far as is possible, a selection of the language really spoken by men; that this selection, wherever it is made with true taste and feeling, will of itself form a distinction far greater than would at first be imagined, and will entirely separate the composition from the vulgarity and meanness of ordinary life; and, if metre be superadded thereto, I believe that a dissimilitude will be produced altogether sufficient for the gratification of a rational mind. What other distinction would we have? Whence is it to come? And where is it to exist? Not, surely, where the Poet speaks through the mouths of his characters: it cannot be necessary here, either for elevation of style, or any of its supposed ornaments: for, if the Poet's subject be judiciously chosen, it will naturally, and upon fit occasion, lead him to passions, the language of which, if selected truly and judiciously, must necessarily be dignified and variegated, and alive with metaphors and figures. I for-

PREFACE TO LYRICAL BALLADS

bear to speak of an incongruity which would shock the intelligent Reader, should the Poet interweave any foreign splendour of his own with that which the passion naturally suggests: it is sufficient to say that such addition is unnecessary. And, surely, it is more probable that those passages, which with propriety abound with metaphors and figures, will have their due effect, if, upon other occasions where the passions are of a milder character, the style also be subdued and temperate.

But, as the pleasure which I hope to give by the Poems now presented to the Reader must depend entirely on just notions upon this subject, and, as it is in itself of high importance to our taste and moral feelings, I cannot content myself with these detached remarks. And if, in what I am about to say, it shall appear to some that my labour is unnecessary, and that I am like a man fighting a battle without enemies, such persons may be reminded that, whatever be the language outwardly holden by men, a practical faith in the opinions which I am wishing to establish is almost unknown. If my conclusions are admitted, and carried as far as they must be carried if admitted at all, our judgments concerning the works of the greatest Poets, both ancient and modern, will be far different from what they are at present, both when we pra'se and when we censure: and our moral feelings influencing and influenced by these judgments will, I believe, be corrected and purified.

Taking up the subject, then, upon general grounds, let me ask, what is meant by the word Poet? What is a Poet? To whom does he address himself? And what language is to be expected from him?—He is a man speaking to men: a man, it is true, endowed with more lively sensibility, more enthusiasm and tenderness, who has a greater knowledge of human nature, and a more comprehensive soul, than are supposed to be common among mankind; a man pleased with his own passions and volitions, and who rejoices more than other men in the spirit of life that is in him; delighting to contemplate similar volitions and passions as manifested in the goings-on of the Universe, and habitually impelled to create them where he does not find them. To these qualities he has added a disposition to be affected more than other men by absent things as if they were present; an ability of conjuring up in himself passions, which are indeed far from being the same as those produced by real events, yet (especially in those parts of the general sympathy which are pleasing and delightful) do more nearly resemble the passions produced by real events than anything which, from the motions of their own minds merely, other men are accustomed to feel in themselves:—whence, and from practice, he has acquired a greater readiness and power in expressing what he thinks and feels, and especially those thoughts and feelings which, by his own choice, or from the structure of his own mind, arise in him without immediate external excitement.

But whatever portion of this faculty we may suppose even the greatest Poet to possess, there cannot be a doubt that the language which it will suggest to him, must often, in liveliness and truth, fall short of that which is uttered by men in real life, under the actual pressure of those passions, certain shadows of which the Poet thus produces, or feels to be produced, in himself.

However exalted a notion we would wish to cherish of the character of a Poet, it is obvious that, while he describes and imitates passions, his employment is in some degree mechanical, compared with the freedom and power of real and substantial action and suffering. So that it will be the wish of the Poet to bring his feelings

PREFACE TO LYRICAL BALLADS

near to those of the persons whose feelings he describes, nay, for short spaces of time, perhaps, to let himself slip into an entire delusion, and even confound and identify his own feelings with theirs; modifying only the language which is thus suggested to him by a consideration that he describes for a particular purpose, that of giving pleasure. Here, then, he will apply the principle of selection which has been already insisted upon. He will depend upon this for removing what would otherwise be painful or disgusting in the passion; he will feel that there is no necessity to trick out or to elevate nature: and the more industriously he applies this principle, the deeper will be his faith that no words, which *his* fancy or imagination can suggest, will be to be compared with those which are the emanations of reality and truth.

But it may be said by those who do not object to the general spirit of these remarks, that, as it is impossible for the Poet to produce upon all occasions language as exquisitely fitted for the passion as that which the real passion itself suggests, it is proper that he should consider himself as in the situation of a translator, who does not scruple to substitute excellencies of another kind for those which are unattainable by him; and endeavours occasionally to surpass his original, in order to make some amends for the general inferiority to which he feels that he must submit. But this would be to encourage idleness and unmanly despair. Further, it is the language of men who speak of what they do not understand; who talk of Poetry as of a matter of amusement and idle pleasure; who will converse with us as gravely about a *taste* for Poetry, as they express it, as if it were a thing as indifferent as a taste for rope-dancing, or Frontiniac or Sherry. Aristotle, I have been told, has said, that Poetry is the most philosophic of all writing:

it is so: its object is truth, not individual and local, but general, and operative; not standing upon external testimony, but carried alive into the heart by passion; truth which is its own testimony, which gives competence and confidence to the tribunal to which it appeals, and receives them from the same tribunal. Poetry is the image of man and nature. The obstacles which stand in the way of the fidelity of the Biographer and Historian, and of their consequent utility, are incalculably greater than those which are to be encountered by the Poet who comprehends the dignity of his art. The Poet writes under one restriction only, namely, the necessity of giving immediate pleasure to a human Being possessed of that information which may be expected from him, not as a lawyer, a physician, a mariner, an astronomer, or a natural philosopher, but as a Man. Except this one restriction, there is no object standing between the Poet and the image of things; between this, and the Biographer and Historian, there are a thousand.

Nor let this necessity of producing immediate pleasure be considered as a degradation of the Poet's art. It is far otherwise. It is an acknowledgment of the beauty of the universe, an acknowledgment the more sincere because not formal, but indirect; it is a task light and easy to him who looks at the world in the spirit of love: further, it is a homage paid to the native and naked dignity of man, to the grand elementary principle of pleasure, by which he knows, and feels, and lives, and moves. We have no sympathy but what is propagated by pleasure: I would not be misunderstood; but wherever we sympathise with pain, it will be found that the sympathy is produced and carried on by subtle combinations with pleasure. We have no knowledge, that is, no general principles drawn from the contemplation of particular facts, but what has been built up by pleasure, and exists in us by pleasure alone. The Man of science, the Chemist and Mathematician, whatever difficulties and disgusts they may have had to struggle with, know and feel this. However painful may be the objects with which the Anatomist's knowledge is connected, he feels that his knowledge is pleasure; and where he has no pleasure he has no knowledge. What then does the Poet? He considers man and the objects that surround him as acting and reacting upon each other, so as to produce an infinite complexity of pain and pleasure; he considers man in his own nature and in his ordinary life as contemplating this with a certain quantity of immediate knowledge, with certain convictions, intuitions, and deductions, which from habit acquire the quality of intuitions; he considers him as looking upon this complex scene of ideas and sensations, and finding everywhere objects that immediately excite in him sympathies which, from the necessities of his nature, are accompanied by an overbalance of enjoyment.

To this knowledge which all men carry about with them, and to these sympathies in which, without any other discipline than that of our daily life, we are fitted to take delight, the Poet principally directs his attention. He considers man and nature as essentially adapted to each other, and the mind of man as naturally the mirror of the fairest and most interesting properties of nature. And thus the Poet, prompted by this feeling of pleasure, which accompanies him through the whole course of his studies, converses with general nature, with affections akin to those which, through labour and length of time, the Man of science has raised up in himself, by conversing with those particular parts of nature which are the objects of his studies. The knowledge both of the Poet and the Man of science is pleasure; but the knowledge of the one cleaves to us as a necessary part of our us in his own person and character. To this I answer by referring the Reader to the description before given of a Poet. Among the qualities there enumerated as principally conducing to form a Poet, is implied nothing differing in kind from other men, but only in degree. The sum of what was said is, that the Poet is chiefly distinguished from other men by a greater promptness to think and feel without immediate external excitement, and a greater power in expressing such thoughts and feelings as are produced in him in that manner. But these passions and thoughts and feelings are the general passions and thoughts and feelings of men. And with what are they connected? Undoubtedly with our moral sentiments and animal sensations, and with the causes which excite these; with the operations of the elements, and the appearances of the visible universe; with storm and sunshine, with the revolutions of the seasons, with cold and heat, with loss of friends and kindred, with injuries and resentments, gratitude and hope, with fear and sorrow. These, and the like, are the sensations and objects which the Poet describes, as they are the sensations of other men, and the objects which interest them. The Poet thinks and feels in the spirit of human passions. How, then, can his language differ in any material degree from that of all other men who feel vividly and see clearly? It might be *proved* that it is impossible. But supposing that this were not the case, the Poet might then be allowed to use a peculiar language when expressing his feelings for his own gratification, or that of men like himself. But Poets do not write for Poets alone, but for men. Unless therefore we are advocates for that admiration which subsists upon ignorance, and that pleasure which arises from hearing what we do not understand, the Poet must descend from this supposed height; and, in order to excite rational sym-

PREFACE TO LYRICAL BALLADS 181

pathy, he must express himself as other men express themselves. To this it may be added, that while he is only selecting from the real language of men, or, which amounts to the same thing, composing accurately in the spirit of such selection, he is treading upon safe ground, and we know what we are to expect from him. Our feelings are the same with respect to metre; for, as it may be proper to remind the Reader, the distinction of metre is regular and uniform, and not, like that which is produced by what is usually called POETIC DICTION, arbitrary, and subject to infinite caprices upon which no calculation whatever can be made. In the one case, the Reader is utterly at the mercy of the Poet, respecting what imagery or diction he may choose to connect with the passion; whereas, in the other, the metre obeys certain laws, to which the Poet and Reader both willingly submit because they are certain, and because no interference is made by them with the passion but such as the concurring testimony of ages has shown to heighten and improve the pleasure which co-exists with it.

It will now be proper to answer an obvious question, namely, Why, professing these opinions, have I written in verse? To this, in addition to such answer as is included in what has been already said, I reply, in the first place, Because, however I may have restricted myself, there is still left open to me what confessedly constitutes the most valuable object of all writing, whether in prose or verse; the great and universal passions of men, the most general and interesting of their occupations, and the entire world of nature before me—to supply endless combinations of forms and imagery. Now, supposing for a moment that whatever is interesting n these objects may be as vividly described in prose, why should I be condemned for attempting to superadd to such description the charm which, by the consent of all nations, is acknowledged to exist in metrical language? To this, by such as are yet unconvinced, it may be answered that a very small part of the pleasure given by Poetry depends upon the metre, and that it is injudicious to write in metre, unless it be accompanied with the other artificial distinctions of style with which metre is usually accompanied, and that, by such deviation, more will be lost from the shock which will thereby be given to the Reader's associations than will be counterbalanced by any pleasure which he can derive from the general power of numbers. In answer to those who still contend for the necessity of accompanying metre with certain appropriate colours of style in order to the accomplishment of its appropriate end, and who also, in my opinion, greatly underrate the power of metre in itself, it might, perhaps, as far as relates to these Volumes, have been almost sufficient to observe, that poems are extant, written upon more humble subjects, and in a still more naked and simple style, which have continued to give pleasure from generation to generation. Now, if nakedness and simplicity be a defect, the fact here mentioned affords a strong presumption that poems somewhat less naked and simple are capable of affording pleasure at the present day; and, what I wished *chiefly* to attempt, at present, was to justify myself for having written under the impression of this belief.

But various causes might be pointed out why, when the style is manly, and the subject of some importance, words metrically arranged will long continue to impart such a pleasure to mankind as he who proves the extent of that pleasure will be desirous to impart. The end of Poetry is to produce excitement in co-existence with an overbalance of pleasure; but, by the supposition, ex-

PREFACE TO LYRICAL BALLADS

citement is an unusual and irregular state of the mind; ideas and feelings do not, in that state, succeed each other in accustomed order. If the words, however, by which this excitement is produced be in themselves powerful, or the images and feelings have an undue proportion of pain connected with them, there is some danger that the excitement may be carried beyond its proper bounds. Now the co-presence of something regular, something to which the mind has been accustomed in various moods and in a less excited state, cannot but have great efficacy in tempering and restraining the passion by an intertexture of ordinary feeling, and of feeling not strictly and necessarily connected with the passion. This is unquestionably true; and hence, though the opinion will at first appear paradoxical, from the tendency of metre to divest language, in a certain degree, of its reality, and thus to throw a sort of half-consciousness of unsubstantial existence over the whole composition, there can be little doubt but that more pathetic situations and sentiments, that is, those which have a greater proportion of pain connected with them, may be endured in metrical composition, especially in rhyme, than in prose. The metre of the old ballads is very artless; yet they contain many passages which would illustrate this opinion; and, I hope, if the following Poems be attentively perused, similar instances will be found in them. This opinion may be further illustrated by appealing to the Reader's own experience of the reluctance with which he comes to the re-perusal of the distressful parts of *Clarissa Harlowe,* or *The Gamester;* while Shakspeare's writings, in the most pathetic scenes, never act upon us, as pathetic, beyond the bounds of pleasure—an effect which, in a much greater degree than might at first be imagined, is to be ascribed to small, but continual and regular impulses of pleasurable surprise from the metrical arrangement.—On the other hand (what it must be allowed will much more frequently happen) if the Poet's words should be incommensurate with the passion, and inadequate to raise the Reader to a height of desirable excitement, then (unless the Poet's choice of his metre has been grossly injudicious) in the feelings of pleasure which the Reader has been accustomed to connect with metre in general, and in the feeling, whether cheerful or melancholy, which he has been accustomed to connect with that particular movement of metre, there will be found something which will greatly contribute to impart passion to the words, and to effect the complex end which the Poet proposes to himself.

If I had undertaken a SYSTEMATIC defence of the theory here maintained, it would have been my duty to develope the various causes upon which the pleasure received from metrical language depends. Among the chief of these causes is to be reckoned a principle which must be well known to those who have made any of the Arts the object of accurate reflection; namely, the pleasure which the mind derives from the perception of similitude in dissimilitude. This principle is the great spring of the activity of our minds, and their chief feeder. From this principle the direction of the sexual appetite, and all the passions connected with it, take their origin: it is the life of our ordinary conversation; and upon the accuracy with which similitude in dissimilitude, and dissimilitude in similitude are perceived, depend our taste and our moral feelings. It would not be a useless employment to apply this principle to the consideration of metre, and to show that metre is hence enabled to afford much pleasure, and to point out in what manner that pleasure is produced. But my limits will not permit me

PREFACE TO LYRICAL BALLADS

to enter upon this subject, and I must content myself with a general summary.

I have said that poetry is the spontaneous overflow of powerful feelings: it takes its origin from emotion recollected in tranquillity: the emotion is contemplated till, by a species of reaction, the tranquillity gradually disappears, and an emotion, kindred to that which was before the subject of contemplation, is gradually produced, and does itself actually exist in the mind. In this mood successful composition generally begins, and in a mood similar to this it is carried on; but the emotion, of whatever kind, and in whatever degree, from various causes, is qualified by various pleasures, so that in describing any passions whatsoever, which are voluntarily described, the mind will, upon the whole, be in a state of enjoyment. If Nature be thus cautious to preserve in a state of enjoyment a being so employed, the Poet ought to profit by the lesson held forth to him, and ought especially to take care, that, whatever passions he communicates to his Reader, those passions, if his Reader's mind be sound and vigorous, should always be accompanied with an over-balance of pleasure. Now the music of harmonious metrical language, the sense of difficulty overcome, and the blind association of pleasure which has been previously received from works of rhyme or metre of the same or similar construction, an indistinct perception perpetually renewed of language closely resembling that of real life, and yet, in the circumstance of metre, differing from it so widely—all these imperceptibly make up a complex feeling of delight, which is of the most important use in tempering the painful feeling always found intermingled with powerful descriptions of the deeper passions. This effect is always produced in pathetic and impassioned poetry; while, in lighter compositions, the ease and gracefulness with which the Poet manages his numbers are themselves confessedly a principal source of the gratification of the Reader. All that it is *necessary* to say, however, upon this subject, may be effected by affirming, what few persons will deny, that of two descriptions, either of passions, manners, or characters, each of them equally well executed, the one in prose and the other in verse, the verse will be read a hundred times where the prose is read once.

Having thus explained a few of my reasons for writing in verse, and why I have chosen subjects from common life, and endeavoured to bring my language near to the real language of men, if I have been too minute in pleading my own cause, I have at the same time been treating a subject of general interest; and for this reason a few words shall be added with reference solely to these particular poems, and to some defects which will probably be found in them. I am sensible that my associations must have sometimes been particular instead of general, and that, consequently, giving to things a false importance, I may have sometimes written upon unworthy subjects; but I am less apprehensive on this account, than that my language may frequently have suffered from those arbitrary connections of feelings and ideas with particular words and phrases from which no man can altogether protect himself. Hence I have no doubt, that, in some instances, feelings, even of the ludicrous, may be given to my Readers by expressions which appeared to me tender and pathetic. Such faulty expressions, were I convinced they were faulty at present, and that they must necessarily continue to be so, I would willingly take all reasonable pains to correct. But it is dangerous to make these alterations on the simple authority of a few individuals, or even of certain classes of men; for where the understanding of an

Author is not convinced, or his feelings altered, this cannot be done without great injury to himself: for his own feelings are his stay and support; and, if he set them aside in one instance, he may be induced to repeat this act till his mind shall lose all confidence in itself, and become utterly debilitated. To this it may be added, that the critic ought never to forget that he is himself exposed to the same errors as the Poet, and, perhaps, in a much greater degree: for there can be no presumption in saying of most readers, that it is not probable they will be so well acquainted with the various stages of meaning through which words have passed, or with the fickleness or stability of the relations of particular ideas to each other; and, above all, since they are so much less interested in the subject, they may decide lightly and carelessly.

Long as the Reader has been detained, I hope he will permit me to caution him against a mode of false criticism which has been applied to Poetry, in which the language closely resembles that of life and nature. Such verses have been triumphed over in parodies, of which Dr. Johnson's stanza is a fair specimen:—

> "I put my hat upon my head
> And walked into the Strand,
> And there I met another man
> Whose hat was in his hand."

Immediately under these lines let us place one of the most justly-admired stanzas of the *Babes in the Woods*.

> "These pretty Babes with hand in hand
> Went wandering up and down;
> But never more they saw the Man
> Approaching from the Town."

In both these stanzas the words, and the order of the words, in no respect differ from the most unimpassioned conversation. There are words in both, for example, "the Strand," and "the Town," connected with none but the most familiar ideas; yet the one stanza we admit as admirable, and the other as a fair example of the superlatively contemptible. Whence arises this difference? Not from the metre, not from the language, not from the order of the words; but the *matter* expressed in Dr. Johnson's stanza is contemptible. The proper method of treating trivial and simple verses, to which Dr. Johnson's stanza would be a fair parallelism, is not to say, this is a bad kind of poetry, or, this is not poetry; but, this wants sense; it is neither interesting in itself, nor can *lead* to anything interesting; the images neither originate in that sane state of feeling which arises out of thought, nor can excite thought or feeling in the Reader. This is the only sensible manner of dealing with such verses. Why trouble yourself about the species till you have previously decided upon the genus? Why take pains to prove that an ape is not a Newton, when it is self-evident that he is not a man?

One request I must make of my Reader, which is, that in judging these Poems he would decide by his own feelings genuinely, and not by reflection upon what will probably be the judgment of others. How common is it to hear a person say, I myself do not object to this style of composition, or this or that expression, but, to such and such classes of people it will appear mean or ludicrous! This mode of criticism, so destructive of all sound unadulterated judgment, is almost universal: let the Reader then abide independently, by his own feelings, and, if he finds himself affected, let him not suffer such conjectures to interfere with his pleasure.

If an Author, by any single composition, has impressed us with respect for his talents, it is useful to consider this as affording a presumption that on other occasions where we have been displeased, he, nevertheless, may not have written ill or absurdly; and further, to give him so much credit for this one composition as may induce us to review what has displeased us, with more care than we should otherwise have bestowed upon it. This is not only an act of justice, but, in our decisions upon poetry especially, may conduce, in a high degree, to the improvement of our own taste; for an *accurate* taste in poetry, and in all the other arts, as Sir Joshua Reynolds has observed, is an *acquired* talent, which can only be produced by thought and a long-continued intercourse with the best models of composition. This is mentioned, not with so ridiculous a purpose as to prevent the most inexperienced Reader from judging for himself (I have already said that I wish him to judge for himself), but merely to temper the rashness of decision, and to suggest that, if Poetry be a subject on which much time has not been bestowed, the judgment may be erroneous; and that, in many cases, it necessarily will be so.

Nothing would, I know, have so effectually contributed to further the end which I have in view, as to have shown of what kind the pleasure is, and how that pleasure is produced, which is confessedly produced by metrical composition essentially different from that which I have here endeavoured to recommend: for the Reader will say that he has been pleased by such composition; and what more can be done for him? The power of any art is limited; and he will suspect that, if it be proposed to furnish him with new friends, that can be only upon condition of his abandoning his old friends. Besides, as I have said, the Reader is himself conscious of the pleasure which he has received from such composition, composition to which he has peculiarly attached the endearing name of Poetry; and all men feel an habitual gratitude, and something of an honourable bigotry, for the objects which have long continued to please them: we not only wish to be pleased, but to be pleased in that particular way in which we have been accustomed to be pleased. There is in these feelings enough to resist a host of arguments; and I should be the less able to combat them successfully, as I am willing to allow that, in order entirely to enjoy the Poetry which I am recommending, it would be necessary to give up much of what is ordinarily enjoyed. But would my limits have permitted me to point out how this pleasure is produced, many obstacles might have been removed, and the Reader assisted in perceiving that the powers of language are not so limited as he may suppose; and that it is possible for poetry to give other enjoyments, of a purer, more lasting, and more exquisite nature. This part of the subject has not been altogether neglected, but it has not been so much my present aim to prove, that the interest excited by some other kinds of poetry is less vivid, and less worthy of the nobler powers of the mind, as to offer reasons for presuming that if my purpose were fulfilled, a species of poetry would be produced which is genuine poetry; in its nature well adapted to interest mankind permanently, and likewise important in the multiplicity and quality of its moral relations.

From what has been said, and from a perusal of the Poems, the Reader will be able clearly to perceive the object which I had in view: he will determine how far it has been attained, and, what is a much more important question, whether it be worth attaining: and upon the decision of these two questions will rest my claim to the approbation of the Public.

1800

SAMUEL TAYLOR COLERIDGE (1772-1834)

THIS LIME-TREE BOWER MY PRISON

In June of 1797, some long-expected friends paid a visit to the author's cottage; and on the morning of their arrival, he met with an accident, which disabled him from walking during the whole time of their stay. One evening, when they had left him for a few hours, he composed the following lines in the garden-bower.

WELL, they are gone, and here must I remain,
This lime-tree bower my prison! I have lost
Beauties and feelings such as would have been
Most sweet to my remembrance even when age
Had dimmed mine eyes to blindness! They, meanwhile,
Friends, whom I never more may meet again,
On springy heath, along the hill-top edge,
Wander in gladness, and wind down, perchance,
To that still roaring dell, of which I told;
The roaring dell, o'er-wooded, narrow, deep,   10
And only speckled by the mid-day sun;
Where its slim trunk the ash from rock to rock
Flings arching like a bridge;—that branchless ash,
Unsunned and damp, whose few poor yellow leaves
Ne'er tremble in the gale, yet tremble still,
Fanned by the water-fall! and there my friends
Behold the dark green file of long lank weeds,[1]

---

[1] *Of long lank weeds.*] The asplenium scolopendrium, called in some countries the Adder's Tongue, in others the Hart's Tongue: but Withering gives the Adder's Tongue as the trivial name of the ophioglossum only.

That all at once (a most fantastic sight!)
Still nod and drip beneath the dripping edge
Of the blue clay-stone.

      Now, my friends emerge   20
Beneath the wide, wide Heaven—and view again
The many-steepled tract magnificent
Of hilly fields and meadows, and the sea,
With some fair bark, perhaps, whose sails light up
The slip of smooth clear blue betwixt two Isles
Of purple shadow! Yes! they wander on
In gladness all; but thou, methinks, most glad,
My gentle-hearted Charles! for thou hast pined
And hungered after Nature, many a year,
In the great City pent, winning thy way   30
With sad yet patient soul, through evil and pain
And strange calamity! Ah! slowly sink
Behind the western ridge, thou glorious Sun!
Shine in the slant beams of the sinking orb,
Ye purple heath-flowers! richlier burn, ye clouds!
Live in the yellow light, ye distant groves!
And kindle, thou blue Ocean! So my Friend
Struck with deep joy may stand, as I have stood,
Silent with swimming sense; yea, gazing round
On the wide landscape, gaze till all doth seem   40
Less gross than bodily; and of such hues
As veil the Almighty Spirit, when yet he makes
Spirits perceive his presence.

      A delight
Comes sudden on my heart, and I am glad
As I myself were there! Nor in this bower,
This little lime-tree bower, have I not marked
Much that has soothed me. Pale beneath the blaze
Hung the transparent foliage; and I watched

Some broad and sunny leaf, and loved to see
The shadow of the leaf and stem above 50
Dappling its sunshine! And that walnut-tree
Was richly tinged, and a deep radiance lay
Full on the ancient ivy, which usurps
Those fronting elms, and now, with blackest mass
Makes their dark branches gleam a lighter hue
Through the late twilight: and though now the bat
Wheels silent by, and not a swallow twitters,
Yet still the solitary humble-bee
Sings in the bean-flower! Henceforth I shall know
That Nature ne'er deserts the wise and pure; 60
No plot so narrow, be but Nature there,
No waste so vacant, but may well employ
Each faculty of sense, and keep the heart
Awake to Love and Beauty! and sometimes
'Tis well to be bereft of promised good,
That we may lift the Soul, and contemplate
With lively joy the joys we cannot share.
My gentle-hearted Charles! when the last rook
Beat its straight path along the dusky air
Homewards, I blest it! deeming, its black wing 70
(Now a dim speck, now vanishing in light)
Had crossed the mighty orb's dilated glory,
While thou stood'st gazing; or when all was still,
Flew creeking o'er thy head, and had a charm
For thee, my gentle-hearted Charles, to whom
No sound is dissonant which tells of Life.
  1797   1800

KUBLA KHAN: OR, A VISION IN A DREAM

A FRAGMENT

The following fragment is here published at the request of a poet of great and deserved celebrity [Lord Byron, presumably], and as far as the Author's own opinions are concerned, rather as a psychological curiosity, than on the ground of any supposed poetic merits.

In the summer of the year 1797, the Author, then in ill health, had retired to a lonely farm-house between Porlock and Linton, on the Exmoor confines of Somerset and Devonshire. In consequence of a slight indisposition, an anodyne had been prescribed, from the effect of which he fell asleep in his chair at the moment that he was reading the following sentence, or words of the same substance, in "Purchas's Pilgrimage": "Here the Khan Kubla commanded a palace to be built, and a stately garden thereunto: and thus ten miles of fertile ground were inclosed with a wall." The Author continued for about three hours in a profound sleep, at least of the external senses, during which time he has the most vivid confidence that he could not have composed less than from two to three hundred lines; if that indeed can be called composition in which all the images rose up before him as *things,* with a parallel production of the correspondent expressions, without any sensation or consciousness of effort. On awaking he appeared to himself to have a distinct recollection of the whole, and taking his pen, ink, and paper, instantly and eagerly wrote down the lines that are here preserved. At this moment he was unfortunately called out by a person on business from Porlock, and detained by him above an hour, and on his return to his room, found, to his no small surprise and mortification, that though he still retained some vague and dim recollection of the general purport of the vision, yet, with the exception of some eight or ten scattered lines and images, all the rest had passed away like the images on the surface of a stream into which a stone had been cast, but alas! without the after restoration of the latter:

>   Then all the charm
> Is broken—all that phantom-world so fair
> Vanishes, and a thousand circlets spread,
> And each mis-shape the other. Stay awhile,
> Poor youth! who scarcely dar'st lift up thine eyes—
> The stream will soon renew its smoothness, soon
> The visions will return! And lo! he stays,
> And soon the fragments dim of lovely forms
> Come trembling back, unite, and now once more
> The pool becomes a mirror.

Yet from the still surviving recollections in his mind, the Author has frequently purposed to finish for himself what had been originally, as it were, given to him. but the to-morrow is yet to come. . . .

Αὔριον ἅδιον ἄσω:
—(Coleridge)

KUBLA KHAN

In XANADU did Kubla Khan
A stately pleasure-dome decree:
Where Alph, the sacred river, ran
Through caverns measureless to man
   Down to a sunless sea.
So twice five miles of fertile ground
With walls and towers were girdled round:
And there were gardens bright with sinuous rills
Where blossomed many an incense-bearing tree;
And here were forests ancient as the hills,   10
Enfolding sunny spots of greenery.

But oh! that deep romantic chasm which slanted
Down the green hill athwart a cedarn cover!
A savage place! as holy and enchanted
As e'er beneath a waning moon was haunted
By woman wailing for her demon-lover!
And from this chasm, with ceaseless turmoil seething,
As if this earth in fast thick pants were breathing,
A mighty fountain momently was forced:
Amid whose swift half-intermitted burst   20
Huge fragments vaulted like rebounding hail,
Or chaffy grain beneath the thresher's flail:
And 'mid these dancing rocks at once and ever
It flung up momently the sacred river.
Five miles meandering with a mazy motion
Through wood and dale the sacred river ran,
Then reached the caverns measureless to man,
And sank in tumult to a lifeless ocean:

And 'mid this tumult Kubla heard from far
Ancestral voices prophesying war! 30

    The shadow of the dome of pleasure
    Floated midway on the waves;
    Where was heard the mingled measure
    From the fountain and the caves.
It was a miracle of rare device,
A sunny pleasure-dome with caves of ice!

    A damsel with a dulcimer
    In a vision once I saw:
    It was an Abyssinian maid,
    And on her dulcimer she played, 40
    Singing of Mount Abora.
    Could I revive within me
    Her symphony and song,
    To such a deep delight 't would win me,
That with music loud and long,
I would build that dome in air,
That sunny dome! those caves of ice!
And all who heard should see them there,
And all should cry, Beware! Beware!
His flashing eyes, his floating hair! 50
Weave a circle round him thrice,
And close your eyes with holy dread,
For he on honey-dew hath fed,
And drunk the milk of Paradise.
    1797   1816

THE RIME OF THE ANCIENT MARINER

IN SEVEN PARTS

Facile credo, plures esse Naturas invisibiles quam visibiles in rerum universitate. Sed horum omnium familiam quis nobis enarrabit? et gradus et cognationes et discrimina et singulorum munera? Quid agunt? quæ loca habitant? Harum rerum notitiam semper ambivit ingenium humanum, nunquam attigit. Juvat, interea, non diffiteor, quandoque in animo, tanquam in Tabulâ, majoris et melioris mundi imaginem contemplari: ne mens assuefacat hodiernæ vitæ minutiis se contrahat nimis, et tota subsidat in pusillas cogitationes. Sed veritati interea invigilandum est, modusque servandus, ut certa ab incertis, diem a nocte, distinguamus.

T. Burnet: Archæol. Phil., p. 68.

[I can easily believe, that there are more Invisible than Visible Beings in the Universe. But who will declare to us the Family of all these, and acquaint us with the Agreements, Differences, and peculiar Talents which are to be found among them; what their employments are, and in what mansions they dwell? I will own that it is very profitable, sometimes to contemplate in the Mind, as in a Draught, the Image of the greater and better World; lest the Soul being accustomed to the Trifles of this present Life, should contract itself too much, and altogether rest in mean Cogitations; but, in the mean Time, we must take care to keep to the Truth, and observe moderation, that we may distinguish certain from uncertain Things, and Day from Night.—"Made English from the Latin Original by Mr. Mead and Mr. Fontin," 1736.]

ARGUMENT

How a Ship having passed the Line was driven by Storms to the cold Country towards the South Pole; and how from thence she made her course to the tropical Latitude of the Great Pacific Ocean; and of the strange things that befell; and in what manner the Ancyent Mariner came back to his own Country. [1798.]

Part I

An ancient Mariner meeteth three Gallants bidden to a wedding-feast, and detaineth one.

It is an ancient Mariner,
And he stoppeth one of three,
"By thy long gray beard and glittering eye,
Now wherefore stopp'st thou me?

The Bridegroom's doors are opened wide,
And I am next of kin;
The guests are met, the feast is set:
May'st hear the merry din."

He holds him with his skinny hand,
"There was a ship," quoth he.   10
"Hold off! unhand me, gray-beard loon!"
Eftsoons[1] his hand dropt he.

<small>The Wedding-Guest is spellbound by the eye of the old seafaring man, and constrained to hear his tale</small>

He holds him with his glittering eye—
The wedding-guest stood still,
And listens like a three years' child:
The Mariner hath his will.

The wedding-guest sat on a stone:
He cannot choose but hear;
And thus spake on that ancient man,
The bright-eyed Mariner.   20

"The ship was cheered, the harbour cleared,
Merrily did we drop
Below the kirk, below the hill,
Below the lighthouse top.

<small>The Mariner tells how the ship sailed southward with a good wind and fair weather, till it reached the Line.</small>

The sun came up upon the left,
Out of the sea came he!
And he shone bright, and on the right
Went down into the sea.

Higher and higher every day,
Till over the mast at noon—"   30
The wedding-guest here beat his breast,
For he heard the loud bassoon.

---

[1] immediately

THE ANCIENT MARINER

The Wedding-Guest heareth the bridal music; but the Mariner continueth his tale.

The bride hath paced into the hall,
Red as a rose is she;
Nodding their heads before her goes
The merry minstrelsy.

The wedding-guest he beat his breast,
Yet he cannot choose but hear;
And thus spake on that ancient man,
The bright-eyed Mariner.   40

The ship drawn by a storm toward the south pole.

"And now the storm-blast came, and he
Was tyrannous and strong:
He struck with his o'ertaking wings,
And chased us south along.

With sloping masts and dipping prow,
As who pursued with yell and blow
Still treads the shadow of his foe,
And forward bends his head,
The ship drove fast, loud roared the blast,
And southward aye we fled.   50

And now there came both mist and snow,
And it grew wondrous cold;
And ice, mast-high, came floating by,
As green as emerald;

The land of ice, and of fearful sounds, where no living thing was to be seen.

And through the drifts the snowy clifts [1]
Did send a dismal sheen:
Nor shapes of men nor beasts we ken [2]—
The ice was all between.

The ice was here, the ice was there,
The ice was all around: 60

---

[1] cliffs   [2] perceive

It cracked and growled, and roared and howled,
Like noises in a swound![1]

'Till a great sea-bird, called the Albatross, came through the snow-fog, and was received with great joy and hospitality.

At length did cross an Albatross:
Thorough[2] the fog it came:
As if it had been a Christian soul,
We hailed it in God's name.

It ate the food it ne'er had eat,
And round and round it flew.
The ice did split with a thunder-fit;
The helmsman steered us through! 70

And lo! the Albatross proveth a bird of good omen, and followeth the ship as it returned northward through fog and floating ice.

And a good south wind sprung up behind;
The Albatross did follow,
And every day, for food or play,
Came to the mariners' hollo!

In mist or cloud, on mast or shroud,
It perched for vespers nine;
Whiles all the night, through fog-smoke white,
Glimmered the white moon-shine."

The ancient Mariner inhospitably killeth the pious bird of good omen

"God save thee, ancient Mariner!
From the fiends, that plague thee thus!— 80
Why look'st thou so?"—"With my cross-bow
I shot the Albatross!

Part II

The sun now rose upon the right:
Out of the sea came he,

---

[1] swoon   [2] through

THE ANCIENT MARINER

Still hid in mist, and on the left
Went down into the sea.

And the good south wind still blew behind,
But no sweet bird did follow,
Nor any day, for food or play,
Came to the mariners' hollo! 90

<small>His shipmates cry out against the ancient Mariner, for killing the bird of good luck.</small>

And I had done a hellish thing,
And it would work 'em woe;
For all averred, I had killed the bird
That made the breeze to blow.
Ah wretch! said they, the bird to slay
That made the breeze to blow!

<small>But when the fog cleared off, they justify the same, and thus make themselves accomplices in the crime.</small>

Nor dim nor red, like God's own head,
The glorious sun uprist:[1]
Then all averred, I had killed the bird
That brought the fog and mist. 100
'Twas right, said they, such birds to slay,
That bring the fog and mist.

<small>The fair breeze continues; the ship enters the Pacific Ocean and sails northward, even till it reaches the Line.</small>

The fair breeze blew, the white foam flew,
The furrow followed free:
We were the first that ever burst
Into that silent sea.

<small>The ship hath been suddenly becalmed.</small>

Down dropt the breeze, the sails dropt down
'Twas sad as sad could be;
And we did speak only to break
The silence of the sea! 110

All in a hot and copper sky,
The bloody Sun, at noon,

---

[1] uprose

> Right up above the mast did stand,
> No bigger than the Moon.
>
> Day after day, day after day,
> We stuck, nor breath nor motion;
> As idle as a painted ship
> Upon a painted ocean.

And the Albatross begins to be avenged.

> Water, water, every where,
> And all the boards did shrink;   120
> Water, water, every where,
> Nor any drop to drink.
>
> The very deep did rot: O Christ!
> That ever this should be!
> Yea, slimy things did crawl with legs
> Upon the slimy sea.
>
> About, about, in reel and rout,
> The death-fires danced at night;
> The water, like a witch's oils,
> Burnt green, and blue and white.   130

A Spirit had followed them; one of the invisible inhabitants of this planet, neither departed souls nor angels; concerning whom the learned Jew, Josephus, and the Platonic Constantinopolitan, Michael Psellus, may be consulted. They are very numerous, and there is no climate or element without one or more.

> And some in dreams assured were
> Of the Spirit that plagued us so:
> Nine fathom deep he had followed us,
> From the land of mist and snow.
>
> And every tongue, through utter drought,
> Was withered at the root;
> We could not speak, no more than if
> We had been choked with soot.
>
> Ah! well-a-day! what evil looks
> Had I from old and young!   140

THE ANCIENT MARINER

<small>The shipmates, in their sore distress, would fain throw the whole guilt on the ancient Mariner: in sign whereof they hang the dead sea-bird round his neck.</small>

Instead of the cross, the Albatross
About my neck was hung.

Part III

There passed a weary time. Each throat
Was parched, and glazed each eye.
A weary time! A weary time!
How glazed each weary eye!
<small>The ancient Mariner beholdeth a sign in the element afar off.</small>
When looking westward I beheld
A something in the sky.

At first it seemed a little speck,
And then it seemed a mist;   150
It moved and moved, and took at last
A certain shape, I wist.[1]

A speck, a mist, a shape, I wist!
And still it neared and neared:
As if it dodged a water-sprite,
It plunged and tacked and veered.

<small>At its nearer approach, it seemeth him to be a ship; and at a dear ransom he freeth his speech from the bonds of thirst.</small>
With throats unslaked, with black lips baked,
We could nor laugh nor wail;
Through utter drought all dumb we stood!
I bit my arm, I sucked the blood,   160
And cried, A sail! a sail!

With throats unslaked, with black lips baked,
Agape they heard me call:
<small>A flash of joy;</small>
Gramercy![2] they for joy did grin,

---
[1] I perceived
[2] Many thanks!

And all at once their breath drew in,
As they were drinking all.

<small>And horror follows. For can it be a *sh p* that comes onward without wind or tide?</small>

'See! see! (I cried) she tacks no more!
Hither to work us weal,
Without a breeze, without a tide,
She steadies with upright keel!'   170

The western wave was all a-flame:
The day was well nigh done:
Almost upon the western wave
Rested the broad bright Sun;
When that strange shape drove suddenly
Betwixt us and the Sun.

<small>It seemeth him but the skeleton of a ship.</small>

And straight the Sun was flecked with bars,
(Heaven's Mother send us grace!)
As if through a dungeon-grate he peered,
With broad and burning face.   180

Alas! (thought I, and my heart beat loud)
How fast she nears and nears!
Are those her sails that glance in the Sun,
Like restless gossameres?

<small>And its ribs are seen as bars on the face of the setting sun. The spectre-woman and her death-mate, and no other on board the skeleton ship.</small>

Are those her ribs through which the Sun
Did peer, as through a grate?
And is that Woman all her crew?
Is that a Death? and are there two?
Is Death that woman's mate?

<small>Like vessel, like crew!</small>

Her lips were red, her looks were free, 190
Her locks were yellow as gold:
Her skin was as white as leprosy,

THE ANCIENT MARINER

The night-mare Life-in-Death was she,
Who thicks man's blood with cold.

Death, and Life-in-Death, have diced for the ship's crew, and she (the latter) winneth the ancient Mariner.

The naked hulk alongside came,
And the twain were casting dice;
'The game is done! I've, I've **won!**'
Quoth she, and whistles thrice.

No twilight within the courts of the sun.

The Sun's rim dips; the stars rush out:
At one stride comes the dark;   200
With far-heard whisper, o'er the sea,
Off shot the spectre-bark.

At the rising of the moon,

We listened and looked sideways up!
Fear at my heart, as at a cup,
My life-blood seemed to sip!
The stars were dim, and thick the night,
The steersman's face by his lamp gleamed white;
From the sails the dew did drip—
Till clomb [1] above the eastern bar
The hornèd Moon, with one bright star 210
Within the nether tip.

One after another,

One after one, by the star-dogged Moon,
Too quick for groan or sigh,
Each turned his face with a ghastly pang,
And cursed me with his eye.

His shipmates drop down dead.

Four times fifty living men,
(And I heard nor sigh nor groan)
With heavy thump, a lifeless lump,
They dropped down one by one.

[1] climbed

SAMUEL TAYLOR COLERIDGE

<small>But Life-in-Death begins her work on the ancient Mariner.</small>

The souls did from their bodies fly,— 220
They fled to bliss or woe!
And every soul, it passed me by,
Like the whizz of my cross-bow!"

Part IV

<small>The Wedding-Guest feareth that a spirit is talking to him.</small>

"I fear thee, ancient Mariner!
I fear thy skinny hand!
And thou art long, and lank, and brown,
As is the ribbed sea-sand.

I fear thee, and thy glittering eye,
And thy skinny hand, so brown."—
"Fear not, fear not, thou Wedding-
 Guest! 230
This body dropt not down.

<small>But the ancient Mariner assureth him of his bodily life, and proceedeth to relate his horrible penance.</small>

Alone, alone, all, all alone,
Alone on a wide wide sea!
And never a saint took pity on
My soul in agony.

<small>He despiseth the creatures of the calm,</small>

The many men, so beautiful!
And they all dead did lie;
And a thousand thousand slimy things
Lived on; and so did I.

<small>And envieth that *they* should live, and so many lie dead.</small>

I looked upon the rotting sea, 240
And drew my eyes away;
I looked upon the rotting deck,
And there the dead men lay.

I looked to Heaven, and tried to pray;
But or ever a prayer had gusht,

THE ANCIENT MARINER 207

A wicked whisper came, and made
My heart as dry as dust.

I closed my lids, and kept them close,
And the balls like pulses beat;
For the sky and the sea, and the sea and
   the sky,   250
Lay like a load on my weary eye,
And the dead were at my feet.

But the curse liveth for him in the eye of the dead men.

The cold sweat melted from their limbs,
Nor rot nor reek [1] did they:
The look with which they looked on me
Had never passed away.

In his loneliness and fixedness he yearneth towards the journeying Moon, and the stars that still sojourn, yet still move onward; and everywhere the blue sky belongs to them, and is their appointed rest, and their native country and their own natural homes, which they enter unannounced, as lords that are certainly expected and yet there is a silent joy at their arrival.

An orphan's curse would drag to hell
A spirit from on high;
But oh! more horrible than that
Is a curse in a dead man's eye!   260
Seven days, seven nights, I saw that curse,
And yet I could not die.

The moving Moon went up the sky,
And no where did abide:
Softly she was going up,
And a star or two beside—
Her beams bemocked the sultry main,
Like April hoar-frost spread;
But where the ship's huge shadow lay,
The charmèd water burnt alway   270
A still and awful red.

By the light of the Moon he beholdeth God's creatures of the great calm.

Beyond the shadow of the ship,
I watched the water-snakes:

---

[1] give off vapor

> They moved in tracks of shining white,
> And when they reared, the elfish light
> Fell off in hoary flakes.
>
> Within the shadow of the ship
> I watched their rich attire:
> Blue, glossy green, and velvet black,
> They coiled and swam; and every track   280
> Was a flash of golden fire.
>
> O happy living things! no tongue
> Their beauty might declare:
> A spring of love gushed from my heart,
> And I blessed them unaware:
> Sure my kind saint took pity on me,
> And I blessed them unaware.
>
> The selfsame moment I could pray;
> And from my neck so free
> The Albatross fell off, and sank   290
> Like lead into the sea.

Their beauty and their happiness.

He blesseth them in his heart.

The spell begins to break.

Part V

> Oh sleep! it is a gentle thing,
> Beloved from pole to pole!
> To Mary Queen the praise be given!
> She sent the gentle sleep from Heaven,
> That slid into my soul.
>
> The silly¹ buckets on the deck,
> That had so long remained,
> I dreamt that they were filled with dew;
> And when I awoke, it rained.   300

By grace of the holy Mother, the ancient Mariner is refreshed with rain.

¹ empty

THE ANCIENT MARINER

My lips were wet, my throat was cold,
My garments all were dank;
Sure I had drunken in my dreams,
And still my body drank.

I moved, and could not feel my limbs:
I was so light—almost
I thought that I had died in sleep,
And was a blessèd ghost.

He heareth sounds and seeth strange sights and commotions in the sky and the element.

And soon I heard a roaring wind:
It did not come anear;
But with its sound it shook the sails,
That were so thin and sere.[1]

The upper air burst into life!
And a hundred fire-flags sheen,[2]
To and fro they were hurried about;
And to and fro, and in and out,
The wan stars danced between.

And the coming wind did roar more loud,
And the sails did sigh like sedge;
And the rain poured down from one black
    cloud;
The Moon was at its edge.

The thick black cloud was cleft, and still
The Moon was at its side:
Like waters shot from some high crag,
The lightning fell with never a jag,
A river steep and wide.

---

[1] withered (worn with age)   [2] resplendent

The Sun, right up above the mast,
Had fixed her to the ocean:
But in a minute she 'gan stir,
With a short uneasy motion—
Backwards and forwards half her length
With a short uneasy motion.

Then like a pawing horse let go,
She made a sudden bound: 390
It flung the blood into my head,
And I fell down in a swound.

The Polar Spirit's fellow demons, the invisible inhabitants of the element, take part in his wrong; and two of them relate, one to the other, that penance long and heavy for the ancient Mariner hath been accorded to the Polar Spirit, who returneth southward.

How long in that same fit I lay,
I have not to declare;
But ere my living life returned,
I heard, and in my soul discerned
Two voices in the air.

'Is it he?' quoth one, 'is this the man?
By Him who died on cross,
With his cruel bow he laid full low 400
The harmless Albatross.

'The spirit who bideth by himself
In the land of mist and snow,
He loved the bird that loved the man
Who shot him with his bow.'

The other was a softer voice,
As soft as honey-dew:
Quoth he, 'The man hath penance done,
And penance more will do.'

Part VI

First Voice

'But tell me, tell me! speak again,   410
Thy soft response renewing—
What makes that ship drive on so fast?
What is the ocean doing?'

Second Voice

'Still as a slave before his lord,
The ocean hath no blast;
His great bright eye most silently
Up to the Moon is cast—

If he may know which way to go;
For she guides him, smooth or grim.
See, brother, see! how graciously   420
She looketh down on him.'

First Voice

The Mariner hath been cast into a trance; for the angelic power causeth the vessel to drive northward, faster than human life could endure.

'But why drives on that ship so fast,
Without or wave or wind?'

Second Voice

'The air is cut away before,
And closes from behind.
Fly, brother, fly! more high, more high!
Or we shall be belated:
For slow and slow that ship will go,
When the Mariner's trance is abated.'

<small>The supernatural motion is retarded; the Mariner awakes, and his penance begins anew.</small>

I woke, and we were sailing on,   430
As in a gentle weather:
'Twas night, calm night, the moon was high;
The dead men stood together.

All stood together on the deck,
For a charnel-dungeon fitter:
All fixed on me their stony eyes,
That in the moon did glitter.

The pang, the curse, with which they died,
Had never passed away:
I could not draw my eyes from theirs, 440
Nor turn them up to pray.

<small>The curse is finally expiated.</small>

And now this spell was snapt: once more
I viewed the ocean green,
And looked far forth, yet little saw
Of what had else been seen—

Like one, that on a lonesome road
Doth walk in fear and dread,
And having once turned round walks on
And turns no more his head;
Because he knows, a frightful fiend   450
Doth close behind him tread.

But soon there breathed a wind on me,
Nor sound nor motion made:
Its path was not upon the sea,
In ripple or in shade.

It raised my hair, it fanned my cheek
Like a meadow-gale of spring—

THE ANCIENT MARINER

It mingled strangely with my fears,
Yet it felt like a welcoming.

Swiftly, swiftly flew the ship, 460
Yet she sailed softly too:
Sweetly, sweetly blew the breeze—
On me alone it blew.

And the ancient Mariner beholdeth his native country.

Oh! dream of joy! is this indeed
The light-house top I see?
Is this the hill? is this the kirk?
Is this mine own countree?

We drifted o'er the harbor-bar,
And I with sobs did pray—
O let me be awake, my God! 470
Or let me sleep alway.

The harbor-bay was clear as glass,
So smoothly it was strewn!
And on the bay the moonlight lay
And the shadow of the Moon.

The rock shone bright, the kirk no less,
That stands above the rock:
The moonlight steeped in silentness
The steady weathercock.

And the bay was white with silent light, 480
Till rising from the same,

The angelic Spirits leave the dead bodies,

Full many shapes, that shadows were,
In crimson colors came.

And appear in their own forms of light.

A little distance from the prow
Those crimson shadows were:

I turned my eyes upon the deck—
Oh, Christ! what saw I there!

Each corse lay flat, lifeless and flat,
And, by the holy rood!
A man all light, a seraph-man, 490
On every corse there stood.

This seraph-band, each waved his hand:
It was a heavenly sight!
They stood as signals to the land,
Each one a lovely light:

This seraph-band, each waved his hand,
No voice did they impart—
No voice; but oh! the silence sank
Like music on my heart.

But soon I heard the dash of oars, 500
I heard the pilot's cheer;
My head was turned perforce away,
And I saw a boat appear.

The Pilot, and the Pilot's boy,
I heard them coming fast:
Dear Lord in Heaven! it was a joy
The dead men could not blast.

I saw a third—I heard his voice:
It is the Hermit good!
He singeth loud his godly hymns 510
That he makes in the wood.
He'll shrieve my soul, he'll wash away
The Albatross's blood.

Part VII

The Hermit of the Wood

This Hermit good lives in that wood
Which slopes down to the sea.
How loudly his sweet voice he rears!
He loves to talk with marineres
That come from a far countree.

He kneels at morn, and noon, and eve—
He hath a cushion plump: 520
It is the moss that wholly hides
The rotted old oak-stump.

The skiff-boat neared: I heard them talk,
'Why, this is strange, I trow![1]
Where are those lights so many and fair,
That signal made but now?'

Approacheth the ship with wonder.

'Strange, by my faith!' the Hermit said—
'And they answered not our cheer!
The planks look warped! and see those sails,
How thin they are and sere! 530
I never saw aught like to them,
Unless perchance it were

Brown skeletons of leaves that lag
My forest-brook along;
When the ivy-tod[2] is heavy with snow,
And the owlet whoops to the wolf below
That eats the she-wolf's young.'

[1] think
[2] ivy-bush

'Dear Lord! it hath a fiendish look'
(The pilot made reply)
'I am a-feared'—'Push on, push on!'   540
Said the Hermit cheerily.

The boat came closer to the ship,
But I nor spake nor stirred;
The boat came close beneath the ship,
And straight a sound was heard.

The ship suddenly sinketh.

Under the water it rumbled on,
Still louder and more dread:
It reached the ship, it split the bay;
The ship went down like lead.

The ancient Mariner is saved in the pilot's boat.

Stunned by that loud and dreadful sound,
Which sky and ocean smote,   [550
Like one that hath been seven days drowned,
My body lay afloat;
But swift as dreams, myself I found
Within the pilot's boat.

Upon the whirl, where sank the ship,
The boat spun round and round;
And all was still, save that the hill
Was telling of the sound.

I moved my lips—the Pilot shrieked   560
And fell down in a fit;
The holy Hermit raised his eyes
And prayed where he did sit.

I took the oars: the Pilot's boy,
Who now doth crazy go,

THE ANCIENT MARINER

Laughed loud and long, and all the while
His eyes went to and fro.
'Ha! ha!' quoth he, 'full plain I see,
The Devil knows how to row.'

And now, all in my own countree, 570
I stood on the firm land!
The Hermit stepped forth from the boat,
And scarcely he could stand.

The ancient Mariner earnestly entreateth the Hermit to shrieve him; and the penance of life falls on him.

'O shrieve me, shrieve me, holy man!'
The Hermit crossed his brow.
'Say quick,' quoth he, 'I bid thee say—
What manner of man art thou?'

Forthwith this frame of mine was wrenched
With a woeful agony,
Which forced me to begin my tale; 580
And then it left me free.

And ever and anon throughout his future life an agony constraineth him to travel from land to land;

Since then at an uncertain hour,
That agony returns;
And till my ghastly tale is told,
This heart within me burns.

I pass, like night, from land to land:
I have strange power of speech;
That moment that his face I see,
I know the man that must hear me:
To him my tale I teach. 590

What loud uproar bursts from that door!
The wedding-guests are there;
But in the garden-bower the bride
And bride-maids singing are:

And hark the little vesper bell,
Which biddeth me to prayer!

O Wedding-Guest! this soul hath been
Alone on a wide wide sea:
So lonely 'twas, that God himself
Scarce seemèd there to be.   600

O sweeter than the marriage-feast,
'Tis sweeter far to me,
To walk together to the kirk
With a goodly company!—

To walk together to the kirk,
And all together pray,
While each to his great Father bends,
Old men, and babes, and loving friends,
And youths and maidens gay!

And to teach, by his own example, love and reverence to all things that God made and loveth.

Farewell, farewell! but this I tell   610
To thee, thou Wedding-Guest!
He prayeth well, who loveth well
Both man and bird and beast.

He prayeth best, who loveth best
All things both great and small;
For the dear God who loveth us,
He made and loveth all."

The Mariner, whose eye is bright,
Whose beard with age is hoar,
Is gone; and now the Wedding-Guest   620
Turned from the bridegroom's door.

He went like one that hath been stunned,
And is of sense forlorn:
A sadder and a wiser man
He rose the morrow morn.

1798   1798 1800

FROST AT MIDNIGHT

THE Frost performs its secret ministry,
Unhelped by any wind. The owlet's cry
Came loud—and hark, again! loud as before.
The inmates of my cottage, all at rest,
Have left me to that solitude, which suits
Abstruser musings: save that at my side
My cradled infant slumbers peacefully.
'Tis calm indeed! so calm, that it disturbs
And vexes meditation with its strange
And extreme silentness. Sea, hill, and wood,   10
This populous village! Sea, and hill, and wood,
With all the numberless goings-on of life,
Inaudible as dreams! the thin blue flame
Lies on my low-burnt fire, and quivers not;
Only that film,[1] which fluttered on the grate,
Still flutters there, the sole unquiet thing.
Methinks, its motion in this hush of nature
Gives it dim sympathies with me who live,
Making it a companionable form,
Whose puny flaps and freaks the idling Spirit   20
By its own moods interprets, everywhere
Echo or mirror seeking of itself,
And makes a toy of Thought.

[1] *Only that film.* In all parts of the kingdom these films are called *strangers* and supposed to portend the arrival of some absent friend.

                              But O! how oft,
How oft, at school, with most believing mind,
Presageful, have I gazed upon the bars,
To watch that fluttering *stranger!* and as oft,
With unclosed lids, already had I dreamt
Of my sweet birth-place, and the old church-tower,
Whose bells, the poor man's only music, rang
From morn to evening, all the hot Fair-day,   30
So sweetly, that they stirred and haunted me
With a wild pleasure, falling on mine ear
Most like articulate sounds of things to come!
So gazed I, till the soothing things I dreamt,
Lulled me to sleep, and sleep prolonged my dreams!
And so I brooded all the following morn,
Awed by the stern preceptor's face, mine eye
Fixed with mock study on my swimming book:
Save if the door half opened, and I snatched
A hasty glance, and still my heart leaped up,   40
For still I hoped to see the *stranger's* face,
Townsman, or aunt, or sister more beloved,
My play-mate when we both were clothed alike!

   Dear Babe, that sleepest cradled by my side,
Whose gentle breathings, heard in this deep calm,
Fill up the interspersèd vacancies
And momentary pauses of the thought!
My babe so beautiful! it thrills my heart
With tender gladness, thus to look at thee,
And think that thou shalt learn far other lore,   50
And in far other scenes! For I was reared
In the great city, pent 'mid cloisters dim,
And saw nought lovely but the sky and stars.
But *thou,* my babe! shalt wander like a breeze
By lakes and sandy shores, beneath the crags
Of ancient mountain, and beneath the clouds,
Which image in their bulk both lakes and shores

And mountain crags: so shalt thou see and hear
The lovely shapes and sounds intelligible
Of that eternal language, which thy God 60
Utters, who from eternity doth teach
Himself in all, and all things in himself.
Great universal Teacher! he shall mould
Thy spirit, and by giving make it ask.

  Therefore all seasons shall be sweet to thee,
Whether the summer clothe the general earth
With greenness, or the redbreast sit and sing
Betwixt the tufts of snow on the bare branch
Of mossy apple-tree, while the nigh thatch
Smokes in the sun-thaw; whether the eave-drops fall 70
Heard only in the trances of the blast,
Or if the secret ministry of frost
Shall hang them up in silent icicles,
Quietly shining to the quiet Moon.

1798   1798

FRANCE: AN ODE

I

Ye Clouds! that far above me float and pause,
  Whose pathless march no mortal may controul!
  Ye Ocean-Waves! that, wheresoe'er ye roll,
Yield homage only to eternal laws!
Ye Woods! that listen to the night-birds singing,
  Midway the smooth and perilous slope reclined,
Save when your own imperious branches swinging,
  Have made a solemn music of the wind!
Where, like a man beloved of God,
Through glooms, which never woodman trod,   10
    How oft, pursuing fancies holy,

My moonlight way o'er flowering weeds I wound,
    Inspired, beyond the guess of folly,
By each rude shape and wild unconquerable sound!
O ye loud Waves! and O ye Forests high!
    And O ye Clouds that far above me soared!
Thou rising Sun! thou blue rejoicing Sky!
    Yea, every thing that is and will be free!
    Bear witness for me, wheresoe'er ye be,
    With what deep worship I have still adored   20
        The spirit of divinest Liberty.

II

When France in wrath her giant-limbs upreared,
    And with that oath, which smote air, earth, and sea,
    Stamped her strong foot and said she would be free,
Bear witness for me, how I hoped and feared!
With what a joy my lofty gratulation
    Unawed I sang, amid a slavish band:
And when to whelm the disenchanted nation,
    Like fiends embattled by a wizard's wand,
        The Monarchs marched in evil day,   30
        And Britain joined the dire array;
    Though dear her shores and circling ocean,
Though many friendships, many youthful loves
    Had swoln the patriot emotion
And flung a magic light o'er all her hills and groves;
Yet still my voice, unaltered, sang defeat
    To all that braved the tyrant-quelling lance,
And shame too long delayed and vain retreat!
For ne'er O Liberty! with partial aim
I dimmed thy light or damped thy holy flame;   40
    But blessed the pæans of delivered France,
And hung my head and wept at Britain's name.

III

"And what," I said, "though Blasphemy's loud scream
  With that sweet music of deliverance strove!
  Though all the fierce and drunken passions wove
A dance more wild than e'er was maniac's dream!
  Ye storms, that round the dawning East assembled,
The Sun was rising, though ye hid his light!"
  And when, to soothe my soul, that hoped and trembled,
The dissonance ceased, and all seemed calm and bright; 50
  When France her front deep-scarr'd and gory
  Concealed with clustering wreaths of glory;
    When, insupportably advancing,
  Her arm made mockery of the warrior's ramp;
    While timid looks of fury glancing,
  Domestic treason, crushed beneath her fatal stamp,
Writhed like a wounded dragon in his gore;
  Then I reproached my fears that would not flee;
"And soon," I said, "shall Wisdom teach her lore
In the low huts of them that toil and groan! 60
And, conquering by her happiness alone,
  Shall France compel the nations to be free,
Till Love and Joy look round, and call the Earth their own."

IV

Forgive me, Freedom! O forgive those dreams!
  I hear thy voice, I hear thy loud lament,
  From bleak Helvetia's icy caverns sent—
I hear thy groans upon her blood-stained streams!
  Heroes, that for your peaceful country perished,

And ye that, fleeing, spot your mountain-snows
  With bleeding wounds; forgive me, that I cherished 70
One thought that ever blessed your cruel foes!
  To scatter rage, and traitorous guilt,
  Where Peace her jealous home had built;
    A patriot-race to disinherit
Of all that made their stormy wilds so dear;
    And with inexpiable spirit
To taint the bloodless freedom of the mountaineer—
O France, that mockest Heaven, adulterous, blind,
  And patriot only in pernicious toils!
Are these thy boasts, Champion of human kind? 80
  To mix with Kings in the low lust of sway,
Yell in the hunt, and share the murderous prey;
To insult the shrine of Liberty with spoils
  From freemen torn; to tempt and to betray?

V

  The Sensual and the Dark rebel in vain,
  Slaves by their own compulsion! In mad game
  They burst their manacles and wear the name
    Of Freedom, graven on a heavier chain!
    O Liberty! with profitless endeavour
Have I pursued thee, many a weary hour; 90
  But thou nor swell'st the victor's strain, nor ever
Didst breathe thy soul in forms of human power.
    Alike from all, howe'er they praise thee,
    (Nor prayer, nor boastful name delays thee)
    Alike from Priestcraft's harpy minions,
  And factious Blasphemy's obscener slaves,
    Thou speedest on thy subtle pinions,
The guide of homeless winds, and playmate of the waves!

And there I felt thee!—on that sea-cliff's verge,
  Whose pines, scarce travelled by the breeze above, 100
Had made one murmur with the distant surge!
Yes, while I stood and gazed, my temples bare,
And shot my being through earth, sea, and air,
  Possessing all things with intensest love,
    O Liberty! my spirit felt thee there.

1798   1798

CHRISTABEL

PREFACE

The first part of the following poem was written in the year one thousand seven hundred and ninety-seven, at Stowey, in the county of Somerset. The second part, after my return from Germany, in the year one thousand eight hundred, at Keswick, Cumberland. Since the latter date, my poetic powers have been, till very lately, in a state of suspended animation. But as, in my very first conception of the tale, I had the whole present to my mind, with the wholeness, no less than with the liveliness of a vision; I trust that I shall yet be able to embody in verse the three parts yet to come, in the course of the present year.

It is probable, that if the poem had been finished at either of the former periods, or if even the first and second part had been finished in the year 1800, the impression of its originality would have been much greater than I dare at present expect. But for this, I have only my own indolence to blame. The dates are mentioned for the exclusive purpose of precluding charges of plagiarism or servile imitation from myself. For there is among us a set of critics, who seem to hold that every possible thought and image is traditional;

who have no notion that there are such things as fountains in the world, small as well as great; and who would, therefore, charitably derive every rill they behold flowing, for a perforation made in some other man's tank. I am confident, however, that as far as the present poem is concerned, the celebrated poets whose writings I might be suspected of having imitated, either in particular passages, or in the tone and the spirit of the whole, would be among the first to vindicate me from the charge, and who, on any striking coincidence, would permit me to address them in this doggerel version of two monkish Latin hexameters:

> 'Tis mine and it is likewise yours,
> But an if this will not do,
> Let it be mine, good friend! for I
> Am the poorer of the two.

I have only to add, that the metre of the Christabel is not, properly speaking, irregular, though it may seem so from its being founded on a new principle: namely, that of counting in each line the accents, not the syllables. Though the latter may vary from seven to twelve, yet in each line the accents will be found to be only four. Nevertheless, this occasional variation in number of syllables is not introduced wantonly, or for the mere ends of convenience, but in correspondence with some transition in the nature of the imagery or passion.

PART I

'Tis the middle of the night by the castle clock,
And the owls have awakened the crowing cock!
Tu—whit!——Tu—whoo!

CHRISTABEL

And hark, again! the crowing cock,
How drowsily it crew.

Sir Leoline, the Baron rich,
Hath a toothless mastiff bitch;
From her kennel beneath the rock
She maketh answer to the clock,
Four for the quarters, and twelve for the hour; 10
Ever and aye, by shine and shower,
Sixteen short howls, not over loud;
Some say, she sees my lady's shroud.

Is the night chilly and dark?
The night is chilly, but not dark.
The thin gray cloud is spread on high,
It covers but not hides the sky.
The moon is behind, and at the full;
And yet she looks both small and dull.
The night is chill, the cloud is gray: 20
'Tis a month before the month of May,
And the Spring comes slowly up this way.

The lovely lady, Christabel,
Whom her father loves so well,
What makes her in the wood so late,
A furlong from the castle gate?
She had dreams all yestern'ght
Of her own betrothèd knight;
And she in the midnight wood will pray
For the weal of her lover that's far away. 30

She stole along, she nothing spoke,
The sighs she heaved were soft and low,
And naught was green upon the oak
But moss and rarest misletoe·

She kneels beneath the huge oak tree,
And in silence prayeth she.

The lady sprang up suddenly,
The lovely lady, Christabel!
It moaned as near, as near can be,
But what it is she cannot tell.—   40
On the other side it seems to be,
Of the huge, broad-breasted, old oak tree.

The night is chill; the forest bare;
Is it the wind that moaneth bleak?
There is not wind enough in the air
To move away the ringlet curl
From the lovely lady's cheek—
There is not wind enough to twirl
The one red leaf, the last of its clan,
That dances as often as dance it can,   50
Hanging so light, and hanging so high,
On the topmost twig that looks up at the sky.

Hush, beating heart of Christabel!
Jesu, Maria, shield her well!
She folded her arms beneath her cloak,
And stole to the other side of the oak.
    What sees she there?

There she sees a damsel bright,
Drest in a silken robe of white,
That shadowy in the moonlight shone: 60
The neck that made that white robe wan,
Her stately neck, and arms were bare;
Her blue-veined feet unsandaled were,
And wildly glittered here and there
The gems entangled in her hair.

CHRISTABEL

I guess, 't was frightful there to see
A lady so richly clad as she—
Beautiful exceedingly!

"Mary mother, save me now!"
(Said Christabel), "And who art thou?" 70

The lady strange made answer meet,
And her voice was faint and sweet:—
"Have pity on my sore distress,
I scarce can speak for weariness:
Stretch forth thy hand, and have no fear!"
Said Christabel, "How camest thou here?"
And the lady, whose voice was faint and sweet,
Did thus pursue her answer meet:—

"My sire is of a noble line,
And my name is Geraldine: 80
Five warriors seized me yestermorn,
Me, even me, a maid forlorn:
They choked my cries with force and fright,
And tied me on a palfrey white.
The palfrey was as fleet as wind,
And they rode furiously behind.
They spurred amain, their steeds were white:
And once we crossed the shade of night.
As sure as Heaven shall rescue me,
I have no thought what men they be; 90
Nor do I know how long it is
(For I have lain entranced I wis)
Since one, the tallest of the five,
Took me from the palfrey's back,
A weary woman, scarce alive.
Some muttered words his comrades spoke:
He placed me underneath this oak;

He swore they would return with haste:
Whither they went I cannot tell—
I thought I heard, some minutes past, 100
Sounds as of a castle bell.
Stretch forth thy hand (thus ended she),
And help a wretched maid to flee."

Then Christabel stretched forth her hand,
And comforted fair Geraldine:
"O well, bright dame! may you command
The service of Sir Leoline;
And gladly our stout chivalry
Will he send forth and friends withal
To guide and guard you safe and free 110
Home to your noble father's hall."

She rose: and forth with steps they passed
That strove to be, and were not, fast.

Her gracious stars the lady blest,
And thus spake on sweet Christabel:
"All our household are at rest,
The hall as silent as the cell;
Sir Leoline is weak in health,
And may not well awakened be,
But we will move as if in stealth, 120
And I beseech your courtesy,
This night, to share your couch with me."

They crossed the moat, and Christabel
Took the key that fitted well;
A little door she opened straight,
All in the middle of the gate;
The gate that was ironed within and without,
Where an army in battle array had marched out.

The lady sank, belike through pain,
And Christabel with might and main   130
Lifted her up, a weary weight,
Over the threshold of the gate:
Then the lady rose again,
And moved, as she were not in pain.

So free from danger, free from fear,
They crossed the court: right glad they were.
And Christabel devoutly cried
To the lady by her side,
"Praise we the Virgin all divine
Who hath rescued thee from thy distress!"   140
"Alas, alas!" said Geraldine,
"I cannot speak for weariness."
So free from danger, free from fear,
They crossed the court: right glad they were.

Outside her kennel, the mastiff old
Lay fast asleep, in moonshine cold.
The mastiff old did not awake,
Yet she an angry moan did make!
And what can ail the mastiff bitch?
Never till now she uttered yell   150
Beneath the eye of Christabel.
Perhaps it is the owlet's scritch:
For what can ail the mastiff bitch?

They passed the hall, that echoes still,
Pass as lightly as you will!
The brands were flat, the brands were dying,
Amid their own white ashes lying;
But when the lady passed, there came
A tongue of light, a fit of flame;
And Christabel saw the lady's eye,   160

And nothing else saw she thereby,
Save the boss of the shield of Sir Leoline tall,
Which hung in a murky old niche in the wall.
"O softly tread," said Christabel,
"My father seldom sleepeth well."

Sweet Christabel her feet doth bare,
And jealous of the listening air
They steal their way from stair to stair,
Now in glimmer, and now in gloom,
And now they pass the Baron's room, 170
As still as death, with stifled breath!
And now have reached her chamber door;
And now doth Geraldine press down
The rushes of the chamber floor.

The moon shines dim in the open air,
And not a moonbeam enters here.
But they without its light can see
The chamber carved so curiously,
Carved with figures strange and sweet,
All made out of the carver's brain, 180
For a lady's chamber meet:
The lamp with twofold silver chain
Is fastened to an angel's feet.

The silver lamp burns dead and dim;
But Christabel the lamp will trim.
She trimmed the lamp, and made it bright,
And left it swinging to and fro,
While Geraldine, in wretched plight,
Sank down upon the floor below.

"O weary lady, Geraldine, 190
I pray you, drink this cordial wine!

It is a wine of virtuous powers;
My mother made it of wild flowers."

"And will your mother pity me,
Who am a maiden most forlorn?"
Christabel answered—"Woe is me!
She died the hour that I was born.
I have heard the grey-haired friar tell
How on her death-bed she did say,
That she should hear the castle-bell   200
Strike twelve upon my wedding-day.
O mother dear! that thou wert here!"
"I would," said Geraldine, "she were!"

But soon with altered voice, said she—
"Off, wandering mother! Peak and pine!
I have power to bid thee flee."
Alas! what ails poor Geraldine?
Why stares she with unsettled eye?
Can she the bodiless dead espy?
And why with hollow voice cries she,   210
"Off, woman, off! this hour is mine—
Though thou her guardian spirit be,
Off, woman, off! 't is given to me."

Then Christabel knelt by the lady's side,
And raised to heaven her eyes so blue—
"Alas!" said she, "this ghastly ride—
Dear lady! it hath wildered you!"
The lady wiped her moist cold brow,
And faintly said, "'t is over now!"

Again the wild-flower wine she drank: 220
Her fair large eyes 'gan glitter bright,
And from the floor whereon she sank,
The lofty lady stood upright:

She was most beautiful to see,
Like a lady of a far countrée.

And thus the lofty lady spake—
"All they who live in the upper sky,
Do love you, holy Christabel!
And you love them, and for their sake
And for the good which me befel,   230
Even I in my degree will try,
Fair maiden, to requite you well.
But now unrobe yourself; for I
Must pray, ere yet in bed I lie."

Quoth Christabel, "So let it be!"
And as the lady bade, did she.
Her gentle limbs did she undress,
And lay down in her loveliness.

But through her brain of weal and woe
So many thoughts moved to and fro,   240
That vain it were her lids to close;
So half-way from the bed she rose,
And on her elbow did recline
To look at the lady Geraldine.

Beneath the lamp the lady bowed,
And slowly rolled her eyes around;
Then drawing in her breath aloud,
Like one that shuddered, she unbound
The cincture from beneath her breast:
Her silken robe, and inner vest,   250
Dropt to her feet, and full in view,
Behold! her bosom and half her side ——
A sight to dream of, not to tell!
O shield her! shield sweet Christabel!

Yet Geraldine nor speaks nor stirs;
Ah! what a stricken look was hers!
Deep from within she seems half-way
To lift some weight with sick assay,
And eyes the maid and seeks delay;
Then suddenly, as one defied, 260
Collects herself in scorn and pride,
And lay down by the Maiden's side!—
And in her arms the maid she took,
      Ah wel-a-day!
And with low voice and doleful look
These words did say:
"In the touch of this bosom there worketh a spell,
Which is lord of thy utterance, Christabel!
Thou knowest to-night, and wilt know to-morrow,
This mark of my shame, this seal of my sorrow; 270

    But vainly thou warrest,
      For this is alone in
    Thy power to declare,
      That in the dim forest
    Thou heard'st a low moaning,
And found'st a bright lady, surpassingly fair;
And didst bring her home with thee in love and in charity,
To shield her and shelter her from the damp air."

THE CONCLUSION TO PART I

It was a lovely sight to see
The lady Christabel, when she 280
Was praying at the old oak tree.
    Amid the jaggèd shadows
      Of mossy leafless boughs,
    Kneeling in the moonlight,
    To make her gentle vows;

Her slender palms together prest,
Heaving sometimes on her breast;
Her face resigned to bliss or bale—
Her face, oh call it fair not pale,
And both blue eyes more bright than clear,   290
Each about to have a tear.

With open eyes (ah woe is me!)
Asleep, and dreaming fearfully,
Fearfully dreaming, yet, I wis,
Dreaming that alone, which is—
O sorrow and shame! Can this be she,
The lady, who knelt at the old oak tree?
And lo! the worker of these harms,
That holds the maiden in her arms,
Seems to slumber still and mild,   300
As a mother with her child.

A star hath set, a star hath risen,
O Geraldine! since arms of thine
Have been the lovely lady's prison.
O Geraldine! one hour was thine—
Thou'st had thy will! By tairn and rill,
The night-birds all that hour were still.
But now they are jubilant anew,
From cliff and tower, tu—whoo! tu—whoo!
Tu—whoo! tu—whoo! from wood and fell!   310

And see! the lady Christabel
Gathers herself from out her trance;
Her limbs relax, her countenance
Grows sad and soft; the smooth thin lids
Close o'er her eyes; and tears she sheds—
Large tears that leave the lashes bright!

And oft the while she seems to smile
As infants at a sudden light!

Yea, she doth smile, and she doth weep,
Like a youthful hermitess, 320
Beauteous in a wilderness,
Who, praying always, prays in sleep.
And, if she move unquietly,
Perchance, 't is but the blood so free
Comes back and tingles in her feet.
No doubt, she hath a vision sweet.
What if her guardian spirit 't were,
What if she knew her mother near?
But this she knows, in joys and woes,
That saints will aid if men will call: 330
For the blue sky bends over all!

PART II

Each matin bell, the Baron saith,
Knells us back to a world of death.
These words Sir Leoline first said,
When he rose and found his lady dead:
These words Sir Leoline will say
Many a morn to his dying day!

And hence the custom and law began
That still at dawn the sacristan,
Who duly pulls the heavy bell, 340
Five and forty beads must tell
Between each stroke—a warning knell,
Which not a soul can choose but hear
From Bratha Head to Wyndermere.

Saith Bracy the bard: "So let it knell!
And let the drowsy sacristan
Still count as slowly as he can!
There is no lack of such, I ween,
As well fill up the space between.
In Langdale Pike and Witch's Lair,   350
And Dungeon-ghyll so foully rent,
With ropes of rock and bells of air
Three sinful sexton's ghosts are pent,
Who all give back, one after t' other,
The death-note to their living brother;
And oft too, by the knell offended,
Just as their one! two! three! is ended,
The devil mocks the doleful tale
With a merry peal from Borodale."

The air is still! through mist and cloud   360
That merry peal comes ringing loud;
And Geraldine shakes off her dread,
And rises lightly from the bed;
Puts on her silken vestments white,
And tricks her hair in lovely plight,
And nothing doubting of her spell
Awakens the lady Christabel.
"Sleep you, sweet lady Christabel?
I trust that you have rested well."

And Christabel awoke and spied   370
The same who lay down by her side—
O rather say, the same whom she
Raised up beneath the old oak tree!
Nay, fairer yet! and yet more fair!
For she belike hath drunken deep
Of all the blessedness of sleep!
And while she spake, her looks, her air

CHRISTABEL

Such gentle thankfulness declare,
That (so it seemed) her girded vests
Grew tight beneath her heaving breasts.
"Sure I have sinned!" said Christabel,
"Now heaven be praised if all be well!"
And in low faltering tones, yet sweet,
Did she the lofty lady greet
With such perplexity of mind
As dreams too lively leave behind.

So quickly she rose, and quickly arrayed
Her maiden limbs, and having prayed
That He, who on the cross did groan,
Might wash away her sins unknown,
She forthwith led fair Geraldine
To meet her sire, Sir Leoline.

The lovely maid and the lady tall
Are pacing both into the hall,
And pacing on through page and groom,
Enter the Baron's presence-room.

The Baron rose, and while he prest
His gentle daughter to his breast,
With cheerful wonder in his eyes
The lady Geraldine espies,
And gave such welcome to the same,
As might beseem so bright a dame!

But when he heard the lady's tale,
And when she told her father's name,
Why waxed Sir Leoline so pale,
Murmuring o'er the name again,
Lord Roland de Vaux of Tryermaine?

Alas! they had been friends in youth;
But whispering tongues can poison truth;
And constancy lives in realms above;   410
And life is thorny; and youth is vain;
And to be wroth with one we love
Doth work like madness in the brain.
And thus it chanced, as I divine,
With Roland and Sir Leoline.
Each spake words of high disdain
And insult to his heart's best brother:
They parted—ne'er to meet again!
But never either found another
To free the hollow heart from paining—   420
They stood aloof, the scars remaining,
Like cliffs which had been rent asunder;
A dreary sea now flows between;—
But neither heat, nor frost, nor thunder,
Shall wholly do away, I ween,
The marks of that which once hath been.

Sir Leoline, a moment's space,
Stood gazing on the damsel's face:
And the youthful Lord of Tryermaine
Came back upon his heart again.   430

O then the Baron forgot his age,
His noble heart swelled high with rage;
He swore by the wounds in Jesu's side
He would proclaim it far and wide,
With trump and solemn heraldry,
That they, who thus had wronged the dame,
Were base as spotted infamy!
"And if they dare deny the same,
My herald shall appoint a week,
And let the recreant traitors seek   440

My tourney court—that there and then
I may dislodge their reptile souls
From the bodies and forms of men!"
He spake: his eye in lightning rolls!
For the lady was ruthlessly seized; and he kenned
In the beautiful lady the child of his friend!

And now the tears were on his face,
And fondly in his arms he took
Fair Geraldine, who met the embrace,
Prolonging it with joyous look. 450
Which when she viewed, a vision fell
Upon the soul of Christabel,
The vision of fear, the touch and pain!
She shrunk and shuddered, and saw again—
(Ah, woe is me! Was it for thee,
Thou gentle maid! such sights to see?)

Again she saw that bosom old,
Again she felt that bosom cold,
And drew in her breath with a hissing sound:
Whereat the Knight turned wildly round, 460
And nothing saw, but his own sweet maid
With eyes upraised, as one that prayed.

The touch, the sight, had passed away,
And in its stead that vision blest,
Which comforted her after-rest
While in the lady's arms she lay,
Had put a rapture in her breast,
And on her lips and o'er her eyes
Spread smiles like light!
      With new surprise,
"What ails then my belovèd child?" 470
The Baron said—His daughter mild

Made answer, "All will yet be well!"
I ween, she had no power to tell
Aught else: so mighty was the spell.

Yet he, who saw this Geraldine,
Had deemed her sure a thing divine:
Such sorrow with such grace she blended,
As if she feared she had offended
Sweet Christabel, that gentle maid!
And with such lowly tones she prayed   480
She might be sent without delay
Home to her father's mansion.
        "Nay!
Nay, by my soul!" said Leoline.
"Ho! Bracy the bard, the charge be thine!
Go thou, with music sweet and loud,
And take two steeds with trappings proud,
And take the youth whom thou lov'st best
To bear thy harp, and learn thy song,
And clothe you both in solemn vest,
And over the mountains haste along,   490
Lest wandering folk, that are abroad,
Detain you on the valley road.

"And when he has crossed the Irthing flood,
My merry bard! he hastes, he hastes
Up Knorren Moor, through Halegarth Wood,
And reaches soon that castle good
Which stands and threatens Scotland's wastes.

"Bard Bracy! bard Bracy! your horses are fleet,
Ye must ride up the hall, your music so sweet,
More loud than your horses' echoing feet!   500
And loud and loud to Lord Roland call,
Thy daughter is safe in Langdale hall!

CHRISTABEL

Thy beautiful daughter is safe and free—
Sir Leoline greets thee thus through me!
He bids thee come without delay
With all thy numerous array
And take thy lovely daughter home:
And he will meet thee on the way
With all his numerous array
White with their panting palfreys' foam:
And, by mine honour! I will say,
That I repent me of the day
When I spake words of fierce disdain
To Roland de Vaux of Tryermaine!—
—For since that evil hour hath flown,
Many a summer's sun hath shone;
Yet ne'er found I a friend again
Like Roland de Vaux of Tryermaine."

The lady fell, and clasped his knees,
Her face upraised, her eyes o'erflowing;
And Bracy replied, with faltering voice,
His gracious Hail on all bestowing!—
"Thy words, thou sire of Christabel,
Are sweeter than my harp can tell;
Yet might I gain a boon of thee,
This day my journey should not be,
So strange a dream hath come to me,
That I had vowed with music loud
To clear yon wood from thing unblest,
Warned by a vision in my rest!
For in my sleep I saw that dove,
That gentle bird, whom thou dost love,
And call'st by thy own daughter's name—
Sir Leoline! I saw the same
Fluttering, and uttering fearful moan,
Among the green herbs in the forest alone.

Which when I saw and when I heard,
I wondered what might ail the bird;
For nothing near it could I see,
Save the grass and green herbs underneath the old
    tree.   540

"And in my dream methought I went
To search out what might there be found;
And what the sweet bird's trouble meant,
That thus lay fluttering on the ground.
I went and peered, and could descry
No cause for her distressful cry;
But yet for her dear lady's sake
I stooped, methought, the dove to take,
When lo! I saw a bright green snake
Coiled around its wings and neck.   550
Green as the herbs on which it couched,
Close by the dove's its head it crouched;
And with the dove it heaves and stirs,
Swelling its neck as she swelled hers!
I woke; it was the midnight hour,
The clock was echoing in the tower;
But though my slumber was gone by,
This dream it would not pass away—
It seems to live upon my eye!
And thence I vowed this self-same day   560
With music strong and saintly song
To wander through the forest bare,
Lest aught unholy loiter there."

Thus Bracy said: the Baron, the while,
Half-listening heard him with a smile;
Then turned to Lady Geraldine,
His eyes made up of wonder and love;
And said in courtly accents fine,

"Sweet maid, Lord Roland's beauteous dove,
With arms more strong than harp or song, 570
Thy sire and I will crush the snake!"
He kissed her forehead as he spake,
And Geraldine in maiden wise
Casting down her large bright eyes,
With blushing cheek and courtesy fine
She turned her from Sir Leoline;
Softly gathering up her train,
That o'er her right arm fell again;
And folded her arms across her chest,
And couched her head upon her breast, 580
And looked askance at Christabel ——
Jesu, Maria, shield her well!

A snake's small eye blinks dull and shy;
And the lady's eyes they shrunk in her head,
Each shrunk up to a serpent's eye,
And with somewhat of malice, and more of dread,
At Christabel she looked askance!—
One moment—and the sight was fled!
But Christabel in dizzy trance
Stumbling on the unsteady ground 590
Shuddered aloud, with a hissing sound;
And Geraldine again turned round,
And like a thing, that sought relief,
Full of wonder and full of grief,
She rolled her large bright eyes divine
Wildly on Sir Leoline.

The maid, alas! her thoughts are gone,
She nothing sees—no sight but one!
The maid, devoid of guile and sin,
I know not how, in fearful wise, 600
So deeply had she drunken in

That look, those shrunken serpent eyes,
That all her features were resigned
To this sole image in her mind:
And passively did imitate
That look of dull and treacherous hate!
And thus she stood, in dizzy trance,
Still picturing that look askance
With forced unconscious sympathy
Full before her father's view —— 510
As far as such a look could be
In eyes so innocent and blue!

And when the trance was o'er, the maid
Paused awhile, and inly prayed:
Then falling at the Baron's feet,
"By my mother's soul do I entreat
That thou this woman send away!"
She said: and more she could not say:
For what she knew she could not tell,
O'er-mastered by the mighty spell. 620

Why is thy cheek so wan and wild,
Sir Leoline? Thy only child
Lies at thy feet, thy joy, thy pride,
So fair, so innocent, so mild;
The same, for whom thy lady died!
O by the pangs of her dear mother
Think thou no evil of thy child!
For her, and thee, and for no other,
She prayed the moment ere she died:
Prayed that the babe for whom she died, 630
Might prove her dear lord's joy and pride!
   That prayer her deadly pangs beguiled,
      Sir Leoline!

CHRISTABEL

And wouldst thou wrong thy only child,
  Her child and thine?

Within the Baron's heart and brain
If thoughts, like these, had any share,
They only swelled his rage and pain,
And did but work confusion there.
His heart was cleft with pain and rage,   640
His cheeks they quivered, his eyes were wild,
Dishonoured thus in his old age;
Dishonoured by his only child,
And all his hospitality
To the wronged daughter of his friend
By more than woman's jealousy
Brought thus to a disgraceful end—
He rolled his eye with stern regard
Upon the gentle minstrel bard,
And said in tones abrupt, austere—   650
"Why, Bracy! dost thou loiter here?
I bade thee hence!" The bard obeyed;
And turning from his own sweet maid,
The agèd knight, Sir Leoline,
Led forth the lady Geraldine!

THE CONCLUSION TO PART II

A little child, a limber elf,
Singing, dancing to itself,
A fairy thing with red round cheeks,
That always finds, and never seeks,
Makes such a vision to the sight   660
As fills a father's eyes with light;
And pleasures flow in so thick and fast
Upon his heart, that he at last
Must needs express his love's excess

With words of unmeant bitterness.
Perhaps 't is pretty to force together
Thoughts so all unlike each other;
To mutter and mock a broken charm,
To dally with wrong that does no harm.
Perhaps 't is tender too and pretty   670
At each wild word to feel within
A sweet recoil of love and pity.
And what, if in a world of sin
(O sorrow and shame should this be true!)
Such giddiness of heart and brain
Comes seldom save from rage and pain,
So talks as it 's most used to do.
    1797-1800   1816

DEJECTION: AN ODE

> Late, late yestreen I saw the new Moon,
> With the old Moon in her arms;
> And I fear, I fear, my Master dear!
> We shall have a deadly storm.
>   —*Ballad of Sir Patrick Spence*

Well! If the Bard was weather-wise, who made
  The grand old ballad of Sir Patrick Spence,
  This night, so tranquil now, will not go hence
Unroused by winds, that ply a busier trade
Than those which mould yon cloud in lazy flakes,
Or the dull sobbing draft, that moans and rakes
Upon the strings of this Æolian lute,
    Which better far were mute.
  For lo! the New-moon winter-bright!
  And overspread with phantom light,   10
    (With swimming phantom light o'erspread
But rimmed and circled by a silver thread)

DEJECTION: AN ODE

I see the old Moon in her lap, foretelling
   The coming-on of rain and squally blast.
And oh! that even now the gust were swelling,
   And the slant night-shower driving loud and fast!
Those sounds which oft have raised me, whilst they awed,
      And sent my soul abroad,
Might now perhaps their wonted impulse give,
Might startle this dull pain, and make it move and live!   20

A grief without a pang, void, dark, and drear,
   A stifled, drowsy, unimpassioned grief,
   Which finds no natural outlet, no relief,
      In word, or sigh, or tear—
O Lady! in this wan and heartless mood,
To other thoughts by yonder throstle wooed,
   All this long eve, so balmy and serene,
Have I been gazing on the western sky,
   And its peculiar tint of yellow green:
And still I gaze—and with how blank an eye!   30
And those thin clouds above, in flakes and bars,
That give away their motion to the stars;
Those stars, that glide behind them or between,
Now sparkling, now bedimmed, but always seen:
Yon crescent Moon, as fixed as if it grew
In its own cloudless, starless lake of blue;
I see them all so excellently fair,
I see, not feel, how beautiful they are!

      My genial spirits fail;
      And what can these avail   40
To lift the smothering weight from off my breast?
      It were a vain endeavour,
      Though I should gaze for ever

On that green light that lingers in the west:
I may not hope from outward forms to win
The passion and the life, whose fountains are within.

O Lady! we receive but what we give,
And in our life alone does Nature live:
Ours is her wedding garment, ours her shroud!
    And would we aught behold, of higher worth,   50
Than that inanimate cold world allowed
To the poor loveless ever-anxious crowd,
    Ah! from the soul itself must issue forth
A light, a glory, a fair luminous cloud
        Enveloping the Earth—
And from the soul itself must there be sent
    A sweet and potent voice, of its own birth,
Of all sweet sounds the life and element!

O pure of heart! thou need'st not ask of me
What this strong music in the soul may be!   60
What, and wherein it doth exist,
This light, this glory, this fair luminous mist,
This beautiful and beauty-making power.
    Joy, virtuous Lady! Joy that ne'er was given,
Save to the pure, and in their purest hour,
Life, and Life's effluence, cloud at once and shower,
Joy, Lady! is the spirit and the power,
Which, wedding Nature to us, gives in dower
    A new Earth and new Heaven,
Undreamt of by the sensual and the proud—   70
Joy is the sweet voice, Joy the luminous cloud—
    We in ourselves rejoice!
And thence flows all that charms or ear or sight,
    All melodies the echoes of that voice,
All colours a suffusion from that light.

DEJECTION: AN ODE

There was a time when, though my path was rough,
  This joy within me dallied with distress,
And all misfortunes were but as the stuff
  Whence Fancy made me dreams of happiness:
For hope grew round me, like the twining vine,   80
And fruits, and foliage, not my own, seemed mine.
But now afflictions bow me down to earth:
Nor care I that they rob me of my mirth;
    But oh! each visitation
Suspends what nature gave me at my birth,
  My shaping spirit of Imagination.
For not to think of what I needs must feel,
  But to be still and patient, all I can;
And haply by abstruse research to steal
  From my own nature all the natural man—   90
  This was my sole resource, my only plan:
Till that which suits a part infects the whole,
And now is almost grown the habit of my soul.

Hence, viper thoughts, that coil around my mind,
    Reality's dark dream!
I turn from you, and listen to the wind,
  Which long has raved unnoticed. What a scream
Of agony by torture lengthened out
That lute sent forth! Thou Wind, that rav'st without,
Bare crag, or mountain-tairn, or blasted tree,   100
Or pine-grove whither woodman never clomb,
Or lonely house, long held the witches' home,
  Methinks were fitter instruments for thee,
Mad Lutanist! who in this month of showers,
Of dark-brown gardens, and of peeping flowers,
Mak'st Devils' yule, with worse than wintry song,
The blossoms, buds, and timorous leaves among.
    Thou Actor, perfect in all tragic sounds!

Thou mighty Poet, e'en to frenzy bold!
    What tell'st thou now about?   110
  'T is of the rushing of an host in rout,
With groans of trampled men, with smarting wounds—
At once they groan with pain, and shudder with the cold!
But hush! there is a pause of deepest silence!
  And all that noise, as of a rushing crowd,
With groans, and tremulous shudderings—all is over—
  It tells another tale, with sounds less deep and loud!
    A tale of less affright,
    And tempered with delight,
As Otway's self had framed the tender lay,—   120
    'T is of a little child
    Upon a lonesome wild,
Not far from home, but she hath lost her way:
And now moans low in bitter grief and fear,
And now screams loud, and hopes to make her mother hear.

'T is midnight, but small thoughts have I of sleep:
Full seldom may my friend such vigils keep!
Visit her, gentle Sleep! with wings of healing,
  And may this storm be but a mountain-birth,
May all the stars hang bright above her dwelling,   130
  Silent as though they watched the sleeping Earth!
    With light heart may she rise,
    Gay fancy, cheerful eyes,
  Joy lift her spirit, joy attune her voice;
To her may all things live, from pole to pole,
Their life the eddying of her living soul!
  O simple spirit, guided from above,
Dear Lady! friend devoutest of my choice,
Thus mayest thou ever, evermore rejoice.
  1802   1802

HYMN BEFORE SUN-RISE, IN THE VALE OF CHAMOUNI

Besides the Rivers, Arve and Arveiron, which have their sources in the foot of Mont Blanc, five conspicuous torrents rush down its sides; and within a few paces of the Glaciers, the Gentiana Major grows in immense numbers, with its flowers of loveliest blue.

Hast thou a charm to stay the morning-star
In his steep course? So long he seems to pause
On thy bald awful head, O sovran Blanc,
The Arve and Arveiron at thy base
Rave ceaselessly; but thou, most awful Form!
Risest from forth thy silent sea of pines,
How silently! Around thee and above
Deep is the air and dark, substantial, black,
An ebon mass: methinks thou piercest it,
As with a wedge! But when I look again,　　　　10
It is thine own calm home, thy crystal shrine,
Thy habitation from eternity!
O dread and silent Mount! I gazed upon thee,
Till thou, still present to the bodily sense,
Didst vanish from my thought: entranced in prayer
I worshipped the Invisible alone.

　Yet, like some sweet beguiling melody,
So sweet, we know not we are listening to it,
Thou, the meanwhile, wast blending with my Thought,
Yea, with my Life and Life's own secret joy:　　20
Till the dilating Soul, enrapt, transfused,
Into the mighty vision passing—there
As in her natural form, swelled vast to Heaven!

　Awake, my soul! not only passive praise
Thou owest! not alone these swelling tears,
Mute thanks and secret ecstasy! Awake,

Voice of sweet song! Awake, my heart, awake!
Green vales and icy cliffs, all join my Hymn.

    Thou first and chief, sole sovereign of the Vale!
O struggling with the darkness all the night,   30
And visited all night by troops of stars,
Or when they climb the sky or when they sink:
Companion of the morning-star at dawn,
Thyself Earth's rosy star, and of the dawn
Co-herald: wake, O wake, and utter praise!
Who sank thy sunless pillars deep in Earth?
Who filled thy countenance with rosy light?
Who made thee parent of perpetual streams?

    And you, ye five wild torrents fiercely glad!
Who called you forth from night and utter death,   40
From dark and icy caverns called you forth,
Down those precipitous, black, jaggèd rocks,
For ever shattered and the same for ever?
Who gave you your invulnerable life,
Your strength, your speed, your fury, and your joy,
Unceasing thunder and eternal foam?
And who commanded (and the silence came),
Here let the billows stiffen, and have rest?

Ye Ice-falls! ye that from the mountain's brow
Adown enormous ravines slope amain—   50
Torrents, methinks, that heard a mighty voice,
And stopped at once amid their maddest plunge!
Motionless torrents! silent cataracts!
Who made you glorious as the Gates of Heaven
Beneath the keen full moon? Who bade the sun
Clothe you with rainbows? Who, with living flowers
Of loveliest blue, spread garlands at your feet?—
God! let the torrents, like a shout of nations,
Answer! and let the ice-plains echo, God!
God! sing ye meadow-streams with gladsome voice!   60
Ye pine-groves, with your soft and soul-like sounds!

And they too have a voice, yon piles of snow,
And in their perilous fall shall thunder, God!
  Ye living flowers that skirt the eternal frost!
Ye wild goats sporting round the eagle's nest!
Ye eagles, play-mates of the mountain-storm!
Ye lightnings, the dread arrows of the clouds!
Ye signs and wonders of the element!
Utter forth God, and fill the hills with praise!
  Thou too, hoar Mount! with thy sky-pointing peaks, 70
Oft from whose feet the avalanche, unheard,
Shoots downward, glittering through the pure serene
Into the depth of clouds, that veil thy breast—
Thou too again, stupendous Mountain! thou
That as I raise my head, awhile bowed low
In adoration, upward from thy base
Slow travelling with dim eyes suffused with tears,
Solemnly seemest, like a vapoury cloud,
To rise before me—Rise, O ever rise,
Rise like a cloud of incense from the Earth!   80
Thou kingly Spirit throned among the hills,
Thou dread ambassador from Earth to Heaven,
Great Hierarch! tell thou the silent sky,
And tell the stars, and tell yon rising sun
Earth, with her thousand voices, praises God.
  1802   1802

WORK WITHOUT HOPE

ALL Nature seems at work. Slugs leave their lair—
The bees are stirring—birds are on the wing—
And Winter slumbering in the open air,
Wears on his smiling face a dream of Spring!
And I the while, the sole unbusy thing,
Nor honey make, nor pair, nor build, nor sing.

Yet well I ken the banks where amaranths blow,
Have traced the fount whence streams of nectar flow.
Bloom, O ye amaranths! bloom for whom ye may,
For me ye bloom not! Glide, rich streams, away! 10
With lips unbrightened, wreathless brow, I stroll:
And would you learn the spells that drowse my soul?
Work without Hope draws nectar in a sieve,
And Hope without an object cannot live.

1825   1828

EPITAPH

Stop, Christian passer-by!—Stop, child of God,
And read with gentle breast. Beneath this sod
A poet lies, or that which once seemed he.
O, lift one thought in prayer for S. T. C.;
That he who many a year with toil of breath
Found death in life, may here find life in death!
Mercy for praise—to be forgiven for fame
He asked, and hoped, through Christ. Do thou the same!

1833   1834

BIOGRAPHIA LITERARIA

Chapter XIV

During the first year that Mr. Wordsworth and I were neighbors, our conversations turned frequently on the two cardinal points of poetry, the power of exciting the sympathy of the reader by a faithful adherence to the truth of nature, and the power of giving the interest of novelty by the modifying colors of imagination. The sudden charm which accidents of light and shade, which moonlight or sunset diffused over a known and familiar landscape, appeared to represent the practicability of combining both. These are the poetry of nature. The thought suggested itself—(to which of us I do not recollect)—that a series of poems might be composed of two sorts. In the one, the incidents and agents were to be, in part at least, supernatural; and the excellence aimed at was to consist in the interesting of the affections by the dramatic truth of such emotions, as would naturally accompany such situations, supposing them real. And real in this sense they have been to every human being who, from whatever source of delusion, has at any time believed himself under supernatural agency. For the second class, subjects were to be chosen from ordinary life; the characters and incidents were to be such as will be found in every village and its vicinity, where there is a meditative and feeling mind to seek after them, or to notice them, when they present themselves.

In this idea originated the plan of the *Lyrical Ballads;* in which it was agreed, that my endeavors should be directed to persons and characters supernatural, or at least romantic; yet so as to transfer from our inward nature a human interest and a semblance of truth sufficient to procure for these shadows of imagination that willing suspension of disbelief for the moment, which constitutes poetic faith. Mr. Wordsworth, on the other hand, was to propose to himself as his object, to give the charm of novelty to things of every day, and to excite a feeling analogous to the supernatural, by awakening the mind's attention to the lethargy of custom, and directing it to the loveliness and the wonders of the world before us; an inexhaustible treasure, but for which, in consequence of the film of familiarity and selfish solicitude, we have eyes, yet see not, ears that hear not, and hearts that neither feel nor understand.

With this view I wrote the *Ancient Mariner,* and was

preparing among other poems, *The Dark Ladie,* and the *Christabel,* in which I should have more nearly realized my ideal than I had done in my first attempt. But Mr. Wordsworth's industry had proved so much more successful, and the number of his poems so much greater, that my compositions, instead of forming a balance, appeared rather an interpolation of heterogeneous matter. Mr. Wordsworth added two or three poems written in his own character, in the impassioned, lofty, and sustained diction, which is characteristic of his genius. In this form the *Lyrical Ballads* were published; and were presented by him, as an experiment, whether subjects, which from their nature rejected the usual ornaments and extra-colloquial style of poems in general, might not be so managed in the language of ordinary life as to produce the pleasurable interest, which it is the peculiar business of poetry to impart. To the second edition he added a preface of considerable length; in which, notwithstanding some passages of apparently a contrary import, he was understood to contend for the extension of this style to poetry of all kinds, and to reject as vicious and indefensible all phrases and forms of speech that were not included in what he (unfortunately, I think, adopting an equivocal expression) called the language of real life. From this preface, prefixed to poems in which it was impossible to deny the presence of original genius, however mistaken its direction might be deemed, arose the whole long-continued controversy. For from the conjunction of perceived power with supposed heresy I explain the inveteracy and in some instances, I grieve to say, the acrimonious passions, with which the controversy has been conducted by the assailants.

Had Mr. Wordsworth's poems been the silly, the childish things, which they were for a long time de-

BIOGRAPHIA LITERARIA

scribed as being; had they been really distinguished from the compositions of other poets merely by meanness of language and inanity of thought; had they indeed contained nothing more than what is found in the parodies and pretended imitations of them; they must have sunk at once, a dead weight, into the slough of oblivion, and have dragged the preface along with them. But year after year increased the number of Mr. Wordsworth's admirers. They were found too not in the lower classes of the reading public, but chiefly among young men of strong sensibility and meditative minds; and their admiration (inflamed perhaps in some degree by opposition) was distinguished by its intensity, I might almost say, by its religious fervor. These facts, and the intellectual energy of the author, which was more or less consciously felt, where it was outwardly and even boisterously denied, meeting with sentiments of aversion to his opinions, and of alarm at their consequences, produced an eddy of criticism, which would of itself have borne up the poems by the violence with which it whirled them round and round. With many parts of this preface in the sense attributed to them and which the words undoubtedy seem to authorize, I never concurred; but on the contrary objected to them as erroneous in principle, and as contradictory (in appearance at least) both to other parts of the same preface, and to the author's own practice in the greater part of the poems themselves. Mr. Wordsworth in his recent collection has, I find, degraded this prefatory disquisition to the end of his second volume, to be read or not at the reader's choice. But he has not, as far as I can discover, announced any change in his poetic creed. At all events, considering it as the source of a controversy, in which I have been honored more than I deserve by the frequent conjunction of my name with his, I think it expedient to declare once for all, in what points I coincide with the opinions supported in that preface, and in what points I altogether differ. But in order to render myself intelligible I must previously, in as few words as possible, explain my views, first, of a Poem; and secondly, of Poetry itself, in kind, and in essence.

The office of philosophical disquisition consists in just distinction; while it is the privilege of the philosopher to preserve himself constantly aware, that distinction is not division. In order to obtain adequate notions of any truth, we must intellectually separate its distinguishable parts; and this is the technical process of philosophy. But having so done, we must then restore them in our conceptions to the unity, in which they actually co-exist; and this is the result of philosophy. A poem contains the same elements as a prose composition; the difference therefore must consist in a different combination of them, in consequence of a different object being proposed. According to the difference of the object will be the difference of the combination. It is possible, that the object may be merely to facilitate the recollection of any given facts or observations by artificial arrangement; and the composition will be a poem, merely because it is distinguished from prose by metre, or by rhyme, or by both conjointly. In this, the lowest sense, a man might attribute the name of a poem to the well-known enumeration of the days in the several months:

'Thirty days hath September,
April, June, and November,' &c.

and others of the same class and purpose. And as a particular pleasure is found in anticipating the recurrence of sound and quantities, all compositions that have this charm superadded, whatever be their contents, *may* be entitled poems.

So much for the superficial form. A difference of object and contents supplies an additional ground of distinction. The immediate purpose may be the communication of truths; either of truth absolute and demonstrable, as in works of science; or of facts experienced and recorded, as in history. Pleasure, and that of the highest and most permanent kind, may result from the attainment of the end; but it is not itself the immediate end. In other works the communication of pleasure may be the immediate purpose; and though truth, either moral or intellectual, ought to be the ultimate end, yet this will distinguish the character of the author, not the class to which the work belongs. Blest indeed is that state of society, in which the immediate purpose would be baffled by the perversion of the proper ultimate end; in which no charm of diction or imagery could exempt the *Bathyllus* even of an Anacreon, or the *Alexis* of Virgil, from disgust and aversion!

But the communication of pleasure may be the immediate object of a work not metrically composed; and that object may have been in a high degree attained, as in novels and romances. Would then the mere superaddition of metre, with or without rhyme, entitle these to the name of poems? The answer is, that nothing can permanently please, which does not contain in itself the reason why it is so, and not otherwise. If metre be superadded, all other parts must be made consonant with it. They must be such, as to justify the perpetual and distinct attention to each part, which an exact correspondent recurrence of accent and sound are calculated to excite. The final definition then, so deduced, may be thus worded. A poem is that species of composition, which is opposed to works of science, by proposing for its *immediate* object pleasure, not truth; and from all other species—(having *this* object in common with it)—it is discriminated by proposing to itself such delight from the *whole,* as is compatible with a distinct gratification from each component *part.*

Controversy is not seldom excited in consequence of the disputants attaching each a different meaning to the same word; and in few instances has this been more striking, than in disputes concerning the present subject. If a man chooses to call every composition a poem, which is rhyme, or measure, or both, I must leave his opinion uncontroverted. The distinction is at least competent to characterize the writer's intention. If it were subjoined, that the whole is likewise entertaining or affecting, as a tale, or as a series of interesting reflections, I of course admit this as another fit ingredient of a poem, and an additional merit. But if the definition sought for be that of a *legitimate* poem, I answer, it must be one, the parts of which mutually support and explain each other; all in their proportion harmonizing with, and supporting the purpose and known influences of metrical arrangement. The philosophic critics of all ages coincide with the ultimate judgment of all countries, in equally denying the praises of a just poem, on the one hand, to a series of striking lines or distiches, each of which, absorbing the whole attention of the reader to itself, becomes disjoined from its context, and forms a separate whole, instead of a harmonizing part; and on the other hand, to an unsustained composition, from which the reader collects rapidly the general result unattracted by the component parts. The reader should be carried forward, not merely or chiefly by the mechanical impulse of curiosity, or by a restless desire to arrive at the final solution; but by the pleasurable activity of mind excited by the attractions of the journey itself. Like the motion of a serpent, which the Egyptians made the emblem of intellectual power; or like the path of sound through the air:—at every step he pauses and half recedes, and from the retrogressive movement collects the force which again carries him onward, *Praecipitandus est liber spiritus,* says Petronius most happily. The epithet, *liber,* here balances the preceding verb; and it is not easy to conceive more meaning condensed in fewer words.

But if this should be admitted as a satisfactory character of a poem, we have still to seek for a definition of poetry. The writings of Plato and Jeremy Taylor, and Burnet's *Theory of the Earth,* furnish undeniable proofs that poetry of the highest kind may exist without metre, and even without the contra-distinguishing objects of a poem. The first chapter of Isaiah—(indeed a very large proportion of the whole book)—is poetry in the most emphatic sense; yet it would be not less irrational than strange to assert, that pleasure, and not truth was the immediate object of the prophet. In short, whatever specific import we attach to the word Poetry, there will be found involved in it, as a necessary consequence, that a poem of any length neither can be, nor ought to be, all poetry. Yet if an harmonious whole is to be produced, the remaining parts must be preserved in keeping with the poetry; and this can be no otherwise effected than by such a studied selection and artificial arrangement, as will partake of one, though not a peculiar property of poetry. And this again can be no other than the property of exciting a more continuous and equal attention than the language of prose aims at, whether colloquial or written.

My own conclusions on the nature of poetry, in the strictest use of the word, have been in part anticipated in some of the remarks on the Fancy and Imagination in the first part of this work. What is poetry?—is so nearly the same question with, what is a poet?—that the answer to the one is involved in the solution of the other. For it is a distinction resulting from the poetic genius itself, which sustains and modifies the images, thoughts, and emotions of the poet's own mind.

The poet, described in ideal perfection, brings the whole soul of man into activity, with the subordination of its faculties to each other according to their relative worth and dignity. He diffuses a tone and spirit of unity, that blends, and (as it were) *fuses,* each into each, by that synthetic and magical power, to which I would exclusively appropriate the name of Imagination. This power, first put in action by the will and understanding, and retained under their irremissive, though gentle and unnoticed, control, *laxis effertur habenis,* reveals itself in the balance or reconcilement of opposite or discordant qualities: of sameness with difference; of the general with the concrete; the idea with the image; the individual with the representative; the sense of novelty and freshness with old and familiar objects; a more than usual state of emotion with more than usual order; judgment ever awake and steady self-possession with enthusiasm and feeling profound or vehement; and while it blends and harmonizes the natural and the artificial, still subordinates art to nature; the manner to the matter; and our admiration of the poet to our sympathy with the poetry. Doubtless, as Sir John Davies observes of the soul—(and his words may with slight alteration be applied, and even more appropriately, to the poetic Imagination)—

"Doubtless this could not be, but that she turns
  Bodies to *spirit* by sublimation strange,

As fire converts to fire the things it burns,
As we our food into our nature change.

From their gross matter she abstracts *their* forms,
And draws a kind of quintessence from things;
Which to her proper nature she transforms
To bear them light on her celestial wings.

Thus does she, when from *individual states*
She doth abstract the universal kinds;
Which then re-clothed in divers names and fates
Steal access through our senses to our minds."

Finally, Good Sense is the Body of poetic genius, Fancy its Drapery, Motion its Life, and Imagination the Soul that is everywhere, and in each; and forms all into one graceful and intelligent whole.

1817

ROBERT SOUTHEY (1774-1843)

THE BATTLE OF BLENHEIM

It was a summer evening,
   Old Kaspar's work was done,
And he before his cottage door
   Was sitting in the sun,
And by him sported on the green
His little grandchild Wilhelmine.

She saw her brother Peterkin
   Roll something large and round,
Which he beside the rivulet
   In playing there had found;   10
He came to ask what he had found,
That was so large, and smooth, and round.

Old Kaspar took it from the boy,
　　Who stood expectant by;
And then the old man shook his head,
　　And, with a natural sigh,
" 'T is some poor fellow's skull," said he,
"Who fell in the great victory.

"I find them in the garden,
　　For there's many here about;　　　　　　　　　　20
And often when I go to plough,
　　The ploughshare turns them out!
For many thousand men," said he,
"Were slain in that great victory."

"Now tell me what 't was all about,"
　　Young Peterkin, he cries;
And little Wilhelmine looks up
　　With wonder-waiting eyes;
"Now tell us all about the war,
And what they fought each other for."　　　　　　　30

"It was the English," Kaspar cried,
　　"Who put the French to rout;
But what they fought each other for,
　　I could not well make out;
But everybody said," quoth he,
"That 't was a famous victory.

"My father lived at Blenheim then,
　　Yon little stream hard by;
They burnt his dwelling to the ground,
　　And he was forced to fly;　　　　　　　　　　　　40
So with his wife and child he fled,
Nor had he where to rest his head.

"With fire and sword the country round
   Was wasted far and wide,
And many a childing mother then,
   And new-born baby died;
But things like that, you know, must be
At every famous victory.

"They say it was a shocking sight
   After the field was won;
For many thousand bodies here
   Lay rotting in the sun;
But things like that, you know, must be
After a famous victory.

"Great praise the Duke of Marlbro' won,
   And our good Prince Eugene."
"Why 't was a very wicked thing!"
   Said little Wilhelmine.
"Nay, nay, my little girl," quoth he,
"It was a famous victory.

"And everybody praised the Duke
   Who this great fight did win."
   "But what good came of it at last?"
   Quoth little Peterkin.
"Why that I cannot tell," said he,
"But 't was a famous victory."

1798   1798

BISHOP BRUNO

Bishop Bruno awoke in the dead midnight,
And he heard his heart beat loud with affright;
He dreamt he had rung the palace bell,
And the sound it gave was his passing knell.

Bishop Bruno smiled at his fears so vain,
He turned to sleep and he dreamt again:—
He rang at the palace gate once more,
And Death was the porter that opened the door.

He started up at the fearful dream,
And he heard at his window the screech-owl scream; 10
Bishop Bruno slept no more that night,—
Oh, glad was he when he saw the day-light!

Now he goes forth in proud array,
For he with the Emperor dines to-day;
There was not a baron in Germany
That went with a nobler train than he.

Before and behind his soldiers ride,
The people thronged to see their pride;
They bowed the head, and the knee they bent,
But nobody blest him as he went. 20

So he went on stately and proud,
When he heard a voice that cried aloud,
"Ho! ho! Bishop Bruno! you travel with glee;
But I would have you know, you travel to me!"

Behind and before and on either side,
He looked, but nobody he espied;
And the Bishop at that grew cold with fear,
For he heard the words distinct and clear.

And when he rang at the palace bell,
He almost expected to hear his knell; 30
And when the porter turned the key,
He almost expected Death to see.

BISHOP BRUNO

But soon the Bishop recovered his glee,
For the Emperor welcomed him royally;
And now the tables were spread, and there
Were choicest wines and dainty fare.

And now the Bishop had blest the meat,
When a voice was heard as he sat in his seat:
"With the Emperor now you are dining with glee;
But know, Bishop Bruno! you sup with me!"   40

The Bishop then grew pale with affright,
And suddenly lost his appetite;
All the wine and dainty cheer
Could not comfort his heart that was sick with fear.

But by little and little recovered he,
For the wine went flowing merrily,
Till at length he forgot his former dread,
And his cheeks again grew rosy red.

When he sat down to the royal fare,
Bishop Bruno was the saddest man there;   50
But when the masquers entered the hall,
He was the merriest man of all.

Then from amid the masquers' crowd
There went a voice hollow and loud:
"You have passed the day, Bishop Bruno, in glee;
But you must pass the night with me!"

His cheek grows pale, and his eye-balls glare,
And stiff round his tonsure bristled his hair;
With that there came one from the masquers' band,
And took the Bishop by the hand.   60

The bony hand suspended his breath,
His marrow grew cold at the touch of Death;
On saints in vain he attempted to call—
Bishop Bruno fell dead in the palace hall.
   1798   1799

MY DAYS AMONG THE DEAD ARE PAST

My days among the Dead are past;
  Around me I behold,
Where'er these casual eyes are cast,
  The mighty minds of old;
My never-failing friends are they,
With whom I converse day by day.

With them I take delight in weal,
  And seek relief in woe;
And while I understand and feel
  How much to them I owe,   10
My cheeks have often been bedewed
With tears of thoughtful gratitude.

My thoughts are with the Dead, with them
  I live in long-past years,
Their virtues love, their faults condemn,
  Partake their hopes and fears,
And from their lessons seek and find
Instruction with an humble mind.

My hopes are with the Dead, anon
  My place with them will be,   20
And I with them will travel on
  Through all Futurity;

Yet leaving here a name, I trust,
That will not perish in the dust.

1818   1823

SIR WALTER SCOTT (1771-1832)

CALEDONIA

From THE LAY OF THE LAST MINSTREL: CANTO VI

BREATHES there the man, with soul so dead,
Who never to himself hath said,
　This is my own, my native land!
Whose heart hath ne'er within him burn'd,
As home his footsteps he hath turn'd,
　From wandering on a foreign strand!
If such there breathe, go, mark him well;
For him no Minstrel raptures swell;
High though his titles, proud his name,
Boundless his wealth as wish can claim;　　　　10
Despite those titles, power, and pelf,
The wretch, concentred all in self,
Living, shall forfeit fair renown,
And, doubly dying, shall go down
To the vile dust, from whence he sprung,
Unwept, unhonour'd, and unsung.

O Caledonia! stern and wild,
Meet nurse for a poetic child!
Land of brown heath and shaggy wood,
Land of the mountain and the flood,　　　　　20
Land of my sires! what mortal hand
Can ere untie the filial band

That knits me to thy rugged strand!
Still as I view each well-known scene,
Think what is now, and what hath been,
Seems as, to me, of all bereft,
Sole friend thy woods and streams were left:
And thus I love them better still,
Even in extremity of ill.
By Yarrow's streams still let me stray, 30
Though none should guide my feeble way;
Still feel the breeze down Ettrick break,
Although it chill my wither'd cheek;
Still lay my head by Teviot Stone,
Though there forgotten and alone,
The Bard may draw his parting groan.

1802-1804   1805

LOCHINVAR

(Lady Heron's Song)

From MARMION, CANTO V

O, YOUNG Lochinvar is come out of the west,
Through all the wide Border his steed was the best;
And save his good broadsword he weapons had none,
He rode all unarmed, and he rode all alone.
So faithful in love, and so dauntless in war,
There never was knight like the young Lochinvar.

He stayed not for brake, and he stopped not for stone,
He swam the Eske river where ford there was none;
But ere he alighted at Netherby gate,
The bride had consented, the gallant came late: 10

LOCHINVAR

For a laggard in love, and a dastard in war,
Was to wed the fair Ellen of brave Lochinvar.

So boldly he entered the Netherby Hall,
Among bride's-men, and kinsmen, and brothers, and all:
Then spoke the bride's father, his hand on his sword,
(For the poor craven bridegroom said never a word,)
"O come ye in peace here, or come ye in war,
Or to dance at our bridal, young Lord Lochinvar?"

"I long wooed your daughter, my suit you denied;—
Love swells like the Solway, but ebbs like its tide— 20
And now am I come, with this lost love of mine,
To lead but one measure, drink one cup of wine.
There are maidens in Scotland more lovely by far,
That would gladly be bride to the young Lochinvar."

The bride kissed the goblet: the knight took it up,
He quaffed off the wine, and he threw down the cup.
She looked down to blush, and she looked up to sigh,
With a smile on her lips, and a tear in her eye.
He took her soft hand, ere her mother could bar,—
"Now tread we a measure!" said young Lochinvar. 30

So stately his form, and so lovely her face,
That never a hall such a galliard did grace;
While her mother did fret, and her father did fume,
And the bridegroom stood dangling his bonnet and plume;
And the bride-maidens whispered, " 'T were better by far,
To have matched our fair cousin with young Lochinvar."

One touch to her hand, and one word in her ear,
When they reached the hall-door, and the charger stood near;

So light to the croupe the fair lady he swung,
So light to the saddle before her he sprung! 40
"She is won! we are gone, over bank, bush, and scaur;[1]
They'll have fleet steeds that follow," quoth young Lochinvar.

There was mounting 'mong Graemes of the Netherby clan;
Forsters, Fenwicks, and Musgraves, they rode and they ran:
There was racing and chasing on Cannobie Lee,
But the lost bride of Netherby ne'er did they see.
So daring in love, and so dauntless in war,
Have ye e'er heard of gallant like young Lochinvar?
   1806-1808   1808

HUNTING SONG

Waken, lords and ladies gay,
On the mountain dawns the day,
All the jolly chase is here,
With hawk, and horse, and hunting-spear!
Hounds are in their couples yelling,
Hawks are whistling, horns are knelling,
Merrily, merrily, mingle they,
"Waken, lords and ladies gay."

Waken, lords and ladies gay,
The mist has left the mountain grey, 10
Springlets in the dawn are steaming,
Diamonds on the brake are gleaming;
And foresters have busy been,
To track the buck in thicket green;

[1] jutting cliff

Now we come to chant our lay,
"Waken, lords and ladies gay."

Waken, lords and ladies gay,
To the green-wood haste away;
We can show you where he lies,
Fleet of foot, and tall of size;   20
We can show the marks he made,
When 'gainst the oak his antlers fray'd;
You shall see him brought to bay,
"Waken, lords and ladies gay."

Louder, louder chant the lay,
Waken, lords and ladies gay!
Tell them youth, and mirth, and glee,
Run a course as well as we;
Time, stern huntsman! who can baulk,
Stanch as hound, and fleet as hawk;   30
Think of this, and rise with day,
Gentle lords and ladies gay.

1808   1814

SOLDIER, REST

(*Ellen's Song*)

From THE LADY OF THE LAKE, CANTO I

SOLDIER, rest! thy warfare o'er,
  Sleep the sleep that knows not breaking;
Dream of battled fields no more,
  Days of danger, nights of waking.
In our isle's enchanted hall,
  Hands unseen thy couch are strewing,

SIR WALTER SCOTT

Fairy strains of music fall,
  Every sense in slumber dewing
Soldier, rest! thy warfare o'er,
Dream of fighting fields no more: 10
Sleep the sleep that knows not breaking,
Morn of toil, nor night of waking.

No rude sound shall reach thine ear,
  Armour's clang, or war-steed champing,
Trump nor pibroch summon here
  Mustering clan, or squadron tramping.
Yet the lark's shrill fife may come
  At the day-break from the fallow,
And the bittern sound his drum,
  Booming from the sedgy shallow.   20
Ruder sounds shall none be near,
Guards nor warders challenge here,
Here's no war-steed's neigh and champing,
Shouting clans, or squadrons stamping.

Huntsman, rest! thy chase is done;
  While our slumbrous spells assail ye,
Dream not, with the rising sun,
  Bugles here shall sound reveillé.
Sleep! the deer is in his den;
  Sleep! thy hounds are by thee lying;   30
Sleep! nor dream in yonder glen,
  How thy gallant steed lay dying.
Huntsman, rest! thy chase is done;
Think not of the rising sun,
For at dawning to assail ye,
Here no bugles sound reveillé.

1809-1810   1810

CORONACH [1]

From THE LADY OF THE LAKE, CANTO III

HE IS gone on the mountain,
   He is lost to the forest,
Like a summer-dried fountain,
   When our need was the sorest.
The font, reappearing,
   From the rain-drops shall borrow,
But to us comes no cheering,
   To Duncan no morrow!

The hand of the reaper
   Takes the ears that are hoary,   10
But the voice of the weeper
   Wails manhood in glory.
The autumn winds rushing
   Waft the leaves that are searest.
But our flower was in flushing,
   When blighting was nearest.

Fleet foot on the correi,[2]
   Sage counsel in cumber,[3]
Red hand in the foray,
   How sound is thy slumber!   20
Like the dew on the mountain,
   Like the foam on the river,
Like the bubble on the fountain,
   Thou art gone, and forever!

1809-1810   1810

[1] Scotch funeral dirge
[2] hillside for hunting
[3] trouble

BRIGNALL BANKS

(Edmund's Song)

From ROKEBY, CANTO III

O, BRIGNALL banks are wild and fair,
   And Greta woods are green,
And you may gather garlands there
   Would grace a summer queen.
And as I rode by Dalton-hall,
   Beneath the turrets high,
A maiden on the castle wall
   Was singing merrily,—
"O, Brignall banks are fresh and fair,
   And Greta woods are green;   10
I'd rather rove with Edmund there,
   Than reign our English queen."

"If, maiden, thou wouldst wend with me,
   To leave both tower and town,
Thou first must guess what life lead we,
   That dwell by dale and down.
And if thou canst that riddle read,
   As read full well you may,
Then to the greenwood shalt thou speed,
   As blithe as Queen of May."   20
Yet sung she, "Brignall banks are fair,
   And Greta woods are green;
I'd rather rove with Edmund there,
   Than reign our English queen.

BRIGNALL BANKS

"I read[1] you, by your bugle-horn,
   And by your palfrey good,
I read you for a ranger sworn,
   To keep the king's greenwood."
"A ranger, lady, winds his horn,
   And 't is at peep of light;   30
His blast is heard at merry morn,
   And mine at dead of night."
Yet sung she, "Brignall banks are fair,
   And Greta woods are gay;
I would I were with Edmund there,
   To reign his Queen of May!

"With burnished brand and musketoon,[2]
   So gallantly you come,
I read you for a bold dragoon,
   That lists the tuck of drum."   40
"I list no more the tuck of drum,
   No more the trumpet hear;
But when the beetle sounds his hum,
   My comrades take the spear.
And O! though Brignall banks be fair,
   And Greta woods be gay,
Yet mickle must the maiden dare,
   Would reign my Queen of May!

"Maiden! a nameless life I lead,
   A nameless death I'll die;   50
The fiend, whose lantern lights the mead,
   Were better mate than I!
And when I'm with my comrades met
   Beneath the greenwood bough,
What once we were we all forget,
   Nor think what we are now.

[1] guess   [2] short musket

Yet Brignall banks are fresh and fair,
   And Greta woods are green,
And you may gather garlands there
   Would grace a summer queen." 60

1811-1813   1813

THE CAVALIER

(*Edmund's Song*)

From ROKEBY, CANTO V

WHILE the dawn on the mountain was misty and gray,
My true love has mounted his steed and away,
Over hill, over valley, o'er dale, and o'er down;
Heaven shield the brave Gallant that fights for the Crown!

He has doff'd the silk doublet the breast-plate to bear,
He has placed the steel cap o'er his long-flowing hair,
From his belt to his stirrup his broadsword hangs down,—
Heaven shield the brave Gallant that fights for the Crown!

For the rights of fair England that broadsword he draws,
Her King is his leader, her Church is his cause; 10
His watchword is honour, his pay is renown,—
God strike with the Gallant that strikes for the Crown!

They may boast of their Fairfax, their Waller, and all
The roundheaded rebels of Westminster Hall;
But tell these bold traitors of London's proud town,
That the spears of the North have encircled the Crown.

There's Derby and Cavendish, dread of their foes;
There's Erin's high Ormond and Scotland's Montrose!
Would you match the base Skippon, and Massey, and Brown,
With the Barons of England that fight for the Crown?   20

Now joy to the crest of the brave Cavalier!
Be his banner unconquer'd, resistless his spear,
Till in peace and in triumph his toils he may drown,
In a pledge to fair England, her Church, and her Crown.
   1811-1813   1813

JOCK OF HAZELDEAN

"Why weep ye by the tide, ladie?
  Why weep ye by the tide?
I'll wed ye to my youngest son,
  And ye sall be his bride:
And ye sall be his bride, ladie,
  Sae comely to be seen"—
But aye she loot[1] the tears down fa'
  For Jock of Hazeldean.

"Now let this wilfu' grief be done,
  And dry that cheek so pale;   10
Young Frank is chief of Errington
  And lord of Langley-dale;
His step is first in peaceful ha',
  His sword in battle keen"—
But aye she loot the tears down fa'
  For Jock of Hazeldean.

[1] let

"A chain of gold ye sall not lack,
  Nor braid to bind your hair;
Nor mettled hound, nor managed hawk,
  Nor palfrey fresh and fair;   20
And you, the foremost o' them a',
  Shall ride our forest queen."—
But aye she loot the tears down fa'
  For Jock of Hazeldean.

The kirk was decked at morning-tide,
  The tapers glimmered fair;
The priest and bridegroom wait the bride,
  And dame and knight are there.
They sought her baith [1] by bower and ha';
  The ladie was not seen!   30
She's o'er the Border and awa'
  Wi' Jock of Hazeldean.

1816

PIBROCH OF DONUIL DHU

Pibroch [2] of Donuil Dhu,[3]
  Pibroch of Donuil,
Wake thy wild voice anew,
  Summon Clan-Conuil.
Come away, come away,
  Hark to the summons!
Come in your war array,
  Gentles and commons.

Come from deep glen, and
  From mountain so rocky,   10

---

[1] both
[2] war music played on the bagpipe
[3] Donald the Black

PIBROCH OF DONUIL DHU

The war-pipe and pennon
    Are at Inverlochy.
Come every hill-plaid, and
    True heart that wears one,
Come every steel blade, and
    Strong hand that bears one.

Leave untended the herd,
    The flock without shelter;
Leave the corpse uninterr'd,
    The bride at the altar;
Leave the deer, leave the steer,
    Leave nets and barges:
Come with your fighting gear,
    Broadswords and targes.

Come as the winds come, when
    Forests are rended,
Come as the waves come, when
    Navies are stranded:
Faster come, faster come,
    Faster and faster,
Chief, vassal, page and groom,
    Tenant and master.

Fast they come, fast they come;
    See how they gather!
Wide waves the eagle plume,
    Blended with heather.
Cast your plaids, draw your blades,
    Forward each man set!
Pibroch of Donuil Dhu,
    Knell for the onset!

1816

PROUD MAISIE

From THE HEART OF MIDLOTHIAN, CHAPTER XI

PROUD Maisie is in the wood,
    Walking so early;
Sweet Robin sits on the bush,
    Singing so rarely.

"Tell me, thou bonny bird,
    When shall I marry me?"
"When six braw [1] gentlemen
    Kirkwood shall carry ye."

"Who makes the bridal bed,
    Birdie, say truly?"
"The grey-headed sexton
    That delves the grave duly.

"The glow-worm o'er grave and stone
    Shall light thee steady.
The owl from the steeple sing,
    'Welcome, proud lady.'"

1818   1818

COUNTY GUY

From QUENTIN DURWARD, CHAPTER IV

AH! County [2] Guy, the hour is nigh,
    The sun has left the lea,
The orange flower perfumes the bower,
    The breeze is on the sea.

---

[1] fine   [2] earl

A HEALTH TO KING CHARLES

The lark, his lay who thrill'd all day,
  Sits hush'd his partner nigh;
Breeze, bird, and flower, confess the hour,
  But where is County Guy?

The village maid steals through the shade,
  Her shepherd's suit to hear;
To beauty shy, by lattice high,
  Sings high-born Cavalier.
The star of Love, all stars above,
  Now reigns o'er earth and sky;
And high and low the influence know—
  But where is County Guy?

1823   1823

HERE'S A HEALTH TO KING CHARLES

From WOODSTOCK, CHAPTER XX

BRING the bowl which you boast,
  Fill it up to the brim;
'Tis to him we love most,
  And to all who love him.
Brave gallants, stand up,
  And avaunt, ye base carles!
Were there death in the cup,
  Here's a health to King Charles!

Though he wanders through dangers,
  Unaided, unknown,
Dependent on strangers,
  Estranged from his own;
Though 'tis under our breath,
  Amidst forfeits and perils,

Here's to honour and faith,
  And a health to King Charles!

Let such honours abound
  As the time can afford,
The knee on the ground,
  And the hand on the sword: 20
But the time shall come round,
  When, 'mid Lords, Dukes, and Earls,
The loud trumpets shall sound
  Here's a health to King Charles!

1826   1826

THOMAS CAMPBELL (1777-1844)

YE MARINERS OF ENGLAND

A NAVAL ODE

Ye mariners of England
That guard our native seas,
Whose flag has braved a thousand years
The battle and the breeze!
Your glorious standard launch again
To match another foe!
And sweep through the deep,
While the stormy winds do blow;
While the battle rages loud and long,
And the stormy winds do blow.   10

The spirits of your fathers
Shall start from every wave!—
For the deck it was their field of fame,
And Ocean was their grave:
Where Blake and mighty Nelson fell,

Your manly hearts shall glow,
As ye sweep through the deep,
While the stormy winds do blow;
While the battle rages loud and long,
And the stormy winds do blow.

Britannia needs no bulwarks,
No towers along the steep;
Her march is o'er the mountain waves,
Her home is on the deep.
With thunders from her native oak
She quells the floods below—
As they roar on the shore,
When the stormy winds do blow;
When the battle rages loud and long,
And the stormy winds do blow.

The meteor flag of England
Shall yet terrific burn,
Till danger's troubled night depart,
And the star of peace return.
Then, then, ye ocean-warriors!
Our song and feast shall flow
To the fame of your name,
When the storm has ceased to blow;
When the fiery fight is heard no more,
And the storm has ceased to blow.

1799-1800   1801

HOHENLINDEN

On Linden, when the sun was low,
All bloodless lay the untrodden snow,
And dark as winter was the flow
Of Iser, rolling rapidly.

But Linden saw another sight,
When the drum beat at dead of night,
Commanding fires of death to light
The darkness of her scenery.

By torch and trumpet fast arrayed,
Each horseman drew his battle-blade,
And furious every charger neighed,
To join the dreadful revelry.

Then shook the hills with thunder riven,
Then rushed the steed to battle driven,
And louder than the bolts of heaven,
Far flashed the red artillery.

But redder yet that light shall glow
On Linden's hills of stainèd snow,
And bloodier yet the torrent flow
Of Iser, rolling rapidly.

'T is morn, but scarce yon level sun
Can pierce the war-clouds, rolling dun,
Where furious Frank and fiery Hun
Shout in their sulphurous canopy.

The combat deepens. On, ye brave,
Who rush to glory, or the grave!
Wave, Munich! all thy banners wave,
And charge with all thy chivalry!

Few, few shall part where many meet!
The snow shall be their winding-sheet,
And every turf beneath their feet
Shall be a soldier's sepulchre.

1802   1802

LORD ULLIN'S DAUGHTER

A CHIEFTAIN to the Highlands bound
   Cries, "Boatman, do not tarry!
And I'll give thee a silver pound
   To row us o'er the ferry!"

"Now who be ye would cross Lochgyle,
   This dark and stormy water?"
"O, I'm the chief of Ulva's isle,
   And this Lord Ullin's daughter.

"And fast before her father's men
   Three days we've fled together,   10
For should he find us in the glen,
   My blood would stain the heather.

"His horsemen hard behind us ride;
   Should they our steps discover,
Then who will cheer my bonnie bride
   When they have slain her lover?"

Out spoke the hardy Highland wight,
   "I'll go, my chief—I'm ready;
It is not for your silver bright,
   But for your winsome lady: 20

"And by my word! the bonny bird
   In danger shall not tarry;
So though the waves are raging white,
   I'll row you o'er the ferry."

By this the storm grew loud apace,
   The water-wraith was shrieking;

And in the scowl of heaven each face
   Grew dark as they were speaking.

But still as wilder blew the wind,
   And as the night grew drearer,
Adown the glen rode armèd men,
   Their trampling sounded nearer.

"Oh, haste thee, haste!" the lady cries,
   "Though tempests round us gather;
I'll meet the raging of the skies,
   But not an angry father."

The boat has left a stormy land,
   A stormy sea before her—
When, oh! too strong for human hand,
   The tempest gathered o'er her.

And still they rowed amidst the roar
   Of waters fast prevailing:
Lord Ullin reached that fatal shore,
   His wrath was changed to wailing.

For sore dismayed, through storm and shade,
   His child he did discover:
One lovely hand she stretched for aid,
   And one was round her lover.

"Come back! come back!" he cried in grief,
   "Across this stormy water:
And I'll forgive your Highland chief,
   My daughter!—oh, my daughter!"

'T was vain: the loud waves lashed the shore,
   Return or aid preventing:

The waters wild went o'er his child—
   And he was left lamenting.

1805   1809

THOMAS MOORE (1779-1852)

THE HARP THAT ONCE THROUGH TARA'S HALLS

The harp that once through Tara's halls
   The soul of music shed,
Now hangs as mute on Tara's walls,
   As if that soul were fled.—
So sleeps the pride of former days,
   So glory's thrill is o'er,
And hearts that once beat high for praise
   Now feel that pulse no more!

No more to chiefs and ladies bright
   The harp of Tara swells;   10
The chord alone, that breaks at night,
   Its tale of ruin tells.
Thus Freedom now so seldom wakes,
   The only throb she gives
Is when some heart indignant breaks,
   To show that still she lives.

                                                                       1808

'T IS THE LAST ROSE OF SUMMER

   'T is the last rose of summer
      Left blooming alone;
   All her lovely companions
      Are faded and gone;
   No flower of her kindred,

No rose-bud is nigh,
   To reflect back her blushes,
      Or give sigh for sigh.

I'll not leave thee, thou lone one!
   To pine on the stem;   10
Since the lovely are sleeping,
   Go, sleep thou with them.
Thus kindly I scatter
   Thy leaves o'er the bed,
Where thy mates of the garden
   Lie scentless and dead.

So soon may *I* follow,
   When friendships decay,
And from Love's shining circle
   The gems drop away.   20
When true hearts lie withered,
   And fond ones are flown,
Oh! who would inhabit
   This bleak world alone?

                                                1808

OFT IN THE STILLY NIGHT

Oft in the stilly night,
   Ere Slumber's chain has bound me,
Fond Memory brings the light
   Of other days around me;
      The smiles, the tears,
      Of boyhood's years,
   The words of love then spoken;
      The eyes that shone,
      Now dimmed and gone,
   The cheerful hearts now broken!   10

Thus, in the stilly night,
   Ere Slumber's chain has bound me,
Sad Memory brings the light
   Of other days around me.

When I remember all
   The friends, so linked together,
I've seen around me fall,
   Like leaves in wintry weather;
      I feel like one
         Who treads alone
Some banquet-hall deserted,
   Whose lights are fled,
   Whose garland's dead,
And all but he departed!
Thus, in the stilly night,
   Ere Slumber's chain has bound me,
Sad Memory brings the light
   Of other days around me.

1816

GEORGE GORDON, LORD BYRON (1788-1824)

OH! SNATCH'D AWAY IN BEAUTY'S BLOOM

OH! SNATCH'D away in beauty's bloom,
On thee shall press no ponderous tomb;
   But on thy turf shall roses rear
   Their leaves, the earliest of the year;
And the wild cypress wave in tender gloom:

And oft by yon blue gushing stream
   Shall Sorrow lean her drooping head,
And feed deep thought with many a dream,

And lingering pause and lightly tread;
Fond wretch! as if her step disturb'd the dead!   10

Away! we know that tears are vain,
  That death nor heeds nor hears distress:
Will this unteach us to complain?
  Or make one mourner weep the less?
And thou—who tell'st me to forget,
Thy looks are wan, thine eyes are wet.
1814   1815

SHE WALKS IN BEAUTY

From HEBREW MELODIES

She walks in beauty, like the night
  Of cloudless climes and starry skies;
And all that's best of dark and bright
  Meet in her aspect and her eyes:
Thus mellowed to that tender light
  Which heaven to gaudy day denies.

One shade the more, one ray the less,
  Had half impaired the nameless grace
Which waves in every raven tress,
  Or softly lightens o'er her face;   10
Where thoughts serenely sweet express
  How pure, how dear their dwelling-place.

And on that cheek, and o'er that brow,
  So soft, so calm, yet eloquent,
The smiles that win, the tints that glow,
  But tell of days in goodness spent,

A mind at peace with all below,
    A heart whose love is innocent!

1814   1815

THE DESTRUCTION OF SENNACHERIB

From HEBREW MELODIES

THE Assyrian came down like the wolf on the fold,
And his cohorts were gleaming in purple and gold;
And the sheen of their spears was like stars on the sea,
When the blue wave rolls nightly on deep Galilee.

Like the leaves of the forest when Summer is green,
That host with their banners at sunset were seen:
Like the leaves of the forest when Autumn hath blown,
That host on the morrow lay withered and strown.

For the Angel of Death spread his wings on the blast,
And breathed in the face of the foe as he passed;   10
And the eyes of the sleepers waxed deadly and chill,
And their hearts but once heaved, and for ever grew still!

And there lay the steed with his nostril all wide,
But through it there rolled not the breath of his pride;
And the foam of his gasping lay white on the turf,
And cold as the spray of the rock-beating surf.

And there lay the rider distorted and pale,
With the dew on his brow, and the rust on his mail:
And the tents were all silent, the banners alone,
The lances unlifted, the trumpet unblown.   20

And the widows of Ashur are loud in their wail,
And the idols are broke in the temple of Baal;
And the might of the Gentile, unsmote by the sword,
Hath melted like snow in the glance of the Lord!
 1814   1815

STANZAS FOR MUSIC

I

There be none of Beauty's daughters
 With a magic like thee;
And like music on the waters
 Is thy sweet voice to me:
When, as if its sound were causing
The charmèd ocean's pausing,
The waves lie still and gleaming,
And the lull'd winds seem dreaming.

II

And the midnight moon is weaving
 Her bright chain o'er the deep;   10
Whose breast is gently heaving,
 As an infant's asleep:
So the spirit bows before thee,
To listen and adore thee;
With a full but soft emotion,
Like the swell of Summer's ocean.
 1815   1816

SONNET ON CHILLON

Eternal Spirit of the chainless Mind!
 Brightest in dungeons, Liberty! thou art,
 For there thy habitation is the heart—

The heart which love of thee alone can bind;
And when thy sons to fetters are consign'd—
　　To fetters, and the damp vault's dayless gloom,
　　Their country conquers with their martyrdom,
And Freedom's fame finds wings on every wind.
Chillon! thy prison is a holy place,
　　And thy sad floor an altar—for 'twas trod,　　10
Until his very steps have left a trace
　　Worn, as if thy cold pavement were a sod,
By Bonnivard! May none those marks efface!
　　For they appeal from tyranny to God.

THE PRISONER OF CHILLON

I

My hair is grey, but not with years,
　　Nor grew it white
　　In a single night,
As men's have grown from sudden fears:
My limbs are bowed, though not with toil,
　　But rusted with a vile repose,
For they have been a dungeon's spoil,
　　And mine has been the fate of those
To whom the goodly earth and air
Are banned, and barred—forbidden fare:　　10
But this was for my father's faith
I suffered chains and courted death;
That father perished at the stake
For tenets he would not forsake;
And for the same his lineal race
In darkness found a dwelling-place;
We were seven—who now are one,
　　Six in youth, and one in age,

Finished as they had begun,
  Proud of Persecution's rage;
One in fire, and two in field,
Their belief with blood have sealed,
Dying as their father died,
For the God their foes denied;
Three were in a dungeon cast,
Of whom this wreck is left the last.

II

There are seven pillars of Gothic mould,
In Chillon's dungeons deep and old,
There are seven columns, massy and grey,
Dim with a dull imprisoned ray,
A sunbeam which hath lost its way,
And through the crevice and the cleft
Of the thick wall is fallen and left;
Creeping o'er the floor so damp,
Like a marsh's meteor lamp:
And in each pillar there is a ring,
  And in each ring there is a chain;
That iron is a cankering thing,
  For in these limbs its teeth remain,
With marks that will not wear away,
Till I have done with this new day,
Which now is painful to these eyes,
Which have not seen the sun so rise
For years—I cannot count them o'er,
I lost their long and heavy score
When my last brother drooped and died,
And I lay living by his side.

III

They chained us each to a column stone,
And we were three—yet, each alone;
We could not move a single pace,
We could not see each other's face,
But with that pale and livid light
That made us strangers in our sight:
And thus together—yet apart,
Fettered in hand, but joined in heart,
'T was still some solace, in the dearth
Of the pure elements of earth,
To hearken to each other's speech,
And each turn comforter to each
With some new hope, or legend old,
Or song heroically bold;
But even these at length grew cold.
Our voices took a dreary tone,
An echo of the dungeon stone,
   A grating sound, not full and free,
   As they of yore were wont to be:
   It might be fancy, but to me
They never sounded like our own.

IV

I was the eldest of the three,
   And to uphold and cheer the rest
   I ought to do—and did my best—
And each did well in his degree.
   The youngest, whom my father loved,
Because our mother's brow was given
To him, with eyes as blue as heaven—
   For him my soul was sorely moved;

And truly might it be distressed
To see such bird in such a nest;
For he was beautiful as day—
   (When day was beautiful to me   80
   As to young eagles, being free)—
   A polar day, which will not see
A sunset till its summer's gone,
   Its sleepless summer of long light,
The snow-clad offspring of the sun:
   And thus he was as pure and bright,
And in his natural spirit gay,
With tears for nought but others' ills,
And then they flowed like mountain rills,
Unless he could assuage the woe   90
Which he abhorred to view below.

v

The other was as pure of mind,
But formed to combat with his kind;
Strong in his frame, and of a mood
Which 'gainst the world in war had stood,
And perished in the foremost rank
   With joy:—but not in chains to pine:
His spirit withered with their clank,
   I saw it silently decline—
   And so perchance in sooth did mine: 100
But yet I forced it on to cheer
Those relics of a home so dear.
He was a hunter of the hills,
   Had followed there the deer and wolf;
   To him this dungeon was a gulf,
And fettered feet the worst of ills.

VI

Lake Leman lies by Chillon's walls:
A thousand feet in depth below
Its massy waters meet and flow;
Thus much the fathom-line was sent   110
From Chillon's snow-white battlement,
  Which round about the wave enthrals:
A double dungeon wall and wave
Have made—and like a living grave
Below the surface of the lake
The dark vault lies wherein we lay:
We heard it ripple night and day;
  Sounding o'er our heads it knocked;
And I have felt the winter's spray
Wash through the bars when winds were high   120
And wanton in the happy sky;
  And then the very rock hath rocked,
  And I have felt it shake, unshocked,
Because I could have smiled to see
The death that would have set me free.

VII

I said my nearer brother pined,
I said his mighty heart declined,
He loathed and put away his food;
It was not that 't was coarse and rude,
For we were used to hunter's fare,   130
And for the like had little care:
The milk drawn from the mountain goat
Was changed for water from the moat,
Our bread was such as captives' tears
Have moistened many a thousand years.

Since man first pent his fellow men
Like brutes within an iron den;
But what were these to us or him?
These wasted not his heart or limb;
My brother's soul was of that mould 140
Which in a palace had grown cold,
Had his free breathing been denied
The range of the steep mountain's side;
But why delay the truth?—he died.
I saw, and could not hold his head,
Nor reach his dying hand—nor dead,—
Though hard I strove, but strove in vain,
To rend and gnash my bonds in twain.
He died—and they unlocked his chain,
And scooped for him a shallow grave 150
Even from the cold earth of our cave.
I begged them, as a boon, to lay
His corse in dust whereon the day
Might shine—it was a foolish thought,
But then within my brain it wrought,
That even in death his freeborn breast
In such a dungeon could not rest.
I might have spared my idle prayer—
They coldly laughed—and laid him there:
The flat and turfless earth above 160
The being we so much did love;
His empty chain above it leant,
Such Murder's fitting monument!

VIII

But he, the favourite and the flower,
Most cherished since his natal hour,
His mother's image in fair face,
The infant love of all his race,

THE PRISONER OF CHILLON

His martyred father's dearest thought,
My latest care, for whom I sought
To hoard my life, that his might be
Less wretched now, and one day free;
He, too, who yet had held untired
A spirit natural or inspired—
He, too, was struck, and day by day
Was withered on the stalk away.
Oh, God! it is a fearful thing
To see the human soul take wing
In any shape, in any mood:
I've seen it rushing forth in blood,
I've seen it on the breaking ocean
Strive with a swoln convulsive motion,
I've seen the sick and ghastly bed
Of Sin delirious with its dread;
But these were horrors—this was woe
Unmixed with such—but sure and slow:
He faded, and so calm and meek,
So softly worn, so sweetly weak,
So tearless, yet so tender, kind,
And grieved for those he left behind;
With all the while a cheek whose bloom
Was as a mockery of the tomb,
Whose tints as gently sunk away
As a departing rainbow's ray;
An eye of most transparent light,
That almost made the dungeon bright;
And not a word of murmur, not
A groan o'er his untimely lot,—
A little talk of better days,
A little hope my own to raise,
For I was sunk in silence—lost
In this last loss, of all the most;
And then the sighs he would suppress

Of fainting nature's feebleness,
More slowly drawn, grew less and less:
I listened, but I could not hear:
I called, for I was wild with fear;
I knew 't was hopeless, but my dread
Would not be thus admonishèd;
I called, and thought I heard a sound—
I burst my chain with one strong bound,   210
And rushed to him:—I found him not,
I only stirred in this black spot,
I only lived, *I* only drew
The accursèd breath of dungeon-dew;
The last, the sole, the dearest link
Between me and the eternal brink,
Which bound me to my failing race,
Was broken in this fatal place.
One on the earth, and one beneath—
My brothers—both had ceased to breathe: 220
I took that hand which lay so still,
Alas! my own was full as chill;
I had not strength to stir, or strive,
But felt that I was still alive—
A frantic feeling, when we know
That what we love shall ne'er be so.
    I know not why
    I could not die,
I had no early hope—but faith,
And that forbade a selfish death.   230

IX

What next befell me then and there
    I know not well—I never knew—
First came the loss of light, and air,
    And then of darkness too:

THE PRISONER OF CHILLON

I had no thought, no feeling—none—
Among the stones I stood a stone,
And was, scarce conscious what I wist,
As shrubless crags within the mist;
For all was blank, and bleak, and grey;
It was not night—it was not day;
It was not even the dungeon-light,
So hateful to my heavy sight,
But vacancy absorbing space,
And fixedness—without a place;
There were no stars—no earth—no time—
No check—no change—no good—no crime—
But silence, and a stirless breath
Which neither was of life nor death;
A sea of stagnant idleness,
Blind, boundless, mute, and motionless!

x

A light broke in upon my brain,—
   It was the carol of a bird;
It ceased, and then it came again,
   The sweetest song ear ever heard,
And mine was thankful till my eyes
Ran over with the glad surprise,
And they that moment could not see
I was the mate of misery;
But then by dull degrees came back
My senses to their wonted track;
I saw the dungeon walls and floor
Close slowly round me as before,
I saw the glimmer of the sun
Creeping as it before had done,

But through the crevice where it came
That bird was perched, as fond and tame,
   And tamer than upon the tree;
A lovely bird, with azure wings,
And song that said a thousand things,
   And seemed to say them all for me!   270
I never saw its like before,
I ne'er shall see its likeness more:
It seemed like me to want a mate,
But was not half so desolate,
And it was come to love me when
None lived to love me so again,
And cheering from my dungeon's brink,
Had brought me back to feel and think.
I know not if it late were free,
   Or broke its cage to perch on mine,   280
But knowing well captivity,
   Sweet bird! I could not wish for thine!
Or if it were, in wingèd guise,
A visitant from Paradise;
For—Heaven forgive that thought! the while
Which made me both to weep and smile—
I sometimes deemed that it might be
My brother's soul come down to me;
But then at last away it flew,
And then 't was mortal well I knew,   290
For he would never thus have flown,
And left me twice so doubly lone,
Lone—as the corse within its shroud,
Lone—as a solitary cloud,
   A single cloud on a sunny day,
While all the rest of heaven is clear,
A frown upon the atmosphere,
That hath no business to appear
   When skies are blue, and earth is gay.

XI

A kind of change came in my fate, 300
My keepers grew compassionate;
I know not what had made them so,
They were inured to sights of woe,
But so it was:—my broken chain
With links unfastened did remain,
And it was liberty to stride
Along my cell from side to side,
And up and down, and then athwart,
And tread it over every part;
And round the pillars one by one, 310
Returning where my walk begun,
Avoiding only, as I trod,
My brothers' graves without a sod;
For if I thought with heedless tread
My step profaned their lowly bed,
My breath came gaspingly and thick,
And my crushed heart fell blind and sick.

XII

I made a footing in the wall,
   It was not therefrom to escape,
For I had buried one and all 320
   Who loved me in a human shape;
And the whole earth would henceforth be
A wider prison unto me:
No child—no sire—no kin had I,
No partner in my misery;
I thought of this, and I was glad,
For thought of them had made me mad;
But I was curious to ascend

To my barred windows, and to bend
Once more, upon the mountains high,   330
The quiet of a loving eye.

XIII

I saw them, and they were the same,
They were not changed like me in frame;
I saw their thousand years of snow
On high—their wide long lake below,
And the blue Rhone in fullest flow;
I heard the torrents leap and gush
O'er channelled rock and broken bush;
I saw the white-walled distant town,
And whiter sails go skimming down;   340
And then there was a little isle,
Which in my very face did smile,
    The only one in view;
A small green isle, it seemed no more,
Scarce broader than my dungeon floor,
But in it there were three tall trees,
And o'er it blew the mountain breeze,
And by it there were waters flowing,
And on it there were young flowers growing,
    Of gentle breath and hue.   350
The fish swam by the castle wall,
And they seemed joyous each and all;
The eagle rode the rising blast,
Methought he never flew so fast
As then to me he seemed to fly;
And then new tears came in my eye,
And I felt troubled—and would fain
I had not left my recent chain;
And when I did descend again,
The darkness of my dim abode   360

Fell on me as a heavy load;
It was as is a new-dug grave,
Closing o'er one we sought to save,—
And yet my glance, too much opprest,
Had almost need of such a rest.

XIV

It might be months, or years, or days,
   I kept no count, I took no note—
I had no hope my eyes to raise,
   And clear them of their dreary mote;
At last men came to set me free;   370
   I asked not why, and recked not where;
It was at length the same to me,
Fettered or fetterless to be,
   I learned to love despair.
And thus when they appeared at last,
And all my bonds aside were cast,
These heavy walls to me had grown
A hermitage—and all my own!
And half I felt as they were come
To tear me from a second home: 380
With spiders I had friendship made,
And watched them in their sullen trade,
Had seen the mice by moonlight play,
And why should I feel less than they?
We were all inmates of one place,
And I, the monarch of each race,
Had power to kill—yet, strange to tell!
In quiet we had learned to dwell;
My very chains and I grew friends,
So much a long communion tends   390

To make us what we are:—even I
Regained my freedom with a sigh.

1816   1816

CHILDE HAROLD'S PILGRIMAGE

CANTO III

I

Is thy face like thy mother's, my fair child!
Ada! sole daughter of my house and heart?
When last I saw thy young blue eyes they smiled,
And then we parted,—not as now we part,
But with a hope.—
                 Awaking with a start,
The waters heave around me; and on high
The winds lift up their voices: I depart,
Whither I know not; but the hour's gone by,
When Albion's lessening shores could grieve or glad mine
    eye.

II

Once more upon the waters! yet once more!   10
And the waves bound beneath me as a steed
That knows his rider. Welcome to their roar!
Swift be their guidance, whereso'er it lead!
Though the strained mast should quiver as a reed,
And the rent canvas fluttering strew the gale,
Still must I on; for I am as a weed,
Flung from the rock, on Ocean's foam to sail
Where'er the surge may sweep, the tempest's breath pre-
    vail.

III

In my youth's summer I did sing of One,
The wandering outlaw of his own dark mind;   20
Again I seize the theme, then but begun,
And bear it with me, as the rushing wind
Bears the cloud onwards: in that Tale I find
The furrows of long thought, and dried-up tears,
Which, ebbing, leave a sterile track behind,
O'er which all heavily the journeying years
Plod the last sands of life,—where not a flower appears.

IV

Since my young days of passion—joy or pain—
Perchance my heart and harp have lost a string
And both may jar: it may be that in vain   30
I would essay, as I have sung, to sing.
Yet, though a dreary strain, to this I cling;
So that it wean me from the weary dream
Of selfish grief or gladness—so it fling
Forgetfulness around me—it shall seem
To me, though to none else, a not ungrateful theme.

V

He, who grown agèd in this world of woe,
In deeds, not years, piercing the depths of life,
So that no wonder waits him; nor below
Can love or sorrow, fame, ambition, strife,   40
Cut to his heart again with the keen knife
Of silent, sharp endurance: he can tell
Why thought seeks refuge in lone caves, yet rife

With airy images, and shapes which dwell
Still unimpaired, though old, in the soul's haunted cell.

VI

'T is to create, and in creating live
A being more intense that we endow
With form our fancy, gaining as we give
The life we image, even as I do now.
What am I? Nothing: but not so art thou,
Soul of my thought! with whom I traverse earth,
Invisible but gazing, as I glow
Mixed with thy spirit, blended with thy birth,
And feeling still with thee in my crushed feelings' dearth.

VII

Yet must I think less wildly:—I *have* thought
Too long and darkly, till my brain became,
In its own eddy boiling and o'erwrought,
A whirling gulf of phantasy and flame:
And thus, untaught in youth my heart to tame,
My springs of life were poisoned. 'T is too late!
Yet am I changed; though still enough the same
In strength to bear what time cannot abate,
And feed on bitter fruits without accusing Fate.

VIII

Something too much of this:—but now 't is past,
And the spell closes with its silent seal.
Long absent Harold re-appears at last;
He of the breast which fain no more would feel,
Wrung with the wounds which kill not, but ne'er heal;

CHILDE HAROLD'S PILGRIMAGE

Yet Time, who changes all, had altered him
In soul and aspect as in age: years steal
Fire from the mind as vigour from the limb;
And life's enchanted cup but sparkles near the brim.

IX

His had been quaffed too quickly, and he found
The dregs were wormwood; but he filled again,
And from a purer fount, on holier ground,
And deemed its spring perpetual; but in vain!
Still round him clung invisibly a chain
Which galled for ever, fettering though unseen,
And heavy though it clanked not; worn with pain,
Which pined although it spoke not, and grew keen,
Entering with every step he took through many a scene.

X

Secure in guarded coldness, he had mixed
Again in fancied safety with his kind,
And deemed his spirit now so firmly fixed
And sheathed with an invulnerable mind,
That, if no joy, no sorrow lurked behind;
And he, as one, might 'midst the many stand
Unheeded, searching through the crowd to find
Fit speculation; such as in strange land
He found in wonder-works of God and Nature's hand.

XI

But who can view the ripened rose, nor seek
To wear it? who can curiously behold
The smoothness and the sheen of beauty's cheek,
Nor feel the heart can never all grow old?

Who can contemplate Fame through clouds unfold
The star which rises o'er her steep, nor climb?
Harold, once more within the vortex, rolled
On with the giddy circle, chasing Time,
Yet with a nobler aim than in his youth's fond prime.

XII

But soon he knew himself the most unfit 100
Of men to herd with Man; with whom he held
Little in common; untaught to submit
His thoughts to others, though his soul was quelled
In youth by his own thoughts; still uncompelled,
He would not yield dominion of his mind
To spirits against whom his own rebelled;
Proud though in desolation; which could find
A life within itself, to breathe without mankind.

XIII

Where rose the mountains, there to him were friends;
Where rolled the ocean, thereon was his home; 110
Where a blue sky, and glowing clime, extends,
He had the passion and the power to roam;
The desert, forest, cavern, breaker's foam,
Were unto him companionship; they spake
A mutual language, clearer than the tome
Of his land's tongue, which he would oft forsake
For Nature's pages glassed by sunbeams on the lake.

XIV

Like the Chaldean, he could watch the stars,
Till he had peopled them with beings bright
As their own beams; and earth, and earth-born jars. 120

And human frailties, were forgotten quite:
Could he have kept his spirit to that flight
He had been happy; but this clay will sink
Its spark immortal, envying it the light
To which it mounts, as if to break the link
That keeps us from yon heaven which woos us to its brink.

XV

But in Man's dwellings he became a thing
Restless and worn, and stern and wearisome,
Drooped as a wild-born falcon with clipt wing,
To whom the boundless air alone were home: 130
Then came his fit again, which to o'ercome,
As eagerly the barred-up bird will beat
His breast and beak against his wiry dome
Till the blood tinge his plumage, so the heat
Of his impeded soul would through his bosom eat.

XVI

Self-exiled Harold wanders forth again,
With nought of hope left, but with less of gloom;
The very knowledge that he lived in vain,
That all was over on this side the tomb,
Had made Despair a smilingness assume, 140
Which, though 't were wild,—as on the plundered wreck
When mariners would madly meet their doom
With draughts intemperate on the sinking deck,—
Did yet inspire a cheer, which he forbore to check.

XVII

Stop!—for thy tread is on an Empire's dust!
An Earthquake's spoil is sepulchred below!

Is the spot marked with no colossal bust?
Nor column trophied for triumphal show?
None; but the moral's truth tells simpler so,
As the ground was before, thus let it be;— 150
How that red rain hath made the harvest grow!
And is this all the world has gained by thee,
Thou first and last of fields! king-making Victory?

XVIII

And Harold stands upon this place of skulls,
The grave of France, the deadly Waterloo!
How in an hour the power which gave annuls
Its gifts, transferring fame as fleeting too!
In "pride of place" here last the eagle flew,
Then tore with bloody talon the rent plain,
Pierced by the shaft of banded nations through; 160
Ambition's life and labours all were vain;
He wears the shattered links of the world's broken chain.

XIX

Fit retribution! Gaul may champ the bit
And foam in fetters;—but is Earth more free?
Did nations combat to make *One* submit;
Or league to teach all kings true sovereignty?
What! shall reviving Thraldom again be
The patched-up idol of enlightened days?
Shall we, who struck the Lion down, shall we
Pay the Wolf homage? proffering lowly gaze 170
And servile knees to thrones? No; *prove* before ye praise!

XX

If not, o'er one fallen despot boast no more!
In vain fair cheeks were furrowed with hot tears
For Europe's flowers long rooted up before
The trampler of her vineyards; in vain years
Of death, depopulation, bondage, fears,
Have all been borne, and broken by the accord
Of roused-up millions; all that most endears
Glory, is when the myrtle wreathes a sword
Such as Harmodius drew on Athens' tyrant lord.   180

XXI

There was a sound of revelry by night,
And Belgium's capital had gathered then
Her Beauty and her Chivalry, and bright
The lamps shone o'er fair women and brave men;
A thousand hearts beat happily; and when
Music arose with its voluptuous swell,
Soft eyes looked love to eyes which spake again,
And all went merry as a marriage bell;
But hush! hark! a deep sound strikes like a rising knell!

XXII

Did ye not hear it?—No; 't was but the wind,   190
Or the car rattling o'er the stony street;
On with the dance! let joy be unconfined;
No sleep till morn, when Youth and Pleasure meet
To chase the glowing Hours with flying feet—
But hark!—that heavy sound breaks in once more,
As if the clouds its echo would repeat;

And nearer, clearer, deadlier than before!
Arm! Arm! it is—it is—the cannon's opening roar

XXIII

Within a windowed niche of that high hall
Sate Brunswick's fated chieftain; he did hear
That sound the first amidst the festival,
And caught its tone with Death's prophetic ear;
And when they smiled because he deemed it near,
His heart more truly knew that peal too well
Which stretched his father on a bloody bier,
And roused the vengeance blood alone could quell;
He rushed into the field, and, foremost fighting, fell.

XXIV

Ah! then and there was hurrying to and fro,
And gathering tears, and tremblings of distress,
And cheeks all pale, which but an hour ago
Blushed at the praise of their own loveliness;
And there were sudden partings, such as press
The life from out young hearts, and choking sighs
Which ne'er might be repeated; who could guess
If ever more should meet those mutual eyes,
Since upon night so sweet such awful morn could rise!

XXV

And there was mounting in hot haste: the steed,
The mustering squadron, and the clattering car,
Went pouring forward with impetuous speed,
And swiftly forming in the ranks of war;
And the deep thunder peal on peal afar;
And near, the beat of the alarming drum

Roused up the soldier ere the morning star;
While thronged the citizens with terror dumb,
Or whispering, with white lips—"The foe! they come! they come!"

XXVI

And wild and high the "Cameron's gathering" rose!
The war-note of Lochiel, which Albyn's hills
Have heard, and heard, too, have her Saxon foes:—
How in the noon of night that pibroch thrills,
Savage and shrill! But with the breath which fills　230
Their mountain-pipe, so fill the mountaineers
With the fierce native daring which instils
The stirring memory of a thousand years,
And Evan's, Donald's fame rings in each clansman's ears!

XXVII

And Ardennes waves above them her green leaves,
Dewy with nature's tear-drops as they pass,
Grieving, if aught inanimate e'er grieves,
Over the unreturning brave,—alas!
Ere evening to be trodden like the grass
Which now beneath them, but above shall grow　240
In its next verdure, when this fiery mass
Of living valour, rolling on the foe
And burning with high hope shall moulder cold and low.

XXVIII

Last noon beheld them full of lusty life,
Last eve in Beauty's circle proudly gay,

Yet withers on till all without is old,
Showing no visible sign, for such things are untold.

XXXIV

There is a very life in our despair,
Vitality of poison,—a quick root
Which feeds these deadly branches; for it were   300
As nothing did we die; but Life will suit
Itself to Sorrow's most detested fruit,
Like to the apples on the Dead Sea's shore,
All ashes to the taste: Did man compute
Existence by enjoyment, and count o'er
Such hours 'gainst years of life,—say, would he name threescore?

XXXV

The Psalmist numbered out the years of man:
They are enough; and if thy tale be *true*,
Thou, who didst grudge him even that fleeting span,
More than enough, thou fatal Waterloo!   310
Millions of tongues record thee, and anew
Their children's lips shall echo them, and say—
"Here, where the sword united nations drew,
Our countrymen were warring on that day!"
And this is much, and all which will not pass away.

XXXVI

There sunk the greatest, nor the worst of men,
Whose spirit, antithetically mixt,
One moment of the mightiest, and again
On little objects with like firmness fixt;
Extreme in all things! hadst thou been betwixt,   320
Thy throne had still been thine, or never been;

For daring made thy rise as fall: thou seek'st
Even now to re-assume the imperial mien,
And shake again the world, the Thunderer of the scene!

XXXVII

Conqueror and captive of the earth art thou!
She trembles at thee still, and thy wild name
Was ne'er more bruited in men's minds than now
That thou art nothing, save the jest of Fame,
Who wooed thee once, thy vassal, and became
The flatterer of thy fierceness, till thou wert   330
A god unto thyself; nor less the same
To the astounded kingdoms all inert,
Who deemed thee for a time whate'er thou didst assert.

XXXVIII

Oh, more or less than man—in high or low,
Battling with nations, flying from the field;
Now making monarchs' necks thy footstool, now
More than thy meanest soldier taught to yield;
An empire thou couldst crush, command, rebuild,
But govern not thy pettiest passion, nor,
However deeply in men's spirits skilled,   340
Look through thine own, nor curb the lust of war,
Nor learn that tempted Fate will leave the loftiest star.

XXXIX

Yet well thy soul hath brooked the turning tide
With that untaught innate philosophy,
Which, be it wisdom, coldness, or deep pride,
Is gall and wormwood to an enemy.
When the whole host of hatred stood hard by,

To watch and mock thee shrinking, thou hast smiled
With a sedate and all-enduring eye;—
When Fortune fled her spoiled and favourite child,   350
He stood unbowed beneath the ills upon him piled.

XL

Sager than in thy fortunes; for in them
Ambition steeled thee on too far to show
That just habitual scorn, which could contemn
Men and their thoughts; 't was wise to feel, not so
To wear it ever on thy lip and brow,
And spurn the instruments thou wert to use
Till they were turned unto thine overthrow:
'T is but a worthless world to win or lose;
So hath it proved to thee, and all such lot who choose.   360

XLI

If, like a tower upon a headland rock,
Thou hast been made to stand or fall alone,
Such scorn of man had helped to brave the shock;
But men's thoughts were the steps which paved thy throne,
Their admiration thy best weapon shone;
The part of Philip's son was thine, not then
(Unless aside thy purple had been thrown)
Like stern Diogenes to mock at men;
For sceptred cynics earth were far too wide a den.

XLII

But quiet to quick bosoms is a hell,   370
And *there* hath been thy bane; there is a fire
And motion of the soul which will not dwell

In its own narrow being, but aspire
Beyond the fitting medium of desire;
And, but once kindled, quenchless evermore,
Preys upon high adventure, nor can tire
Of aught but rest; a fever at the core,
Fatal to him who bears, to all who ever bore.

XLIII

This makes the madmen who have made men mad
By their contagion; Conquerors and Kings,
Founders of sects and systems, to whom add
Sophists, Bards, Statesmen, all unquiet things
Which stir too strongly the soul's secret springs,
And are themselves the fools to those they fool;
Envied, yet how unenviable! what stings
Are theirs! One breast laid open were a school
Which would unteach mankind the lust to shine or rule:

XLIV

Their breath is agitation, and their life
A storm whereon they ride, to sink at last,
And yet so nursed and bigoted to strife,
That should their days, surviving perils past,
Melt to calm twilight, they feel overcast
With sorrow and supineness, and so die;
Even as a flame unfed, which runs to waste
With its own flickering, or a sword laid by,
Which eats into itself, and rusts ingloriously.

XLV

He who ascends to mountain-tops, shall find
The loftiest peaks most wrapt in clouds and snow;

He who surpasses or subdues mankind,
Must look down on the hate of those below.   400
Though high *above* the sun of glory glow,
And far *beneath* the earth and ocean spread,
Round him are icy rocks, and loudly blow
Contending tempest on his naked head,
And thus reward the toils which to those summits led.

XLVI

Away with these! true Wisdom's world will be
Within its own creation, or in thine,
Maternal Nature! for who teems like thee,
Thus on the banks of thy majestic Rhine?
There Harold gazes on a work divine,   410
A blending of all beauties; streams and dells,
Fruit, foliage, crag, wood, cornfield, mountain, vine,
And chiefless castles breathing stern farewells
From gray but leafy walls, where Ruin greenly dwells.

XLVII

And there they stand, as stands a lofty mind,
Worn, but unstooping to the baser crowd,
All tenantless, save to the crannying wind,
Or holding dark communion with the crowd.
There was a day when they were young and proud;
Banners on high, and battles passed below;   420
But they who fought are in a bloody shroud,
And those which waved are shredless dust ere now,
And the bleak battlements shall bear no future blow

XLVIII

Beneath those battlements, within those walls,
Power dwelt amidst her passions; in proud state

Each robber chief upheld his armèd halls,
Doing his evil will, nor less elate
Than mightier heroes of a longer date.
What want these outlaws conquerors should have
But history's purchased page to call them great?   430
A wider space, an ornamented grave?
Their hopes were not less warm, their souls were full
   as brave.

XLIX

In their baronial feuds and single fields,
What deeds of prowess unrecorded died!
And Love, which lent a blazon to their shields,
With emblems well devised by amorous pride,
Through all the mail of iron hearts would glide;
But still their flame was fierceness, and drew on
Keen contest and destruction near allied,
And many a tower for some fair mischief won,   440
Saw the discoloured Rhine beneath its ruin run.

L

But Thou, exulting and abounding river!
Making thy waves a blessing as they flow
Through banks whose beauty would endure for ever
Could man but leave thy bright creation so,
Nor its fair promise from the surface mow
With the sharp scythe of conflict,—then to see
Thy valley of sweet waters, were to know
Earth paved like Heaven; and to seem such to me,
Even now what wants thy stream?—that it should Lethe
   be.   450

LI

A thousand battles have assailed thy banks,
But these and half their fame have passed away,
And Slaughter heaped on high his weltering ranks;
Their very graves are gone, and what are they?
Thy tide washed down the blood of yesterday,
And all was stainless, and on thy clear stream
Glassed, with its dancing light, the sunny ray;
But o'er the blackened memory's blighting dream
Thy waves would vainly roll, all sweeping as they seem.

LII

Thus Harold inly said, and passed along,   460
Yet not insensible to all which here
Awoke the jocund birds to early song
In glens which might have made even exile dear:
Though on his brow were graven lines austere,
And tranquil sternness, which had ta'en the place
Of feelings fierier far but less severe,
Joy was not always absent from his face,
But o'er it in such scenes would steal with transient trace.

LIII

Nor was all love shut from him, though his days
Of passion had consumed themselves to dust.   470
It is in vain that we would coldly gaze
On such as smile upon us; the heart must
Leap kindly back to kindness, though disgust
Hath weaned it from all worldlings: thus he felt,
For there was soft remembrance, and sweet trust

In one fond breast, to which his own would melt,
And in its tenderer hour on that his bosom dwelt.

LIV

And he had learned to love,—I know not why,
For this in such as him seems strange of mood,—
The helpless looks of blooming infancy, 480
Even in its earliest nurture; what subdued,
To change like this, a mind so far imbued
With scorn of man, it little boots to know;
But thus it was; and though in solitude
Small power the nipped affections have to grow,
In him this glowed when all beside had ceased to glow.

LV

And there was one soft breast, as hath been said,
Which unto his was bound by stronger ties
Than the church links withal; and, though unwed,
That love was pure, and, far above disguise, 490
Had stood the test of mortal enmities
Still undivided, and cemented more
By peril, dreaded most in female eyes;
But this was firm, and from a foreign shore
Well to that heart might his these absent greetings pour!

1

The castled crag of Drachenfels
Frowns o'er the wide and winding Rhine,
Whose breast of waters broadly swells
Between the banks which bear the vine,
And hills all rich with blossomed trees, 500
And fields which promise corn and wine,

And scattered cities crowning these,
Whose far white walls along them shine,
Have strewed a scene, which I should see
With double joy wert *thou* with me.

2

And peasant girls, with deep blue eyes,
And hands which offer early flowers,
Walk smiling o'er this paradise;
Above, the frequent feudal towers
Through green leaves lift their walls of gray; 510
And many a rock which steeply lowers,
And noble arch in proud decay,
Look o'er this vale of vintage-bowers;
But one thing want these banks of Rhine,—
Thy gentle hand to clasp in mine!

3

I send the lilies given to me;
Though long before thy hand they touch,
I know that they must withered be,
But yet reject them not as such;
For I have cherished them as dear, 520
Because they yet may meet thine eye,
And guide thy soul to mine even here,
When thou behold'st them drooping nigh,
And know'st them gathered by the Rhine,
And offered from my heart to thine!

4

The river nobly foams and flows,
The charm of this enchanted ground,
And all its thousand turns disclose

Some fresher beauty varying round:
The haughtiest breast its wish might bound 530
Through life to dwell delighted here;
Nor could on earth a spot be found
To nature and to me so dear,
Could thy dear eyes in following mine
Still sweeten more these banks of Rhine!

LVI

By Coblentz, on a rise of gentle ground,
There is a small and simple pyramid,
Crowning the summit of the verdant mound;
Beneath its base are heroes' ashes hid,
Our enemy's—but let not that forbid 540
Honour to Marceau! o'er whose early tomb
Tears, big tears, gushed from the rough soldier's lid,
Lamenting and yet envying such a doom,
Falling for France, whose rights he battled to resume.

LVII

Brief, brave, and glorious was his young career,—
His mourners were two hosts, his friends and foes;
And fitly may the stranger lingering here
Pray for his gallant spirit's bright repose;
For he was Freedom's champion, one of those,
The few in number, who had not o'er-stept 550
The charter to chastise which she bestows
On such as wield her weapons; he had kept
The whiteness of his soul, and thus men o'er him wept

LVIII

Here Ehrenbreitstein, with her shattered wall
Black with the miner's blast, upon her height

Yet shows of what she was, when shell and ball
Rebounding idly on her strength did light:
A tower of victory! from whence the flight
Of baffled foes was watched along the plain:
But Peace destroyed what War could never blight, 560
And laid those proud roofs bare to Summer's rain—
On which the iron shower for years had poured in vain.

LIX

Adieu to thee, fair Rhine! How long delighted
The stranger fain would linger on his way!
Thine is a scene alike where souls united
Or lonely Contemplation thus might stray;
And could the ceaseless vultures cease to prey
On self-condemning bosoms, it were here,
Where Nature, nor too sombre nor too gay,
Wild but not rude, awful yet not austere,   570
Is to the mellow Earth as Autumn to the year.

LX

Adieu to thee again! a vain adieu!
There can be no farewell to scene like thine;
The mind is coloured by thy every hue;
And if reluctantly the eyes resign
Their cherished gaze upon thee, lovely Rhine!
'Tis with the thankful heart of parting praise;
More mighty spots may rise, more glaring shine,
But none unite in one attaching maze
The brilliant, fair, and soft,—the glories of old days. 580

LXI

The negligently grand, the fruitful bloom
Of coming ripeness, the white city's sheen,

CHILDE HAROLD'S PILGRIMAGE

The rolling stream, the precipice's gloom,
The forest's growth, and Gothic walls between,
The wild rocks shaped as they had turrets been,
In mockery of man's art; and these withal
A race of faces happy as the scene,
Whose fertile bounties here extend to all,
Still springing o'er thy banks, though Empires near them fall.

LXII

But these recede. Above me are the Alps,   590
The palaces of Nature, whose vast walls
Have pinnacled in clouds their snowy scalps,
And throned Eternity in icy halls
Of cold sublimity, where forms and falls
The avalanche—the thunderbolt of snow!
All that expands the spirit, yet appals,
Gather around these summits, as to show
How Earth may pierce to Heaven, yet leave vain man below.

LXIII

But ere these matchless heights I dare to scan,
There is a spot should not be passed in vain,—   600
Morat! the proud, the patriot field! where man
May gaze on ghastly trophies of the slain,
Nor blush for those who conquered on that plain;
Here Burgundy bequeathed his tombless host,
A bony heap, through ages to remain,
Themselves their monument;—the Stygian coast
Unsepulchred they roamed, and shrieked each wandering ghost.

LXIV

While Waterloo with Cannæ's carnage vies,
Morat and Marathon twin names shall stand;
They were true Glory's stainless victories,   610
Won by the unambitious heart and hand
Of a proud, brotherly, and civic band,
All unbought champions in no princely cause
Of vice-entailed Corruption; they no land
Doomed to bewail the blasphemy of laws
Making kings' rights divine, by some Draconic clause.

LXV

By a lone wall a lonelier column rears
A gray and grief-worn aspect of old days;
'T is the last remnant of the wreck of years,
And looks as with the wild-bewildered gaze   620
Of one to stone converted by amaze,
Yet still with consciousness; and there it stands
Making a marvel that it not decays,
When the coeval pride of human hands,
Levelled Adventicum, hath strewed her subject lands.

LXVI

And there—oh! sweet and sacred be the name!—
Julia—the daughter, the devoted—gave
Her youth to Heaven; her heart, beneath a claim
Nearest to Heaven's, broke o'er a father's grave.
Justice is sworn 'gainst tears, and hers would crave 630
The life she lived in; but the judge was just,
And then she died on him she could not save.

CHILDE HAROLD'S PILGRIMAGE

Their tomb was simple, and without a bust,
And held within their urn one mind, one heart, one dust.

LXVII

But these are deeds which should not pass away,
And names that must not wither, though the earth
Forgets her empires with a just decay,
The enslavers and the enslaved, their death and birth;
The high, the mountain-majesty of worth
Should be, and shall, survivor of its woe,   640
And from its immortality look forth
In the sun's face, like yonder Alpine snow,
Imperishably pure beyond all things below.

LXVIII

Lake Leman woos me with its crystal face,
The mirror where the stars and mountains view
The stillness of their aspect in each trace
Its clear depth yields of their far height and hue:
There is too much of man here, to look through
With a fit mind the might which I behold;
But soon in me shall Loneliness renew   650
Thoughts hid, but not less cherished than of old,
Ere mingling with the herd had penned me in their fold.

LXIX

To fly from, need not be to hate, mankind:
All are not fit with them to stir and toil,
Nor is it discontent to keep the mind
Deep in its fountain, lest it overboil
In the hot throng, where we become the spoil
Of our infection, till too late and long

We may deplore and struggle with the coil,
In wretched interchange of wrong for wrong   660
Midst a contentious world, striving where none are strong.

LXX

There, in a moment we may plunge our years
In fatal penitence, and in the blight
Of our own soul turn all our blood to tears,
And colour things to come with hues of Night;
The race of life becomes a hopeless flight
To those that walk in darkness: on the sea
The boldest steer but where their ports invite;
But there are wanderers o'er Eternity
Whose bark drives on and on, and anchored ne'er shall be.   670

LXXI

Is it not better, then, to be alone,
And love Earth only for its earthly sake?
By the blue rushing of the arrowy Rhone,
Or the pure bosom of its nursing lake,
Which feeds it as a mother who doth make
A fair but froward infant her own care,
Kissing its cries away as these awake;—
Is it not better thus our lives to wear,
Than join the crushing crowd, doomed to inflict or bear?

LXXII

I live not in myself, but I become   680
Portion of that around me; and to me
High mountains are a feeling, but the hum
Of human cities torture: I can see
Nothing to loathe in nature, save to be

A link reluctant in a fleshly chain,
Classed among creatures, when the soul can flee,
And with the sky, the peak, the heaving plain
Of ocean, or the stars, mingle, and not in vain.

LXXIII

And thus I am absorbed, and this is life:
I look upon the peopled desert past, 690
As on a place of agony and strife,
Where, for some sin, to sorrow I was cast,
To act and suffer, but remount at last
With a fresh pinion; which I feel to spring,
Though young, yet waxing vigorous as the blast
Which it would cope with, on delighted wing,
Spurning the clay-cold bonds which round our being cling.

LXXIV

And when, at length, the mind shall be all free
From what it hates in this degraded form,
Reft of its carnal life, save what shall be 700
Existent happier in the fly and worm,—
When elements to elements conform,
And dust is as it should be, shall I not
Feel all I see, less dazzling, but more warm?
The bodiless thought? the Spirit of each spot?
Of which, even now, I share at times the immortal lot?

LXXV

Are not the mountains, waves, and skies, a part
Of me and of my soul, as I of them?
Is not the love of these deep in my heart
With a pure passion? should I not contemn 710

All objects, if compared with these? and stem
A tide of suffering, rather than forego
Such feelings for the hard and worldly phlegm
Of those whose eyes are only turned below,
Gazing upon the ground, with thoughts which dare not glow?

LXXVI

But this is not my theme; and I return
To that which is immediate, and require
Those who find contemplation in the urn,
To look on One, whose dust was once all fire,
A native of the land where I respire 720
The clear air for a while—a passing guest,
Where he became a being,—whose desire
Was to be glorious; 't was a foolish quest,
The which to gain and keep, he sacrificed all rest.

LXXVII

Here the self-torturing sophist, wild Rousseau,
The apostle of affliction, he who threw
Enchantment over passion, and from woe
Wrung overwhelming eloquence, first drew
The breath which made him wretched; yet he knew
How to make madness beautiful, and cast 730
O'er erring deeds and thoughts a heavenly hue
Of words, like sunbeams, dazzling as they past
The eyes, which o'er them shed tears feelingly and fast.

LXXVIII

His love was passion's essence:—as a tree
On fire by lightning, with ethereal flame
Kindled he was, and blasted; for to be

Thus, and enamoured, were in him the same.
But his was not the love of living dame,
Nor of the dead who rise upon our dreams,
But of ideal beauty, which became 740
In him existence, and o'erflowing teems
Along his burning page, distempered though it seems.

LXXIX

This breathed itself to life in Julie, *this*
Invested her with all that's wild and sweet;
This hallowed, too, the memorable kiss
Which every morn his fevered lip would greet,
From hers, who but with friendship his would meet;
But to that gentle touch through brain and breast
Flashed the thrilled spirit's love-devouring heat;
In that absorbing sigh perchance more blest 750
Than vulgar minds may be with all they seek possest.

LXXX

His life was one long war with self-sought foes,
Or friends by him self-banished; for his mind
Had grown Suspicion's sanctuary, and chose,
For its own cruel sacrifice, the kind,
'Gainst whom he raged with fury strange and blind.
But he was phrensied,—wherefore, who may know?
Since cause might be which skill could never find;
But he was phrensied by disease or woe,
To that worst pitch of all, which wears a reasoning show. 760

LXXXI

For then he was inspired, and from him came,
As from the Pythian's mystic cave of yore,

Those oracles which set the world in flame,
Nor ceased to burn till kingdoms were no more:
Did he not this for France? which lay before
Bowed to the inborn tyranny of years?
Broken and trembling to the yoke she bore,
Till by the voice of him and his compeers
Roused up to too much wrath, which follows o'ergrown fears?

LXXXII

They made themselves a fearful monument! 770
The wreck of old opinions—things which grew,
Breathed from the birth of time: the veil they rent,
And what behind it lay, all earth shall view.
But good with ill they also overthrew,
Leaving but ruins, wherewith to rebuild
Upon the same foundation, and renew
Dungeons and thrones, which the same hour refilled,
As heretofore, because ambition was self-willed.

LXXXIII

But this will not endure, nor be endured!
Mankind have felt their strength, and made it felt. 780
They might have used it better, but allured
By their new vigor, sternly have they dealt
On one another; pity ceased to melt
With her once natural charities. But they
Who in oppression's darkness caved had dwelt,
They were not eagles, nourished with the day;
What marvel then, at times, if they mistook their prey?

LXXXIV

What deep wounds ever closed without a scar?
The heart's bleed longest, and but heal to wear

That which disfigures it; and they who war   790
With their own hopes, and have been vanquished, bear
Silence, but not submission: in his lair
Fixed Passion holds his breath, until the hour
Which shall atone for years; none need despair:
It came, it cometh, and will come,—the power
To punish or forgive—in *one* we shall be slower.

LXXXV

Clear, placid Leman! thy contrasted lake,
With the wild world I dwelt in, is a thing
Which warns me, with its stillness, to forsake
Earth's troubled waters for a purer spring.   800
This quiet sail is as a noiseless wing
To waft me from distraction; once I loved
Torn ocean's roar, but thy soft murmuring
Sounds sweet as if a Sister's voice reproved,
That I with stern delights should e'er have been so moved.

LXXXVI

It is the hush of night, and all between
Thy margin and the mountains, dusk, yet clear,
Mellowed and mingling, yet distinctly seen,
Save darkened Jura, whose capt heights appear
Precipitously steep; and drawing near,   810
There breathes a living fragrance from the shore,
Of flowers yet fresh with childhood; on the ear
Drops the light drip of the suspended oar,
Or chirps the grasshopper one good-night carol more;

LXXXVII

He is an evening reveller, who makes
His life an infancy, and sings his fill;

At intervals, some bird from out the brakes
Starts into voice a moment, then is still.
There seems a floating whisper on the hill,
But that is fancy, for the starlight dews   820
All silently their tears of love instil,
Weeping themselves away, till they infuse
Deep into nature's breast the spirit of her hues.

LXXXVIII

Ye stars! which are the poetry of heaven!
If in your bright leaves we would read the fate
Of men and empires,—'t is to be forgiven,
That in our aspirations to be great,
Our destinies o'erleap their mortal state,
And claim a kindred with you; for ye are
A beauty and a mystery, and create   830
In us such love and reverence from afar,
That fortune, fame, power, life, have named themselves
    a star.

LXXXIX

All heaven and earth are still—though not in sleep,
But breathless, as we grow when feeling most;
And silent, as we stand in thoughts too deep:—
All heaven and earth are still: From the high host
Of stars, to the lulled lake and mountain-coast,
All is concentered in a life intense,
Where not a beam, nor air, nor leaf is lost,
But hath a part of being, and a sense   840
Of that which is of all Creator and defence.

XC

Then stirs the feeling infinite, so felt
In solitude, where we are *least* alone;

A truth, which through our being then doth melt,
And purifies from self: it is a tone,
The soul and source of music, which makes known
Eternal harmony, and sheds a charm
Like to the fabled Cytherea's zone,
Binding all things with beauty;—'t would disarm
The spectre Death, had he substantial power to harm. 850

XCI

Not vainly did the early Persian make
His altar the high places, and the peak
Of earth-o'ergazing mountains, and thus take
A fit and unwalled temple, there to seek
The Spirit, in whose honour shrines are weak,
Upreared of human hands. Come, and compare
Columns and idol-dwellings, Goth or Greek,
With Nature's realms of worship, earth and air,
Nor fix on fond abodes to circumscribe thy pray'r!

XCII

The sky is changed!—and such a change! Oh night, 860
And storm, and darkness, ye are wondrous strong,
Yet lovely in your strength, as is the light
Of a dark eye in woman! Far along,
From peak to peak, the rattling crags among
Leaps the live thunder! Not from one lone cloud,
But every mountain now hath found a tongue,
And Jura answers, through her misty shroud,
Back to the joyous Alps, who call to her aloud!

XCIII

And this is in the night:—Most glorious night!
Thou wert not sent for slumber! let me be 870

A sharer in thy fierce and far delight,—
A portion of the tempest and of thee!
How the lit lake shines, a phosphoric sea,
And the big rain comes dancing to the earth!
And now again 't is black,—and now, the glee
Of the loud hills shakes with its mountain-mirth,
As if they did rejoice o'er a young earthquake's birth.

XCIV

Now, where the swift Rhone cleaves his way between
Heights which appear as lovers who have parted
In hate, whose mining depths so intervene, 880
That they can meet no more, though broken-hearted;
Though in their souls, which thus each other thwarted,
Love was the very root of the fond rage
Which blighted their life's bloom, and then departed:
Itself expired, but leaving them an age
Of years all winters.—war within themselves to wage.

XCV

Now, where the quick Rhone thus hath cleft his way,
The mightiest of the storms hath ta'en his stand:
For here, not one, but many, make their play,
And fling their thunder-bolts from hand to hand, 890
Flashing and cast around; of all the band,
The brightest through these parted hills hath forked
His lightnings,—as if he did understand,
That in such gaps as desolation worked,
There the hot shaft should blast whatever therein lurked.

XCVI

Sky, mountains, river, winds, lake, lightnings! ye!
With night, and clouds, and thunder, and a soul

To make these felt and feeling, well may be
Things that have made me watchful; the far roll
Of your departing voices, is the knoll 900
Of what in me is sleepless,—if I rest.
But where of ye, O tempests! is the goal?
Are ye like those within the human breast?
Or do ye find, at length, like eagles, some high nest?

XCVII

Could I embody and unbosom now
That which is most within me,—could I wreak
My thoughts upon expression, and thus throw
Soul, heart, mind, passions, feelings, strong or weak,
All that I would have sought, and all I seek,
Bear, know, feel, and yet breathe—into *one* word, 910
And that one word were Lightning, I would speak;
But as it is, I live and die unheard,
With a most voiceless thought, sheathing it as a sword.

XCVIII

The morn is up again, the dewy morn,
With breath all incense, and with cheek all bloom,
Laughing the clouds away with playful scorn,
And living as if earth contained no tomb,—
And glowing into day: we may resume
The march of our existence: and thus I,
Still on thy shores, fair Leman! may find room 920
And food for meditation, nor pass by
Much, that may give us pause, if pondered fittingly.

XCIX

Clarens! sweet Clarens, birthplace of deep Love!
Thine air is the young breath of passionate thought;

Thy trees take root in Love; the snows above
The very Glaciers have his colours caught,
And sun-set into rose-hues sees them wrought
By rays which sleep there lovingly: the rocks,
The permanent crags, tell here of Love, who sought
In them a refuge from the worldly shocks,   930
Which stir and sting the soul with hope that woos, then
    mocks.

C

Clarens! by heavenly feet thy paths are trod,—
Undying Love's, who here ascends a throne
To which the steps are mountains; where the god
Is a pervading life and light,—so shown
Not on those summits solely, nor alone
In the still cave and forest; o'er the flower
His eye is sparkling, and his breath hath blown,
His soft and summer breath, whose tender power
Passes the strength of storms in their most desolate
    hour.   940

CI

All things are here of *him*; from the black pines,
Which are his shade on high, and the loud roar
Of torrents, where he listeneth, to the vines
Which slope his green path downward to the shore,
Where the bowed waters meet him, and adore,
Kissing his feet with murmurs; and the wood,
The covert of old trees, with trunks all hoar,
But light leaves, young as joy, stands where it stood,
Offering to him, and his, a populous solitude.

CII

A populous solitude of bees and birds, 950
And fairy-formed and many-coloured things,
Who worship him with notes more sweet than words,
And innocently open their glad wings,
Fearless and full of life: the gush of springs,
And fall of lofty fountains, and the bend
Of stirring branches, and the bud which brings
The swiftest thought of beauty, here extend,
Mingling, and made by Love, unto one mighty end.

CIII

He who hath loved not, here would learn that lore,
And make his heart a spirit; he who knows 960
That tender mystery, will love the more;
For this is Love's recess, where vain men's woes,
And the world's waste, have driven him far from those,
For 't is his nature to advance or die;
He stands not still, but or decays, or grows
Into a boundless blessing, which may vie
With the immortal lights, in its eternity!

CIV

'T was not for fiction chose Rousseau this spot,
Peopling it with affections; but he found
It was the scene which Passion must allot 970
To the mind's purified beings; 't was the ground
Where early Love his Psyche's zone unbound,
And hallowed it with loveliness: 't is lone,
And wonderful, and deep, and hath a sound,

And sense, and sight of sweetness; here the Rhone
Hath spread himself a couch, the Alps have reared a throne.

CV

Lausanne! and Ferney! ye have been the abodes
Of names which unto you bequeathed a name;
Mortals, who sought and found, by dangerous roads,
A path to perpetuity of fame: 980
They were gigantic minds, and their steep aim
Was, Titan-like, on daring doubts to pile
Thoughts which should call down thunder, and the flame
Of Heaven again assailed, if Heaven the while
On man and man's research could deign do more than smile.

CVI

The one was fire and fickleness, a child
Most mutable in wishes, but in mind
A wit as various,—gay, grave, sage, or wild,—
Historian, bard, philosopher, combined;
He multiplied himself among mankind, 990
The Proteus of their talents: But his own
Breathed most in ridicule,—which, as the wind,
Blew where it listed, laying all things prone,—
Now to o'erthrow a fool, and now to shake a throne.

CVII

The other, deep and slow, exhausting thought,
And hiving wisdom with each studious year,
In meditation dwelt, with learning wrought,
And shaped his weapon with an edge severe,

Sapping a solemn creed with solemn sneer;
The lord of irony,—that master-spell, 1000
Which stung his foes to wrath, which grew from fear,
And doomed him to the zealot's ready Hell,
Which answers to all doubts so eloquently well.

CVIII

Yet, peace be with their ashes,—for by them,
If merited, the penalty is paid;
It is not ours to judge,—far less condemn;
The hour must come when such things shall be made
Known unto all, or hope and dread allayed
By slumber, on one pillow, in the dust,
Which, thus much we are sure, must lie decayed; 1010
And when it shall revive, as is our trust,
'T will be to be forgiven, or suffer what is just.

CIX

But let me quit man's works, again to read
His Maker's, spread around me, and suspend
This page, which from my reveries I feed,
Until it seems prolonging without end.
The clouds above me to the white Alps tend,
And I must pierce them, and survey whate'er
May be permitted, as my steps I bend
To their most great and growing region, where 1020
The earth to her embrace compels the powers of air.

CX

Italia! too, Italia! looking on thee,
Full flashes on the soul the light of ages,
Since the fierce Carthaginian almost won thee.

To the last halo of the chiefs and sages
Who glorify thy consecrated pages;
Thou wert the throne and grave of empires; still,
The fount at which the panting mind assuages
Her thirst of knowledge, quaffing there her fill,
Flows from the eternal source of Rome's imperial hill.   1030

CXI

Thus far have I proceeded in a theme
Renewed with no kind auspices:—to feel
We are not what we have been, and to deem
We are not what we should be, and to steel
The heart against itself; and to conceal,
With a proud caution, love, or hate, or aught,—
Passion or feeling, purpose, grief or zeal,—
Which is the tyrant spirit of our thought,
Is a stern task of soul:—No matter,—it is taught.

CXII

And for these words, thus woven into song,   1040
It may be that they are a harmless wile,—
The colouring of the scenes which fleet along,
Which I would seize, in passing, to beguile
My breast, or that of others, for a while.
Fame is the thirst of youth, but I am not
So young as to regard men's frown or smile,
As loss or guerdon of a glorious lot;
I stood and stand alone,—remembered or forgot.

CXIII

I have not loved the world, nor the world me;
I have not flattered its rank breath, nor bowed   1050

CHILDE HAROLD'S PILGRIMAGE

To its idolatries a patient knee,
Nor coined my cheek to smiles, nor cried aloud
In worship of an echo; in the crowd
They could not deem me one of such; I stood
Among them, but not of them; in a shroud
Of thoughts which were not their thoughts, and still could,
Had I not filed my mind, which thus itself subdued.

CXIV

I have not loved the world, nor the world me,—
But let us part fair foes; I do believe,
Though I have found them not, that there may be
Words which are things, hopes which will not deceive,
And virtues which are merciful, nor weave
Snares for the failing; I would also deem
O'er others' griefs that some sincerely grieve;
That two, or one, are almost what they seem,
That goodness is no name, and happiness no dream.

CXV

My daughter! with thy name this song begun;
My daughter! with thy name thus much shall end;
I see thee not, I hear thee not, but none
Can be so wrapt in thee; thou art the friend
To whom the shadows of far years extend:
Albeit my brow thou never shouldst behold,
My voice shall with thy future visions blend,
And reach into thy heart, when mine is cold,
A token and a tone, even from thy father's mould.

CXVI

To aid thy mind's development, to watch
Thy dawn of little joys, to sit and see
Almost thy very growth, to view thee catch
Knowledge of objects,—wonders yet to thee!
To hold thee lightly on a gentle knee,　　　　　1080
And print on thy soft cheek a parent's kiss,—
This, it should seem, was not reserved for me;
Yet this was in my nature: as it is,
I know not what is there, yet something like to this.

CXVII

Yet, though dull Hate as duty should be taught,
I know that thou wilt love me; though my name
Should be shut from thee, as a spell still fraught
With desolation, and a broken claim:
Though the grave closed between us, 't were the same,
I know that thou wilt love me; though to drain　　1090
My blood from out thy being were an aim,
And an attainment,—all would be in vain,—
Still thou wouldst love me, still that more than life retain.

CXVIII

The child of love, though born in bitterness,
And nurtured in convulsion. Of thy sire
These were the elements, and thine no less.
As yet such are around thee, but thy fire
Shall be more tempered, and thy hope far higher.
Sweet be thy cradled slumbers! O'er the sea
And from the mountains where I now respire,　　1100

Fain would I waft such blessing upon thee,
As, with a sigh, I deem thou might'st have been to me.

1816   1816

TO THOMAS MOORE

My boat is on the shore,
   And my bark is on the sea;
But, before I go, Tom Moore,
   Here's a double health to thee!

Here's a sigh to those who love me,
   And a smile to those who hate;
And, whatever sky's above me,
   Here's a heart for every fate.

Though the ocean roar around me,
   Yet it still shall bear me on;
Though a desert should surround me,
   It hath springs that may be won.

Were 't the last drop in the well,
   As I gasped upon the brink,
Ere my fainting spirit fell,
   'T is to thee that I would drink.

With that water, as this wine,
   The libation I would pour
Should be—peace with thine and mine,
   And a health to thee, Tom Moore.

1817   1821

DON JUAN

CANTO THE THIRD: STANZAS 85 TO END

LXXXV

Thus, usually, when he was asked to sing,
  He gave the different nations something national;
'T was all the same to him—"God save the king,"
  Or "Ça Ira," according to the fashion all:
His muse made increment of anything,
  From the high lyric down to the low rational;
If Pindar sang horse-races, what should hinder
Himself from being as pliable as Pindar?

LXXXVI

In France, for instance, he would write a chanson;
  In England, a six canto quarto tale;   680
In Spain he'd make a ballad or romance on
  The last war—much the same in Portugal;
In Germany, the Pegasus he'd prance on
  Would be old Goethe's—(see what says De Staël);
In Italy, he'd ape the "Trecentisti";
In Greece, he'd sing some sort of hymn like this t'ye:

1

The isles of Greece, the isles of Greece!
  Where burning Sappho loved and sung,
Where grew the arts of war and peace,—
  Where Delos rose, and Phœbus sprung!   690
Eternal summer gilds them yet,
But all, except their sun, is set.

2

The Scian and the Teian muse,
   The hero's harp, the lover's lute,
Have found the fame your shores refuse:
   Their place of birth alone is mute
To sounds which echo further west
Than your sires' "Islands of the Blest."

3

The mountains look on Marathon—
   And Marathon looks on the sea;
And musing there an hour alone,
   I dreamed that Greece might still be free;
For standing on the Persian's grave,
I could not deem myself a slave.

4

A king sate on the rocky brow
   Which looks o'er sea-born Salamis;
And ships, by thousands, lay below,
   And men in nations;—all were his!
He counted them at break of day—
And when the sun set, where were they?

5

And where are they? and where art thou,
   My country? On thy voiceless shore
The heroic lay is tuneless now—
   The heroic bosom beats no more!

GEORGE GORDON, LORD BYRON

And must thy lyre, so long divine,
Degenerate into hands like mine?

6

'T is something, in the dearth of fame,
   Though linked among a fettered race,
To feel at least a patriot's shame,
   Even as I sing, suffuse my face;   720
For what is left the poet here?
For Greeks a blush—for Greece a tear.

7

Must *we* but weep o'er days more blest?
   Must *we* but blush?—Our fathers bled.
Earth! render back from out thy breast
   A remnant of our Spartan dead!
Of the three hundred grant but three.
To make a new Thermopylæ!

8

What, silent still? and silent all?
   Ah! no;—the voices of the dead   730
Sound like a distant torrent's fall,
   And answer, "Let one living head,
But one arise,—we come, we come!"
'T is but the living who are dumb.

9

In vain—in vain: strike other chords:
   Fill high the cup with Samian wine!
Leave battles to the Turkish hordes,
   And shed the blood of Scio's vine!

DON JUAN

Hark! rising to the ignoble call—
How answers each bold Bacchanal!   **740**

10

You have the Pyrrhic dance as yet:
  Where is the Pyrrhic phalanx gone?
Of two such lessons, why forget
  The nobler and the manlier one?
You have the letters Cadmus gave—
Think ye he meant them for a slave?

11

Fill high the bowl with Samian wine!
  We will not think of themes like these!
It made Anacreon's song divine;
  He served—but served Polycrates—   **750**
A tyrant; but our masters then
Were still, at least, our countrymen.

12

The tyrant of the Chersonese
  Was freedom's best and bravest friend;
That tyrant was Miltiades!
  Oh! that the present hour would lend
Another despot of the kind!
Such chains as his were sure to bind.

13

Fill high the bowl with Samian wine!
  On Suli's rock, and Parga's shore,   **760**
Exists the remnant of a line

Such as the Doric mothers bore;
And there, perhaps, some seed is sown,
The Heracleidan blood might own.

14

Trust not for freedom to the Franks—
  They have a king who buys and sells;
In native swords and native ranks,
  The only hope of courage dwells:
But Turkish force, and Latin fraud,
Would break your shield, however broad.   770

15

Fill high the bowl with Samian wine!
  Our virgins dance beneath the shade—
I see their glorious black eyes shine;
  But gazing on each glowing maid,
My own the burning tear-drop laves,
To think such breasts must suckle slaves.

16

Place me on Sunium's marbled steep,
  Where nothing, save the waves and I,
May hear our mutual murmurs sweep;
  There, swan-like, let me sing and die: 780
A land of slaves shall ne'er be mine—
Dash down yon cup of Samian wine!

LXXXVII

Thus sung, or would, or could, or should have sung,
  The modern Greek, in tolerable verse:

If not like Orpheus quite, when Greece was young,
  Yet in these times he might have done much worse:
His strain displayed some feeling—right or wrong;
    And feeling, in a poet, is the source
Of others' feeling; but they are such liars,
And take all colours—like the hands of dyers.   790

LXXXVIII

But words are things, and a small drop of ink,
  Falling like dew, upon a thought, produces
That which makes thousands, perhaps millions, think;
    'T is strange, the shortest letter which man uses
Instead of speech, may form a lasting link
    Of ages; to what straits old Time reduces
Frail man when paper—even a rag like this,
Survives himself, his tomb, and all that's his!

LXXXIX

And when his bones are dust, his grave a blank,
  His station, generation, even his nation,   800
Become a thing, or nothing, save to rank
    In chronological commemoration,
Some dull MS. oblivion long has sank.
    Or graven stone found in a barrack's station
In digging the foundation of a closet,
May turn his name up, as a rare deposit.

XC

And glory long has made the sages smile;
  'T is something, nothing, words, illusion, wind—
Depending more upon the historian's style
    Than on the name a person leaves behind: 810

Troy owes to Homer what whist owes to Hoyle:
  The present century was growing blind
To the great Marlborough's skill in giving knocks,
Until his late Life by Archdeacon Coxe.

XCI

Milton's the prince of poets—so we say;
  A little heavy, but no less divine:
An independent being in his day—
  Learned, pious, temperate in love and wine;
But his life falling into Johnson's way,
  We're told this great high priest of all the Nine
Was whipt at college—a harsh sire—odd spouse,
For the first Mrs. Milton left his house.

XCII

All these are, *certes,* entertaining facts,
  Like Shakspere's stealing deer, Lord Bacon's bribes;
Like Titus' youth, and Cæsar's earliest acts;
  Like Burns (whom Doctor Currie well describes);
Like Cromwell's pranks:—but although truth exacts
  These amiable descriptions from the scribes,
As most essential to their hero's story,
They do not much contribute to his glory.

XCIII

All are not moralists, like Southey, when
  He prated to the world of 'Pantisocracy:'
Or Wordsworth unexcised, unhired, who then
  Seasoned his peddler poems with democracy;

Or Coleridge, long before his flighty pen
    Let to the Morning Post its aristocracy;
When he and Southey, following the same path,
Espoused two partners (milliners of Bath).

XCIV

Such names at present cut a convict figure,
    The very Botany Bay in moral geography;
Their loyal treason, renegado rigour,
    Are good manure for their more bare biography,
Wordsworth's last quarto, by the way, is bigger
    Than any since the birthday of typography;
A drowsy frowsy poem, call'd the "Excursion,"
Writ in a manner which is my aversion.

XCV

He there builds up a formidable dyke
    Between his own and others' intellect:
But Wordsworth's poem, and his followers, like
    Joanna Southcote's Shiloh, and her sect,
Are things which in this century don't strike
    The public mind,—so few are the elect;
And the new births of both their stale virginities
Have proved but dropsies, taken for divinities.

XCVI

But let me to my story: I must own,
    If I have any fault, it is digression,
Leaving my people to proceed alone,
    While I soliloquize beyond expression:
But these are my addresses from the throne,
    Which put off business to the ensuing session:

Forgetting each omission is a loss to
The world, not quite so great as Ariosto.

XCVII

I know that what our neighbours call *"longueurs,"*
    (We've not so good a *word,* but have the *thing,*
In that complete perfection which insures
    An epic from Bob Southey every Spring—)
Form not the true temptation which allures
    The reader; but 'twould not be hard to bring
Some fine examples of the *epopée,*
To prove its grand ingredient is *ennui.*   870

XCVIII

We learn from Horace, "Homer sometimes sleeps;"
    We feel without him, Wordsworth sometimes wakes,—
To show with what complacency he creeps,
    With his dear *"Waggoners,"* around his lakes.
He wishes for "a boat" to sail the deeps—
    Of ocean?—No, of air; and then he makes
Another outcry for "a little boat,"
And drivels seas to set it well afloat.

XCIX

If he must fain sweep o'er the ethereal plain,
    And Pegasus runs restive in his "Wagon,"   880
Could he not beg the loan of Charles's Wain?
    Or pray Medea for a single dragon?
Or if, too classic for his vulgar brain,
    He fear'd his neck to venture such a nag on,
And he must needs mount nearer to the moon,
Could not the blockhead ask for a balloon?

C

"Pedlars," and "Boats," and "Wagons!" Oh! ye shades
　Of Pope and Dryden, are we come to this?
That trash of such sort not alone evades
　Contempt, but from the bathos' vast abyss　　　　890
Floats scumlike uppermost, and these Jack Cades
　Of sense and song above your graves may hiss—
The "little boatman" and his *Peter Bell*
Can sneer at him who drew "Achitophel!"

CI

T' our tale.—The feast was over, the slaves gone,
　The dwarfs and dancing girls had all retired:
The Arab lore and poet's song were done,
　And every sound of revelry expired;
The lady and her lover, left alone,
　The rosy flood of twilight's sky admired:　　　　900
Ave Maria! o'er the earth and sea,
That heavenliest hour of Heaven is worthiest thee!

CII

Ave Maria! blessed be the hour!
　The time, the clime, the spot, where I so oft
Have felt that moment in its fullest power
　Sink o'er the earth so beautiful and soft,
While swung the deep bell in the distant tower,
　Or the faint dying day-hymn stole aloft,
And not a breath crept through the rosy air,
And yet the forest leaves seemed stirred with prayer.　　　　910

CIII

Ave Maria! 't is the hour of prayer!
  Ave Maria! 't is the hour of love!
Ave Maria! may our spirits dare
  Look up to thine and to thy Son's above!
Ave Maria! oh, that face so fair!
  Those downcast eyes beneath the Almighty dove—
What though 't is but a pictured image strike,
That painting is no idol,—'t is too like.

CIV

Some kinder casuists are pleased to say,
  In nameless print—that I have no devotion;   920
But set those persons down with me to pray,
  And you shall see who has the properest notion
Of getting into heaven the shortest way;
  My altars are the mountains and the ocean,
Earth, air, stars,—all that springs from the great Whole,
Who hath produced, and will receive the soul.

CV

Sweet hour of twilight!—in the solitude
Of the pine forest and the silent shore
Which bounds Ravenna's immemorial wood,
  Rooted where once the Adrian wave flowed o'er.   930
To where the last Cæsarean fortress stood,
  Evergreen forest! which Boccaccio's lore
And Dryden's lay made haunted ground to me,
How have I loved the twilight hour and thee!

CVI

The shrill cicalas, people of the pine,
    Making their summer lives one ceaseless song,
Were the sole echoes, save my steed's and mine,
    And vesper bell's that rose the boughs along;
The spectre huntsman of Onesti's line,
    His hell-dogs, and their chase, and the fair throng
Which learn'd from his example not to fly
From a true lover,—shadow'd my mind's eye.

CVII

Oh, Hesperus! thou bringest all good things—
    Home to the weary, to the hungry cheer,
To the young bird the parent's brooding wings,
    The welcome stall to the o'erlabour'd steer;
Whate'er of peace about our hearthstone clings,
    Whate'er our household gods protect of dear,
Are gather'd round us by thy look of rest;
Thou bring'st the child, too, to the mother's breast.

CVIII

Soft hour! which wakes the wish and melts the heart
    Of those who sail the seas, on the first day
When they from their sweet friends are torn apart;
    Or fills with love the pilgrim on his way
As the far bell of vesper makes him start,
    Seeming to weep the dying day's decay;
Is this a fancy which our reason scorns?
Ah! surely nothing dies but something mourns!

CIX

When Nero perish'd by the justest doom
  Which ever the destroyer yet destroy'd,
Amidst the roar of liberated Rome,
  Of nations freed, and the world overjoy'd,
Some hands unseen strew'd flowers upon his tomb:
  Perhaps the weakness of a heart not void
Of feeling for some kindness done, when power
Had left the wretch an uncorrupted hour.

CX

But I'm digressing; what on earth has Nero,
  Or any such like sovereign buffoons,
To do with the transactions of my hero,
  More than such madmen's fellow man—the moon's?
Sure my invention must be down at zero,
  And I grown one of many "wooden spoons"
Of verse (the name with which we Cantabs please
To dub the last of honours in degrees).

CXI

I feel this tediousness will never do—
  'Tis being *too* epic, and I must cut down
(In copying) this long canto into two;
  They'll never find it out, unless I own
The fact, excepting some experienced few;
  And then as an improvement '' will be shown:
I'll prove that such the opinion of the critic is
From Aristotle *passim.*—See Ποιητικῆς.

1819   1821

STANZAS WRITTEN ON THE ROAD BETWEEN FLORENCE AND PISA

Oh, talk not to me of a name great in story;
The days of our youth are the days of our glory;
And the myrtle and ivy of sweet two-and-twenty
Are worth all your laurels, though ever so plenty.

What are garlands and crowns to the brow that is wrinkled?
'Tis but as a dead flower with May-dew besprinkled.
Then away with all such from the head that is hoary!
What care I for the wreaths that can *only* give glory!

Oh FAME!—if I e'er took delight in thy praises,
'Twas less for the sake of thy high-sounding phrases,   10
Than to see the bright eyes of the dear one discover
She thought that I was not unworthy to love her.

There chiefly I sought thee, *there* only I found thee;
Her glance was the best of the rays that surround thee;
When it sparkled o'er aught that was bright in my story,
I knew it was love, and I felt it was glory.

1821   1821

ON THIS DAY I COMPLETE MY THIRTY-SIXTH YEAR

'T is time this heart should be unmoved,
    Since others it hath ceased to move;
Yet, though I cannot be beloved,
    Still let me love!

My days are in the yellow leaf;
  The flowers and fruits of love are gone;
The worm, the canker, and the grief
    Are mine alone!

The fire that on my bosom preys
  Is lone as some volcanic isle;
No torch is kindled at its blaze—
    A funeral pile.

The hope, the fear, the jealous care,
  The exalted portion of the pain
And power of love, I cannot share,
    But wear the chain.

But 't is not *thus*—and 't is not *here*—
  Such thoughts should shake my soul, nor *now*,
Where glory decks the hero's bier,
    Or binds his brow.

The sword, the banner, and the field,
  Glory and Greece, around me see!
The Spartan, borne upon his shield,
    Was not more free.

Awake! (not Greece—she *is* awake!)
  Awake, my spirit! Think through *whom*
Thy life-blood tracks its parent lake,
    And then strike home!

Tread those reviving passions down,
  Unworthy manhood!—unto thee
Indifferent should the smile or frown
    Of beauty be.

If thou regrett'st thy youth, *why live?*
   The land of honourable death
Is here:—up to the field, and give
      Away thy breath!

Seek out—less often sought than found—
   A soldier's grave, for thee the best;
Then look around, and choose thy ground,
      And take thy rest.   40

1824   1824

PERCY BYSSHE SHELLEY (1792-1822)

HYMN TO INTELLECTUAL BEAUTY

I

The awful shadow of some unseen Power
   Floats though unseen among us,—visiting
   This various world with as inconstant wing
As summer winds that creep from flower to flower,—
Like moonbeams that behind some piny mountain shower,
     It visits with inconstant glance
     Each human heart and countenance;
Like hues and harmonies of evening,—
     Like clouds in starlight widely spread,—
     Like memory of music fled,—   10
     Like aught that for its grace may be
Dear, and yet dearer for its mystery.

II

Spirit of Beauty, that dost consecrate
   With thine own hues all thou dost shine upon
   Of human thought or form,—where art thou gone?

Why dost thou pass away and leave our state,
This dim vast vale of tears, vacant and desolate?
    Ask why the sunlight not for ever
    Weaves rainbows o'er yon mountain-river,
Why aught should fail and fade that once is shown,   20
    Why fear and dream and death and birth
    Cast on the daylight of this earth
    Such gloom,—why man has such a scope
For love and hate, despondency and hope?

III

No voice from some sublimer world hath ever
    To sage or poet these responses given—
    Therefore the names of Demon, Ghost, and Heaven,
Remain the records of their vain endeavour,
Frail spells—whose uttered charm might not avail to sever,
    From all we hear and all we see,   30
    Doubt, chance, and mutability.
Thy light alone—like mist o'er mountains driven,
    Or music by the night-wind sent
    Through strings of some still instrument,
    Or moonlight on a midnight stream,
Gives grace and truth to life's unquiet dream.

IV

Love, Hope, and Self-esteem, like clouds depart
    And come, for some uncertain moments lent.
    Man were immortal, and omnipotent,
Didst thou, unknown and awful as thou art,   40
Keep with thy glorious train firm state within his heart.
    Thou messenger of sympathies,
    That wax and wane in lovers' eyes—

Thou—that to human thought art nourishment,
  Like darkness to a dying flame!
  Depart not as thy shadow came,
  Depart not—lest the grave should be,
Like life and fear, a dark reality.

v

While yet a boy I sought for ghosts, and sped
  Through many a listening chamber, cave and ruin, 50
  And starlight wood, with fearful steps pursuing
Hopes of high talk with the departed dead.
I called on poisonous names with which our youth is fed;
  I was not heard—I saw them not—
  When musing deeply on the lot
Of life, at that sweet time when winds are wooing
  All vital things that wake to bring
  News of birds and blossoming,—
  Sudden, thy shadow fell on me;
I shrieked, and clasped my hands in ecstasy!   60

vi

I vowed that I would dedicate my powers
  To thee and thine—have I not kept the vow?
  With beating heart and streaming eyes, even now
I call the phantoms of a thousand hours
Each from his voiceless grave: they have in visioned bowers
  Of studious zeal or love's delight
  Outwatched with me the envious night—
They know that never joy illumed my brow
  Unlinked with hope that thou wouldst free
  This world from its dark slavery,   70
  That thou—O awful Loveliness,
Wouldst give whate'er these words cannot express.

VII

The day becomes more solemn and serene
  When noon is past—there is a harmony
  In autumn, and a lustre in its sky,
Which through the summer is not heard or seen,
As if it could not be, as if it had not been!
    Thus let thy power, which like the truth
    Of nature on my passive youth
  Descended, to my onward life supply   80
    Its calm—to one who worships thee,
    And every form containing thee,
    Whom, Spirit fair, thy spells did bind
To fear himself, and love all human kind.
  1816   1817

OZYMANDIAS

I MET a traveller from an antique land
Who said: "Two vast and trunkless legs of stone
Stand in the desert . . . Near them, on the sand,
Half sunk, a shattered visage lies, whose frown,
And wrinkled lip, and sneer of cold command,
Tell that its sculptor well those passions read
Which yet survive, stamped on these lifeless things,
The hand that mocked them, and the heart that fed.
And on the pedestal these words appear:
'My name is Ozymandias, king of kings: 10
Look on my works, ye Mighty, and despair!'
Nothing beside remains. Round the decay
Of that colossal wreck, boundless and bare
The lone and level sands stretch far away."
  1817   1818

STANZAS

WRITTEN IN DEJECTION, NEAR NAPLES

The sun is warm, the sky is clear,
   The waves are dancing fast and bright,
Blue isles and snowy mountains wear
   The purple noon's transparent might;
   The breath of the moist earth is light
Around its unexpanded buds;
   Like many a voice of one delight,
The winds, the birds, the ocean floods,
The City's voice itself, is soft like Solitude's.

I see the Deep's untrampled floor
   With green and purple seaweeds strown;
I see the waves upon the shore,
   Like light dissolved in star-showers, thrown:
   I sit upon the sands alone,—
The lightning of the noontide ocean
   Is flashing round me, and a tone
Arises from its measured motion,
How sweet! did any heart now share in my emotion.

Alas! I have nor hope nor health,
   Nor peace within nor calm around,
Nor that content surpassing wealth
   The sage in meditation found,
   And walked with inward glory crowned—
Nor fame, nor power, nor love, nor leisure.
   Others I see whom these surround—
Smiling they live, and call life pleasure;—
To me that cup has been dealt in another measure.

    Yet now despair itself is mild,
        Even as the winds and waters are;
    I could lie down like a tired child,   30
        And weep away the life of care
        Which I have borne and yet must bear,
    Till death like sleep might steal on me,
        And I might feel in the warm air
    My cheek grow cold, and hear the sea
Breathe o'er my dying brain its last monotony.

    Some might lament that I were cold,
        As I, when this sweet day is gone,
    Which my lost heart, too soon grown old,
        Insults with this untimely moan;   40
        They might lament—for I am one
    Whom men love not,—and yet regret,
        Unlike this day, which, when the sun
    Shall on its stainless glory set,
Will linger, though enjoyed, like joy in memory yet.
    1818   1824

THE TRANSFORMATION OF ASIA

PROMETHEUS UNBOUND, ACT II, SCENE 5

SCENE V.—*The Car pauses within a Cloud on the top of a snowy Mountain.* ASIA, PANTHEA, *and the* SPIRIT OF THE HOUR.

Spirit.
On the brink of the night and the morning
    My coursers are wont to respire;
But the Earth has just whispered a warning
    That their flight must be swifter than fire:
They shall drink the hot speed of desire!

PROMETHEUS UNBOUND

Asia. Thou breathest on their nostrils, but my breath
Would give them swifter speed.
    Spirit.   Alas! it could not.
    Panthea. Oh Spirit! pause, and tell whence is the light
Which fills this cloud? the sun is yet unrisen.
    Spirit. The sun will rise not until noon. Apollo
Is held in heaven by wonder; and the light
Which fills this vapour, as the aëreal hue
Of fountain-gazing roses fills the water,
Flows from thy mighty sister.
    Panthea.   Yes, I feel—
    Asia. What is it with thee, sister? Thou art pale.
    Panthea. How thou art changed! I dare not look on thee;
I feel but see thee not. I scarce endure
The radiance of thy beauty. Some good change
Is working in the elements, which suffer
Thy presence thus unveiled. The Nereids tell
That on the day when the clear hyaline
Was cloven at thine uprise, and thou didst stand
Within a veinèd shell, which floated on
Over the calm floor of the crystal sea,
Among the Ægean isles, and by the shores
Which bear thy name; love, like the atmosphere
Of the sun's fire filling the living world,
Burst from thee, and illumined earth and heaven
And the deep ocean and the sunless caves
And all that dwells within them; till grief cast
Eclipse upon the soul from which it came:
Such art thou now; nor is it I alone,
Thy sister, thy companion, thine own chosen one,
But the whole world which seeks thy sympathy.
Hearest thou not sounds i' the air which speak the love

Of all articulate beings? Feelest thou not
The inanimate winds enamoured of thee? List! [*Music.*

Asia. Thy words are sweeter than aught else but his
Whose echoes they are: yet all love is sweet,
Given or returned. Common as light is love, 40
And its familiar voice wearies not ever.
Like the wide heaven, the all-sustaining air,
It makes the reptile equal to the God:
They who inspire it most are fortunate,
As I am now; but those who feel it most
Are happier still, after long sufferings,
As I shall soon become.
    Panthea.   List! Spirits speak.

        Voice in the Air, singing.
Life of Life! thy lips enkindle
   With their love the breath between them;
And thy smiles before they dwindle 50
   Make the cold air fire; then screen them
In those looks, where whoso gazes
Faints, entangled in their mazes.

Child of Light! thy limbs are burning
   Through the vest which seems to hide them;
As the radiant lines of morning
   Through the clouds ere they divide them;
And this atmosphere divinest
Shrouds thee wheresoe'er thou shinest.

Fair are others; none beholds thee, 60
   But thy voice sounds low and tender
Like the fairest, for it folds thee
   From the sight, that liquid splendour,
And all feel, yet see thee never,
As I feel now, lost for ever!

Lamp of Earth! where'er thou movest
  Its dim shapes are clad with brightness,
And the souls of whom thou lovest
  Walk upon the winds with lightness,
Till they fail, as I am failing,
Dizzy, lost, yet unbewailing!

Asia.

  My soul is an enchanted boat,
  Which, like a sleeping swan, doth float
Upon the silver waves of thy sweet singing;
  And thine doth like an angel sit
  Beside a helm conducting it,
Whilst all the winds with melody are ringing.
  It seems to float ever, for ever,
  Upon that many-winding river,
  Between mountains, woods, abysses,
  A paradise of wildernesses!
Till, like one in slumber bound,
Borne to the ocean, I float down, around,
Into a sea profound of ever-spreading sound.

  Meanwhile thy spirit lifts its pinions
  In music's most serene dominions,
Catching the winds that fan that happy heaven.
  And we sail on, away, afar,
  Without a course, without a star,
But by the instinct of sweet music driven;
  Till through Elysian garden islets
  By thee, most beautiful of pilots,
  Where never mortal pinnace glided,
  The boat of my desire is guided:
Realms where the air we breathe is love,
Which in the winds and on the waves doth move,
Harmonizing this earth with what we feel above.

We have passed Age's icy caves,
  And Manhood's dark and tossing waves,
And Youth's smooth ocean, smiling to betray: 100
  Beyond the glassy gulfs we flee
  Of shadow-peopled Infancy,
Through Death and Birth to a diviner day;
  A paradise of vaulted bowers,
  Lit by downward-gazing flowers,
  And watery paths that wind between
  Wildernesses calm and green,
Peopled by shapes too bright to see,
And rest, having beheld; somewhat like thee;
Which walk upon the sea, and chant melodiously! 110
1818-1819   1820

ODE TO THE WEST WIND

I

O WILD West Wind, thou breath of Autumn's being,
Thou, from whose unseen presence the leaves dead
Are driven, like ghosts from an enchanter fleeing,

Yellow, and black, and pale, and hectic red,
Pestilence-stricken multitudes: O thou,
Who chariotest to their dark wintry bed

The wingèd seeds, where they lie cold and low,
Each like a corpse within its grave, until
Thine azure sister of the Spring shall blow

Her clarion o'er the dreaming earth, and fill   10
(Driving sweet buds like flocks to feed in air)
With living hues and odours plain and hill:

ODE TO THE WEST WIND

Wild Spirit, which art moving everywhere;
Destroyer and preserver; hear, oh, hear!

II

Thou on whose stream, mid the steep sky's commotion,
Loose clouds like earth's decaying leaves are shed,
Shook from the tangled boughs of Heaven and Ocean,

Angels of rain and lightning: there are spread
On the blue surface of thine aëry surge,
Like the bright hair uplifted from the head   20

Of some fierce Maenad, even from the dim verge
Of the horizon to the zenith's height,
The locks of the approaching storm. Thou dirge

Of the dying year, to which this closing night
Will be the dome of a vast sepulchre,
Vaulted with all thy congregated might

Of vapours, from whose solid atmosphere
Black rain, and fire, and hail will burst: oh, hear!

III

Thou who didst waken from his summer dreams
The blue Mediterranean, where he lay,   30
Lulled by the coil of his crystalline streams,

Beside a pumice isle in Baiae's bay,
And saw in sleep old palaces and towers
Quivering within the wave's intenser day,

All overgrown with azure moss and flowers
So sweet, the sense faints picturing them! Thou
For whose path the Atlantic's level powers

Cleave themselves into chasms, while far below
The sea-blooms and the oozy woods which wear
The sapless foliage of the ocean, know   40

Thy voice, and suddenly grow gray with fear,
And tremble and despoil themselves: oh, hear!

IV

If I were a dead leaf thou mightest bear;
If I were a swift cloud to fly with thee;
A wave to pant beneath thy power, and share

The impulse of thy strength, only less free
Than thou, O uncontrollable! If even
I were as in my boyhood, and could be

The comrade of thy wanderings over Heaven,
As then, when to outstrip thy skiey speed   50
Scarce seemed a vision; I would ne'er have striven

As thus with thee in prayer in my sore need.
Oh, lift me as a wave, a leaf, a cloud!
I fall upon the thorns of life! I bleed!

A heavy weight of hours has chained and bowed
One too like thee: tameless, and swift, and proud.

V

Make me thy lyre, even as the forest is:
What if my leaves are falling like its own!
The tumult of thy mighty harmonies

Will take from both a deep, autumnal tone,   60
Sweet though in sadness. Be thou, Spirit fierce,
My spirit! Be thou me, impetuous one!

Drive my dead thoughts over the universe
Like withered leaves to quicken a new birth!
And, by the incantation of this verse,

Scatter, as from an unextinguished hearth
Ashes and sparks, my words among mankind!
Be through my lips to unawakened earth

The trumpet of a prophecy! O, Wind,
If Winter comes, can Spring be far behind?   70
  1819   1820

THE INDIAN SERENADE

    I ARISE from dreams of thee
    In the first sweet sleep of night,
    When the winds are breathing low,
    And the stars are shining bright:
    I arise from dreams of thee,
    And a spirit in my feet
    Hath led me—who knows how?
    To thy chamber window, Sweet!

The wandering airs they faint
On the dark, the silent stream—
The Champak odors fail
Like sweet thoughts in a dream;
The nightingale's complaint,
It dies upon her heart;—
As I must on thine,
O! belovèd as thou art!

O lift me from the grass!
I die! I faint! I fail!
Let thy love in kisses rain
On my lips and eyelids pale.
My cheek is cold and white, alas!
My heart beats loud and fast;—
Oh! press it to thine own again,
Where it will break at last.

1819   1822

THE CLOUD

I BRING fresh showers for the thirsting flowers,
  From the seas and the streams;
I bear light shade for the leaves when laid
  In their noonday dreams.
From my wings are shaken the dews that waken
  The sweet buds every one,
When rocked to rest on their mother's breast,
  As she dances about the sun.
I wield the flail of the lashing hail,
  And whiten the green plains under,
And then again I dissolve it in rain,
  And laugh as I pass in thunder.

THE CLOUD

I sift the snow on the mountains below,
   And their great pines groan aghast;
And all the night 't is my pillow white,
   While I sleep in the arms of the blast.
Sublime on the towers of my skiey bowers,
   Lightning my pilot sits;
In a cavern under is fettered the thunder,
   It struggles and howls at fits;   20
Over earth and ocean, with gentle motion,
   This pilot is guiding me,
Lured by the love of the genii that move
   In the depths of the purple sea;
Over the rills, and the crags, and the hills,
   Over the lakes and the plains,
Wherever he dream, under mountain or stream,
   The Spirit he loves remains;
And I all the while bask in Heaven's blue smile,
   Whilst he is dissolving in rains.   30

The sanguine Sunrise, with his meteor eyes,
   And his burning plumes outspread,
Leaps on the back of my sailing rack,
   When the morning star shines dead;
As on the jag of a mountain crag,
   Which an earthquake rocks and swings,
An eagle alit one moment may sit
   In the light of its golden wings.
And when Sunset may breathe, from the lit sea beneath,
   Its ardours of rest and of love,   40
And the crimson pall of eve may fall
   From the depth of Heaven above,
With wings folded I rest, on mine aëry nest,
   As still as a brooding dove.

That orbèd maiden with white fire laden,
  Whom mortals call the Moon,
Glides glimmering o'er my fleece-like floor,
  By the midnight breezes strewn;
And wherever the beat of her unseen feet,
  Which only the angels hear, 50
May have broken the woof of my tent's thin roof,
  The stars peep behind her and peer;
And I laugh to see them whirl and flee,
  Like a swarm of golden bees,
When I widen the rent in my wind-built tent,
  Till the calm rivers, lakes, and seas,
Like strips of the sky fallen through me on high,
  Are each paved with the moon and these.

I bind the Sun's throne with a burning zone,
  And the Moon's with a girdle of pearl; 60
The volcanoes are dim, and the stars reel and swim,
  When the whirlwinds my banner unfurl.
From cape to cape, with a bridge-like shape,
  Over a torrent sea,
Sunbeam-proof, I hang like a roof,—
  The mountains its columns be.
The triumphal arch through which I march
  With hurricane, fire, and snow,
When the Powers of the air are chained to my chair,
  Is the million-coloured bow; 70
The sphere-fire above its soft colours wove,
  While the moist Earth was laughing below.

I am the daughter of Earth and Water,
  And the nursling of the Sky;
I pass through the pores of the ocean and shores;
  I change, but I cannot die.

For after the rain when with never a stain
   The pavilion of Heaven is bare,
And the winds and sunbeams with their convex gleams
   Build up the blue dome of air,   80
I silently laugh at my own cenotaph,
   And out of the caverns of rain,
Like a child from the womb, like a ghost from the tomb,
   I arise and unbuild it again.
1820   1820

TO A SKYLARK

   Hail to thee, blithe Spirit!
      Bird thou never wert,
   That from Heaven, or near it,
      Pourest thy full heart
In profuse strains of unpremeditated art.

   Higher still and higher
      From the earth thou springest
   Like a cloud of fire;
      The blue deep thou wingest,
And singing still dost soar, and soaring ever singest. 10

   In the golden lightning
      Of the sunken sun,
   O'er which clouds are bright'ning,
      Thou dost float and run;
Like an unbodied joy whose race is just begun.

   The pale purple even
      Melts around thy flight;
   Like a star of Heaven,
      In the broad daylight
Thou art unseen, but yet I hear thy shrill delight,   20

With thy clear keen joyance
  Languor cannot be:
Shadow of annoyance
  Never came near thee:
Thou lovest—but ne'er knew love's sad satiety.　　80

Waking or asleep,
  Thou of death must deem
Things more true and deep
  Than we mortals dream,
Or how could thy notes flow in such a crystal stream?

We look before and after,
  And pine for what is not:
Our sincerest laughter
  With some pain is fraught;
Our sweetest songs are those that tell of saddest
  thought.　　90

Yet if we could scorn
  Hate, and pride, and fear;
If we were things born
  Not to shed a tear,
I know not how thy joy we ever should come near.

Better than all measures
  Of delightful sound,
Better than all treasures
  That in books are found,
Thy skill to poet were, thou scorner of the ground! 100

Teach me half the gladness
  That thy brain must know,
Such harmonious madness
  From my lips would flow

The world should listen then—as I am listening now.
1820   1820

TO NIGHT

I

Swiftly walk o'er the western wave,
        Spirit of Night!
Out of the misty eastern cave,
Where, all the long and lone daylight,
Thou wovest dreams of joy and fear,
Which make thee terrible and dear,—
        Swift be thy flight!

II

Wrap thy form in a mantle gray,
        Star-inwrought!
Blind with thine hair the eyes of Day;   10
Kiss her until she be wearied out,
Then wander o'er city, and sea, and land,
Touching all with thine opiate wand—
        Come, long-sought!

III

When I arose and saw the dawn,
        I sighed for thee;
When light rode high, and the dew was gone,
And noon lay heavy on flower and tree,
And the weary Day turned to his rest,
Lingering like an unloved guest,   20
        I sighed for thee.

IV

Thy brother Death came, and cried,
        Wouldst thou me?
Thy sweet child Sleep, the filmy-eyed,
Murmured like a noontide bee,
Shall I nestle near thy side?
Wouldst thou me?—And I replied,
        No, not thee!

V

Death will come when thou art dead,
        Soon, too soon—
Sleep will come when thou art fled;
Of neither would I ask the boon
I ask of thee, belovèd Night—
Swift be thine approaching flight,
        Come soon, soon!

1821   1824

TIME

UNFATHOMABLE Sea! whose waves are years,
  Ocean of Time, whose waters of deep woe
Are brackish with the salt of human tears!
  Thou shoreless flood, which in thy ebb and flow
Claspest the limits of mortality,
And sick of prey, yet howling on for more,
Vomitest thy wrecks on its inhospitable shore;
  Treacherous in calm, and terrible in storm,
      Who shall put forth on thee,
      Unfathomable Sea?

1821   1824

SONG

I

Rarely, rarely, comest thou,
  Spirit of Delight!
Wherefore hast thou left me now
  Many a day and night?
Many a weary night and day
'T is since thou art fled away.

II

How shall ever one like me
  Win thee back again?
With the joyous and the free
  Thou wilt scoff at pain.   10
Spirit false! thou hast forgot
All but those who need thee not.

III

As a lizard with the shade
  Of a trembling leaf,
Thou with sorrow art dismayed;
  Even the sighs of grief
Reproach thee, that thou art not near,
And reproach thou wilt not hear.

IV

Let me set my mournful ditty
  To a merry measure;   20

Thou wilt never come for pity,
  Thou wilt come for pleasure;
Pity then will cut away
Those cruel wings, and thou wilt stay.

V

I love all that thou lovest,
  Spirit of Delight!
The fresh Earth in new leaves dressed,
  And the starry night;
Autumn evening, and the morn
When the golden mists are born.   30

VI

I love snow, and all the forms
  Of the radiant frost;
I love waves, and winds, and storms,
  Everything almost
Which is Nature's, and may be
Untainted by man's misery.

VII

I love tranquil solitude,
  And such society
As is quiet, wise, and good;
  Between thee and me   40
What difference? but thou dost possess
The things I seek, not love them less.

VIII

I love Love—though he has wings,
  And like light can flee,

MUTABILITY

But above all other things,
   Spirit, I love thee—
Thou art love and life! Oh, come,
Make once more my heart thy home.

1821   1824

MUTABILITY

THE flower that smiles to-day
      To-morrow dies;
All that we wish to stay
      Tempts and then flies.
What is this world's delight?
Lightning that mocks the night,
      Brief even as bright.

Virtue, how frail it is!
      Friendship how rare!
Love, how it sells poor bliss   10
      For proud despair!
But we, though soon they fall,
Survive their joy, and all
      Which ours we call.

Whilst skies are blue and bright,
      Whilst flowers are gay,
Whilst eyes that change ere night
      Make glad the day;
Whilst yet the calm hours creep,
Dream thou—and from thy sleep   20
      Then wake to weep.

1821   1824

A LAMENT

O WORLD! O life! O time!
On whose last steps I climb,
   Trembling at that where I had stood before;
When will return the glory of your prime?
      No more—Oh, never more!

Out of the day and night
A joy has taken flight;
   Fresh spring, and summer, and winter hoar,
Move my faint heart with grief, but with delight
      No more—Oh, never more!

1821   1824

ADONAIS

AN ELEGY ON THE DEATH OF JOHN KEATS, AUTHOR OF
ENDYMION, HYPERION, ETC.

PREFACE

It is my intention to subjoin to the London edition of this poem a criticism upon the claims of its lamented object to be classed among the writers of the highest genius who have adorned our age. My known repugnance to the narrow principles of taste on which several of his earlier compositions were modelled prove at least that I am an impartial judge. I consider the fragment of *Hyperion* as second to nothing that was ever produced by a writer of the same years.

John Keats died at Rome of a consumption, in his [twenty-sixth] year, on the [twenty-third] of [February], 1821; and was buried in the romantic and lonely cemetery of the Protestants in that city, under the pyramid which is the tomb of Cestius, and the massy walls and towers, now mouldering and desolate, which formed the circuit of ancient Rome. The cemetery is an open space among the ruins, covered in winter with violets and daisies. It might make one in love with death, to think that one should be buried in so sweet a place.

The genius of the lamented person to whose memory I have dedicated these unworthy verses was not less delicate and fragile than it was beautiful; and where cankerworms abound, what wonder if its young flower was blighted in the bud? The savage criticism on his *Endymion,* which appeared in the *Quarterly Review,* produced the most violent effect on his susceptible mind; the agitation thus originated ended in the rupture of a blood-vessel in the lungs; a rapid consumption ensued, and the succeeding acknowledgements from more candid critics of the true greatness of his powers were ineffectual to heal the wound thus wantonly inflicted.

It may be well said that these wretched men know not what they do. They scatter their insults and their slanders without heed as to whether the poisoned shaft lights on a heart made callous by many blows or one like Keats's composed of more penetrable stuff. One of their associates is, to my knowledge, a most base and unprincipled calumniator. As to *Endymion,* was it a poem, whatever might be its defects, to be treated contemptuously by those who had celebrated, with various degrees of complacency and panegyric, *Paris,* and *Woman,* and a *Syrian Tale,* and Mrs. Lefanu, and Mr. Barrett, and Mr. Howard Payne, and a long list of the illustrious obscure? Are these the men who in their venal good nature presumed to draw a parallel between the Rev. Mr. Milman and Lord Byron? What gnat did they strain at here, after having swallowed all those camels? Against what woman taken in adultery dares the foremost of these literary prostitutes to cast his opprobrious stone? Miserable man! you, one of the meanest, have wantonly defaced one of the noblest specimens of the workmanship of God. Nor shall it be your excuse, that, murderer as you are, you have spoken daggers, but used none.

The circumstances of the closing scene of poor Keats's life were not made known to me until the *Elegy* was ready for the press. I am given to understand that the wound which his sensitive spirit had received from the criticism of *Endymion* was exasperated by the bitter sense of unrequited benefits; the poor fellow seems to have been hooted from the stage of life, no less by those on whom he had wasted the promise of his genius, than those on whom he had lavished his fortune and his care. He was accompanied to Rome, and attended in his last illness by Mr. Severn, a young artist of the highest promise, who, I have been informed, "almost risked his own life, and sacrificed every prospect to unwearied attendance upon his dying friend." Had I known these circumstances before the completion of my poem, I should have been tempted to add my feeble tribute of applause to the more solid recompense which the virtuous man finds in the recollection of his own motives. Mr. Severn can dispense with a reward from "such stuff as dreams are made of." His conduct is a golden augury of the success of his future career—may the unextinguished Spirit of his illustrious friend animate the creations of his pencil, and plead against Oblivion for his name!—*Shelley*.

ADONAIS

I

I WEEP for Adonais—he is dead!
O, weep for Adonais! though our tears
Thaw not the frost which binds so dear a head!
And thou, sad Hour, selected from all years
To mourn our loss, rouse thy obscure compeers,
And teach them thine own sorrow, say: "With me
Died Adonais; till the Future dares
Forget the Past, his fate and fame shall be
An echo and a light unto eternity!"

II

Where wert thou, mighty Mother, when he lay,
When thy Son lay, pierced by the shaft which flies
In darkness? where was lorn Urania
When Adonais died? With veilèd eyes,
'Mid listening Echoes, in her Paradise
She sate, while one, with soft enamoured breath,
Rekindled all the fading melodies,
With which, like flowers that mock the corse beneath,
He had adorned and hid the coming bulk of Death.

III

Oh, weep for Adonais—he is dead!
Wake, melancholy Mother, wake and weep!
Yet wherefore? Quench within their burning bed
Thy fiery tears, and let thy loud heart keep
Like his, a mute and uncomplaining sleep;
For he is gone, where all things wise and fair
Descend;—oh, dream not that the amorous Deep

Will yet restore him to the vital air;
Death feeds on his mute voice, and laughs at our despair.

IV

Most musical of mourners, weep again!
Lament anew, Urania!—He died,
Who was the Sire of an immortal strain, 30
Blind, old, and lonely, when his country's pride,
The priest, the slave, and the liberticide,
Trampled and mocked with many a loathèd rite
Of lust and blood; he went, unterrified,
Into the gulf of death; but his clear Sprite
Yet reigns o'er earth; the third among the sons of light

V

Most musical of mourners, weep anew!
Not all to that bright station dared to climb;
And happier they their happiness who knew,
Whose tapers yet burn through that night of time 40
In which suns perished; others more sublime,
Struck by the envious wrath of man or god,
Have sunk, extinct in their refulgent prime;
And some yet live, treading the thorny road,
Which leads, through toil and hate, to Fame's serene abode.

VI

But now, thy youngest, dearest one, has perished—
The nursling of thy widowhood, who grew,
Like a pale flower by some sad maiden cherished,
And fed with true-love tears, instead of dew;
Most musical of mourners, weep anew! 50

Thy extreme hope, the loveliest and the last,
The bloom, whose petals nipped before they blew
Died on the promise of the fruit, is waste;
The broken lily lies—the storm is overpast.

VII

To that high Capital, where kingly Death
Keeps his pale court in beauty and decay,
He came; and bought, with price of purest breath,
A grave among the eternal.—Come away!
Haste, while the vault of blue Italian day
Is yet his fitting charnel-roof! while still   60
He lies, as if in dewy sleep he lay;
Awake him not! surely he takes his fill
Of deep and liquid rest, forgetful of all ill.

VIII

He will awake no more, oh, never more!—
Within the twilight chamber spreads apace
The shadow of white Death, and at the door
Invisible Corruption waits to trace
His extreme way to her dim dwelling-place;
The eternal Hunger sits, but pity and awe
Soothe her pale rage, nor dares she to deface   70
So fair a prey, till darkness, and the law
Of change, shall o'er his sleep the mortal curtain draw.

IX

Oh, weep for Adonais!—The quick Dreams,
The passion-wingèd Ministers of thought,
Who were his flocks, whom near the living streams
Of his young spirit he fed, and whom he taught

The love which was its music, wander not,—
Wander no more, from kindling brain to brain,
But droop there, whence they sprung; and mourn their lot
Round the cold heart, where, after their sweet pain, 80
They ne'er will gather strength, or find a home again.

X

And one with trembling hands clasps his cold head,
And fans him with her moonlight wings, and cries;
"Our love, our hope, our sorrow, is not dead;
See, on the silken fringe of his faint eyes,
Like dew upon a sleeping flower, there lies
A tear some Dream has loosened from his brain."
Lost Angel of a ruined Paradise!
She knew not 't was her own; as with no stain
She faded, like a cloud which had outwept its rain. 90

XI

One from a lucid urn of starry dew
Washed his light limbs as if embalming them;
Another clipped her profuse locks, and threw
The wreath upon him, like an anadem,
Which frozen tears instead of pearls begem;
Another in her wilful grief would break
Her bow and wingèd reeds, as if to stem
A greater loss with one which was more weak;
And dull the barbèd fire against his frozen cheek.

XII

Another Splendour on his mouth alit, 100
That mouth, whence it was wont to draw the breath

ADONAIS

Which gave it strength to pierce the guarded wit,
And pass into the panting heart beneath
With lightning and with music: the damp death
Quenched its caress upon his icy lips;
And, as a dying meteor stains a wreath
Of moonlight vapour, which the cold night clips,
It flushed through his pale limbs, and passed to its
    eclipse.

XIII

And others came . . . Desires and Adorations,
Wingèd Persuasions and veiled Destinies, 110
Splendours, and Glooms, and glimmering Incarnations
Of hopes and fears, and twilight Phantasies;
And Sorrow, with her family of Sighs,
And Pleasure, blind with tears, led by the gleam
Of her own dying smile instead of eyes,
Came in slow pomp;—the moving pomp might seem
Like pageantry of mist on an autumnal stream.

XIV

All he had loved, and moulded into thought,
From shape, and hue, and odour, and sweet sound,
Lamented Adonais. Morning sought 120
Her eastern watch-tower, and her hair unbound,
Wet with the tears which should adorn the ground,
Dimmed the aëreal eyes that kindle day;
Afar the melancholy thunder moaned,
Pale Ocean in unquiet slumber lay,
And the wild Winds flew round, sobbing in their dis-
    may.

XV

Lost Echo sits amid the voiceless mountains,
And feeds her grief with his remembered lay,
And will no more reply to winds or fountains,
Or amorous birds perched on the young green spray, 130
Or herdsman's horn, or bell at closing day;
Since she can mimic not his lips, more dear
Than those for whose disdain she pined away
Into a shadow of all sounds:—a drear
Murmur, between their songs, is all the woodmen hear.

XVI

Grief made the young Spring wild, and she threw down
Her kindling buds, as if she Autumn were,
Or they dead leaves; since her delight is flown,
For whom should she have waked the sullen year?
To Phoebus was not Hyacinth so dear 140
Nor to himself Narcissus, as to both
Thou, Adonais: wan they stand and sere
Amid the faint companions of their youth,
With dew all turned to tears; odour, to sighing ruth.

XVII

Thy spirit's sister, the lorn nightingale
Mourns not her mate with such melodious pain;
Not so the eagle, who like thee could scale
Heaven, and could nourish in the sun's domain
Her mighty youth with morning, doth complain,
Soaring and screaming round her empty nest, 150
As Albion wails for thee: the curse of Cain

Light on his head who pierced thy innocent breast,
And scared the angel soul that was its earthly guest!

XVIII

Ah, woe is me! Winter is come and gone,
But grief returns with the revolving year;
The airs and streams renew their joyous tone;
The ants, the bees, the swallows reappear;
Fresh leaves and flowers deck the dead Seasons' bier;
The amorous birds now pair in every brake,
And build their mossy homes in field and brere; 160
And the green lizard, and the golden snake,
Like unimprisoned flames, out of their trance awake.

XIX

Through wood and stream and field and hill and Ocean
A quickening life from the Earth's heart has burst
As it has ever done, with change and motion,
From the great morning of the world when first
God dawned on Chaos; in its stream immersed,
The lamps of Heaven flash with a softer light;
All baser things pant with life's sacred thirst;
Diffuse themselves; and spend in love's delight, 170
The beauty and the joy of their renewèd might.

XX

The leprous corpse, touched by this spirit tender,
Exhales itself in flowers of gentle breath;
Like incarnations of the stars, when splendour
Is changed to fragrance, they illumine death
And mock the merry worm that wakes beneath;
Nought we know, dies. Shall that alone which knows

Be as a sword consumed before the sheath
By sightless lightning?—the intense atom glows
A moment, then is quenched in a most cold repose.   180

XXI

Alas! that all we loved of him should be,
But for our grief, as if it had not been,
And grief itself be mortal! Woe is me!
Whence are we, and why are we? of what scene
The actors or spectators? Great and mean
Meet massed in death, who lends what life must borrow.
As long as skies are blue, and fields are green,
Evening must usher night, night urge the morrow,
Month follow month with woe, and year wake year to sorrow.

XXII

He will awake no more, oh, never more!   190
"Wake thou," cried Misery, "childless Mother, rise
Out of thy sleep, and slake, in thy heart's core,
A wound more fierce than his, with tears and sighs."
And all the Dreams that watched Urania's eyes,
And all the Echoes whom their sister's song
Had held in holy silence, cried: "Arise!"
Swift as a Thought by the snake Memory stung,
From her ambrosial rest the fading Splendour sprung.

XXIII

She rose like an autumnal Night, that springs
Out of the East, and follows wild and drear   200
The golden Day, which, on eternal wings,
Even as a ghost abandoning a bier,

Had left the Earth a corpse. Sorrow and fear
So struck, so roused, so rapped Urania;
So saddened round her like an atmosphere
Of stormy mist; so swept her on her way
Even to the mournful place where Adonais lay.

XXIV

Out of her secret Paradise she sped,
Through camps and cities rough with stone, and steel,
And human hearts, which to her aery tread   210
Yielding not, wounded the invisible
Palms of her tender feet where'er they fell:
And barbèd tongues, and thoughts more sharp than they,
Rent the soft Form they never could repel,
Whose sacred blood, like the young tears of May,
Paved with eternal flowers that undeserving way.

XXV

In the death-chamber for a moment Death,
Shamed by the presence of that living Might,
Blushed to annihilation, and the breath
Revisited those lips, and Life's pale light   220
Flashed through those limbs, so late her dear delight.
"Leave me not wild and drear and comfortless,
As silent lightning leaves the starless night!
Leave me not!" cried Urania: her distress
Roused Death: Death rose and smiled, and met her vain caress.

XXVI

"Stay yet awhile! speak to me once again;
Kiss me, so long but as a kiss may live;
And in my heartless breast and burning brain

That word, that kiss, shall all thoughts else survive,
With food of saddest memory kept alive, 230
Now thou art dead, as if it were a part
Of thee, my Adonais! I would give
All that I am to be as thou now art!
But I am chained to Time, and cannot thence depart!

XXVII

"O gentle child, beautiful as thou wert,
Why didst thou leave the trodden paths of men
Too soon, and with weak hands though mighty heart
Dare the unpastured dragon in his den?
Defenceless as thou wert, oh, where was then
Wisdom the mirrored shield, or scorn the spear? 240
Or hadst thou waited the full cycle, when
Thy spirit should have filled its crescent sphere,
The monsters of life's waste had fled from thee like deer.

XXVIII

"The herded wolves, bold only to pursue;
The obscene ravens, clamorous o'er the dead;
The vultures to the conqueror's banner true
Who feed where Desolation first has fed,
And whose wings rain contagion;—how they fled,
When, like Apollo, from his golden bow
The Pythian of the age one arrow sped 250
And smiled!—The spoilers tempt no second blow,
They fawn on the proud feet that spurn them lying low.

XXIX

"The sun comes forth, and many reptiles spawn;
He sets, and each ephemeral insect then

ADONAIS

Is gathered into death without a dawn,
And the immortal stars awake again;
So is it in the world of living men:
A godlike mind soars forth, in its delight
Making earth bare and veiling heaven, and when
It sinks, the swarms that dimmed or shared its light 260
Leave to its kindred lamps the spirit's awful night."

XXX

Thus ceased she: and the mountain shepherds came,
Their garlands sere, their magic mantles rent;
The Pilgrim of Eternity, whose fame
Over his living head like Heaven is bent,
An early but enduring monument,
Came, veiling all the lightnings of his song
In sorrow; from her wilds Ierne sent
The sweetest lyrist of her saddest wrong,
And Love taught Grief to fall like music from his tongue. 270

XXXI

Midst others of less note, came one frail Form,
A phantom among men; companionless
As the last cloud of an expiring storm
Whose thunder is its knell; he, as I guess,
Had gazed on Nature's naked loveliness,
Actaeon-like, and now he fled astray
With feeble steps o'er the world's wilderness,
And his own thoughts, along that rugged way,
Pursued, like raging hounds, their father and their prey.

XXXII

A pardlike Spirit beautiful and swift— 280
A Love in desolation masked;—a Power
Girt round with weakness;—it can scarce uplift
The weight of the superincumbent hour;
It is a dying lamp, a falling shower,
A breaking billow;—even whilst we speak
Is it not broken? On the withering flower
The killing sun smiles brightly: on a cheek
The life can burn in blood, even while the heart may break.

XXXIII

His head was bound with pansies overblown,
And faded violets, white, and pied, and blue; 290
And a light spear topped with a cypress cone,
Round whose rude shaft dark ivy-tresses grew
Yet dripping with the forest's noonday dew,
Vibrated, as the ever-beating heart
Shook the weak hand that grasped it; of that crew
He came the last, neglected and apart;
A herd-abandoned deer struck by the hunter's dart.

XXXIV

All stood aloof, and at his partial moan
Smiled through their tears; well knew that gentle band
Who in another's fate now wept his own, 300
As in the accents of an unknown land
He sung new sorrow; sad Urania scanned
The Stranger's mien, and murmured: "Who art thou?"
He answered not, but with a sudden hand

Made bare his branded and ensanguined brow,
Which was like Cain's or Christ's—oh! that it should
    be so!

XXXV

What softer voice is hushed over the dead?
Athwart what brow is that dark mantle thrown?
What form leans sadly o'er the white death-bed,
In mockery of monumental stone,
The heavy heart heaving without a moan?
If it be He, who, gentlest of the wise,
Taught, soothed, loved, honoured the departed one,
Let me not vex, with inharmonious sighs,
The silence of that heart's accepted sacrifice.

XXXVI

Our Adonais has drunk poison—oh!
What deaf and viperous murderer could crown
Life's early cup with such a draught of woe?
The nameless worm would now itself disown:
It felt, yet could escape, the magic tone
Whose prelude held all envy, hate, and wrong,
But what was howling in one breast alone,
Silent with expectation of the song,
Whose master's hand is cold, whose silver lyre unstrung.

XXXVII

Live thou, whose infamy is not thy fame!
Live! fear no heavier chastisement from me,
Thou noteless blot on a remembered name!
But be thyself, and know thyself to be!
And ever at thy season be thou free

To spill the venom when thy fangs o'erflow: 330
Remorse and Self-contempt shall cling to thee;
Hot Shame shall burn upon thy secret brow,
And like a beaten hound tremble thou shalt—as now.

XXXVIII

Nor let us weep that our delight is fled
Far from these carrion kites that scream below;
He wakes or sleeps with the enduring dead;
Thou canst not soar where he is sitting now—
Dust to the dust! but the pure spirit shall flow
Back to the burning fountain whence it came,
A portion of the Eternal, which must glow 340
Through time and change, unquenchably the same,
Whilst thy cold embers choke the sordid hearth of shame.

XXXIX

Peace, peace! he is not dead, he doth not sleep—
He hath awakened from the dream of life—
'T is we, who lost in stormy visions, keep
With phantoms an unprofitable strife,
And in mad trance, strike with our spirit's knife
Invulnerable nothings.—*We* decay
Like corpses in a charnel; fear and grief
Convulse us and consume us day by day, 350
And cold hopes swarm like worms within our living clay.

XL

He has outsoared the shadow of our night;
Envy and calumny and hate and pain,
And that unrest which men miscall delight,
Can touch him not and torture not again;

ADONAIS

From the contagion of the world's slow stain
He is secure, and now can never mourn
A heart grown cold, a head grown gray in vain;
Nor, when the spirit's self has ceased to burn,
With sparkless ashes load an unlamented urn.

XLI

He lives, he wakes—'t is Death is dead, not he;
Mourn not for Adonais.—Thou young Dawn,
Turn all thy dew to splendour, for from thee
The spirit thou lamentest is not gone;
Ye caverns and ye forests, cease to moan!
Cease, ye faint flowers and fountains, and thou Air,
Which like a mourning veil thy scarf hadst thrown
O'er the abandoned Earth, now leave it bare
Even to the joyous stars which smile on its despair!

XLII

He is made one with Nature: there is heard
His voice in all her music, from the moan
Of thunder, to the song of night's sweet bird;
He is a presence to be felt and known
In darkness and in light, from herb and stone,
Spreading itself where'er that Power may move
Which has withdrawn his being to its own;
Which wields the world with never-wearied love,
Sustains it from beneath, and kindles it above.

XLIII

He is a portion of the loveliness
Which once he made more lovely: he doth bear
His part, while the one Spirit's plastic stress

Sweeps through the dull dense world, compelling there,
All new successions to the forms they wear;
Torturing th' unwilling dross that checks its flight
To its own likeness, as each mass may bear;
And bursting in its beauty and its might
From trees and beasts and men into the Heaven's light.

XLIV

The splendours of the firmament of time
May be eclipsed, but are extinguished not;
Like stars to their appointed height they climb,   390
And death is a low mist which cannot blot
The brightness it may veil. When lofty thought
Lifts a young heart above its mortal lair,
And love and life contend in it, for what
Shall be its earthly doom, the dead live there
And move like winds of light on dark and stormy air.

XLV

The inheritors of unfulfilled renown
Rose from their thrones, built beyond mortal thought,
Far in the Unapparent. Chatterton
Rose pale,—his solemn agony had not   400
Yet faded from him; Sidney, as he fought
And as he fell and as he lived and loved
Sublimely mild, a Spirit without spot,
Arose; and Lucan, by his death approved:
Oblivion as they rose shrank like a thing reproved.

XLVI

And many more, whose names on Earth are dark,
But whose transmitted effluence cannot die

ADONAIS

So long as fire outlives the parent spark,
Rose, robed in dazzling immortality.
"Thou art become as one of us," they cry,
"It was for thee yon kingless sphere has long
Swung blind in unascended majesty,
Silent alone amid an Heaven of Song.
Assume thy wingèd throne, thou Vesper of our throng!"

XLVII

Who mourns for Adonais? Oh, come forth,
Fond wretch! and know thyself and him aright.
Clasp with thy panting soul the pendulous Earth;
As from a centre, dart thy spirit's light
Beyond all worlds, until its spacious might
Satiate the void circumference: then shrink
Even to a point within our day and night;
And keep thy heart light lest it make thee sink
When hope has kindled hope, and lured thee to the brink.

XLVIII

Or go to Rome, which is the sepulchre,
Oh, not of him, but of our joy: 't is nought
That ages, empires, and religions there
Lie buried in the ravage they have wrought;
For such as he can lend,—they borrow not
Glory from those who made the world their prey;
And he is gathered to the kings of thought
Who waged contention with their time's decay,
And of the past are all that cannot pass away.

XLIX

Go thou to Rome,—at once the Paradise,
The grave, the city, and the wilderness;
And where its wrecks like shattered mountains rise,
And flowering weeds, and fragrant copses dress
The bones of Desolation's nakedness,
Pass, till the spirit of the spot shall lead
Thy footsteps to a slope of green access,
Where, like an infant's smile, over the dead   440
A light of laughing flowers along the grass is spread;

L

And gray walls moulder round, on which dull Time
Feeds, like slow fire upon a hoary brand;
And one keen pyramid with wedge sublime,
Pavilioning the dust of him who planned
This refuge for his memory, doth stand
Like flame transformed to marble; and beneath,
A field is spread, on which a newer band
Have pitched in Heaven's smile their camp of death,
Welcoming him we lose with scarce extinguished
    breath.   450

LI

Here pause: these graves are all too young as yet
To have outgrown the sorrow which consigned
Its charge to each; and if the seal is set,
Here, on one fountain of a mourning mind,
Break it not thou! too surely shalt thou find
Thine own well full, if thou returnest home,
Of tears and gall. From the world's bitter wind

ADONAIS

Seek shelter in the shadow of the tomb.
What Adonais is, why fear we to become?

LII

The One remains, the many change and pass; 460
Heaven's light forever shines, Earth's shadows fly;
Life, like a dome of many-coloured glass,
Stains the white radiance of Eternity,
Until Death tramples it to fragments.—Die,
If thou wouldst be with that which thou dost seek!
Follow where all is fled!—Rome's azure sky,
Flowers, ruins, statues, music, words, are weak
The glory they tranfuse with fitting truth to speak.

LIII

Why linger, why turn back, why shrink, my Heart?
Thy hopes are gone before: from all things here 470
They have departed; thou shouldst now depart!
A light is passed from the revolving year,
And man, and woman; and what still is dear
Attracts to crush, repels to make thee wither.
The soft sky smiles,—the low wind whispers near:
'T is Adonais calls! oh, hasten thither,
No more let Life divide what Death can join together.

LIV

That Light whose smile kindles the Universe,
That Beauty in which all things work and move,
That Benediction which the eclipsing Curse 480
Of birth can quench not, that sustaining Love
Which through the web of being blindly wove
By man and beast and earth and air and sea,

Burns bright or dim, as each are mirrors of
The fire for which all thirst—now beams on me,
Consuming the last clouds of cold mortality.

LV

The breath whose might I have invoked in song
Descends on me; my spirit's bark is driven,
Far from the shore, far from the trembling throng
Whose sails were never to the tempest given; 490
The massy earth and spherèd skies are riven!
I am borne darkly, fearfully, afar;
Whilst, burning through the inmost veil of Heaven,
The soul of Adonais, like a star,
Beacons from the abode where the Eternal are.
   1821   1821

THE FINAL CHORUS FROM HELLAS

THE world's great age begins anew,
    The golden years return,
The earth doth like a snake renew
    Her winter weeds outworn:
Heaven smiles, and faith and empires gleam,
Like wrecks of a dissolving dream.

A brighter Hellas rears its mountains
    From waves serener far;
A new Peneus rolls his fountains
    Against the morning star.   10
Where fairer Tempes bloom, there sleep
Young Cyclads on a sunnier deep.

A loftier Argo cleaves the main,
    Fraught with a later prize;

FINAL CHORUS FROM HELLAS

Another Orpheus sings again,
   And loves, and weeps, and dies.
A new Ulysses leaves once more
Calypso for his native shore.

Oh, write no more the tale of Troy,
   If earth Death's scroll must be!
Nor mix with Laian rage the joy
   Which dawns upon the free:
Although a subtler Sphinx renew
Riddles of death Thebes never knew.

Another Athens shall arise,
   And to remoter time
Bequeath, like sunset to the skies,
   The splendor of its prime;
And leave, if naught so bright may live,
All earth can take or Heaven can give.

Saturn and Love their long repose
   Shall burst, more bright and good
Than all who fell, than One who rose,
   Than many unsubdued:
Not gold, not blood, their altar dowers,
But votive tears and symbol flowers.

O cease! must hate and death return?
   Cease! must men kill and die?
Cease! drain not to its dregs the urn
   Of bitter prophecy.
The world is weary of the past,
O might it die or rest at last!

1821   1822

TO ——

One word is too often profaned
    For me to profane it,
One feeling too falsely disdained
    For thee to disdain it;
One hope is too like despair
    For prudence to smother,
And pity from thee more dear
    Than that from another.

I can give not what men call love,
    But wilt thou accept not
The worship the heart lifts above
    And the Heavens reject not,—
The desire of the moth for the star,
    Of the night for the morrow,
The devotion to something afar
    From the sphere of our sorrow?

1821   1824

LINES: WHEN THE LAMP IS SHATTERED

I

When the lamp is shattered,
The light in the dust lies dead—
    When the cloud is scattered
The rainbow's glory is shed.
    When the lute is broken,
Sweet tones are remembered not;
    When the lips have spoken,
Loved accents are soon forgot.

WHEN THE LAMP IS SHATTERED

II

   As music and splendor
Survive not the lamp and the lute,   10
   The heart's echoes render
No song when the spirit is mute:—
   No song but sad dirges,
Like the wind through a ruined cell,
   Or the mournful surges
That ring the dead seaman's knell.

III

   When hearts have once mingled,
Love first leaves the well-built nest,
   The weak one is singled
To endure what it once possessed.   20
   O Love! who bewailest
The frailty of all things here,
   Why choose you the frailest
For your cradle, your home, and your bier?

IV

   Its passions will rock thee
As the storms rock the ravens on high:
   Bright reason will mock thee,
Like the sun from a wintry sky.
   From thy nest every rafter
Will rot, and thine eagle home   30
   Leave thee naked to laughter,
When leaves fall and cold winds come.

1822   1824

A DIRGE

Rough wind, that moanest loud
  Grief too sad for song;
Wild wind, when sullen cloud
  Knells all the night long;
Sad storm, whose tears are vain,
Bare woods, whose branches strain,
Deep caves and dreary main,—
  Wail, for the world's wrong!

1822   1824

JOHN KEATS (1795-1821)

KEEN, FITFUL GUSTS

Keen, fitful gusts are whisp'ring here and there
Among the bushes half leafless, and dry;
The stars look very cold about the sky,
And I have many miles on foot to fare.
Yet feel I little of the cool bleak air,
Or of the dead leaves rustling drearily,
Or of those silver lamps that burn on high,
Or of the distance from home's pleasant lair:
For I am brimful of the friendliness
That in a little cottage I have found;   10
Of fair-haired Milton's eloquent distress,
And all his love for gentle Lycid drowned;
Of lovely Laura in her light green dress,
And faithful Petrarch gloriously crowned.

1815   1817

ON FIRST LOOKING INTO CHAPMAN'S HOMER

Much have I travelled in the realms of gold,
And many goodly states and kingdoms seen;
Round many western islands have I been
Which bards in fealty to Apollo hold.
Oft of one wide expanse had I been told
That deep-browed Homer ruled as his demesne;
Yet did I never breathe its pure serene
Till I heard Chapman speak out loud and bold:
Then felt I like some watcher of the skies
When a new planet swims into his ken;   10
Or like stout Cortez when with eagle eyes
He stared at the Pacific—and all his men
Looked at each other with a wild surmise—
Silent, upon a peak in Darien.
1816   1817

TO ONE WHO HAS BEEN LONG IN CITY PENT

To one who has been long in city pent,
'Tis very sweet to look into the fair
And open face of heaven,—to breathe a prayer
Full in the smile of the blue firmament.
Who is more happy, when, with heart's content,
Fatigued he sinks into some pleasant lair
Of wavy grass, and reads a debonair
And gentle tale of love and languishment?
Returning home at evening, with an ear
Catching the notes of Philomel,—an eye   10
Watching the sailing cloudlet's bright career,
He mourns that day so soon has glided by:
E'en like the passage of an angel's tear

That falls through the clear ether silently.
1816   1817

PROEM TO ENDYMION

From BOOK I

A THING of beauty is a joy for ever:
Its loveliness increases; it will never
Pass into nothingness; but still will keep
A bower quiet for us, and a sleep
Full of sweet dreams, and health, and quiet breathing.
Therefore, on every morrow, are we wreathing
A flowery band to bind us to the earth,
Spite of despondence, of the inhuman dearth
Of noble natures, of the gloomy days,
Of all the unhealthy and o'er-darkened ways   10
Made for our searching: yes, in spite of all,
Some shape of beauty moves away the pall
From our dark spirits. Such the sun, the moon,
Trees old and young, sprouting a shady boon
For simple sheep: and such are daffodils
With the green world they live in; and clear rills
That for themselves a cooling covert make
'Gainst the hot season; the mid-forest brake,
Rich with a sprinkling of fair musk-rose blooms:
And such too is the grandeur of the dooms   20
We have imagined for the mighty dead;
All lovely tales that we have heard or read:
An endless fountain of immortal drink,
Pouring unto us from the heaven's brink.

Nor do we merely feel these essences
For one short hour; no, even as the trees
That whisper round a temple become soon

PROEM TO ENDYMION

Dear as the temple's self, so does the moon,
The passion poesy, glories infinite,
Haunt us till they become a cheering light
Unto our souls, and bound to us so fast,
That, whether there be shine, or gloom o'ercast,
They always must be with us, or we die.

Therefore, 't is with full happiness that I
Will trace the story of Endymion.
The very music of the name has gone
Into my being, and each pleasant scene
Is growing fresh before me as the green
Of our own valleys: so I will begin
Now while I cannot hear the city's din;
Now while the early budders are just new,
And run in mazes of the youngest hue
About old forests; while the willow trails
Its delicate amber; and the dairy pails
Bring home increase of milk. And, as the year
Grows lush in juicy stalks, I'll smoothly steer
My little boat, for many quiet hours,
With streams that deepen freshly into bowers.
Many and many a verse I hope to write,
Before the daisies, vermeil rimmed and white,
Hide in deep herbage; and ere yet the bees
Hum about globes of clover and sweet peas,
I must be near the middle of my story.
O may no wintry season, bare and hoary,
See it half finished; but let Autumn bold,
With universal tinge of sober gold,
Be all about me when I make an end.
And now at once, adventuresome, I send
My herald thought into a wilderness:
There let its trumpet blow, and quickly dress
My uncertain path with green, that I may speed

Easily onward, through flowers and weed.
    1817   1818

WHEN I HAVE FEARS

When I have fears that I may cease to be
Before my pen has gleaned my teeming brain,
Before high-pilèd books, in charactery,
Hold like rich garners the full ripened grain;
When I behold, upon the night's starred face,
Huge cloudy symbols of a high romance,
And think that I may never live to trace
Their shadows, with the magic hand of chance;
And when I feel, fair creature of an hour,
That I shall never look upon thee more,   10
Never have relish in the faery power
Of unreflecting love;—then on the shore
Of the wide world I stand alone, and think
Till love and fame to nothingness do sink.
    1818   1848

LINES ON THE MERMAID TAVERN

Souls of Poets dead and gone,
What Elysium have ye known,
Happy field or mossy cavern,
Choicer than the Mermaid Tavern?
Have ye tippled drink more fine
Than mine host's Canary wine?
Or are fruits of Paradise
Sweeter than those dainty pies
Of venison? O generous food!
Drest as though bold Robin Hood   10
Would, with his maid Marian,
Sup and bowse from horn and can.

I have heard that on a day
Mine host's sign-board flew away,
Nobody knew whither, till
An astrologer's old quill
To a sheepskin gave the story,
Said he saw you in your glory,
Underneath a new old sign
Sipping beverage divine,   20
And pledging with contented smack
The Mermaid in the Zodiac.

   Souls of Poets dead and gone,
What Elysium have ye known,
Happy field or mossy cavern,
Choicer than the Mermaid Tavern?

ROBIN HOOD

No! those days are gone away,
And their hours are old and gray,
And their minutes buried all
Under the down-trodden pall
Of the leaves of many years:
Many times have winter's shears,
Frozen North, and chilling East,
Sounded tempests to the feast
Of the forest's whispering fleeces.
Since men knew nor rent nor leases.   10

   No, the bugle sounds no more,
And the twanging bow no more;
Silent is the ivory shrill
Past the heath and up the hill;
There is no mid-forest laugh,

Where lone Echo gives the half
To some wight, amazed to hear
Jesting, deep in forest drear.

  On the fairest time of June
You may go, with sun or moon,   29
Or the seven stars to light you,
Or the polar ray to right you;
But you never may behold
Little John, or Robin bold;
Never one, of all the clan,
Thrumming on an empty can
Some old hunting ditty, while
He doth his green way beguile
To fair hostess Merriment,
Down beside the pasture Trent;   30
For he left the merry tale
Messenger for spicy ale.

  Gone, the merry morris din;
Gone, the song of Gamelyn;
Gone, the tough-belted outlaw
Idling in the "grene shawe;"
All are gone away and past!
And if Robin should be cast
Sudden from his turfèd grave,
And if Marian should have   40
Once again her forest days,
She would weep, and he would craze:
He would swear, for all his oaks,
Fallen beneath the dockyard strokes,
Have rotted on the briny seas;
She would weep that her wild bees
Sang not to her—strange! that honey
Can't be got without hard money!

> So it is: yet let us sing,
> Honor to the old bow-string! 50
> Honor to the bugle-horn!
> Honor to the woods unshorn!
> Honor to the Lincoln green!
> Honor to the archer keen!
> Honor to tight Little John,
> And the horse he rode upon!
> Honor to bold Robin Hood,
> Sleeping in the underwood!
> Honor to Maid Marian,
> And to all the Sherwood-clan! 60
> Though their days have hurried by,
> Let us two a burden try.

1818 1820

THE EVE OF ST. AGNES

I

St. Agnes' Eve—Ah, bitter chill it was!
The owl, for all his feathers, was a-cold;
The hare limped trembling through the frozen grass,
And silent was the flock in woolly fold:
Numb were the Beadsman's fingers, while he told
His rosary, and while his frosted breath,
Like pious incense from a censer old,
Seemed taking flight for heaven, without a death,
Past the sweet Virgin's picture, while his prayer he saith.

II

His prayer he saith, this patient, holy man; 10
Then takes his lamp, and riseth from his knees,

And back returneth, meagre, barefoot, wan,
Along the chapel aisle by slow degrees:
The sculptured dead, on each side, seem to freeze,
Emprisoned in black, purgatorial rails:
Knights, ladies, praying in dumb orat'ries,
He passeth by; and his weak spirit fails
To think how they may ache in icy hoods and mails.

III

Northward he turneth through a little door,
And scarce three steps, ere Music's golden tongue   20
Flattered to tears this agèd man and poor;
But no—already had his deathbell rung:
The joys of all his life were said and sung:
His was harsh penance on St. Agnes' Eve:
Another way he went, and soon among
Rough ashes sat he for his soul's reprieve,
And all night kept awake, for sinners' sake to grieve.

IV

That ancient Beadsman heard the prelude soft;
And so it chanced, for many a door was wide,
From hurry to and fro. Soon, up aloft,   30
The silver, snarling trumpets 'gan to chide:
The level chambers, ready with their pride,
Were glowing to receive a thousand guests:
The carvèd angels, ever eager-eyed,
Stared, where upon their heads the cornice rests,
With hair blown back, and wings put crosswise on their breasts.

V

At length burst in the argent revelry,
With plume, tiara, and all rich array,
Numerous as shadows haunting faerily
The brain, new stuffed, in youth, with triumphs gay   40
Of old romance. These let us wish away,
And turn, sole-thoughted, to one Lady there,
Whose heart had brooded, all that wintry day,
On love, and winged St. Agnes' saintly care,
As she had heard old dames full many times declare.

VI

They told her how, upon St. Agnes' Eve,
Young virgins might have visions of delight,
And soft adorings from their loves receive
Upon the honeyed middle of the night,
If ceremonies due they did aright;   50
As, supperless to bed they must retire,
And couch supine their beauties, lilly white;
Nor look behind, nor sideways, but require
Of Heaven with upward eyes for all that they desire.

VII

Full of this whim was thoughtful Madeline:
The music, yearning like a God in pain,
She scarcely heard: her maiden eyes divine,
Fixed on the floor, saw many a sweeping train
Pass by—she heeded not at all: in vain
Came many a tiptoe, amorous cavalier,   60
And back retired; not cooled by high disdain,

But she saw not: her heart was otherwhere:
She sighed for Agnes' dreams, the sweetest of the year.

VIII

She danced along with vague, regardless eyes,
Anxious her lips, her breathing quick and short:
The hallowed hour was near at hand: she sighs
Amid the timbrels, and the thronged resort
Of whisperers in anger, or in sport;
'Mid looks of love, defiance, hate, and scorn,
Hoodwinked with faery fancy; all amort, 70
Save to St. Agnes and her lambs unshorn,
And all the bliss to be before to-morrow morn.

IX

So, purposing each moment to retire,
She lingered still. Meantime, across the moors,
Had come young Porphyro, with heart on fire
For Madeline. Beside the portal doors,
Buttressed from moonlight, stands he, and implores
All saints to give him sight of Madeline,
But for one moment in the tedious hours,
That he might gaze and worship all unseen; 80
Perchance speak, kneel, touch, kiss—in sooth such things have been.

X

He ventures in: let no buzzed whisper tell:
All eyes be muffled, or a hundred swords
Will storm his heart, Love's fev'rous citadel:
For him, those chambers held barbarian hordes,
Hyena foemen, and hot-blooded lords,

THE EVE OF ST. AGNES

Whose very dogs would execrations howl
Against his lineage: not one breast affords
Him any mercy, in that mansion foul,
Save one old beldame, weak in body and in soul. 90

XI

Ah, happy chance! the agèd creature came,
Shuffling along with ivory-headed wand,
To where he stood, hid from the torch's flame,
Behind a broad hall-pillar, far beyond
The sound of merriment and chorus bland:
He startled her; but soon she knew his face,
And grasped his fingers in her palsied hand,
Saying, "Mercy, Porphyro! hie thee from this place:
They are all here to-night, the whole blood-thirsty race!

XII

"Get hence! get hence! there's dwarfish Hildebrand; 100
He had a fever late, and in the fit
He cursèd thee and thine, both house and land:
Then there's that old Lord Maurice, not a whit
More tame for his gray hairs—Alas me! flit!
Flit like a ghost away."—"Ah, Gossip dear,
We're safe enough; here in this arm-chair sit,
And tell me how"—"Good Saints! not here, not here;
Follow me, child, or else these stones will be thy bier."

XIII

He followed through a lowly archèd way,
Brushing the cobwebs with his lofty plume, 110
And as she muttered "Well-a—well-a-day!"
He found him in a little moonlight room,

Pale, latticed, chill, and silent as a tomb.
"Now tell me where is Madeline," said he,
"O tell me, Angela, by the holy loom
Which none but secret sisterhood may see,
When they St. Agnes' wool are weaving piously."

XIV

"St. Agnes! Ah! it is St. Agnes' Eve—
Yet men will murder upon holy days:
Thou must hold water in a witch's sieve, 120
And be liege-lord of all the Elves and Fays,
To venture so: it fills me with amaze
To see thee, Porphyro!—St. Agnes' Eve!
God's help! my lady fair the conjuror plays
This very night: good angels her deceive!
But let me laugh awhile, I've mickle time to grieve."

XV

Feebly she laugheth in the languid moon,
While Porphyro upon her face doth look,
Like puzzled urchin on an agèd crone
Who keepeth closed a wond'rous riddlebook, 130
As spectacled she sits in chimney nook.
But soon his eyes grew brilliant, when she told
His lady's purpose; and he scarce could brook
Tears, at the thought of those enchantments cold,
And Madeline asleep in lap of legends old.

XVI

Sudden a thought came like a full-blown rose,
Flushing his brow, and in his painèd heart
Made purple riot: then doth he propose

THE EVE OF ST. AGNES

A stratagem, that makes the beldame start:
"A cruel man and impious thou art: 140
Sweet lady, let her pray, and sleep, and dream
Alone with her good angels, far apart
From wicked men like thee. Go, go!—I deem
Thou canst not surely be the same that thou didst seem."

XVII

"I will not harm her, by all saints I swear,"
Quoth Porphyro: "O may I ne'er find grace
When my weak voice shall whisper its last prayer,
If one of her soft ringlets I displace,
Or look with ruffian passion in her face:
Good Angela, believe me by these tears; 150
Or I will, even in a moment's space,
Awake, with horrid shout, my foemen's ears,
And beard them, though they be more fanged than wolves and bears."

XVIII

"Ah! why wilt thou affright a feeble soul?
A poor, weak, palsy-stricken, churchyard thing,
Whose passing-bell may ere the midnight toll;
Whose prayers for thee, each morn and evening,
Were never missed."—Thus plaining, doth she bring
A gentler speech from burning Porphyro;
So woful, and of such deep sorrowing, 160
That Angela gives promise she will do
Whatever he shall wish, betide her weal or woe.

XIX

Which was, to lead him, in close secrecy,
Even to Madeline's chamber, and there hide

Him in a closet, of such privacy
That he might see her beauty unespied,
And win perhaps that night a peerless bride,
While legioned faeries paced the coverlet,
And pale enchantment held her sleepy-eyed.
Never on such a night have lovers met,   170
Since Merlin paid his Demon all the monstrous debt.

XX

"It shall be as thou wishest," said the Dame:
"All cates and dainties shall be storèd there
Quickly on this feast-night: by the tambour frame
Her own lute thou wilt see: no time to spare,
For I am slow and feeble, and scarce dare
On such a catering trust my dizzy head.
Wait here, my child, with patience; kneel in prayer
The while: Ah! thou must needs the lady wed,
Or may I never leave my grave among the dead."   180

XXI

So saying, she hobbled off with busy fear.
The lover's endless minutes slowly passed;
The dame returned, and whispered in his ear
To follow her; with agèd eyes aghast
From fright of dim espial. Safe at last,
Through many a dusky gallery, they gain
The maiden's chamber, silken, hushed, and chaste;
Where Porphyro took covert, pleased amain.
His poor guide hurried back with agues in her brain.

XXII

Her falt'ring hand upon the balustrade,   190
Old Angela was feeling for the stair,

THE EVE OF ST. AGNES

When Madeline, St. Agnes' charmèd maid,
Rose, like a missioned spirit, unaware:
With silver taper's light, and pious care,
She turned, and down the agèd gossip led
To a safe level matting. Now prepare,
Young Porphyro, for gazing on that bed;
She comes, she comes again, like ring-dove frayed and
  fled.

XXIII

Out went the taper as she hurried in;
Its little smoke, in pallid moonshine, died: 200
She closed the door, she panted, all akin
To spirits of the air, and visions wide:
No uttered syllable, or, woe betide!
But to her heart, her heart was voluble,
Paining with eloquence her balmy side;
As though a tongueless nightingale should swell
Her throat in vain, and die, heart-stifled, in her dell.

XXIV

A casement high and triple-arched there was,
All garlanded with carven imag'ries
Of fruits, and flowers, and bunches of knotgrass, 210
And diamonded with panes of quaint device,
Innumerable of stains and splendid dyes,
As are the tiger-moth's deep-damasked wings;
And in the midst, 'mong thousand heraldries,
And twilight saints, and dim emblazonings,
A shielded scutcheon blushed with blood of queens and
  kings.

XXV

Full on this casement shone the wintry moon,
And threw warm gules on Madeline's fair breast,
As down she knelt for heaven's grace and boon;
Rose-bloom fell on her hands, together prest,   220
And on her silver cross soft amethyst,
And on her hair a glory, like a saint:
She seemed a splendid angel, newly drest,
Save wings, for heaven:—Porphyro grew faint:
She knelt, so pure a thing, so free from mortal taint.

XXVI

Anon his heart revives: her vespers done,
Of all its wreathèd pearls her hair she frees;
Unclasps her warmèd jewels one by one;
Loosens her fragrant boddice; by degrees
Her rich attire creeps rustling to her knees: 230
Half-hidden, like a mermaid in sea-weed,
Pensive awhile she dreams awake, and sees,
In fancy, fair St. Agnes in her bed,
But dares not look behind, or all the charm is fled.

XXVII

Soon, trembling in her soft and chilly nest,
In sort of wakeful swoon, perplexed she lay,
Until the poppied warmth of sleep oppressed
Her soothèd limbs, and soul fatigued away;
Flown, like a thought, until the morrow-day;
Blissfully havened both from joy and pain;   240
Clasped like a missal where swart Paynims pray;

THE EVE OF ST. AGNES

Blinded alike from sunshine and from rain,
As though a rose should shut, and be a bud again.

XXVIII

Stol'n to this paradise, and so entranced,
Porphyro gazed upon her empty dress,
And listened to her breathing, if it chanced
To wake into a slumberous tenderness;
Which when he heard, that minute did he bless,
And breathed himself: then from the closet crept,
Noiseless as fear in a wide wilderness, 250
And over the hushed carpet, silent, stept,
And 'tween the curtains peeped, where, lo!—how fast she slept.

XXIX

Then by the bed-side, where the faded moon
Made a dim, silver twilight, soft he set
A table, and, half anguished, threw thereon
A cloth of woven crimson, gold, and jet:—
O for some drowsy Morphean amulet!
The boisterous, midnight, festive clarion,
The kettle-drum, and far-heard clarinet,
Affray his ears, though but in dying tone:— 260
The hall door shuts again, and all the noise is gone.

XXX

And still she slept an azure-lidded sleep,
In blanchèd linen, smooth, and lavendered,
While he from forth the closet brought a heap
Of candied apple, quince, and plum, and gourd;
With jellies soother than the creamy curd,
And lucent syrops, tinct with cinnamon;

Manna and dates, in argosy transferred
From Fez; and spicèd dainties, every one,
From silken Samarcand to cedared Lebanon.

XXXI

These delicates he heaped with glowing hand
On golden dishes and in baskets bright
Of wreathèd silver: sumptuous they stand
In the retirèd quiet of the night,
Filling the chilly room with perfume light.—
"And now, my love, my seraph fair, awake!
Thou art my heaven, and I thine eremite:
Open thine eyes, for meek St. Agnes' sake,
Or I shall drowse beside thee, so my soul doth ache."

XXXII

Thus whispering, his warm, unnervèd arm
Sank in her pillow. Shaded was her dream
By the dusk curtains:—'t was a midnight charm
Impossible to melt as icèd stream:
The lustrous salvers in the moonlight gleam;
Broad golden fringe upon the carpet lies:
It seemed he never, never could redeem
From such a stedfast spell his lady's eyes;
So mused awhile, entoiled in woofèd phantasies.

XXXIII

Awakening up, he took her hollow lute,—
Tumultuous,—and, in chords that tenderest be,
He played an ancient ditty, long since mute,
In Provence called, "La belle dame sans mercy:"
Close to her ear touching the melody;—

THE EVE OF ST. AGNES

Wherewith disturbed, she uttered a soft moan:
He ceased—she panted quick—and suddenly
Her blue affrayèd eyes wide open shone:
Upon his knees he sank, pale as smooth-sculptured stone.

XXXIV

Her eyes were open, but she still beheld,
Now wide awake, the vision of her sleep:
There was a painful change, that night expelled   300
The blisses of her dream so pure and deep
At which fair Madeline began to weep,
And moan forth witless words with many a sigh;
While still her gaze on Porphyro would keep;
Who knelt, with joinèd hands and piteous eye,
Fearing to move or speak, she looked so dreamingly.

XXXV

"Ah, Porphyro!" said she, "but even now
Thy voice was at sweet tremble in mine ear,
Made tuneable with every sweetest vow;
And those sad eyes were spiritual and clear: 310
How changed thou art! how pallid, chill, and drear!
Give me that voice again, my Porphyro,
Those looks immortal, those complainings dear!
Oh leave me not in this eternal woe,
For if thou diest, my Love, I know not where to go."

XXXVI

Beyond a mortal man impassioned far
At these voluptuous accents, he arose,
Ethereal, flushed, and like a throbbing star
Seen mid the sapphire heaven's deep repose;

Into her dream he melted, as the rose 320
Blendeth its odour with the violet,—
Solution sweet: meantime the frost-wind blows
Like Love's alarum pattering the sharp sleet
Against the window-panes; St. Agnes' moon hath set.

XXXVII

'T is dark: quick pattereth the flaw-blown sleet:
"This is no dream, my bride, my Madèline!"
'T is dark: the icèd gusts still rave and beat:
"No dream, alas! alas! and woe is mine!
Porphyro will leave me here to fade and pine.—
Cruel! what traitor could thee hither bring? 330
I curse not, for my heart is lost in thine,
Though thou forsakest a deceivèd thing;—
A dove forlorn and lost with sick unprunèd wing."

XXXVIII

"My Madeline! sweet dreamer! lovely bride!
Say, may I be for aye thy vassal blest?
Thy beauty's shield, heart-shaped and vermeil dyed?
Ah, silver shrine, here will I take my rest
After so many hours of toil and quest,
A famished pilgrim,—saved by miracle.
Though I have found, I will not rob thy nest 340
Saving of thy sweet self; if thou think'st well
To trust, fair Madeline, to no rude infidel.

XXXIX

"Hark! 't is an elfin-storm from faery land,
Of haggard seeming, but a boon indeed:
Arise—arise! the morning is at hand;—

The bloated wassaillers will never heed:—
Let us away, my love, with happy speed;
There are no ears to hear, or eyes to see,—
Drowned all in Rhenish and the sleepy mead:
Awake! arise! my love, and fearless be,   350
For o'er the southern moors I have a home for thee."

XL

She hurried at his words, beset with fears,
For there were sleeping dragons all around,
At glaring watch, perhaps, with ready spears—
Down the wide stairs a darkling way they found.—
In all the house was heard no human sound.
A chain-drooped lamp was flickering by each door;
The arras, rich with horseman, hawk, and hound,
Fluttered in the besieging wind's uproar;
And the long carpets rose along the gusty floor.   360

XLI

They glide, like phantoms, into the wide hall;
Like phantoms, to the iron porch, they glide;
Where lay the Porter, in uneasy sprawl,
With a huge empty flaggon by his side:
The wakeful bloodhound rose, and shook his hide,
But his sagacious eye an inmate owns:
By one, and one, the bolts full easy slide:—
The chains lie silent on the footworn stones;—
The key turns, and the door upon its hinges groans.

XLII

And they are gone: aye, ages long ago   370
These lovers fled away into the storm.

That night the Baron dreamt of many a woe,
And all his warrior-guests, with shade and form
Of witch, and demon, and large coffin-worm,
Were long be-nightmared. Angela the old
Died palsy-twitched, with meagre face deform:
The Beadsman, after thousand aves told,
For aye unsought for slept among his ashes cold.
  1819   1820

LA BELLE DAME SANS MERCI

Ah, what can ail thee, wretched wight,
    Alone and palely loitering;
The sedge is withered from the lake,
    And no birds sing.

Ah, what can ail thee, wretched wight,
    So haggard and so woe-begone?
The squirrel's granary is full,
    And the harvest's done.

I see a lily on thy brow,
    With anguish moist and fever dew;   10
And on thy cheek a fading rose
    Fast withereth too.

I met a lady in the meads
    Full beautiful, a faery's child;
Her hair was long, her foot was light,
    And her eyes were wild.

I set her on my pacing steed,
    And nothing else saw all day long;
For sideways would she lean, and sing
    A faery's song.   20

LA BELLE DAME SANS MERCI

I made a garland for her head,
    And bracelets too, and fragrant zone;
She looked at me as she did love,
    And made sweet moan.

She found me roots of relish sweet,
    And honey wild, and manna dew;
And sure in language strange she said,
    "I love thee true."

She took me to her elfin grot,
    And there she gazed and sighèd deep,   30
And there I shut her wild sad eyes—
    So kissed to sleep.

And there we slumbered on the moss,
    And there I dreamed, ah woe betide,
The latest dream I ever dreamed
    On the cold hill side.

I saw pale kings, and princes too,
    Pale warriors, death-pale were they all;
Who cried—"La belle Dame sans merci
    Hath thee in thrall!"   40

I saw their starved lips in the gloam
    With horrid warning gapèd wide,
And I awoke, and found me here
    On the cold hill side.

And this is why I sojourn here
    Alone and palely loitering,
Though the sedge is withered from the lake,
    And no birds sing.

1819   1820

ODE

Bards of Passion and of Mirth

Bards of Passion and of Mirth,
Ye have left your souls on earth!
Have ye souls in heaven too,
Double-lived in regions new?
Yes, and those of heaven commune
With the spheres of sun and moon;
With the noise of fountains wond'rous,
And the parle of voices thund'rous;
With the whisper of heaven's trees
And one another, in soft ease   10
Seated on Elysian lawns
Browsed by none but Dian's fawns;
Underneath large blue-bells tented,
Where the daisies are rose-scented,
And the rose herself has got
Perfume which on earth is not;
Where the nightingale doth sing
Not a senseless, trancèd thing,
But divine melodious truth;
Philosophic numbers smooth;   20
Tales and golden histories
Of heaven and its mysteries.

 Thus ye live on high, and then
On the earth ye live again;
And the souls ye left behind you
Teach us, here, the way to find you,
Where your other souls are joying,
Never slumbered, never cloying.

ODE TO A NIGHTINGALE

Here, your earth-born souls still speak
To mortals, of their little week;   30
Of their sorrows and delights;
Of their passions and their spites;
Of their glory and their shame;
What doth strengthen and what maim.
Thus ye teach us, every day,
Wisdom, though fled far away.

Bards of Passion and of Mirth,
Ye have left your souls on earth!
Ye have souls in heaven too,
Doubled-lived in regions new!   40

1819   1820

ODE TO A NIGHTINGALE

I

My heart aches, and a drowsy numbness pains
  My sense, as though of hemlock I had drunk,
Or emptied some dull opiate to the drains
  One minute past, and Lethe-wards had sunk:
'T is not through envy of thy happy lot,
  But being too happy in thine happiness,—
    That thou, light-wingèd Dryad of the trees,
      In some melodious plot
Of beechen green, and shadows numberless,
  Singest of summer in full-throated ease.   10

II

O, for a draught of vintage! that hath been
  Cooled a long age in the deep-delvèd earth,

Tasting of Flora and the country green,
  Dance, and Provençal song, and sunburnt mirth!
O for a beaker full of the warm South,
  Full of the true, the blushful Hippocrene,
    With beaded bubbles winking at the brim,
      And purple-stainèd mouth;
  That I might drink, and leave the world unseen,
    And with thee fade away into the forest dim: 20

III

Fade far away, dissolve, and quite forget
  What thou among the leaves hast never known,
The weariness, the fever, and the fret
  Here, where men sit and hear each other groan;
Where palsy shakes a few, sad, last gray hairs,
  Where youth grows pale, and spectre-thin, and dies;
    Where but to think is to be full of sorrow
      And leaden-eyed despairs,
  Where Beauty cannot keep her lustrous eyes,
    Or new Love pine at them beyond to-morrow. 30

IV

Away! away! for I will fly to thee,
  Not charioted by Bacchus and his pards,
But on the viewless wings of Poesy,
  Though the dull brain perplexes and retards:
Already with thee! tender is the night,
  And haply the Queen-Moon is on her throne,
    Clustered around by all her starry Fays;
      But here there is no light,
  Save what from heaven is with the breezes blown
    Through verdurous glooms and winding mossy ways. 40

ODE TO A NIGHTINGALE

V

I cannot see what flowers are at my feet,
  Nor what soft incense hangs upon the boughs,
But, in embalmèd darkness, guess each sweet
  Wherewith the seasonable month endows
The grass, the thicket, and the fruit-tree wild;
  White hawthorn, and the pastoral eglantine;
    Fast fading violets covered up in leaves;
      And mid-May's eldest child,
  The coming musk-rose, full of dewy wine,
    The murmurous haunt of flies on summer eves. 50

VI

Darkling I listen; and, for many a time
  I have been half in love with easeful Death,
Called him soft names in many a musèd rhyme,
  To take into the air my quiet breath;
Now more than ever seems it rich to die,
  To cease upon the midnight with no pain,
    While thou art pouring forth thy soul abroad
      In such an ecstasy!
  Still wouldst thou sing, and I have ears in vain—
    To thy high requiem become a sod. 60

VII

Thou wast not born for death, immortal Bird!
  No hungry generations tread thee down;
The voice I hear this passing night was heard
  In ancient days by emperor and clown:

Perhaps the self-same song that found a path
  Through the sad heart of Ruth, when, sick for home,
    She stood in tears amid the alien corn;
      The same that oft-times hath
  Charmed magic casements, opening on the foam
    Of perilous seas, in faery lands forlorn.   70

VIII

Forlorn! the very word is like a bell
  To toll me back from thee to my sole self!
Adieu! the fancy cannot cheat so well
  As she is famed to do, deceiving elf.
Adieu! adieu! thy plaintive anthem fades
  Past the near meadows, over the still stream,
    Up the hill-side; and now 't is buried deep
      In the next valley-glades:
  Was it a vision, or a waking dream?
    Fled is that music:—Do I wake or sleep?   80
1819   1820

ODE ON A GRECIAN URN

I

THOU still unravished bride of quietness,
  Thou foster-child of silence and slow time,
Sylvan historian, who canst thus express
  A flowery tale more sweetly than our rhyme:
What leaf-fringed legend haunts about thy shape
  Of deities or mortals, or of both,
    In Tempe or the dales of Arcady?
  What men or gods are these? What maidens loth?
What mad pursuit? What struggle to escape?
    What pipes and timbrels? What wild ecstasy?   10

ODE ON A GRECIAN URN

II

Heard melodies are sweet, but those unheard
    Are sweeter; therefore, ye soft pipes, play on;
Not to the sensual ear, but, more endeared,
    Pipe to the spirit ditties of no tone:
Fair youth, beneath the trees, thou canst not leave
    Thy song, nor ever can those trees be bare;
      Bold Lover, never, never canst thou kiss,
Though winning near the goal—yet, do not grieve;
      She cannot fade, though thou hast not thy bliss,
        For ever wilt thou love, and she be fair!   20

III

Ah, happy, happy boughs! that cannot shed
    Your leaves, nor ever bid the Spring adieu;
And, happy melodist, unwearièd,
    For ever piping songs for ever new;
More happy love! more happy, happy love!
    For ever warm and still to be enjoyed,
      For ever panting, and for ever young;
All breathing human passion far above,
    That leaves a heart high-sorrowful and cloyed,
      A burning forehead, and a parching tongue.   30

IV

Who are these coming to the sacrifice?
    To what green altar, O mysterious priest,
Lead'st thou that heifer lowing at the skies,
    And all her silken flanks with garlands drest?

What little town by river or sea shore,
  Or mountain-built with peaceful citadel,
    Is emptied of this folk, this pious morn?
And, little town, thy streets for evermore
  Will silent be; and not a soul to tell
    Why thou art desolate, can e'er return.   40

v

O Attic shape! Fair attitude! with brede
  Of marble men and maidens overwrought,
With forest branches and the trodden weed;
  Thou, silent form, dost tease us out of thought
As doth eternity: Cold Pastoral!
  When old age shall this generation waste,
    Thou shalt remain, in midst of other woe
Than ours, a friend to man, to whom thou say'st,
    "Beauty is truth, truth beauty,"—that is all
      Ye know on earth, and all ye need to know.   50
1819   1820

ODE TO PSYCHE

O Goddess! hear these tuneless numbers, wrung
  By sweet enforcement and remembrance dear,
And pardon that thy secrets should be sung
  Even into thine own soft-conchèd ear:
Surely I dreamt to-day, or did I see
  The wingèd Psyche with awakened eyes?
I wandered in a forest thoughtlessly,
  And, on the sudden, fainting with surprise,
Saw two fair creatures, couchèd side by side
  In deepest grass, beneath the whisp'ring roof   10
    Of leaves and trembled blossoms, where there ran
      A brooklet, scarce espied:

ODE TO PSYCHE

'Mid hushed, cool-rooted flowers, fragrant-eyed,
   Blue, silver-white, and budded Tyrian,
They lay calm-breathing on the bedded grass;
   Their arms embracèd, and their pinions too;
   Their lips touched not, but had not bade adieu,
As if disjoinèd by soft-handed slumber,
And ready still past kisses to outnumber
   At tender eye-dawn of aurorean love:
        The wingèd boy I knew;
   But who wast thou, O happy, happy dove?
        His Psyche true!

O latest born and loveliest vision far
   Of all Olympus' faded hierarchy!
Fairer than Phœbe's sapphire-regioned star,
   Or Vesper, amorous glow-worm of the sky;
Fairer than these, though temple thou hast none,
        Nor altar heaped with flowers;
Nor virgin-choir to make delicious moan
        Upon the midnight hours;
No voice, no lute, no pipe, no incense sweet
   From chain-swung censer teeming;
No shrine, no grove, no oracle, no heat
   Of pale-mouthed prophet dreaming.

O brightest! though too late for antique vows,
   Too, too late for the fond believing lyre,
When holy were the haunted forest boughs,
   Holy the air, the water, and the fire;
Yet even in these days so far retired
   From happy pieties, thy lucent fans,
   Fluttering among the faint Olympians,
I see, and sing, by my own eyes inspired.
So let me be thy choir, and make a moan
        Upon the midnight hours;

Thy voice, thy lute, thy pipe, thy incense sweet
  From swingèd censer teeming;
Thy shrine, thy grove, thy oracle, thy heat
  Of pale-mouthed prophet dreaming.

Yes, I will be thy priest, and build a fane   50
  In some untrodden region of my mind,
Where branchèd thoughts, new grown with pleasant pain,
  Instead of pines shall murmur in the wind:
Far, far around shall those dark-clustered trees
  Fledge the wild-ridgèd mountains steep by steep;
And there by zephyrs, streams, and birds, and bees,
  The moss-lain Dryads shall be lulled to sleep;
And in the midst of this wide quietness
A rosy sanctuary will I dress
With the wreathed trellis of a working brain,   60
  With buds, and bells, and stars without a name,
With all the gardener Fancy e'er could feign,
  Who breeding flowers, will never breed the same:
And there shall be for thee all soft delight
  That shadowy thought can win,
A bright torch, and a casement ope at night,
  To let the warm Love in!
1819   1820

ODE ON MELANCHOLY

I

No, no, go not to Lethe, neither twist
  Wolf's-bane, tight-rooted, for its poisonous wine;
Nor suffer thy pale forehead to be kissed
  By nightshade, ruby grape of Proserpine;

ODE ON MELANCHOLY

Make not your rosary of yew-berries,
  Nor let the beetle, nor the death-moth be
    Your mournful Psyche, nor the downy owl
A partner in your sorrow's mysteries;
  For shade to shade will come too drowsily,
    And drown the wakeful anguish of the soul.   10

II

But when the melancholy fit shall fall
  Sudden from heaven like a weeping cloud,
That fosters the droop-headed flowers all,
  And hides the green hill in an April shroud;
Then glut thy sorrow on a morning rose,
  Or on the rainbow of the salt sand-wave,
    Or on the wealth of globèd peonies;
Or if thy mistress some rich anger shows,
  Emprison her soft hand, and let her rave,
    And feed deep, deep upon her peerless eyes.   20

III

She dwells with Beauty—Beauty that must die;
  And Joy, whose hand is ever at his lips
Bidding adieu; and aching Pleasure nigh,
  Turning to Poison while the bee-mouth sips:
Ay, in the very temple of delight
  Veiled Melancholy has her sovran shrine,
    Though seen of none save him whose strenuous tongue
  Can burst Joy's grape against his palate fine;
His soul shall taste the sadness of her might,
  And be among her cloudy trophies hung.   30

1819   1820

JOHN KEATS

TO AUTUMN

I

Season of mists and mellow fruitfulness,
   Close bosom-friend of the maturing sun;
Conspiring with him how to load and bless
   With fruit the vines that round the thatch-eves run;
To bend with apples the mossed cottage-trees,
   And fill all fruit with ripeness to the core;
     To swell the gourd, and plump the hazel shells
With a sweet kernel; to set budding more,
And still more, later flowers for the bees,
Until they think warm days will never cease,   10
   For Summer has o'er-brimmed their clammy cells.

II

Who hath not seen thee oft amid thy store?
   Sometimes whoever seeks abroad may find
Thee sitting careless on a granary floor,
   Thy hair soft-lifted by the winnowing wind;
Or on a half-reaped furrow sound asleep,
   Drowsed with the fume of poppies, while thy hook
     Spares the next swath and all its twinèd flowers:
And sometimes like a gleaner thou dost keep
   Steady thy laden head across a brook;   20
Or by a cider-press, with patient look,
   Thou watchest the last oozings hours by hours.

III

Where are the songs of Spring? Ay, where are they?
   Think not of them, thou hast thy music too.—

While barrèd clouds bloom the soft-dying day,
  And touch the stubble-plains with rosy hue;
Then in a wailful choir the small gnats mourn
  Among the river sallows, borne aloft
    Or sinking as the light wind lives or dies;
And full-grown lambs loud bleat from hilly bourn;   30
  Hedge-crickets sing; and now with treble soft
The red-breast whistles from a garden-croft;
    And gathering swallows twitter in the skies.
1819   1820

BRIGHT STAR

Bright star, would I were steadfast as thou art—
Not in lone splendour hung aloft the night
And watching, with eternal lids apart,
Like nature's patient, sleepless Eremite,
The moving waters at their priestlike task
Of pure ablution round earth's human shores,
Or gazing on the new soft-fallen mask
Of snow upon the mountains and the moors—
No—yet still steadfast, still unchangeable,
Pillowed upon my fair love's ripening breast,   10
To feel for ever its soft fall and swell,
Awake for ever in a sweet unrest,
Still, still to hear her tender-taken breath,
And so live ever—or else swoon to death.
1820   1846

WALTER SAVAGE LANDOR (1775-1864)

ROSE AYLMER

Ah, what avails the sceptered race,
Ah, what the form divine!

What every virtue, every grace!
  Rose Aylmer, all were thine.
Rose Aylmer, whom these wakeful eyes
  May weep, but never see,
A night of memories and of sighs
  I consecrate to thee.

1806

LYRICS TO IANTHE

MILD IS THE PARTING YEAR

Mild is the parting year, and sweet
  The odor of the falling spray;
Life passes on more rudely fleet,
  And balmless is its closing day.

I wait its close, I court its gloom,
  But mourn that never must there fall
Or on my breast or on my tomb
  The tear that would have soothed it all.

1831

PAST RUINED ILION

Past ruined Ilion Helen lives,
  Alcestis rises from the shades;
Verse calls them forth; 't is verse that gives
  Immortal youth to mortal maids.

Soon shall Oblivion's deepening veil
  Hide all the peopled hills you see,
The gay, the proud, while lovers hail,
  These many summers, you and me.

1831

THE DEATH OF ARTEMIDORA

"ARTEMIDORA! Gods invisible,
While thou art lying faint along the couch,
Have tied the sandal to thy slender feet
And stand beside thee, ready to convey
Thy weary steps where other rivers flow.
Refreshing shades will waft thy weariness
Away, and voices like thy own come near
And nearer, and solicit an embrace."
    Artemidora sighed, and would have pressed
The hand now pressing hers, but was too weak.   10
Iris stood over her dark hair unseen
While thus Elpenor spake. He looked into
Eyes that had given light and life erewhile
To those above them, but now dim with tears
And wakefulness. Again he spake of joy
Eternal. At that word, that sad word, *joy,*
Faithful and fond her bosom heaved once more:
Her head fell back; and now a loud deep sob
Swelled through the darkened chamber; 't was not hers.
                                                      1836

TO ROBERT BROWNING

THERE is delight in singing, though none hear
Beside the singer; and there is delight
In praising, though the praiser sit alone
And see the praised far off him, far above.
Shakespeare is not our poet, but the world's,
Therefore on him no speech! and brief for thee,
Browning! Since Chaucer was alive and hale,
No man hath walkt along our roads with step
So active, so inquiring eye, or tongue

So varied in discourse. But warmer climes 10
Give brighter plumage, stronger wing: the breeze
Of Alpine heights thou playest with, borne on
Beyond Sorrento and Amalfi, where
The Siren waits thee, singing song for song.

1846

IMAGINARY CONVERSATIONS

ADMIRAL BLAKE AND HUMPHREY BLAKE

Blake. Humphrey! it hath pleased God, upon this day, to vouchsafe unto the English arms a signal victory. Brother! it grieves my heart that neither of us can rejoice in it as we should do. Evening is closing on the waters: our crews are returning thanks and offering up prayers to the Almighty. Alas! Alas! that we, who ought to be the most grateful for his protection, and for the spirit he hath breathed into our people, should be the only men in this vast armament whom he hath sorely chastened!—that we of all others should be ashamed to approach the throne of grace among our countrymen and comrades! There are those who accuse you, and they are brave and honest men—there are those, O Humphrey! Humphrey!—was the sound ever heard in our father's house?—who accuse you, brother! brother!—how can I ever find utterance for the word? —yea, of cowardice.

Stand off! I want no help: let me be.

Humphrey. To-day, for the first time in my life, I was in the midst of many ships of superior force firing upon mine, at once and incessantly.

Blake. The very position where most intrepidity was required. Were none with you?—were none in the same 'anger? Shame, shame! You owed many an example,

IMAGINARY CONVERSATIONS

and you defrauded them of it. They could not gain promotion, the poor seamen! they could not hope for glory in the wide world: example they might have hoped for. You would not have robbed them of their prize-money—

Humphrey. Brother! was ever act of dishonesty imputed to a Blake?

Blake. Until now. You have robbed them even of the chance they had of winning it; you have robbed them of the pride, the just and chastened pride, awaiting them at home; you have robbed their children of their richest inheritance, a father's good repute.

Humphrey. Despite of calumniators, there are worthy men ready to speak in my favour, at least in extenuation—

Blake. I will hear them, as becomes me, although I myself am cognizant of your default; for during the conflict how anxiously, as often as I could, did I look toward your frigate! Especial care could not be fairly taken that aid at the trying moment should be at hand: other vessels were no less exposed than yours; and it was my duty to avoid all partiality in giving my support.

Humphrey. Grievous as my short-coming may be, surely I am not precluded from what benefit the testimony of my friends may afford me.

Blake. Friends!—ah, thou hast many, Humphrey! and many hast thou well deserved. In youth, in boyhood, in childhood, thy honied temper brought ever warm friends about thee. Easiness of disposition conciliates bad and good alike; it draws affections to it, and relaxes enmities: but that same easiness renders us, too often, negligent of our graver duties. God knows, I may without the same excuse (if it is any) be impeached of negligence in many of mine; but never where the honour or safety of my country was concerned. Wherefore the Almighty's hand, in this last battle, as in others no less prosperous, hath conducted and sustained me.

Humphrey! did thy heart wax faint within thee through want of confidence in our sole Deliverer?

Humphrey. Truly I have no such plea.

Blake. It were none; it were an aggravation.

Humphrey. I confess I am quite unable to offer any adequate defence for my backwardness, my misconduct. Oh! could the hour return, the battle rage again! How many things are worse than death!—how few things better! I am twelve years younger than you are, brother, and want your experience.

Blake. Is that your only want? Deplorable is it to know, as now I know, that you will never have it, and that you will have a country which you can never serve.

Humphrey. Deplorable it is, indeed. God help me!

Blake. Worse evil soon may follow,—worse to me, remembering thy childhood. Merciful Father! after all the blood that hath been shed this day, must I devote a brother's?

Humphrey. O Robert!—always compassionate, always kind and generous!—do not inflict on yourself so lasting a calamity, so unavailing a regret.

Listen!—not to me—but listen. I hear under your bow the sound of oars. I hear them drawn into boats: verily do I believe that several of the captains are come to intercede for me, as they said they would do.

Blake. Intercession is vain. Honourable men shall judge you. A man to be honourable must be strictly just, at the least. Will brave men spare you? It lies with them. Whatever be their sentence, my duty is (God give me strength!) to execute it.

Gentlemen! who sent for you? [*Officers come aboard*].

Senior Officer. General! we, the captains of your fleet, come before you upon the most painful of duties.

Blake (to himself). I said so: his doom is sealed. (*To Senior Officer.*) Speak, sir! speak out, I say. A man who hath fought so bravely as you have fought to-day ought never to hesitate and falter.

Senior Officer. General! we grieve to say that Captain Humphrey Blake, commanding a frigate in the service of the Commonwealth, is accused of remissness in his duty.

Blake. I know it. Where is the accuser? What! no answer from any of you? Then I am he. Captain Humphrey Blake is here impleaded of neglecting to perform his uttermost in the seizure or destruction of the enemy's galleons. Is the crime—write it, write it down!—no need to speak it here—capital? Negligence? no worse? But worse can there be?

Senior Officer. We would humbly represent—

Blake. Representations, if made at all, must be made elsewhere. He goes forthwith to England. Return each of you to his vessel. Delinquency, grave delinquency, there hath been, of what nature and to what extent you must decide. Take him away. (*Alone.*) Just God! am I the guilty man, that I should drink to the very dregs such a cup of bitterness?

Forgive, forgive, O Lord! the sinful cry of thy servant! Thy will be done! Thou hast shown thy power this day, O Lord! now show, and make me worthy of, thy mercy!

Various and arduous as were Blake's duties, such on all occasions were his circumspection and discretion, that no fault could be detected or invented in him. His victories were won against all calculation but his own. Recollecting, however late, his services; recollecting that in private life, in political, in military, his purity was ever the same,—England will place Robert Blake the foremost and the highest of her defenders. He was the archetype of her Nelsons, Collingwoods, and Pellews. Of all the men that ever bore a sword, none was worthier of that awful trust.

1853

ON HIS SEVENTY-FIFTH BIRTHDAY

I strove with none, for none was worth my strife,
   Nature I loved, and next to Nature, Art;
I warmed both hands before the fire of life,
   It sinks, and I am ready to depart.

1853

TO MY NINTH DECADE

To my ninth decade I have tottered on,
   And no soft arm bends now my steps to steady;
She, who once led me where she would, is gone,
   So when he calls me, Death shall find me ready.

1863

THOMAS HOOD (1799-1845)

THE BRIDGE OF SIGHS

One more Unfortunate,
   Weary of breath,
Rashly importunate,
   Gone to her death!

Take her up tenderly,
   Lift her with care;
Fashioned so slenderly,
   Young, and so fair!

Look at her garments
Clinging like cerements;   10

THE BRIDGE OF SIGHS

Whilst the wave constantly
  Drips from her clothing;
Take her up instantly,
  Loving, not loathing.

Touch her not scornfully;
Think of her mournfully,
  Gently and humanly:
Not of the stains of her,
All that remains of her
  Now is pure womanly. 20

Make no deep scrutiny
Into her mutiny
  Rash and undutiful:
Past all dishonour,
Death has left on her
  Only the beautiful.

Still, for all slips of hers,
  One of Eve's family—
Wipe those poor lips of hers
  Oozing so clammily. 30

Loop up her tresses
  Escaped from the comb,
Her fair auburn tresses;
Whilst wonderment guesses
  Where was her home?

Who was her father?
  Who was her mother?
Had she a sister?
  Had she a brother?
Or was there a dearer one 40

Still, and a nearer one
 Yet, than all other?

Alas! for the rarity
Of Christian charity
 Under the sun!
O, it was pitiful!
Near a whole city full,
 Home she had none.

Sisterly, brotherly,
Fatherly, motherly   50
 Feelings had changed:
Love, by harsh evidence,
Thrown from its eminence;
Even God's providence
 Seeming estranged.

Where the lamps quiver
So far in the river,
 With many a light
From window to casement,
From garret to basement,   60
She stood with amazement,
 Houseless by night.

The bleak wind of March
 Made her tremble and shiver;
But not the dark arch,
 Or the black flowing river:
Mad from life's history,
Glad to death's mystery,
 Swift to be hurled—
Anywhere, anywhere   70
 Out of the world!

THE BRIDGE OF SIGHS

In she plunged boldly—
No matter how coldly
  The rough river ran—
Over the brink of it,
Picture it—think of it,
  Dissolute Man!
Lave in it, drink of it,
  Then, if you can!

Take her up tenderly,
  Lift her with care;
Fashioned so slenderly,
  Young, and so fair!

Ere her limbs frigidly
Stiffen too rigidly,
  Decently, kindly,
Smooth and compose them;
And her eyes, close them,
  Staring so blindly!

Dreadfully staring
  Through muddy impurity,
As when with the daring
Last look of despairing
  Fixed on futurity.

Perishing gloomily,
Spurred by contumely,
Cold inhumanity,
Burning insanity,
  Into her rest—
Cross her hands humbly,
As if praying dumbly,
  Over her breast!

Owning her weakness,
　　Her evil behaviour,
And leaving with meekness,
　　Her sins to her Saviour!

1843

THE SONG OF THE SHIRT

With fingers weary and worn,
　　With eyelids heavy and red,
A woman sat, in unwomanly rags,
　　Plying her needle and thread—
Stitch! stitch! stitch!
　　In poverty, hunger, and dirt,
And still with a voice of dolorous pitch
　　She sang the "Song of the Shirt."

"Work! work! work!
　　While the cock is crowing aloof!
And work—work—work,
　　Till the stars shine through the roof!
It's Oh! to be a slave
　　Along with the barbarous Turk,
Where woman has never a soul to save,
　　If this is Christian work!

"Work—work—work,
　　Till the brain begins to swim;
Work—work—work,
　　Till the eyes are heavy and dim!
Seam, and gusset, and band,
　　Band, and gusset, and seam,
Till over the buttons I fall asleep,
　　And sew them on in a dream!

THE SONG OF THE SHIRT

"Oh, Men, with Sisters dear!
  Oh, Men, with Mothers and Wives!
It is not linen you're wearing out
  But human creatures' lives!
Stitch—stitch—stitch,
  In poverty, hunger, and dirt,   30
Sewing at once, with a double thread,
  A Shroud as well as a Shirt.

"But why do I talk of Death?
  That Phantom of grisly bone,
I hardly fear its terrible shape,
  It seems so like my own—
It seems so like my own,
  Because of the fasts I keep;
Oh, God! that bread should be so dear,
  And flesh and blood so cheap!   40

"Work—work—work!
  My labor never flags;
And what are its wages? A bed of straw,
  A crust of bread—and rags.
That shattered roof—this naked floor—
  A table—a broken chair—
And a wall so blank, my shadow I thank
  For sometimes falling there!

"Work—work—work!
  From weary chime to chime,   50
Work—work—work,
  As prisoners work for crime!
Band, and gusset, and seam,
  Seam, and gusset, and band,
Till the heart is sick, and the brain benumbed,
  As well as the weary hand.

"Work—work—work!
　　In the dull December light,
And work—work—work,
　　When the weather is warm and bright—
While underneath the eaves
　　The brooding swallows cling
As if to show me their sunny backs
　　And twit me with the spring.

"Oh! but to breathe the breath
　　Of the cowslip and primrose sweet—
With the sky above my head,
　　And the grass beneath my feet;
For only one short hour
　　To feel as I used to feel,
Before I knew the woes of want
　　And the walk that costs a meal.

"Oh! but for one short hour!
　　A respite however brief!
No blessèd leisure for Love or Hope,
　　But only time for Grief!
A little weeping would ease my heart,
　　But in their briny bed
My tears must stop, for every drop
　　Hinders needle and thread!"

With fingers weary and worn,
　　With eyelids heavy and red,
A woman sat, in unwomanly rags,
　　Plying her needle and thread—
Stitch! stitch! stitch!
　　In poverty, hunger, and dirt,
And still with a voice of dolorous pitch,—

Would that its tone could reach the Rich!—
She sang this "Song of the Shirt!"

1843

CHARLES LAMB (1775-1834)

DREAM-CHILDREN: A REVERIE

CHILDREN love to listen to stories about their elders, when *they* were children; to stretch their imagination to the conception of a traditionary great-uncle or grandame whom they never saw. It was in this spirit that my little ones crept about me the other evening to hear about their great-grandmother Field, who lived in a great house in Norfolk (a hundred times bigger than that in which they and papa lived) which had been the scene —so at least it was generally believed in that part of the country—of the tragic incidents which they had lately become familiar with from the ballad of the Children in the Wood. Certain it is that the whole story of the children and their cruel uncle was to be seen fairly carved out in wood upon the chimney-piece of the great hall, the whole story down to the Robin Redbreasts, till a foolish rich person pulled it down to set up a marble one of modern invention in its stead, with no story upon it. Here Alice put out one of her dear mother's looks, too tender to be called upbraiding. Then I went on to say how religious and how good their great-grandmother Field was, how beloved and respected by everybody, though she was not indeed the mistress of this great house, but had only the charge of it (and yet in some respects she might be said to be the mistress of it too) committed to her by the owner, who preferred living in a newer and more fashionable mansion which he had purchased somewhere in the adjoining county; but still she lived in it in a manner as if it had been her own, and kept up the dignity of the great house in a sort while she lived, which afterwards came to decay, and was nearly pulled down, and all its old ornaments stripped and carried away to the owner's other house, where they were set up, and looked as awkward as if some one were to carry away the old tombs they had seen lately at the Abbey, and stick them up in Lady C.'s tawdry gilt drawing-room. Here John smiled, as much as to say, "that would be foolish indeed." And then I told how, when she came to die, her funeral was attended by a concourse of all the poor, and some of the gentry too, of the neighborhood for many miles round, to show their respect for her memory, because she had been such a good and religious woman; so good indeed that she knew all the Psaltery by heart, ay, and a great part of the Testament besides. Here little Alice spread her hands. Then I told what a tall, upright, graceful person their great-grandmother Field once was; and how in her youth she was esteemed the best dancer—here Alice's little right foot played an involuntary movement, till, upon my looking grave, it desisted—the best dancer, I was saying, in the county, till a cruel disease, called a cancer, came, and bowed her down with pain; but it could never bend her good spirits, or make them stoop, but they were still upright, because she was so good and religious. Then I told how she was used to sleep by herself in a lone chamber of the great lone house; and how she believed that an apparition of two infants was to be seen at midnight gliding up and down the great staircase near where she slept, but she said "those innocents would do her no harm"; and how frightened I used to be, though in those days I had my maid to sleep

DREAM-CHILDREN

with me, because I was never half so good or religious as she—and yet I never saw the infants. Here John expanded all his eyebrows and tried to look courageous. Then I told how good she was to all her grandchildren, having us to the great house in the holidays, where I in particular used to spend many hours by myself, in gazing upon the old busts of the twelve Cæsars, that had been Emperors of Rome, till the old marble heads would seem to live again, or I to be turned into marble with them; how I never could be tired with roaming about that huge mansion, with its vast empty rooms, with their worn-out hangings, fluttering tapestry, and carved oaken panels, with the gilding almost rubbed out—sometimes in the spacious old-fashioned gardens, which I had almost to myself, unless when now and then a solitary gardening man would cross me; and how the nectarines and peaches hung upon the walls, without my ever offering to pluck them, because they were forbidden fruit, unless now and then—and because I had more pleasure in strolling about among the old melancholy-looking yew-trees, or the firs, and picking up the red berries, and the fir-apples, which were good for nothing but to look at—or in lying about upon the fresh grass with all the fine garden smells around me—or basking in the orangery, till I could almost fancy myself ripening too along with the oranges and the limes in that grateful warmth—or in watching the dace that darted to and fro in the fish-pond at the bottom of the garden, with here and there a great sulky pike hanging midway down the water in silent state, as if it mocked at their impertinent friskings,—I had more pleasure in these busy-idle diversions than in all the sweet flavours of peaches, nectarines, oranges, and such-like common baits of children. Here John slyly deposited back upon the plate a bunch of grapes, which, not unobserved by Alice, he had meditated dividing with her, and both seemed willing to relinquish them for the present as irrelevant. Then, in somewhat a more heightened tone, I told how, though their great-grandmother Field loved all her grandchildren, yet in an especial manner she might be said to love their uncle, John L——, because he was so handsome and spirited a youth, and a king to the rest of us; and, instead of moping about in solitary corners, like some of us, he would mount the most mettlesome horse he could get, when but an imp no bigger than themselves, and make it carry him half over the county in a morning, and join the hunters when there were any out—and yet he loved the old great house and gardens too, but had too much spirit to be always pent up within their boundaries—and how their uncle grew up to man's estate as brave as he was handsome, to the admiration of everybody, but of their great-grandmother Field most especially; and how he used to carry me upon his back when I was a lame-footed boy—for he was a good bit older than me—many a mile when I could not walk for pain; and how in after life he became lame-footed too, and I did not always, I fear, make allowances enough for him when he was impatient, and in pain, nor remember sufficiently how considerate he had been to me when I was lame-footed; and how when he died, though he had not been dead an hour, it seemed as if he had died a great while ago, such a distance there is betwixt life and death; and how I bore his death as I thought pretty well at first, but afterwards it haunted and haunted me; and though I did not cry or take it to heart as some do, and as I think he would have done if I had died, yet I missed him all day long, and knew not till then how much I had loved him. I missed his kindness, and I missed his crossness, and wished him to be alive again, to be quarreling with him (for we quarreled sometimes), rather than not have him again, and was as uneasy without him, as he, their poor uncle, must have been when the doctor took off his limb.—Here the children fell a crying, and asked if their little mourning which they had on was not for Uncle John, and they looked up, and prayed me not to go on about their uncle, but to tell them some stories about their pretty dead mother. Then I told how for seven long years, in hope sometimes, sometimes in despair, yet persisting ever, I courted the fair Alice W———n; and, as much as children could understand, I explained to them what coyness, and difficulty, and denial, meant in maidens—when suddenly, turning to Alice, the soul of the first Alice looked out at her eyes with such a reality of re-presentment, that I became in doubt which of them stood there before me, or whose that bright hair was; and while I stood gazing, both the children gradually grew fainter to my view, receding, and still receding, till nothing at last but two mournful features were seen in the uttermost distance, which, without speech, strangely impressed upon me the effects of speech: "We are not of Alice, nor of thee, nor are we children at all. The children of Alice call Bartrum father. We are nothing; less than nothing, and dreams. We are only what might have been, and must wait upon the tedious shores of Lethe millions of ages before we have existence and a name"————and immediately awaking, I found myself quietly seated in my bachelor arm-chair, where I had fallen asleep, with the faithful Bridget unchanged by my side—but John L. (or James Elia) was gone for ever.

1822

THE SUPERANNUATED MAN

Sera tamen respexit
Libertas. —Virgil

A Clerk I was in London gay.
—O'Keefe

If peradventure, Reader, it has been thy lot to waste the golden years of thy life, thy shining youth, in the irksome confinement of an office; to have thy prison days prolonged through middle age down to decrepitude and silver hairs, without hope of release or respite; to have lived to forget that there are such things as holidays, or to remember them but as the prerogatives of childhood; then, and then only, will you be able to appreciate my deliverance.

It is now six and thirty years since I took my seat at the desk in Mincing Lane. Melancholy was the transition at fourteen from the abundant playtime, and the frequently intervening vacations of school days, to the eight, nine, and sometimes ten hours a-day attendance at the counting-house. But time partially reconciles us to any thing. I gradually became content—doggedly contented, as wild animals in cages.

It is true I had my Sundays to myself; but Sundays, admirable as the institution of them is for purposes of worship, are for that very reason the very worst adapted for days of unbending and recreation. In particular, there is a gloom for me attendant upon a city Sunday, a weight in the air. I miss the cheerful cries of London, the music, and the ballad-singers—the buzz and stirring murmur of the streets. Those eternal bells depress me. The closed shops repel me. Prints, pictures, all the glittering and endless succession of knacks and gewgaws, and ostentatiously displayed wares of trades-

THE SUPERANNUATED MAN

men, which make a week-day saunter through the less busy parts of the metropolis so delightful—are shut out. No book-stalls deliciously to idle over—No busy faces to recreate the idle man who contemplates them ever passing by—the very face of business a charm by contrast to his temporary relaxation from it. Nothing to be seen but unhappy countenances—or half-happy at best—of emancipated 'prentices and little tradesfolk, with here and there a servant maid that has got leave to go out, who, slaving all the week, with the habit has lost almost the capacity of enjoying a free hour, and livelily expressing the hollowness of a day's pleasuring. The very strollers in the fields on that day looked any thing but comfortable.

But besides Sundays I had a day at Easter, and a day at Christmas, with a full week in the summer to go and air myself in my native fields of Hertfordshire. This last was a great indulgence; and the prospect of its recurrence, I believe, alone kept me up through the year, and made my durance tolerable. But when the week came around, did the glittering phantom of the distance keep touch with me? or rather was it not a series of seven uneasy days, spent in restless pursuit of pleasure, and a wearisome anxiety to find out how to make the most of them? Where was the quiet? where the promised rest? Before I had a taste of it, it was vanished. I was at the desk again, counting upon the fifty-one tedious weeks that must intervene before such another snatch would come. Still the prospect of its coming threw something of an illumination upon the darker side of my captivity. Without it, as I have said, I could scarcely have sustained my thraldom.

Independently of the rigours of attendance, I have ever been haunted with a sense (perhaps a mere caprice) of incapacity for business. This, during my latter years, had increased to such a degree, that it was visible in all the lines of my countenance. My health and my good spirits flagged. I had perpetually a dread of some crisis, to which I should be found unequal. Besides my daylight servitude, I served over again all night in my sleep, and would awake with terrors of imaginary false entries, errors in my accounts, and the like. I was fifty years of age, and no prospect of emancipation presented itself. I had grown to my desk, as it were; and the wood had entered into my soul.

My fellows in the office would sometimes rally me upon the trouble legible in my countenance; but I did not know that it had raised the suspicions of any of my employers, when, on the fifth of last month, a day ever to be remembered by me, L——, the junior partner in the firm, calling me on one side, directly taxed me with my bad looks, and frankly inquired the cause of them. So taxed, I honestly made confession of my infirmity, and added that I was afraid I should eventually be obliged to resign his service. He spoke some words of course to hearten me, and there the matter rested. A whole week I remained labouring under the impression that I had acted imprudently in my disclosure; that I had foolishly given a handle against myself, and had been anticipating my own dismissal. A week passed in this manner, the most anxious one, I verily believe, in my whole life, when on the evening of the twelfth of April, just as I was about quitting my desk to go home (it might be about eight o'clock) I received an awful summons to attend the presence of the whole assembled firm in the formidable back parlour. I thought now my time was surely come, I have done for myself, I am going to be told that they have no longer occasion for me. L——, I could see, smiled at the terror I was in, which was a little relief to me,—when to my utter

THE SUPERANNUATED MAN

astonishment B——, the eldest partner, began a formal harangue to me on the length of my services, my very meritorious conduct during the whole of the time (the deuce, thought I, how did he find out that? I protest I never had the confidence to think as much). He went on to descant on the expediency of retiring at a certain time of life (how my heart panted!), and asking me a few questions as to the amount of my own property, of which I have a little, ended with a proposal, to which his three partners nodded a grave assent, that I should accept from the house, which I had served so well, a pension for life to the amount of two-thirds of my accustomed salary—a magnificent offer! I do not know what I answered between surprise and gratitude, but it was understood that I accepted their proposal, and I was told that I was free from that hour to leave their service. I stammered out a bow, and at just ten minutes after eight I went home—for ever. This noble benefit (gratitude forbids me to conceal their names) I owe to the kindness of the most munificent firm in the world—the house of Boldero, Merryweather, Bosanquet, and Lacy.

Esto perpetua!

For the first day or two I felt stunned, overwhelmed. I could only apprehend my felicity; I was too confused to taste it sincerely. I wandered about, thinking I was happy, and knowing that I was not. I was in the condition of a prisoner in the Old Bastile, suddenly let loose after a forty years' confinement. I could scarce trust myself with myself. It was like passing out of Time into Eternity—for it is a sort of Eternity for a man to have his Time all to himself. It seemed to me that I had more time on my hands than I could ever manage.

From a poor man, poor in Time, I was suddenly lifted up into a vast revenue; I could see no end of my possessions: I wanted some steward, or judicious bailiff, to manage my estates in Time for me. And here let me caution persons grown old in active business, not lightly, nor without weighing their own resources, to forego their customary employment all at once, for there may be danger in it. I feel it by myself, but I know that my resources are sufficient; and now that those first giddy raptures have subsided, I have a quiet home-feeling of the blessedness of my condition. I am in no hurry. Having all holidays, I am as though I had none. If Time hung heavy upon me, I could walk it away; but I do *not* walk all day long, as I used to do in those transient holidays, thirty miles a day, to make the most of them. If Time were troublesome, I could read it away; but I do *not* read in that violent measure, with which, having no Time my own but candlelight Time, I used to weary out my head and eye-sight in by-gone winters. I walk, read, or scribble (as now) just when the fit seizes me. I no longer hunt after pleasure; I let it come to me. I am like the man

—"that's born, and has his years come to him,
In some green desert."

"Years!" you will say! "what is that superannuated simpleton calculating upon? He has already told us he is past fifty."

I have indeed lived nominally fifty years; but deduct out of them the hours which I have lived to other people, and not to myself, and you will find me still a young fellow: for *that* is the only true Time which a man can properly call his own, that which he has all to himself; the rest, though in some sense he may be said to live it,

THE SUPERANNUATED MAN

is other people's time, not his. The remnant of my poor days, long or short, is at least multiplied for me threefold. My ten next years, if I stretch so far, will be as long as any preceding thirty. 'T is a fair Rule-of-Three sum.

Among the strange fantasies which beset me at the commencement of my freedom, and of which all traces are not yet gone, one was, that a vast tract of time had intervened since I quitted the Counting House. I could not conceive of it as an affair of yesterday. The partners, and the clerks, with whom I had for so many years and for so many hours in each day of the year been closely associated, being suddenly removed from them, they seemed as dead to me. There is a fine passage, which may serve to illustrate this fancy, in a tragedy by Sir Robert Howard, speaking of a friend's death:—

> ——" 'T was but just now he went away;
> I have not since had time to shed a tear;
> And yet the distance does the same appear
> As if he had been a thousand years from me.
> Time takes no measure in Eternity."

To dissipate this awkward feeling, I have been fain to go among them once or twice since; to visit my old desk-fellows—my co-brethren of the quill—that I had left below in the state militant. Not all the kindness with which they received me could quite restore to me that pleasant familiarity which I had hitherto enjoyed among them. We cracked some of our old jokes, but methought they went off but faintly. My old desk, the peg where I hung my hat, were appropriated to another. I knew it must be, but I could not take it kindly. D——l take me, if I did not feel some remorse—beast, if I had not—at quitting my old compeers, the faithful partners of my toils for six and thirty years, that smoothed for me with their jokes and conundrums the ruggedness of my professional road. Had it been so rugged then, after all? or was I a coward simply? Well, it is too late to repent; and I also know that these suggestions are a common fallacy of the mind on such occasions. But my heart smote me. I had violently broken the bands betwixt us. It was at least not courteous. I shall be some time before I get quite reconciled to the separation. Farewell, old cronies; yet not for long, for again and again I will come among ye, if I shall have your leave. Farewell, Ch——, dry, sarcastic, and friendly! Do——, mild, slow to move, and gentlemanly! Pl——, officious to do and to volunteer, good services!—and thou, thou dreary pile, fit mansion for a Gresham or a Whittington of old, stately House of Merchants; with thy labyrinthine passages, and light-excluding, pent-up offices, where candles for one half the year supplied the place of the sun's light; unhealthy contributor to my weal, stern fosterer of my living, farewell! In thee remain, and not in the obscure collection of some wandering bookseller, my "works!" There let them rest, as I do from my labours, piled on thy massy shelves, more MSS. in folio than ever Aquinas left, and full as useful! My mantle I bequeath among ye.

A fortnight has passed since the date of my first communication. At that period I was approaching to tranquillity, but had not reached it. I boasted of a calm indeed, but it was comparative only. Something of the first flutter was left; an unsettling sense of novelty; the dazzle to weak eyes of unaccustomed light. I missed my old chains, forsooth, as if they had been some necessary part of my apparel. I was a poor Carthusian, from strict cellular discipline suddenly by some revolution re-

THE SUPERANNUATED MAN

turned upon the world. I am now as if I had never been other than my own master. It is natural to me to go where I please, to do what I please. I find myself at eleven o'clock in the day in Bond Street, and it seems to me that I have been sauntering there at that very hour for years past. I digress into Soho, to explore a bookstall. Methinks I have been thirty years a collector. There is nothing strange nor new in it. I find myself before a fine picture in the morning. Was it ever otherwise? What is become of Fish Street Hill? Where is Fenchurch Street? Stones of old Mincing Lane, which I have worn with my daily pilgrimage for six and thirty years, to the footsteps of what toil-worn clerk are your everlasting flints now vocal? I indent the gayer flags of Pall Mall. It is 'Change time, and I am strangely among the Elgin marbles. It was no hyperbole when I ventured to compare the change in my condition to a passing into another world. Time stands still in a manner to me. I have lost all distinction of season. I do not know the day of the week or of the month. Each day used to be individually felt by me in its reference to the foreign post days; in its distance from, or propinquity to, the next Sunday. I had my Wednesday feelings, my Saturday nights' sensations. The genius of each day was upon me distinctly during the whole of it, affecting my appetite, spirits, &c. The phantom of the next day, with the dreary five to follow, sate as a load upon my poor Sabbath recreations. What charm has washed that Ethiop white? What is gone of Black Monday? All days are the same. Sunday itself —that unfortunate failure of a holiday, as it too often proved, what with my sense of its fugitiveness, and overcare to get the greatest quantity of pleasure out of it—is melted down into a week day. I can spare time to go to church now, without grudging the huge cantle which it used to seem to cut out of the holiday. I have Time for everything. I can visit a sick friend. I can interrupt the man of much occupation when he is busiest. I can insult over him with an invitation to take a day's pleasure with me to Windsor this fine May morning. It is Lucretian pleasure to behold the poor drudges, whom I have left behind in the world, carking and caring; like horses in a mill, drudging on in the same eternal round: and what is it all for? A man can never have too much Time to himself, nor too little to do. Had I a little son, I would christen him NOTHING-TO-DO; he should do nothing. Man, I verily believe, is out of his element as long as he is operative. I am altogether for the life contemplative. Will no kindly earthquake come and swallow up those accursed cotton mills? Take me that lumber of a desk there, and bowl it down

"As low as the fiends."

I am no longer ———, clerk to the Firm of, &c. I am Retired Leisure. I am to be met with in trim gardens. I am already come to be known by my vacant face and careless gesture, perambulating at no fixed pace, nor with any settled purpose. I walk about; not to and from. They tell me, a certain *cum dignitate* air, that has been buried so long with my other good parts, has begun to shoot forth in my person. I perceptibly grow into gentility. When I take up a newspaper, it is to read the state of the opera. *Opus operatum est.* I have done all that I came into this world to do. I have worked task-work, and have the rest of the day to myself.

1825

WILLIAM HAZLITT (1778-1830)

ON POETRY IN GENERAL

(*From* LECTURES ON ENGLISH POETS)

* * * * * *

POETRY is the language of the imagination and the passions. It relates to whatever gives immediate pleasure or pain to the human mind. It comes home to the bosoms and businesses of men; for nothing but what so comes home to them in the most general and intelligible shape, can be a subject for poetry. Poetry is the universal language which the heart holds with nature and itself. He who has a contempt for poetry cannot have much respect for himself, or for anything else. It is not a mere frivolous accomplishment (as some persons have been led to imagine), the trifling amusement of a few idle readers or leisure hours—it has been the study and delight of mankind in all ages. Many people suppose that poetry is something to be found only in books, contained in lines of ten syllables, with like endings: but wherever there is a sense of beauty, or power, or harmony, as in the motion of a wave of the sea, in the growth of a flower that "spreads its sweet leaves to the air and dedicates its beauty to the sun,"— *there* is poetry, in its birth. If history is a grave study, poetry may be said to be a graver: its materials lie deeper, and are spread wider. History treats, for the most part, of the cumbrous and unwieldy masses of things, the empty cases in which the affairs of the world are packed, under the heads of intrigue or war, in different states, and from century to century: but there is no thought or feeling that can have entered into the mind of man, which he would be eager to communicate to others, or which they would listen to with delight, that is not a fit subject for poetry. It is not a branch of authorship: it is "the stuff of which our life is made." The rest is "mere oblivion," a dead letter: for all that is worth remembering in life, is the poetry of it. Fear is poetry, hope is poetry, love is poetry, hatred is poetry; contempt, jealousy, remorse, admiration, wonder, pity, despair, or madness, are all poetry. Poetry is that fine particle within us, that expands, rarefies, refines, raises our whole being: without it "man's life is poor as beast's." Man is a poetical animal: and those of us who do not study the principles of poetry, act upon them all our lives, like Molière's *Bourgeois Gentilhomme,* who had always spoken prose without knowing it. The child is a poet in fact, when he first plays at hide-and-seek, or repeats the story of Jack the Giant-killer; the shepherd-boy is a poet, when he first crowns his mistress with a garland of flowers; the countryman, when he stops to look at the rainbow; the city-apprentice, when he gazes after the Lord-Mayor's show; the miser, when he hugs his gold; the courtier, who builds his hopes upon a smile; the savage, who paints his idol with blood; the slave, who worships a tyrant, or the tyrant, who fancies himself a god;—the vain, the ambitious, the proud, the choleric man, the hero and the coward, the beggar and the king, the rich and the poor, the young and the old, all live in a world of their own making; and the poet does no more than describe what all the others think and act.

* * * * * *

If poetry is a dream, the business of life is much the same. If it is a fiction, made up of what we wish things to be, and fancy that they are, because we wish them so, there is no other or better reality. Ariosto has described the loves of Angelica and Medoro: but was not Medoro, who carved the name of his mistress on the barks of trees, as much enamoured of her charms as he? Homer has celebrated the anger of Achilles; but was not the hero as mad as the poet? Plato banished the poets from his commonwealth, lest their descriptions of the natural man should spoil his mathematical man, who was to be without passions and affections, who was neither to laugh nor weep, to feel sorrow nor anger, to be cast down nor elated by any thing. This was a chimera, however, which never existed but in the brain of the inventor; and Homer's poetical world has outlived Plato's philosophical Republic.

Poetry then is an imitation of nature, but the imagination and the passions are a part of man's nature. We shape things according to our wishes and fancies, without poetry; but poetry is the most emphatical language that can be found for those creations of the mind "which ecstasy is very cunning in." Neither a mere description of natural objects, nor a mere delineation of natural feelings, however distinct or forcible, constitutes the ultimate end and aim of poetry, without the heightenings of the imagination. The light of poetry is not only a direct but also a reflected light, that while it shows us the object, throws a sparkling radiance on all around it: the flame of the passions, communicated to the imagination, reveals to us, as with a flash of lightning, the inmost recesses of thought, and penetrates our whole being. Poetry represents forms chiefly as they suggest other forms; feelings, as they suggest forms or other feelings. Poetry puts a spirit of life and motion into the universe. It describes the flowing, not the fixed. It does not define the limits of sense, or analyze the distinctions of the understanding, but signifies the excess of the imagination beyond the actual or ordinary impression of any object or feeling. The poetical impression of any object is that uneasy, exquisite sense of beauty or power that cannot be contained within itself; that is impatient of all limit; that (as flame bends to flame) strives to link itself to some other image of kindred beauty or grandeur; to enshrine itself, as it were, in the highest forms of fancy, and to relieve the aching sense of pleasure by expressing it in the boldest manner, and by the most striking examples of the same quality in other instances. Poetry, according to Lord Bacon, for this reason "has something divine in it, because it raises the mind and hurries it into sublimity, by conforming the shows of things to the desires of the soul, instead of subjecting the soul to external things, as reason and history do." It is strictly the language of the imagination; and the imagination is that faculty which represents objects, not as they are in themselves, but as they are molded by other thoughts and feelings into an infinite variety of shapes and combinations of power. This language is not the less true to nature because it is false in point of fact; but so much the more true and natural, if it conveys the impression which the object under the influence of passion makes on the mind. 1818

* * * * * *

ON FAMILIAR STYLE

It is not easy to write a familiar style. Many people mistake a familiar for a vulgar style, and suppose that to write without affectation is to write at random. On the contrary, there is nothing that requires more precision, and, if I may so say, purity of expression, than the style I am speaking of. It utterly rejects not only all unmeaning pomp, but all low, cant phrases, and loose, unconnected, *slipshod* allusions. It is not to take the first word that offers, but the best word in common use; it is not to throw words together in any combinations we please, but to follow and avail ourselves of the true idiom of the language. To write a genuine familiar or truly English style, is to write as any one would speak in common conversation who had a thorough command and choice of words, or who could discourse with ease, force, and perspicuity, setting aside all pedantic and oratorical flourishes. Or to give another illustration, to write naturally is the same thing in regard to common conversation as to read naturally is in regard to common speech. It does not follow that it is an easy thing to give the true accent and inflection to the words you utter, because you do not attempt to rise above the level of ordinary life and colloquial speaking. You do not assume, indeed, the solemnity of the pulpit, or the tone of stage-declamation: neither are you at liberty to gabble on at a venture, without emphasis or discretion, or to resort to vulgar dialect or clownish pronunciation. You must steer a middle course. You are tied down to a given and appropriate articulation, which is determined by the habitual associations between sense and sound, and which you can only hit by entering into the author's meaning, as you must find the proper words and style to express yourself by fixing your thoughts on the subject you have to write about. Any one may mouth out a passage with a theatrical cadence, or get upon stilts to tell his thoughts; but to write or speak with propriety and simplicity is a more difficult task. Thus it is easy to affect a pompous style, to use a word twice as big as the thing you want to express: it is not so easy to pitch upon the very word that exactly fits it. Out of eight or ten words equally common, equally intelligible, with nearly equal pretensions, it is a matter of some nicety and discrimination to pick out the very one the preferableness of which is scarcely perceptible, but decisive. The reason why I object to Dr. Johnson's style is, that there is no discrimination, no selection, no variety in it. He uses none but "tall, opaque words," taken from the "first row of the rubric;" —words with the greatest number of syllables, or Latin phrases with merely English terminations. If a fine style depended on this sort of arbitrary pretension, it would be fair to judge of an author's elegance by the measurement of his words, and the substitution of foreign circumlocutions (with no precise associations) for the mother-tongue. How simple it is to be dignified without ease, to be pompous without meaning! Surely, it is but a mechanical rule for avoiding what is low, to be always pedantic and affected. It is clear you cannot use a vulgar English word, if you never use a common English word at all. A fine tact is shown in adhering to those which are perfectly common, and yet never falling into any expressions which are debased by disgusting circumstances, or which owe their signification and point to technical or professional allusions. A truly natural or familiar style can never be quaint or vulgar, for this reason, that it is of universal force and applicability, and that quaintness and vulgarity arise out of the immediate connection of certain words with coarse and disagreeable or with confined ideas. The last form what we understand by *cant* or *slang* phrases.—To give an example of what is not very clear in the general statement. I should say that the phrase *To cut with a knife,* or *To cut a piece of wood,* is perfectly free from vulgarity, because it is perfectly common: but *To cut an acquaintance* is not quite unexceptionable, because it is not perfectly common or intelligible, and has hardly yet escaped out of the limits of slang phraseology. I should hardly therefore use the word in this sense without putting it in italics as a license of expression, to be received *cum grano salis*. All provincial or bye-phrases come under the same mark of reprobation—all such as the writer transfers to the page from his fireside or a particular *coterie,* or that he invents for his own sole use and convenience. I conceive that words are like money, not the worse for being common, but that it is the stamp of custom alone that gives them circulation or value. I am fastidious in this respect, and would almost as soon coin the currency of the realm as counterfeit the King's English. I never invented or gave a new and unauthorized meaning to any word but one single one (the term *impersonal* applied to feelings), and that was in an abstruse metaphysical discussion to express a very difficult distinction. I have been (I know) loudly accused of revelling in vulgarisms and broken English. I cannot speak to that point: but so far I plead guilty to the determined use of acknowledged idioms and common elliptical expressions. I am not sure that the critics in question know the one from the other, that is, can distinguish any medium between formal pedantry and the most barbarous solecism. As an author, I endeavor to employ plain words and popular modes of construction, as, were I a chapman and dealer, I should common weights and measures.

The proper force of words lies not in the words themselves, but in their application. A word may be a fine-sounding word, of an unusual length, and very imposing from its learning and novelty, and yet in the connection in which it is introduced may be quite pointless and irrelevant. It is not pomp or pretension, but the adaptation of the expression to the idea that clenches a writer's meaning:—as it is not the size or glossiness of the materials, but their being fitted each to its place, that gives strength to the arch; or as the pegs and nails are as necessary to the support of the building as the larger timbers, and more so than the mere showy, unsubstantial ornaments. I hate anything that occupies more space than it is worth. I hate to see a load of band-boxes go along the street, and I hate to see a parcel of big words without anything in them. A person who does not deliberately dispose of all his thoughts alike in cumbrous draperies and flimsy disguises, may strike out twenty varieties of familiar everyday language, each coming somewhat nearer to the feeling he wants to convey, and at last not hit upon that particular and only one which may be said to be identical with the exact impression in his mind. This would seem to show that Mr. Cobbett is hardly right in saying that the first word that occurs is always the best. It may be a very good one; and yet a better may present itself on reflection or from time to time. It should be suggested naturally, however, and spontaneously, from a fresh and lively conception of the subject. We seldom succeed by trying at improvement, or by merely substituting one word for another that we are not satisfied with, as we cannot recollect the name of a place or person by merely plaguing ourselves about it. We wander farther from the point by persisting in a wrong scent; but it starts up accidentally in the memory when we least expect it, by touching some link in the chain of previous association.

There are those who hoard up and make a cautious display of nothing but rich and rare phraseology;—ancient medals, obscure coins, and Spanish pieces of eight. They are very curious to inspect; but I myself would neither offer nor take them in the course of exchange. A sprinkling of archaisms is not amiss; but a tissue of obsolete expressions is more fit *for keep than wear*. I do not say I would not use any phrase that had been brought into fashion before the middle or the end of the last century; but I should be shy of using any that had not been employed by any approved author during the whole of that time. Words, like clothes, get old-fashioned, or mean and ridiculous, when they have been for some time laid aside. Mr. Lamb is the only imitator of old English style I can read with pleasure; and he is so thoroughly imbued with the spirit of his authors that the idea of imitation is almost done away. There is an inward unction, a marrowy vein both in the thought and feeling, an intuition, deep and lively, of his subject, that carries off any quaintness or awkwardness arising from an antiquated style and dress. The matter is completely his own, though the manner is assumed. Perhaps his ideas are altogether so marked and individual as to require their point and pungency to be neutralised by the affectation of a singular but traditional form of conveyance. Tricked out in the prevailing costume, they would probably seem more startling and out of the way. The old English authors, Burton, Fuller, Coryate, Sir Thomas Browne, are a kind of mediators between us and the more eccentric and whimsical modern, reconciling us to his peculiarities. I do not, however, know how far this is the case or not, till he condescends to write like one of us. I must confess that what I like best of his papers under the signature of Elia (still I do not presume, amidst such excellence, to decide what is most excellent) is the account of "Mrs. Battle's Opinions on Whist," which is also the most free from obsolete allusions and turns of expression—

"A well of native English undefiled."

To those acquainted with his admired prototypes, these Essays of the ingenious and highly gifted author have the same sort of charm and relish that Erasmus's Colloquies or a fine piece of modern Latin have to the classical scholar. Certainly, I do not know any borrowed pencil that has more power of felicity of execution than the one of which I have here been speaking.

It is as easy to write a gaudy style without ideas, as it is to spread a pallet of showy colors, or to smear in a flaunting transparency. "What do you read?"—"Words, words, words."—"What is the matter?"—"*Nothing,*" it might be answered. The florid style is the reverse of the familiar. The last is employed as an unvarnished medium to convey ideas; the first is resorted to as a spangled veil to conceal the want of them. When there is nothing to be set down but words, it costs little to have them fine. Look through the dictionary, and cull out a *florilegium,* rival the *tulipomania. Rouge* high enough, and never mind the natural complexion. The vulgar, who are not in the secret, will admire the look of preternatural health and vigor; and the fashionable, who regard only appearances, will be delighted with the imposition. Keep to your sounding generalities, your tinkling phrases, and all will be well. Swell out an unmeaning truism to a perfect tympany of style. A thought, a distinction, is the rock on which all this brittle cargo of verbiage splits at once. Such writers have merely *verbal* imaginations, that retain nothing but words. Or their puny thoughts have dragon-wings, all green and gold. They soar far above the vulgar failing of the *Sermo humi abrepens*—their most ordinary speech is never short of an hyperbole, splendid, imposing, vague, incomprehensible, magniloquent, a cento of sounding commonplaces. If some of us, whose "ambition is more lowly," pry a little too narrowly into nooks and corners to pick up a number of "unconsidered trifles," they never once direct their eyes or lift their hands to seize on any but the most gorgeous, tarnished, threadbare, patchwork set of phrases, the left-off finery of poetic extravagance, transmitted down through successive generations of barren pretenders. If they criticize actors and actresses, a huddled phantasmagoria of feathers, spangles, floods of light, and oceans of sound float before their morbid sense, which they paint in the style of Ancient Pistol. Not a glimpse can you get of the merits or defects of the performers: they are hidden in a profusion of barbarous epithets and wilful rhodomontade. Our hypercritics are not thinking of these little fantoccini beings—

"That strut and fret their hour upon the stage"—

but of tall phantoms of words, abstractions, *genera* and *species,* sweeping clauses, periods that unite the Poles, forced alliterations, astounding antitheses—

"And on their pens *Fustian* sits plumed."

If they describe kings and queens, it is an Eastern pageant. The Coronation at either House is nothing to it. We get at four repeated images—a curtain, a throne, a sceptre, and a foot-stool. These are with them the wardrobe of a lofty imagination; and they turn their servile strains to servile uses. Do we read a description of pictures? It is not a reflection of tones and hues which "nature's own sweet and cunning hand laid on," but piles of precious stones, rubies, pearls, emeralds, Golconda's mines, and all the blazonry of art. Such persons are in fact besotted with words, and their brains are turned with the glittering but empty and sterile phantoms of things. Personifications, capital letters, seas of sunbeams, visions of glory, shining inscriptions, the figures of a transparency, Britannia with her shield, or Hope leaning on an anchor, make up their stock in trade. They may be considered as *hieroglyphical* writers. Images stand out in their minds isolated and important merely in themselves, without any groundwork of feeling—there is no context in their imaginations. Words affect them in the same way, by the mere sound, that is, by their possible, not by their actual application to the subject in hand. They are fascinated by first appearances, and have no sense of consequences. Nothing more is meant by them than meets the ear: they understand or feel nothing more than meets their eye. The web and texture of the universe, and of the heart of man, is a mystery to them: they have no faculty that strikes a chord in unison with it. They cannot get beyond the daubings of fancy, the varnish of sentiment. Objects are not linked to feelings, words to things, but images revolve in splendid mockery, words represent themselves in their strange rhapsodies. The categories of such a mind are pride and ignorance—pride in outside show, to which they sacrifice everything, and ignorance of the true worth and hidden structure both of words and things. With a sovereign contempt for what is familiar and natural, they are the slaves of vulgar affectation—of a routine of high-flown phrases. Scorning to imitate realities, they are unable to invent anything, to strike out one original idea. They are not copyists of nature, it is true; but they are the poorest of all plagiarists, the plagiarists of words. All is farfetched, dear-bought, artificial, oriental in subject and allusion; all is mechanical, conventional, vapid, formal, pedantic in style and execution. They startle and confound the understanding of the reader by the remoteness and obscurity of their illustrations; they soothe the ear by the monotony of the same everlasting round of circuitous metaphors. They are the *mock-school* in poetry and prose. They flounder about between fustian in expression and bathos in sentiment. They tantalise the fancy, but never reach the head nor touch the heart. Their Temple of Fame is like a shadowy structure raised by Dulness to Vanity, or like Cowper's description of the Empress of Russia's palace of ice, "as worthless as in show 't was glittering"—

"It smiled, and it was cold!"

1821

LEIGH HUNT (1784-1859)

ABOU BEN ADHEM

Abou Ben Adhem (may his tribe increase!)
Awoke one night from a deep dream of peace,
And saw, within the moonlight in his room,
Making it rich, and like a lily in bloom,
An angel writing in a book of gold:—
Exceeding peace had made Ben Adhem bold,
And to the presence in the room he said,
"What writest thou?"—The vision raised its head,
And with a look made of all sweet accord,
Answered, "The names of those who love the Lord." 10
"And is mine one?" said Abou. "Nay, not so,"
Replied the angel. Abou spoke more low,
But cheerly still; and said, "I pray thee, then,
Write me as one that loves his fellow-men."

The angel wrote, and vanished. The next night
It came again with a great wakening light,

And showed the names whom love of God had blessed
And, lo! Ben Adhem's name led all the rest!

1834

GETTING UP ON COLD MORNINGS

An Italian author—Giulio Cordara, a Jesuit—has written a poem upon insects, which he begins by insisting, that those troublesome and abominable little animals were created for our annoyance, and that they were certainly not inhabitants of Paradise. We of the north may dispute this piece of theology; but on the other hand, it is as clear as the snow on the house-tops, that Adam was not under the necessity of shaving; and that when Eve walked out of her delicious bower, she did not step upon ice three inches thick.

Some people say it is a very easy thing to get up of a cold morning. You have only, they tell you, to take the resolution; and the thing is done. This may be very true; just as a boy at school has only to take a flogging, and the thing is over. But we have not at all made up our minds upon it; and we find it a very pleasant exercise to discuss the matter, candidly, before we get up. This at least is not idling, though it may be lying. It affords an excellent answer to those, who ask how lying in bed can be indulged in by a reasoning being—a rational creature. How? Why with the argument calmly at work in one's head, and the clothes over one's shoulder. Oh—it is a fine way of spending a sensible, impartial half-hour.

If these people would be more charitable, they would get on with their argument better. But they are apt to reason so ill, and to assert so dogmatically, that one could wish to have them stand round one's bed of a bitter morning, and *lie* before their faces. They ought to hear

GETTING UP ON COLD MORNINGS

both sides of the bed, the inside and out. If they cannot entertain themselves with their own thoughts for half an hour or so, it is not the fault of those who can. If their will is never pulled aside by the enticing arms of imagination, so much the luckier for the stage-coachman.

Candid inquiries into one's decumbency, besides the greater or less privileges to be allowed a man in proportion to his ability of keeping early hours, the work given his faculties, etc., will at least concede their due merits to such representations as the following. In the first place, says the injured but calm appealer, I have been warm all night, and find my system in a state perfectly suitable to the warm-blooded animal. To get out of this state into the cold, besides the inharmonious and uncritical abruptness of the transition, is so unnatural to such a creature, that the poets, refining upon the tortures of the damned, make one of their greatest agonies consist in being suddenly transported from heat to cold,—from fire to ice. They are "haled" out of their "beds," says Milton, by "harpy-footed furies,"—fellows who come to call them. On my first movement towards the anticipation of getting up, I find that such parts of the sheets and bolster, as are exposed to the air of the room, are stone-cold. On opening my eyes, the first thing that meets them is my own breath rolling forth, as if in the open air, like smoke out of a cottage chimney.

Think of this symptom. Then I turn my eyes sideways and see the window all frozen over. Think of that. Then the servant comes in. "It is very cold this morning, is it not?"—"Very cold, Sir."—"Very cold indeed, isn't it?"—"Very cold indeed, Sir."—"More than usually so, isn't it, even for this weather?" (Here the servant's wit and good-nature are put to a considerable test, and the inquirer lies on thorns for the answer.) "Why, Sir . . . I think it *is.*" (Good creature! There is not a better, or more truth-telling servant going.) "I must rise, however—get me some warm water."—Here comes a fine interval between the departure of the servant and the arrival of the hot water; during which, of course, it is of "no use" to get up. The hot water comes. "Is it quite hot?"—"Yes, Sir."—"Perhaps too hot for shaving: I must wait a little?"—"No, Sir; it will just do." (There is an over-nice propriety sometimes, an officious zeal of virtue, a little troublesome.) "Oh —the shirt—you must air my clean shirt—linen gets very damp this weather."—"Yes, Sir." Here another delicious five minutes. A knock at the door. "Oh, the shirt —very well. My stockings—I think the stockings had better be aired too."—"Very well, Sir."—Here another interval. At length everything is ready, except myself. I now, continues our incumbent (a happy word, by the bye, for a country vicar)—I now cannot help thinking a good deal—who can?—upon the unnecessary and villainous custom of shaving: it is a thing so unmanly (here I nestle closer)—so effeminate (here I recoil from an unlucky step into the colder part of the bed.)—No wonder that the Queen of France took part with the rebels against the degenerate King, her husband, who first affronted her smooth visage with a face like her own. The Emperor Julian never showed the luxuriancy of his genius to better advantage than in reviving the flowing beard. Look at Cardinal Bembo's picture —at Michael Angelo's—at Titian's—at Shakespeare's— at Fletcher's—at Spenser's—at Chaucer's—at Alfred's —at Plato's—I could name a great man for every tick of my watch.—Look at the Turks, a grave and otiose people.—Think of Haroun Al Raschid and Bed-ridden

GETTING UP ON COLD MORNINGS

Hassan.—Think of Wortley Montague, the worthy son of his mother, a man above the prejudice of his time.—Look at the Persian gentlemen, whom one is ashamed of meeting about the suburbs, their dress and appearance are so much finer than our own.—Lastly, think of the razor itself—how totally opposed to every sensation of bed—how cold, how edgy, how hard! how utterly different from anything like the warm and circling amplitude, which

> "Sweetly recommends itself
> Unto our gentle senses."

Add to this, benumbed fingers, which may help you to cut yourself, a quivering body, a frozen towel, and a ewer full of ice; and he that says there is nothing to oppose in all this, only shows, at any rate, that he has no merit in opposing it.

Thomson the poet, who exclaims in his Seasons—

> "Falsely luxurious! Will not man awake?"

used to lie in bed till noon, because he said he had no motive in getting up. He could imagine the good of rising; but then he could also imagine the good of lying still; and his exclamation, it must be allowed, was made upon summer-time, not winter. We must proportion the argument to the individual character. A money-getter may be drawn out of his bed by three and four pence; but this will not suffice for a student. A proud man may say, "What shall I think of myself, if I don't get up?" but the more humble one will be content to waive this prodigious notion of himself, out of respect to his kindly bed. The mechanical man shall get up without any ado at all; and so shall the barometer. An ingenious lier in bed will find hard matter of discussion even on the score of health and longevity. He will ask us for our proofs and precedents of the ill effects of lying later in cold weather; and sophisticate much on the advantages of an even temperature of body; of the natural propensity (pretty universal) to have one's way; and of the animals that roll themselves up, and sleep all the winter. As to longevity, he will ask whether the longest life is of necessity the best; and whether Holborn is the handsomest street in London.

We only know of one confounding, not to say confounded argument, fit to overturn the huge luxury, the "enormous bliss"—of the vice in question. A lier in bed may be allowed to profess a disinterested indifference for his health or longevity; but while he is showing the reasonableness of consulting his own or one person's comfort, he must admit the proportionate claim of more than one; and the best way to deal with him is this, especially for a lady; for we earnestly recommend the use of that sex on such occasions, if not somewhat *over*-persuasive; since extremes have an awkward knack of meeting. First then, admit all the ingeniousness of what he says, telling him that the bar has been deprived of an excellent lawyer. Then look at him in the most good-natured manner in the world, with a mixture of assent and appeal in your countenance, and tell him that you are waiting breakfast for him; that you never like to breakfast without him; that you really want it too; that the servants want theirs; that you shall not know how to get the house into order, unless he rises; and that you are sure he would do things twenty times worse, even than getting out of his warm bed, to put them all into good humour and a state of comfort. Then, after

GETTING UP ON COLD MORNINGS

having said this, throw in the comparatively indifferent matter, to *him,* about his health; but tell him that it is no indifferent matter to you; that the sight of his illness makes more people suffer than one; but that if, nevertheless, he really does feel so very sleepy and so very much refreshed by—Yet stay; we hardly know whether the frailty of a—Yes, yes; say that too, especially if you say it with sincerity; for if the weakness of human nature on the one hand and the *vis inertæ* on the other, should lead him to take advantage of it once or twice, good-humour and sincerity form an irresistible junction at last; and are still better and warmer things than pillows and blankets.

Other little helps of appeal may be thrown in, as occasion requires. You may tell a lover, for instance, that lying in bed makes people corpulent; a father, that you wish him to complete the fine manly example he sets his children; a lady, that she will injure her bloom or her shape, which M. or W. admires so much; and a student or artist, that he is always so glad to have done a good day's work, in his best manner.

Reader. And pray, Mr. Indicator, how do *you* behave yourself in this respect?

Indic. Oh, Madam, perfectly, of course; like all advisers.

Reader. Nay, I allow that your mode of argument does not look quite so suspicious as the old way of sermonizing and severity, but I have my doubts, especially from that laugh of yours. If I should look in to-morrow morning ——

Indic. Ah, Madam, the look in of a face like yours does anything with me. It shall fetch me up at nine, if you please—*six,* I meant to say.

1820

THOMAS DE QUINCEY (1785-1859)

SUSPIRIA DE PROFUNDIS

LEVANA AND OUR LADIES OF SORROW

Oftentimes at Oxford I saw Levana in my dreams. I knew her by her Roman symbols. Who is Levana? Reader, that do not pretend to have leisure for very much scholarship, you will not be angry with me for telling you. Levana was the Roman goddess that performed for the new-born infant the earliest office of ennobling kindness,—typical, by its mode, of that grandeur which belongs to man everywhere, and of that benignity in powers invisible which even in Pagan worlds sometimes descends to sustain it. At the very moment of birth, just as the infant tasted for the first time the atmosphere of our troubled planet, it was laid on the ground. *That* might bear different interpretations. But immediately, lest so grand a creature should grovel there for more than one instant, either the paternal hand, as proxy for the goddess Levana, or some near kinsman, as proxy for the father, raised it upright, bade it look erect as the king of all this world, and presented its forehead to the stars, saying, perhaps, in his heart, "Behold what is greater than yourselves!" This symbolic act represented the function of Levana. And that mysterious lady, who never revealed her face (except to me in dreams), but always acted by delegation, had her name from the Latin verb (as still it is the Italian verb) *levare,* to raise aloft.

This is the explanation of Levana. And hence it has arisen that some people have understood by Levana the tutelary power that controls the education of the nursery.

LEVANA AND OUR LADIES OF SORROW

She, that would not suffer at his birth even a prefigurative or mimic degradation for her awful ward, far less could be supposed to suffer the real degradation attaching to the non-development of his powers. She therefore watches over human education. Now, the word *edŭco,* with the penultimate short, was derived (by a process often exemplified in the crystallization of languages) from the word *edūco,* with the penultimate long. Whatsoever *educes,* or develops, *educates.* By the education of Levana, therefore, is meant,—not the poor machinery that moves by spelling-books and grammars, but that mighty system of central forces hidden in the deep bosom of human life, which by passion, by strife, by temptation, by the energies of resistance, works forever upon children,—resting not day or night, any more than the mighty wheel of day and night themselves, whose moments, like restless spokes, are glimmering for ever as they revolve.

If, then, *these* are the ministries by which Levana works, how profoundly must she reverence the agencies of grief! But you, reader, think that children generally are not liable to grief such as mine. There are two senses in the word *generally,*—the sense of Euclid, where it means *universally* (or in the whole extent of the *genus*), and a foolish sense of this world, where it means *usually.* Now, I am far from saying that children universally are capable of grief like mine. But there are more than you ever heard of who die of grief in this island of ours. I will tell you a common case. The rules of Eton require that a boy on the *foundation* should be there twelve years: he is superannuated at eighteen, consequently he must come at six. Children torn away from mothers and sisters at that age not unfrequently die. I speak of what I know. The complaint is not entered by the registrar as grief; but *that* it is. Grief of that sort, and at that age, has killed more than ever have been counted amongst its martyrs.

Therefore it is that Levana often communes with the powers that shake man's heart: therefore it is that she dotes upon grief. "These ladies," said I softly to myself, on seeing the ministers with whom Levana was conversing, "these are the Sorrows; and they are three in number, as the *Graces* are three, who dress man's life with beauty; the *Parcæ* are three, who weave the dark arras of man's life in their mysterious loom always with colors sad in part, sometimes angry with tragic crimson and black; the *Furies* are three, who visit with retributions called from the other side of the grave offences that walk upon this; and once even the *Muses* were but three, who fit the harp, the trumpet, or the lute, to the great burdens of man's impassioned creations. These are the Sorrows, all three of whom I know." The last words I say *now;* but in Oxford I said, "One of whom I know, and the others too surely I *shall* know." For already, in my fervent youth, I saw (dimly relieved upon the dark back-ground of my dreams) the imperfect lineaments of the awful sisters. These sisters—by what name shall we call them?

If I say simply, "The Sorrows," there will be a chance of mistaking the term; it might be understood of individual sorrow,—separate cases of sorrow,—whereas I want a term expressing the mighty abstractions that incarnate themselves in all individual sufferings of man's heart; and I wish to have these abstractions presented as impersonations, that is, as clothed with human attributes of life, and with functions pointing to flesh. Let us call them, therefore, *Our Ladies of Sorrow.* I know them thoroughly, and have walked in all their kingdoms. Three sisters they are, of one mysterious household; and their paths are wide apart; but of their dominion there is no end. Them I saw often conversing with Levana, and sometimes about myself. Do they talk, then? Oh, no! Mighty phantoms like these disdain the infirmities of language. They may utter voices through the organs of man when they dwell in human hearts, but amongst themselves is no voice nor sound; eternal silence reigns in *their* kingdoms. *They* spoke not, as they talked with Levana; *they* whispered not; *they* sang not; though oftentimes methought they *might* have sung: for I upon earth had heard their mysteries oftentimes deciphered by harp and timbrel, by dulcimer and organ. Like God, whose servants they are, they utter their pleasure not by sounds that perish, or by words that go astray, but by signs in heaven, by changes on earth, by pulses in secret rivers, heraldries painted on darkness, and hieroglyphics written on the tablets of the brain. *They* wheeled in mazes; *I* spelled the steps. *They* telegraphed from afar; *I* read the signals. *They* conspired together; and on the mirrors of darkness *my* eye traced the plots. *Theirs* were the symbols; *mine* are the words.

What is it the sisters are? What is it that they do? Let me describe their form, and their presence; if form it were that still fluctuated in its outline; or presence it were that forever advanced to the front, or forever receded amongst shades.

The eldest of the three is named *Mater Lachrymarum,* Our Lady of Tears. She it is that night and day raves and moans, calling for vanished faces. She stood in Rama, where a voice was heard of lamentation,—Rachel weeping for her children, and refused to be comforted. She it was that stood in Bethlehem on the night when Herod's sword swept its nurseries of Innocents, and the little feet were stiffened forever, which, heard at times as they tottered along floors overhead, woke pulses of love in household hearts that were not unmarked in heaven.

Her eyes are sweet and subtile, wild and sleepy, by turns; oftentimes rising to the clouds, oftentimes challenging the heavens. She wears a diadem round her head. And I knew by childish memories that she could go abroad upon the winds, when she heard that sobbing of litanies, or the thundering of organs, and when she beheld the mustering of summer clouds. This sister, the elder, it is that carries keys more than papal at her girdle, which open every cottage and every palace. She, to my knowledge, sat all last summer by the bedside of the blind beggar, him that so often and so gladly I talked with, whose pious daughter, eight years old with the sunny countenance, resisted the temptations of play and village mirth to travel all day long on dusty roads with her afflicted father. For this did God send her a great reward. In the spring-time of the year, and whilst yet her own spring was budding, He recalled her to himself. But her blind father mourns forever over *her;* still he dreams at midnight that the little guiding hand is locked within his own; and still he wakens to a darkness that is *now* within a second and a deeper darkness. This *Mater Lachrymarum* also has been sitting all this winter of 1844-1845 within the bed-chamber of the Czar, bringing before his eyes a daughter (not less pious) that vanished to God not less suddenly, and left behind her a darkness not less profound. By the power of her keys it is that Our Lady of Tears glides a ghostly intruder into the chambers of sleepless men, sleepless women, sleepless children, from Ganges to the Nile, from Nile to Mississippi. And her, because she is the first-born of her house, and has the widest empire, let us honor with the title of "Madonna."

The second sister is called *Mater Suspiriorum,* Our

Lady of Sighs. She never scales the clouds, nor walks abroad upon the winds. She wears no diadem. And her eyes, if they were ever seen, would be neither sweet nor subtile; no man could read their story; they would be found filled with perishing dreams, and with wrecks of forgotten delirium. But she raises not her eyes; her head, on which sits a dilapidated turban, droops forever, forever fastens on the dust. She weeps not. She groans not. But she sighs inaudibly at intervals. Her sister Madonna is oftentimes stormy and frantic, raging in the highest against heaven, and demanding back her darlings. But Our Lady of Sighs never clamours, never defies, dreams not of rebellious aspirations. She is humble to abjectness. Hers is the meekness that belongs to the hopeless. Murmur she may, but it is in her sleep. Whisper she may, but it is to herself in the twilight. Mutter she does at times, but it is in solitary places that are desolate as she is desolate, in ruined cities, and when the sun has gone down to his rest. This sister is the visitor of the Pariah, of the Jew, of the bondsman to the oar in the Mediterranean galleys; and of the English criminal in Norfolk Island, blotted out from the books of remembrance in sweet far-off England; of the baffled penitent reverting his eyes forever upon a solitary grave, which to him seems the altar overthrown of some past and bloody sacrifice, on which altar no oblations can now be availing, whether towards pardon that he might implore, or towards reparation that he might attempt. Every slave that at noonday looks up to the tropical sun with timid reproach, as he points with one hand to the earth, our general mother, but for *him* a stepmother, as he points with the other hand to the Bible, our general teacher, but against *him* sealed and sequestered; every woman sitting in darkness, without love to shelter her head, or hope to illumine her solitude, because the heaven-born instincts kindling in her nature germs of holy affections, which God implanted in her womanly bosom, having been stifled by social necessities, now burn sullenly to waste, like sepulchral lamps amongst the ancients; every nun defrauded of her unreturning May-time by wicked kinsman, whom God will judge; every captive in every dungeon; all that are betrayed, and all that are rejected; outcasts by traditionary law, and children of *hereditary* disgrace,—all these walk with Our Lady of Sighs. She also carries a key; but she needs it little. For her kingdom is chiefly amongst the tents of Shem, and the houseless vagrant of every clime. Yet in the very highest ranks of man she finds chapels of her own; and even in glorious England there are some that, to the world, carry their heads as proudly as the reindeer, who yet secretly have received her mark upon their foreheads.

But the third sister, who is also the youngest ——! Hush! whisper whilst we talk of *her!* Her kingdom is not large, or else no flesh should live; but within that kingdom all power is hers. Her head, turreted like that of Cybele, rises almost beyond the reach of sight. She droops not; and her eyes rising so high *might* be hidden by distance. But, being what they are, they cannot be hidden; through the treble veil of crape which she wears, the fierce light of a blazing misery, that rests not for matins or for vespers, for noon of day or noon of night, for ebbing or for flowing tide, may be read from the very ground. She is the defier of God. She also is the mother of lunacies, and the suggestress of suicides. Deep lie the roots of her power; but narrow is the nation that she rules. For she can approach only those in whom a profound nature has been upheaved by central convulsions; in whom the heart trembles and the brain rocks under conspiracies of tempest from without and tempest from

LEVANA AND OUR LADIES OF SORROW 511

within. Madonna moves with uncertain steps, fast or slow, but still with tragic grace. Our Lady of Sighs creeps timidly and stealthily. But this youngest sister moves with incalculable motions, bounding, and with a tiger's leaps. She carries no key; for, though coming rarely amongst men, she storms all doors at which she is permitted to enter at all. And *her* name is *Mater Tenebrarum*,—Our Lady of Darkness.

These were the *Semnai Theai,* or Sublime Goddesses, these were the *Eumenides,* or Gracious Ladies (so called by antiquity in shuddering propitiation) of my Oxford dreams. Madonna spoke. She spoke by her mysterious hand. Touching my head, she beckoned to Our Lady of Sighs; and *what* she spoke, translated out of the signs which (except in dreams) no man reads, was this:

"Lo! here is he, whom in childhood I dedicated to my altars. This is he that once I made my darling. Him I led astray, him I beguiled, and from heaven I stole away his young heart to mine. Through me did he become idolatrous; and through me it was, by languishing desires, that he worshipped the worm, and prayed to the wormy grave. Holy was the grave to him; lovely was its darkness; saintly its corruption. Him, this young idolator, I have seasoned for thee, dear gentle Sister of Sighs! Do thou take him now to *thy* heart and season him for our dreadful sister. And thou,"— turning to the *Mater Tenebrarum,* she said,—"wicked sister, that temptest and hatest, do thou take him from *her.* See that thy sceptre lie heavy on his head. Suffer not woman and her tenderness to sit near him in his darkness. Banish the frailties of hope, wither the relenting of love, scorch the fountains of tears, curse him as only thou canst curse. So shall he be accomplished in the furnace; so shall he see the things that ought *not* to be seen. sights that are abominable, and secrets that are unutterable. So shall he read elder truths, sad truths, grand truths, fearful truths. So shall he rise again *before* he dies. And so shall our commission be accomplished which from God we had,—to plague his heart until we had unfolded the capacities of his spirit."

1845

NOTES

WILLIAM COWPER

WILLIAM COWPER, born in 1731 at Great Berkhampstead, in Hertfordshire, was the son of a parish minister and a descendant on both sides from illustrious families. After a period of seven years at Westminster School, where he studied the classics and learned to love Homer, he was "articled" for three years to an attorney in London. Here he fell deeply in love with his cousin Theodora, but her father, Ashley Cowper, refused to sanction the engagement; the disappointment greatly affected his supersensitive nature, and he fell into a state of morbid despondency from which he never wholly recovered. In 1752 he entered as a law student at the Middle Temple, and two years later he was admitted to the bar. Through the influence of friends he secured a position as Commissioner of Bankruptcy at $300 a year, and for the next ten years he was scribbling verse and enjoying the society of the wits at the Nonsense Club. In 1763 his cousin, Major Cowper, offered him a position as Clerk of the Journals to the House of Lords. Conscience-stricken over having wished for the former clerk's death and harassed by fear of the ordeal of a public examination, he lost his mind and attempted to take his life; the disease took the form of religious mania, in which he believed he had committed the unpardonable sin. On his restoration to health, in 1765, he took up lodgings with the family of the Reverend Morley Unwin at Huntingdon. After Mr. Unwin's death, two years later, he continued to live in the home of Mrs. Unwin (the "Mary" of his letters and poems), who became not only a mother and real friend to him but the greatest inspiration of his life. They moved to Olney, in Buckinghamshire, to be near the Reverend John Newton, for whom they had formed a warm attachment. Newton's religious fanaticism had an unwholesome effect on Cowper, resulting, in 1773, in his second attack of insanity. He was nursed back to recovery by Mary Unwin, who succeeded in getting him interested, first, in gardening and in raising tame hares, and then in the exercise of his poetic gifts. In 1781 he met Lady Austen, a bright young widow who came to Olney and inspired *The Task* and the humorous ballad, *The Diverting Ride of John Gilpin*. In 1786, through the generosity of his cousin, Lady Hasketh (sister of Theodora), he was provided with a home at "Weston Lodge," near Olney, where he and Mrs. Unwin spent the remainder of their lives. In 1791 Mrs. Unwin became a paralytic, and died four years later. Cowper's last years were full of despondency

513

and gloom (see *The Castaway*). He died in 1800, and was buried at Dereham Church in Norfolk.

No literary work of importance was produced by Cowper before 1782. In this year appeared a volume of poems, suggested by Mrs. Unwin, on such subjects as *Table Talk, The Progress of Error, Expostulation*, and *Retirement*. These poems, satiric and didactic in content, are written in the heroic couplet in the manner of Pope. In his most important poem, *The Task* (1785), Cowper brought poetry back to nature and the simple life, and began a renaissance in English poetry which reached its culmination in the greater Romantic poets, who immediately followed. The translation of Homer, which required his most exacting labors, appeared in 1791.

Cowper is also known for the simplicity and charm of his personal letters, which some critics have pronounced the best in the English language.

THE OLNEY HYMNS

The Olney Hymns are the joint authorship of Cowper and the Reverend John Newton. Of the 348 in the collection, Cowper wrote 68, which are signed with the letter C. Though Cowper's hymns lack the fire of imaginative passion, they show real simplicity and genuine sincerity; many of them are still popular in the hymn collections of various Protestant churches.

THE LOSS OF THE ROYAL GEORGE

The Royal George was a British flagship under the command of Rear Admiral Kempenfelt. While being repaired at Spithead in Portsmouth Harbor, she suddenly heeled over in a gust of wind with the loss of the brave admiral and 800 of the 1100 souls aboard. The tragedy occurred on August 29, 1782. Cowper wrote the poem, at the suggestion of Lady Austen, in September following; but it was not published until after his death.

3, l. 9. **A land-breeze shook the shrouds.** The wind came from the land side; so the ship turned over in deep water. **Shrouds** are the ropes and tackle which support the masts of the ship.

l. 12. **With all her crew complete.** About 300 of the crew were saved (see above.)

l. 22. **His fingers . . . pen.** When the accident occurred the admiral was sitting in his cabin engaged in writing.

4, l. 25. **Weigh the vessel up.** Unsuccessful attempts were made in 1782 and 1783 to raise the ship by passing huge cables under the keel.

l. 26. **Once dreaded by our foes.** The Royal George had been in several naval conflicts which won notable victories over the French.

NOTES

The Task: Book IV

The following explanation of the title is given by Cowper in the "Advertisement" to the first edition: "The history of the following production is briefly this: A lady [Lady Austen], fond of blank verse, demanded a poem of that kind by the author, and gave him the SOFA for a subject. He obeyed; and, having much leisure, connected another subject with it; and, pursuing the train of thought to which his situation and turn of mind led him, brought forth at length, instead of the trifle which he at first intended, a serious affair—a volume."

The poem, which contains six books, is a picture of Cowper's surroundings at Olney with various reflections on life. The fourth book, the best of the group, is fairly typical.

5, l. 49. **placemen.** A placeman is one who holds an appointive office under the government.

7, l. 86 f. **Katterfelto . . . wonders.** A quack of the eighteenth century who exhibited in London and advertised with the phrase: "Wonders! Wonders!"

9, l. 189 f. **O evenings . . . Sabine bard.** The Sabine or Roman bard was Horace. Compare *Satires* II, 6, 65: *O noctes coenaque Deum* (O nights and suppers of the gods).

12, l. 269. **He of Gath, Goliath.** Compare I Samuel XVII, 23–24.

16, l. 427. **I mean the man.** The benefactor referred to here is the first Lord Carrington, whom Cowper mentions in a letter to Unwin: "How I love and honor that man . . . My bosom burns to immortalize him."

18, l. 473. **Indian fume.** Tobacco smoke.

19, l. 507. **Midas.** A king of Phrygia, who through the gift of Dionysus, turned everything he touched into gold.

l. 515 f. **Arcadian scenes . . . Sidney.** Arcadia was a mountainous district of Greece which was supposed to be inhabited by a simple and contented pastoral people. Virgil (Maro) sings of these people in his *Eclogues;* Sir Philip Sidney (1554–1586) writes in a similar vein in his *Arcadia* (1585).

24, l. 707. **Tityrus.** A shepherd in the first *Eclogue* of Virgil.

ll. 709–730. Note, in these lines, Cowper's indebtedness to Milton (1608–1674) and Cowley (1613–1667).

25, l. 728. **Chertsey's silent bowers.** Chertsey is a village not far from London, where Cowley spent his last years.

26, l. 765. **The Frenchman's darling.** Mignonette, noted for the delicious fragrance of its flower.

On Receipt of My Mother's Picture

In a letter dated February 27, 1790, Cowper writes to his cousin Ann Bodham as follows: "The world could not have furnished you with a present so acceptable to me as the picture which you have so kindly sent me. I received it the night before last, and viewed it with a trepidation of nerves and spirits somewhat akin to what I should have felt had the dear original presented herself to my embraces. I kissed it, and hung it where it is the last that I see at night, and of course the first on which I open my eyes in the morning. She died when I had completed my sixth year; yet I remember her well, and am an ocular witness of the great fidelity of the copy. I remember too a multitude of the maternal tendernesses which I received from her, and which have endeared her memory to me beyond expression."

- 28, l. 19. **Elysian.** Blessed or heavenly. Elysium was the Greek heaven, the dwelling place of souls after death.
- 29, l. 50. **bauble coach.** A toy coach.
- l. 53. **pastoral house.** The rectory at Great Berkhampstead.
- l. 54. **Short lived possession!** Cowper's father died in 1756.
- l. 75 f. **Vesture's tissued flowers . . . pin.** Refers to his childish habit of pricking out the pattern of printed flowers of his mother's dress, on a piece of paper placed under the material.
- 30, l. 102 f. **Me howling blasts, etc.** Refers to a feeling of dreadful despair that Cowper had just experienced. See letter to John Newton dated February 5, 1790.
- l. 108 f. **I deduce my birth . . . rulers of the earth.** Cowper's mother was descended by four different lines from King Henry III.

SONNET TO MRS. UNWIN

This sonnet records Cowper's deep and sincere feeling of the worth of Mary Unwin, his almost life-long companion.

The Castaway

The poem is founded on an incident in Anson's *Voyage Around the World*. Cowper sees a melancholy image of his own destiny in the fate of the poor sailor who was drowned. Of *The Castaway* Southey wrote: "It is the last original piece that he composed, and, all circumstances considered, one of the most affecting that was ever composed."

- 32, l. 8. **he.** Admiral Lord George Anson (1697-1762), noted British naval commander and world voyager.
- l. 11. **He loved them both.** The sailor loved both Lord Anson and England.
- l. 27. **The coop, the floated cord.** Wooden hen-coops were often thrown to drowning sailors. The floated cord was a rope with a buoy attached.
- 33, l. 37. **He.** The pronoun here is used in a demonstrative sense, meaning *that man;* in line 39 "he" refers to the sailor.
- l. 49. **No poet wept him.** As Milton did for Edward King in *Lycidas*, for example.

NOTES

GEORGE CRABBE

GEORGE CRABBE was born in 1754 at Aldeburgh, on the coast of Suffolk, where his father was collector of salt-duties. The cheerless scenes of his native village and the contact with "surly and sordid fishermen, given to hard labor and rough brawl" laid the foundation for his conception of the sterner side of nature and of the suffering poor revealed later in his poetry.

Crabbe's education was very meager. His only schooling consisted of about half a dozen years, first in the village school of Aldeburgh and later in boarding schools at Bungay and Showmarket. Destined for the profession of medicine, he was apprenticed first to a physician at Wickhambrook and later to a doctor at Woodbridge. Failing as a practitioner and encouraged by his early poetic efforts, he went to London to try his fortune in literature. After a season of dire penury and fruitless appeals for aid to Lord North, Lord Shelburne, and Lord Thurlow, he finally won the sympathy of Edmund Burke, who invited him to his home at Beaconsfield and furnished financial backing for the publication of *The Library* (1781) and *The Village* (1783). On the advice of his patron he took orders, became chaplain to the Duke of Rutland at Belvoir Castle (1782–1783), and afterwards served as a parish clergyman in various parts of Southern England. In 1814 he was appointed to a spiritual charge at Trowbridge, in Wiltshire. Here he spent the remainder of his life in comparative ease, winning the affection of his parishioners, and making frequent visits to London. During this period he won the high esteem of Scott (whom he visited in Edinburgh), Wordsworth, Southey, and others. He died at Trowbridge on February 3, 1832.

After the publication of *The Village* (1783) Crabbe published nothing of importance for twenty-four years. In 1807 appeared a volume including, besides reprints of *The Library* and *The Village*, *The Parish Register* (a narration of the lives of the village people), *The Hall of Justice* (the story of a gypsy woman), and *The Birth of Flattery* (an allegory). *The Borough* (another realistic description of life in Aldeburgh) was published in 1810; *The Tales* (containing twenty-one stories) appeared in 1812, and *The Tales of Hall* in 1819. For the last poem Murray paid him $15,000.

Although Crabbe used the heroic couplet of Pope as his medium of expression and was a thorough-going realist to the last, his poetry shows a close observation of nature and a real sympathy for the poor. Crabbe was greatly admired by some of his contemporary poets. Wordsworth praised him highly, and Byron says of him, "Though nature's sternest painter, yet her best."

THE VILLAGE

The Village, Crabbe's best-known work, reveals all the peculiar qualities of his poetry. After completion, the poem was carefully revised under the supervision of Burke; then it was submitted by Sir Joshua Reynolds to Dr. Samuel Johnson, who pronounced it "original, vigorous, and elegant." The poem is a reaction against Goldsmith's *Deserted Village* and Gray's *Elegy*, which in Crabbe's opinion were idealized pictures and not true to fact. Crabbe says (see *The Village*, lines 53-54 in the Text):

> "I paint the Cot,
> As Truth will paint it, and as Bards will not."

34, l. 12. **Corydons.** Shepherds in pastoral poetry, named from a character in Virgil's *Eclogues*.

l. 15 f. **Mincio's bank.** Mincio is a river flowing past Mantua, the home of Virgil.

l. 27. **honest Duck.** A minor poet who was well-known at the time—possibly Stephen Duck, referred to by Johnson in his *Life of Savage*.

37, l. 97. **huge Ajax.** One of the heroes in Homer's *Iliad*. He possessed great strength, and was next to Achilles in prowess and beauty.

42, l. 284. **a drowsy Bench protect.** Refers to the lax laws governing the practice of medicine.

43, l. 303. **"passing rich with forty pounds a year."** The quotation is from Goldsmith's description of the preacher in *The Deserted Village* (line 135).

ROBERT BURNS

Robert Burns, born at Alloway, near Ayr, in 1759, was the son of a pious, hard-headed Scottish peasant. Under John Murdock he received his meager education, which consisted chiefly of instruction in English grammar and in the rudiments of Latin and French; to this was added some practical training in mensuration and surveying. He was an omnivorous reader, his favorite books being the plays of Shakespeare, Jeremy Taylor's *Doctrine of Original Sin*, Lock's *Essay on the Human Understanding*, the poetry of Pope (including the translation of the *Iliad*), Thomson's *Seasons*, and especially the poetry of Allan Ramsay and Robert Fergusson. But his chief inspiration was received from *A Collection of Songs*, which, he says, "was my *vade mecum*. I pored over them driving my cart or walking to labor, song by song, verse by verse, carefully noting the true, tender, sublime or fustian."

Most of Burns's life was spent in drudgery on the farm. This began in 1766 when his father, William Burnes, left the seven-acre croft at Alloway and leased, with borrowed money, the seventy-acre farm at Mount Oliphant. Under the pressure of debt the whole family worked like galley slaves; and upon Robert, the eldest child, fell much of the burden. After a hopeless struggle of eleven years the family moved to Lochlea, some ten or twelve miles from Mount Oliphant. Here they continued the same laborious toil until 1784, when William Burnes, crushed in spirit and broken in health, was released from his suffering by death.

NOTES

On the death of his father, Burns and his brother Gilbert leased a a farm at Mossgiel, about two miles from Lochlea, where the family moved on Whitsunday, 1784. After two crop failures and an unfortunate love affair with Jean Armour, Burns became disgusted with his miserable lot and resolved to go to Jamaica. During these two years he had written a considerable number of poems which he decided to publish to raise money for his passage. This publication, known as the Kilmarnock edition, appeared on July 31, 1786, and resulted in an invitation to visit Edinburgh, then a considerable literary center. At Edinburgh he was lionized by the literati and the world of rank and fashion. In 1787 he published the first Edinburgh edition of his poems, from the profits of which he gave his brother a generous sum. In 1788 he married Jean Armour, and leased a farm in Dumfriesshire. The following year he obtained an appointment as a collector of excise taxes, but because of his sympathy with the French Revolution he lost all hope of promotion in this office. During his last years he composed the songs on which his fame chiefly rests. They were composed without remuneration for love of old Scotland. He died at Dumfries in 1796.

Burns is Scotland's greatest poet. He is primarily the poetic interpreter of the Scottish rustic of the eighteenth century—of his ideals and aspirations; of his joys and sorrows; and of his humor, buffooneries, superstitions, and debaucheries. But his poetry makes a universal appeal to English readers as well. He is supreme as a lyric poet, with love as the favorite theme.

MARY MORISON

The Mary Morison of this poem was probably Ellison Begbie, the daughter of a small farmer near Galston. The poet had previously sung her praises in *Bonie Peggy Alison* (his first lyric) and *The Lass on Cessnock Banks*. In his life of Burns, Shairp says: "Long afterwards, when he had seen much of the world, Burns spoke of this young woman as, of all those on whom he had ever fixed his fickle affections, the one most likely to have made a pleasant partner for life."

44, l. 10. **the lighted ha'.** Refers to the village dancing school at Tarbolton.

GREEN GROW THE RASHES

A song of love expressing, as Burns said, "the genuine language of my heart." The poem was written shortly after he secured a copy of Fergusson's Scottish poems which, he says, inspired him "with emulating vigor."

EPISTLE TO JOHN LAPRAIK

John Lapraik was a genial old farmer who lived near Muirkirk, about fourteen miles east of Burns's farm at Mossgiel, and who had a local reputation for rhymes.

The occasion which produced this poem is described by Gilbert Burns as follows: "It was a rockin, when we had twelve or fifteen people . . . that Lapraik's song was sung, and we were informed that he was the author. Upon this Robert wrote his first epistle to Lapraik." A second "epistle," a reply to Lapraik's answer, was written about three weeks later.

47, l. 21. **Pope or Steele.** The citation of Pope (1688–1744) and Steele (1672–1729) shows the reverence still present for eighteenth-century writers.

l. 22. **Beattie's wark.** James Beattie (1735–1803), Professor of Moral Philosophy at Aberdeen, wrote *The Minstrel* (1771), a poem in the Spenserian stanza.

l. 35. **Inverness and Teviotdale.** Inverness, on the Moray Firth, was then regarded as the northern limit of Scottish civilization. Teviotdale is in Southern Scotland on the English border.

49, ll. 73–78. This stanza sums up Burns's poetic creed.

l. 79–80. **Allan's Glee or Fergusson's.** Allan Ramsay (1686–1758) wrote *The Gentle Shepherd* and numerous songs, tales, and humorous satires—all in the Scottish vernacular. Robert Fergusson (1750–1774) is principally known as the author of *The Farmer's Ingle*. Burns was greatly indebted to both poets.

To a Mouse

This poem was occasioned by a commonplace incident. On a November day, Burns, while plowing, turned up the nest of a field mouse. When a farm hand started with his "pattle" in pursuit of the animal, Burns called to him to let it alone. On the same day he composed this immortal poem.

52, l. 39 f. **The best laid schemes**, etc. Perhaps as often quoted as any other lines in poetry.

The Cotter's Saturday Night

The most elucidating comment on this poem has been made by Professor William Allan Neilson in his *Essentials of Poetry* (pages 205–206): "A poem like *The Cotter's Saturday Night* has gained its great popularity mainly by the diffusion throughout it of those sentiments with which the ordinary man most sympathizes: the feeling of domesticity; the attraction of fireside and children at the end of the day's work; the mild reciprocal inclination of the man to the maid and the maid to the man, love in the stage when it is still impeded by bashfulness; the family exercise of religion, here affecting the reader through old associations rather than conviction; and finally the emotion of patriotism."

More than half the poem is in English, but the more elevated stanzas are in the Scottish dialect. It is written in the Spenserian stanza.

NOTES

and owes something in theme and treatment to Shenstone's *Schoolmistress* and Fergusson's *The Farmer's Ingle*.

57, l. 111. f. **Dundee's,** etc. Names of the favorite psalm melodies, now heard principally in the rural churches.
58, l. 138. **Hope springs,** etc. Compare Pope's *Windsor Forest*, l. 112.
59, l. 166. **An honest man,** etc. From Pope's *Essay on Man* Epistle IV, l. 248.
    l. 182. **Wallace.** William Wallace (1274–1305), a Scottish patriot and hero.

Address to the Unco Guid or the Rigidly Righteous

This poem is a bitter satire against those who think they are more pious than other people; at the same time it is Burns's defense of his own shortcomings.

Of a' the Airts

This poem, one of the most popular of Burns's songs, was composed in honor of Mrs. Burns (Jean Armour).

Auld Lang Syne

This is the favorite re-union song in Scotland, invariably sung at the parting of friends. It is almost as popular in this country.

Tam O'Shanter

This inimitable tale of drink and diablerie is considered by many critics as Burns's masterpiece. Alloway Kirk, the central scene of the story, was only a few yards from the cottage in which the poet was born. In his childhood the place was hoary with age and supernatural associations.

Highland Mary

The Mary of this poem was Mary Campbell, who died in 1786. Burns protested his love for her, and the two were engaged to be married; but the poet seems to have forgotten his vows. The anniversary of her death seemed to bring to him a sense of remorse. This song, together with its companion piece, *To Mary in Heaven*, is perhaps the tenderest of all of Burns's love poems.

Scots Wha Hae

The original title of this poem was *Bruce's March to Bannockburn*. The words are supposed to constitute Bruce's stirring appeal to his soldiers on the eve of the great victory of the Scots over the English under Edward II at Bannockburn, June 24, 1314. Robert Bruce (1274–1329), a national hero, became King of Scotland in 1306.

A Man's a Man for a' That

This poem, which shows Burns's sympathy for the cause of the

French Revolution, is an echo of the Revolutionary cry, "Liberty Equality, Fraternity."

WILLIAM BLAKE

WILLIAM BLAKE was born in 1757 in London, where his father carried on a small hosiery business. After an apprenticeship of seven years to a prominent engraver by the name of Basire, he studied art for a time at the Royal Academy. But he soon gave up the orthodox ways of art, and began to engrave illustrations for various publishers, which he continued throughout the remainder of his life. His best-known engravings were those of Young's *Night Thoughts*, Blair's *Grave*, and *The Book of Job*. Early in life he developed the poetic gift, and later published a considerable body of poetry. Most of his poems were published by himself, and were accompanied by his own engravings. He died in 1827.

Blake is best described by the word mystic. As a child he believed he had seen angels in the trees and in the sky; later he said: "My desire is to converse with my friends throughout eternity, see visions, dream dreams, and prophesy and speak parables unobserved." His poetry falls into two divisions. The first includes the three groups of poems by which he is best known: *Poetical Sketches* (1783), *Songs of Innocence* (1789), and *Songs of Experience* (1794). These lyrics show a remarkable simplicity of diction, and are spontaneous like the voice of a bird; they reveal a love of nature and the lower animals, "stamped by the Divine image," and they show an interest in children and in the simple life. The second group of his poems includes the so-called Prophetic Books, which are so weird and obscure that commentators, after all these years of critical study, have been able to understand them only in part. In his love of children and in his mystical view of nature he anticipates Wordsworth; in his lyrical intensity he suggests Shelley.

WILLIAM WORDSWORTH

WILLIAM WORDSWORTH's long life of eighty years was, except for an occasional outburst of passion, singularly calm and simple. He was born at Cockermouth, in the Lake Region of Northern England, on April 7, 1770. His mother died when he was eight years of age, and his father followed her five years later. After preparing for college at the village school at Hawkshead he entered, in 1787, St. John's College, Cambridge. In the summer of 1790 he made a long tour through France, Switzerland, and Northern Italy; and in 1791, after graduating without honors from Cambridge, he went to France for about a year. Here his imagination, which had already been fired by the teachings of Rousseau, was profoundly stirred, and he threw his sympathy with the French Revolutionists. Disturbed over a love affair with a French girl, **Annette Vallon**, and disillusioned by the trend of events of the French Revolution, he returned home on the eve of England's declaration of war against France. He passed into a

NOTES

tate of melancholy and indecision until, in 1795, he and his sister set up house-keeping at Racedown, where Dorothy's genial personality restored some of his optimism and self-confidence. Two years later they joined the Coleridges at Nether Stowey, Somersetshire. Here Wordsworth and Coleridge planned *The Lyrical Ballads*. After an eight months' sojourn in Germany (1798–1799) he returned to England, rented Dove Cottage, Grasmere, and, in 1802, married Mary Hutchinson. In 1814 he moved to Rydal Mount, where he spent the remainder of his life. On the death of Southey, in 1843, he was appointed poet-laureate. He died in 1850.

In his poetry Wordsworth continues the literary traditions of Cowper, Burns, and Blake. The love of nature, the sympathy for the poor, the interest in the naïveté of children, and the tendency to philosophize about life which are present in the poetry of the early Romanticists are also present in Wordsworth's poetry. But Wordsworth goes beyond these poets, and makes a distinct contribution to English literature. This contribution consists largely of his imaginative vision of man and external nature—the two great themes of his poetry. Not only does he have the power of seeing objects as they are in nature, and, through his selection of details, of making others see them as he does, but by the process of creative imagination he shows the power of nature to transform the mind of man and to reveal the hidden mysteries of life. Moreover, in his philosophic vision he represents external nature as permeated with the presence of a Divine Being, visible in every flower, lake, and mountain. His themes are based on humble life not merely because he had a genuine sympathy for the poor, but because he thought he saw in these lowly people, who "are under less restraint," a better soil for the expression of the elementary passions of man. The simplicity of his diction and his invention of new verse-forms show the reaction against the classical school and the further development of the Romantic Movement.

WE ARE SEVEN

In this poem Wordsworth expresses his belief in the intuitive knowledge of children. The same idea is more fully developed in his *Ode on Intimations of Immortality* (lines 111 f.).

LINES WRITTEN IN EARLY SPRING

This poem is notable as an expression of Wordsworth's idea that Nature is a conscious thing, capable of feeling and sense-perception.

EXPOSTULATION AND REPLY

101, l. 15. **Mathew.** Probably Wordsworth's old teacher, William Taylor.

LINES COMPOSED A FEW MILES ABOVE TINTERN ABBEY

Wordsworth's philosophy of Nature is most fully brought out in this poem. The poem, therefore, is worthy of the most careful study. Lines 22-49 should be memorized.

The Lucy Poems

These five poems form a group which picture the poet's love for Lucy. No one knows whether Lucy really lived or whether she was merely the creation of the poet's imagination.

Michael

Of this poem Wordsworth says: "The Sheepfold, on which so much of the poem turns, remains, or rather the ruins of it. The character and circumstances of Luke were taken from a family to whom had belonged, many years before, the house we lived in at Town-end, along with some fields and Woodlands on the eastern shore at Grasmere. The name of the Evening Star was not in fact given to this house, but to another on the same side of the valley, more to the north."

My Heart Leaps Up

Here we have a succinct statement of Wordsworth's poetic philosophy: it is *The Prelude* condensed into a lyric.

128, l. 9. **Bound each to each,** etc. Bound up in reverence for God as He appears in Nature.

Resolution and Independence

Concerning this poem Wordsworth wrote: "Written at Town-end, Grasmere. This old man I met a few hundred yards from my cottage; and the account of him is taken from his own mouth. I was in the state of feeling described in the beginning of the poem, while crossing over Barton Fell from Mr. Clarkson's, at the foot of Ullswater, towards Askham. The image of the hare I then observed on the ridge of the Fell."

129, l. 43. **Chatterton.** Thomas Chatterton (1752-1770), author of the "forged" Rowley poems, was one of the most pathetic characters in English literature. Penniless and starving, he poisoned himself in his attic on Brooke Street, Holborn, in 1770.
    l. 45. **Of Him who walked,** etc. Robert Burns.

Composed upon Westminster Bridge

This and the six poems following, together with the last three poems of the selections from Wordsworth, are sonnets. Professor Oliver Elton, who reminds us that Wordsworth has left more than 500 examples of this form of poetry, says: "The sonnet, with its freedom of choice in theme and emotion, united to its exacting discipline, and to its special need of a clear intellectual basis and articulation, was a predestined form for Wordsworth."

NOTES

The Solitary Reaper

This poem is a favorite of Wordsworth's admirers. The poem is a fine example of the power of the imagination to reveal the highest truths of life. Its haunting melody and its intense emotional appeal add to its effectiveness.

I Wandered Lonely as a Cloud

The circumstances under which this poem was inspired are set forth in the following entry (dated April 15, 1802) in Dorothy Wordsworth's *Journal:* "When we were in the woods below Gowbarrow Park we saw a few daffodils close to the waterside. . . . I never saw daffodils so beautiful. They grew among the mossy stones, about and above them; some rested their heads on these stones as on a pillow for weariness; and the rest tossed, and reeled, and danced, and seemed as if they verily laughed with the wind that blew upon them over the lake."

139, l. 1. **I wandered lonely,** etc. Nature affects Wordsworth greatest when he is alone. Compare lines 21–22 below.

The Prelude

The Prelude was intended to serve as an introduction to a very long philosophical poem in three parts called *The Recluse*. Only the second part, *The Excursion*, was written; a fragment of the first part was printed after the poet's death; the third part seems never to have been undertaken.

Wordsworth attempts in *The Prelude* to embody, as he says, his "views on man, nature, and society." The poem, as the sub-title states, is autobiographical, setting forth the poet's reactions to the events of his life, and expressing the development of his theories on nature and on the social and political life of the times.

145, l. 105. **O pleasant exercise of hope and joy.** These lines first appeared in Coleridge's magazine, *The Friend*, October 26, 1809, under the title: *French Revolution, as it Appeared to Enthusiasts at its Commencement*.

Elegiac Stanzas

The Peele Castle portrayed in the picture is in Lancashire.

147, l. 1. **I was thy neighbor once.** Refers to a visit, during a summer vacation, to his cousin Mrs. Baker.
148, l. 42. **If he had lived.** The person referred to is Wordsworth's brother, Captain John Wordsworth, who went down with his ship off the coast of Portland, February 5, 1805.

Ode to Duty

Wordsworth says: "This ode is on the model of Gray's *Ode to Adversity*, which is copied from Horace's *Ode to Fortune*. Many and

526 NOTES

many a time have I been twitted by my wife and sister for having forgotten this stern dedication of myself to the stern lawgiver. Transgressor indeed I have been, from hour to hour, from day to day: I would fain hope, however, not more flagrantly or in a worse way than most of my tuneful brethren. But these last words are in a wrong strain. We should be rigorous to ourselves and forbearing, if not indulgent, to others, and if we make comparisons at all, it ought to be with those who have morally excelled us."

The poem is remarkable for its simplicity and beauty. Henry Reed says, "I would rather a child of mine should know and feel the high imaginative teachings of Wordsworth's *Ode to Duty* than any piece of uninspired prose morality in the language."

149, ll. 6–7. **Thou who art victory,** etc. Duty rather than fear is the impelling motive to righteousness.

l. 12. **the genial sense of youth.** The natural impulse of youthful innocence.

150, l. 19. **When love is an unerring light.** This suggests Shelley who believed that the world should be ruled not by law but by the principle of love.

150–151, ll. 41–48. In this fine stanza Wordsworth conceives the whole of nature as under the beneficent influence of the Stern Lawgiver.

The Character of a Happy Warrior

In a prefatory note Wordsworth states that the elements of character indicated in this poem are derived from the lives of Nelson and his brother John. The poem, however, is largely a reflection of Wordsworth's own life and ideals.

Ode on Intimations of Immortality

This poem is generally recognized as one of the highest creations of poetic genius. Of its content Emerson says: "I am a better believer, and all serious souls are better believers, in immortality than we can give grounds for. The real evidence is too subtle, or is higher than we can write down in propositions, and therefore Wordsworth's *Ode* is the best essay on the subject." Note, in reading the poem, that Wordsworth never descends to mere argument in support of immortality, but attempts imaginatively to make us realize the identity of the instincts of childhood and enlightened reason. The chief value of the poem, however, does not consist in the views of immortality or prenatal existence, but rather in its vision of the beauty of nature, and of its influence on the whole life of man.

156, l. 59. **Our birth is but a sleep,** etc. In his preface to this poem Wordsworth says concerning the pre-existence of the soul: "It is far too shadowy a notion to be recommended to faith, as more than an element in our instincts of im-

NOTES

mortality." For Plato's doctrine of pre-existence see *Phaedo*, sections 72-77 (Jowett's translation).

158-9, l. 140 f. those obstinate questionings, etc. "I was often unable to think of external things as having external existence, and I communed with all that I saw as something not apart from, but inherent in, my own immaterial nature. Many times while going to school have I grasped at a wall or tree to recall myself from this abyss of idealism to reality. . . . In later periods of life I have deplored, as we all have reason to do, a subjugation of an opposite character." (From Wordsworth's note.)

160, ll. 202-03. To me the meanest flower, etc. "These lines," says Professor Dowden, "have been often quoted as an illustration of Wordsworth's sensibility to external nature; in reality, they testify to his enriching the sentiment of nature with feeling derived from the heart of man and from the experience of human life."

The World Is Too Much with Us

161, ll. 13-14. Have sight of Proteus, etc. Proteus and Triton were sea-deities of Greek mythology. Wordsworth means he had rather be a heathen with some appreciation of Nature than a professed Christian who is so occupied with wealth and ambition that he has lost all sympathy for the sights and sounds of land and sea.

After Thought

This is the last sonnet of a series which Wordsworth wrote under the title *The River Duddon*. The Duddon is a small stream which rises on the border of Westmoreland and flows into the Irish Sea.

SAMUEL TAYLOR COLERIDGE

Coleridge was born at the vicarage of Ottery, in Devonshire, in 1772. He received his early education from his father, who served in the dual capacity of vicar of the parish and master of the village school. At the age of ten he proceeded to Christ's Hospital, London, where his precocity and marked literary ability soon became evident. Here he met Charles Lamb, who has vividly described their friendship in *Christ's Hospital Five and Thirty Years Ago*. In 1791 he entered Jesus College, Cambridge, as a sizar or needy student. A complication of causes—bad debts, disappointed love, and a generally unsettled state of mind growing out of radical political and religious sympathies—led him, two years later, to leave the University suddenly and to enlist in the King's Regiment of Light Dragoons under the fictitious name of Silas Tomkyn Comberbacke. After being discharged from the army in April, 1794, he returned to Cambridge, but left in December without taking a degree. At this time he fell

528   NOTES

in with the plan of Robert Southey and others to establish a "Pantisocracy" on the banks of the Susquehanna. But in 1795 Coleridge and Southey married Edith and Sarah Fricker, and the Utopian scheme was dropped.

In 1796 appeared his first volume of poems. But lack of money, increasing family responsibilities, bad health, and a consequent habit of taking opium, led to a general depression of spirits, which only the bracing influence of Dorothy and William Wordsworth, whom he met in that year, could alleviate. Toward the close of this year the Coleridges moved into a small cottage at Nether Stowey, where the Wordsworths joined them soon afterward. Here the famous *Lyrical Ballads* was planned.

In 1798 Coleridge joined the Wordsworths on their tour to Germany, but left them early the next year to perfect his knowledge of the language and to study at the University of Göttingen. In November, 1799, he took up residence in London, engaged in journalistic work, and in 1800 went to live at Greta Hall, Keswick.

Soon afterwards Coleridge and his wife separated. Coleridge sank from bad to worse: the opium habit took firm hold on him, his health declined, and he suffered fits of despondency which were only relieved by the advances of money and sympathy from kindly publishers and staunch friends. (See *Dejection: an Ode*, composed in 1802, as a good commentary on Coleridge at this time.) After another trip to the continent and some fruitless literary undertakings, Coleridge finally admitted defeat by placing himself under the care of Dr. Gillman who undertook, not quite successfully, to cure him of his use of narcotics and stimulants. He spent his last years in retirement, the object of a wide circle of admirers, especially among the young and rising generation of litterateurs. He died in 1834.

Coleridge is known as a poet, a philosopher, and a literary critic. The poetry on which his fame chiefly rests was produced before he was thirty years of age, yet the quality of this work is such as to place him among the greatest of the Romantic poets. His greatest prose achievement is the *Biographia Literaria* (1817), which gives illuminating glimpses of his life, of his philosophical opinions, and of his literary theories.

This Lime-Tree Bower My Prison

The "long-expected friends" referred to in Coleridge's note are Charles and Mary Lamb (see line 28). The poem is interesting not so much for its comments on the visit of his friends, but for its beautiful descriptions of nature, based largely on his surroundings at Nether Stowey.

191, l.   3. **Beauties and feelings.** That is, the beauties of the walk, and the feelings which his friends would have inspired.
193, l. 60. **That nature ne'er deserts,** etc. Compare Wordsworth's *Tintern Abbey*, lines 122–3.

NOTES

KUBLA KHAN

For word-music and imagery this is one of the most remarkable poems in the language. Professor William A. Neilson, writing of the poem in his *Essentials of Poetry* (page 43), says: "We have no wrestling with spiritual questions, no lofty solution of the problem of conduct found through brooding on the beauties of nature. Instead, a thousand impressions received from the senses, from records of Oriental travel, from numberless romantic tales, have been taken in by the author, dissolved as in a crucible by the fierce heat of his imagination, and are poured forth a molten stream of sensuous imagery, incalculable in its variety of suggestion, yet homogeneous, unified, and, despite its fragmentary character, the ultimate expression of a whole romantic world."

THE RIME OF THE ANCIENT MARINER

The origin of this poem is given by Wordsworth in his preface to *We Are Seven* (see the Globe Edition of Wordsworth, Macmillan, pages 73-74). Further comments on the poem may be found in Coleridge's *Biographia Literaria*, Chapter XIV (pages 258-260 in the present text).

FROST AT MIDNIGHT

Aside from the charm of its blank verse and beautiful descriptions of nature this poem has an autobiographical value. It was written at Nether Stowey and was "the outcome of a midnight meditation."

221, l. 15. **that film.** Coleridge has the following note on this line, which also throws light on the word "stranger" in line 26: "In all parts of the kingdom these films are called *strangers* and supposed to portend the arrival of some absent friend."

222, l. 25. **at school.** Christ's Hospital, where Coleridge was at school from 1782 to 1791.

222, l. 42. **or sister more beloved.** Coleridge was very fond of his sister, who was five years his senior. She died in 1791.

223, ll. 60-64. These lines contain a succinct statement of Coleridge's philosophy of Nature.

FRANCE: AN ODE

This poem breathes the spirit of the times. Coleridge, like Wordsworth, was at first in sympathy with the French Revolution as a movement toward freedom and democracy. The present ode is a magnificent poetical utterance of the author's reaction against the excesses that followed the triumph of the Revolutionists. The argument of the poem proceeds from stanza to stanza as follows: (1) The poet's invocation to Nature to bear witness that he has ever worshiped "the spirit of divinest Liberty"; (2) his exultation at the beginning of the French Revolution and his abhorrence of the alliance against the Republic; (3) his continued faith in liberty during the wild excesses of the Reign of Terror; (4) his recantation when France invaded free Switzerland; (5) his address to Liberty, expressing the conviction that the ideal of freedom comes to the individual man through love of Nature.

224, l. 30. **The Monarchs marched,** etc. France declared war against Austria and Prussia on April 20, 1792; against England, Holland, and Spain on February 1, 1793.

225, l. 43. **Blasphemy's loud scream.** During the Reign of Terror (1793–1794) women dressed to represent the Goddess of Reason were enthroned in Notre Dame Cathedral.

l. 50. **The dissonance ceased.** The reaction against the Reign of Terror led to the establishment of the Directory (1795), under which the French achieved some of their greatest victories.

l. 66. **From bleak Helvetia's,** etc. The invasion of Switzerland in 1798 was the occasion of Coleridge's Ode.

Christabel

In its mediaeval setting and atmosphere of terror *Christabel* suggests the tales of wonder which German romanticism had made popular. Swinburne writes of Coleridge's early poetry: "When it has been said that such melodies were never heard, such dreams never dreamed, and such speech never spoken, the chief thing remains unsaid and unspeakable. There is a charm in these poems which can only be felt in silent submission to wonder. Were we compelled to the choice, I for one would rather preserve *Kubla Khan* and *Christabel* than any other of Coleridge's poems. . . . The former is the most wonderful of the poems, while the loveliest is assuredly *Christabel*." Coleridge told Gillman that the poem was founded on the notion that "the virtuous of this world save the wicked." The third part referred to in Coleridge's note was never written.

Much of the charm of the poem depends on the meter, which Coleridge invented.

233, l. 129. **The lady sank,** etc. The fact that the lady could not cross the threshold (which had probably been blessed by the church) shows that she is a witch or demon.

l. 142. **I cannot speak.** Observe that Geraldine cannot join in the prayer of line 139,—another proof that she is an evil creature.

l. 149. **What can ail the mastiff bitch?** Animals have a keen sense of the presence of supernatural creatures.

ll. 159–60. **A tongue of light,** etc. The flame of fire connects the witch with the regions of hell, and at the same time reveals the eye of the wicked one.

NOTES 531

235, ll. 205–06. **Off, wandering mother!** etc. The wicked Geraldine has power to drive off the kindly spirit of Christabel's mother.

236, l. 252. **Behold! her bosom and half her side.** Both the Globe and the Oxford editions of Coleridge give the following line from another manuscript: "Are lean and old and fond of hue." This line, which appears between ll. 252–3, gives the key to Geraldine's character.

239, l. 344–51. **From Bratha Head,** etc. The places referred to in these lines are in the lake region, but the scene of *Christabel* is in the land of faery enchantment.

242, ll. 408–26. Coleridge said of these lines, "The best and sweetest I ever wrote."

DEJECTION: AN ODE

This ode was first printed in *The Morning Post* on Wordsworth's wedding day, October 4, 1802. An early manuscript preserved at Coleorton shows that the poem was addressed to Wordsworth (see notes). Later, after the two poets were temporarily estranged, Coleridge revised the poem, reprinting it in 1817. The later edition is used in this text; the first printed form appears in the Globe Edition of Coleridge's works, page 522, and in the Oxford Edition, page 574.

On the poem as reflecting Coleridge's life at this time, see the editor's biographical sketch of Coleridge. In addition to his troubles there mentioned, Coleridge felt that he had lost his most precious endowment—"My shaping spirit of imagination" (l. 86).

250, l. 2. **The grand old ballad,** etc. This ballad was first printed by Thomas Percy in his *Reliques of Ancient English Poetry* (1765). The stanza from this ballad which Coleridge quotes at the beginning of his poem forms the motto of the ode.

251, l. 13. **I see the old moon,** etc. The poem was written on April 4 (1802), the day on which the moon entered its first quarter.

l. 25. **O lady!** In the Coleorton manuscript, "Wordsworth" took the place of "lady"; in the 1802 edition the word "Edmund" occurs.

l. 40. **what can these avail,** etc. The beauties of nature referred to in the preceding stanza.

252, l. 53 f. **Ah! from the soul must issue forth,** etc. Coleridge here expresses the philosophy that it is the mind or soul, through feeling, which colors Nature with the attributes of beauty and sweetness. Compare Wordsworth's philosophy as expressed in the last stanza of *I Wandered Lonely as a Cloud*.

253, l. 76–93. Mr. Arthur Symons says (*The Romantic Movement in English Poetry*, p. 137) that this stanza is the biography of the poet's soul.

254, l. 120 f. **As Otway's self**, etc. The Coleorton manuscript has "William's self"; the 1802 edition has "Edmund's self." The allusion in lines 121-125 is to Wordsworth's *Lucy Gray, or Solitude*. The reference here to Thomas Otway (1652-1685) is less appropriate.

Hymn Before Sunrise

"Printed in *The Morning Post*, 11 Sept. 1802, with a prefatory note which might have been taken as implying that Coleridge was familiar with the scene he was describing. He had, however, never visited Chamouni, and his poem was elaborated from a German original by Frederika Brun, to which he made no acknowledgment." (A. Hamilton Thompson.)

255, l. 3. **O sovran Blanc.** Mount Blanc rises above the Vale of Chamouni.

ll. 17-23. Compare these lines with the lines 53-58 in *Dejection: an Ode*

Work Without Hope

258, l. 9. **Bloom, O ye amaranths!** etc. Amaranths are symbolic of immortality.

ll. 10-14. These lines show the poet's depression over the loss of poetic power, more fully set forth in *Dejection*.

Epitaph

This epitaph is on Coleridge's grave in Highgate Churchyard.

Biographia Literaria

Biographia Literaria is "the most permanent, profound, and distinct" of Coleridge's prose writings; and the fourteenth chapter, given in the text, is the best statement of his literary theory.

Page 265. **Praecipitandus**, etc. A free spirit must be urged forward.

266. **Laxis effertur**, etc. Is borne along with loosened reins.

ROBERT SOUTHEY

It is customary to associate the name of Robert Southey with that of Wordsworth and Coleridge, the other two members of the "Lake Poets." Born at Bristol in 1774, Southey was educated at Westminster and Oxford. Like Wordsworth and Coleridge he was early converted to revolutionary ideas, and, like them also, he veered to the opposite extreme of the scale and became an unbending conservative. While at Oxford he joined Coleridge in the scheme of "Pantisocracy" (see the life of Coleridge), and on its collapse he married Sarah Fricker and became Coleridge's brother-in-law. After a long visit to Spain and Portugal, where he acquired a knowledge of the language and literature of the Peninsula, he returned to England and settled, in 1803, at Greta Hall, Keswick, devoting himself assiduously to literary work. He died as poet-laureate of England in 1843. He was a man of beautiful character—tender, true-hearted, and brave; he gave cheerfully and unstintedly to the support of Coleridge's family, and ungrudgingly provided a home for his wife's widowed sister.

Southey was a prodigious writer; and because of the general inferiority of his work it is not likely to appear in a collected edition. His most pretentious poems are *Thalaba the Destroyer* (1801), *Madoc* (1805), and the *Curse of Kehema* (1810). These oriental tales illustrate "the tendency of Romanticism to go far afield in quest of fresh material." Southey is best remembered for his short poems (three of which appear in this volume), and for his admirable biographies of Nelson and John Wesley.

THE BATTLE OF BLENHEIM

In 1700 the question of Spanish succession brought about a war in which England was involved. The Duke of Marlborough and Prince Eugene Savoy (a distinguished Austrian general) formed an alliance and defeated the French and Bavarians at Blenheim, August 13, 1704.

MY DAYS AMONG THE DEAD ARE PAST

Southey was a great lover of books, and spent much of his time in his library, which contained about 14,000 volumes.

SIR WALTER SCOTT

SIR WALTER SCOTT was born in Edinburgh, in 1771, of an ancient Scottish clan that numbered in its time many a hard rider and good fighter. His father, who was the first member of the clan to abandon country life, was a lawyer of considerable standing. As a child Scott spent much of his time at his grandfather's farm at Sandyknowe, where his early love for nature was developed, and where his mind was stored with the tales of Border feuds which the old women related to him. After graduating from Edinburgh University he studied law, was later admitted to the bar, and practiced his profession for some time in his native city. In 1798, shortly after his marriage, he took up his residence at Lasswade on the Esk. In the following year he was appointed sheriff of Selkirkshire, and through his official contacts with the Scottish highlanders he gathered much of the material for his famous collection of ballads published under the title *The Minstrelsy of the Scottish Border* in 1802. But his literary career really began in 1805 when, at the age of thirty-four, he published *The Lay of the Last Minstrel*. This was followed by the other well-known narrative poems, *Marmion* (1808), *The Lady of the Lake* (1810), and *Rokeby*

(1813). From the proceeds of these poems, and with an annual salary of £1,300 as clerk of session, he bought an estate a few miles down the Tweed at Abbotsford and built a home, where he was to spend the remainder of his life. Because of Byron's extraordinary success as a narrative poet, Scott turned from verse tales to the novel as his future field of labor. Beginning with *Waverley* (1814) and ending with *Castle Dangerous* (1831) he wrote twenty-nine novels—about two a year. During the period of his novel-writing he was made baronet (1820), and was involved in the financial crash of the publishing house of Constable and Ballantyne (1825). Though not legally responsible for the failure, Scott assumed a debt of £130,000 and worked doggedly with his pen, in spite of failing health, to pay it in full. In 1830 he was seized with paralysis; in the following year he had a second stroke, which incapacitated him for further work. He died in 1832, and was buried at Dryburg Abbey.

Scott's literary work falls into three periods: (1) his translations (including Bürger's *Lenore* and Goethe's *Götz von Berlichingen*); (2) his narrative poems, with their stirring scenes of action, their vivid character delineations, and their strong and buoyant meter; and (3) his novels, embodying the spirit of Gothic romance and the historic past. His greatest achievement was in the novel, but to most readers he is best known for his charming lyrics, scattered throughout his novels and narrative poems.

CALEDONIA

These stirring, patriotic lines form the prelude to the concluding part of the minstrel's story. They are, of course, spoken by the minstrel, who is "the last survivor of a bygone age of song." "Caledonia" is the Latin name for Scotland.

LOCHINVAR

This song (found in Canto V, XII) is sung by Lady Heron to James IV and his court at Holyrood. Scott tells us that the story is "in a very slight degree founded on a ballad called *Katharine Janfarie*, which may be found in *The Minstrelsy of the Scottish Border*."

275, l. 20. **Love swells like the Solway.** The Solway Firth, between England and Scotland, is noted for the swift rise of its tides.
276, l. 44. **Forsters, Fenwicks, and Muskgraves.** Names of border families.
    l. 45. **Cannobie Lee.** Cannobie is on the Esk River in Dumfriesshire.

SOLDIER REST

This song (Canto I, xxxi–xxxii) is sung by Ellen to the music of an unseen harp at the close of the evening spent by Fitz-James on the island.

NOTES 535

278, l. 15. **pibroch.** Martial strains played on the bagpipe.
l. 34. **reveillé.** The bugle-note sounded at early morn to awaken soldiers and huntsmen.

Brignall Banks

Brignall Banks referred to here are in the southeast corner of Rokeby Park on the left side of the Greta River in Yorkshire. Greta woods (l. 2) are on the left side of the Greta opposite Brignall. Edmund who sings the song is a young outlaw.

Jock of Hazeldean

Hazeldean, now called Hassendean, is in Roxburghshire. The speaker who pleads the cause of his son is a Northumberland laird.

283, ll. 11-12. Errington and Langley-dale are in the Tyne Valley in Northumberland.

Pibroch of Donuil Dhu

Donuil Dhu, or Donald the Black, was the chieftain of the Campbell clan. Inverlochy (l. 12) is at the head of Loch Linnhe near the boundaries of Argyll and Inverness.

THOMAS CAMPBELL

A minor poet of this period, Thomas Campbell, had considerable influence in furthering the development of Romanticism. He was born in Glasgow in 1777, graduated from the university there, founded the University of London, and later became rector of his Alma Mater. He began his literary career as an imitator of Pope, but a visit to Germany in 1797 brought him under the influence of Bürger and other German Romanticists; and in 1803 he published a group of poems in the new vein, including *Hohenlinden* and *The Exile of Erin*. In addition to writing poetry he did considerable hack-work for the magazines. He died in 1844.

Campbell is best known for his war lyrics, which are full of martial energy and are written in a meter admirably adapted to the theme.

Ye Mariners of England

The popularity of this poem was doubtless increased by the brilliant naval victories which the English had just won over the French.

Hohenlinden

At Hohenlinden, a village near Munich, the French defeated the Austrians, December 2, 1800. Campbell visited the battle field in 1802, in which year he wote his famous poem.

LORD ULLIN'S DAUGHTER

The scene of this poem is the island of Mull, off the west coast of Scotland, where the poet spent several months as a tutor in 1795.

291, l. 5. **Lochgyle.** A small arm of the sea at the west coast of Scotland.
l. 7. **Ulva.** A small island southwest of Mull. "The lovers were fleeing from the island to the highland, on the mainland." (Bronson).

THOMAS MOORE

THOMAS MOORE, Ireland's greatest lyric poet, was born in Dublin in 1779, and was educated at Trinity College. He won the esteem of scholars by his early work, consisting of translations from *Anacreon* (1800), *Poems of the Late Thomas Little* (1801), and *Epistles, Odes and other Poems* (1806). But he is known to the general reader as the author of *Irish Melodies* (1807–1834) and *Lalla Rookh* (1817). The former consists of a group of poems which express the haunting melody of the Celtic race and possess much of the singing quality of the lyrics of Burns; the latter is an oriental tale overloaded with gaudy ornament and "candied sweetness," but full, nevertheless, of beautiful sentiment. Moore is also known for his *Life and Letters of Lord Byron* (1830), which in its day was held in high esteem, and which is still regarded as a standard work. Moore died in 1852.

THE HARP THAT ONCE THROUGH TARA'S HALL

This poem is one of the *Irish Melodies*. Tara (l. 1), near Dublin, was the residence of royalty in the early history of Ireland.

GEORGE GORDON (LORD) BYRON

LORD BYRON, more than any other English romanticist, has come in the popular mind to stand for the very essence of Romanticism. In his figure were combined at once headlong passion, a god-like physical beauty, noble but tumultuous blood, dash, arrogance and hauteur, defiance of the common conventionalities of life, romantic and strange adventures, over all of which he took care to cast a mysteriousness which made him the object of a highly exaggerated and glorified hero-cult.

Born in London in 1788 of a scapegrace father and an erratic mother, Byron was unfortunate in his temperamental inheritance. His childhood was spent in Aberdeen, Scotland. At the age of ten, he became a Lord and the heir to the ancestral home of the Byrons, Newstead Abbey, in Nottinghamshire. After some rather haphazard schooling the boy proceeded to Harrow and in due time to Cambridge. After three years he received, in 1808, the M.A. degree.

In the meantime he had been scribbling verses, which he published in 1807 under the title of *Hours of Idleness*. A harsh review of these

NOTES

juvenile poems in the *Edinburgh Magazine* drew from him a scathing satire, *English Bards and Scotch Reviewers* (frequently called "the *Dunciad* of Romanticism").

In 1809–1811 he made a trip to Southern Europe and the near East, and upon his return published the first two cantos of *Childe Harold's Pilgrimage* (1812). Upon the publication of this poem Byron said, "I awoke one morning and found myself famous." Then followed a period during which Byron reigned as a kind of glorified social lion. He followed up his success with a series of romantic and oriental verse tales. At the height of his fame he married Anne Milbanke (January, 1815). A year later (for reasons not definitely known) they separated. The London, which a year before had bowed in admiration to him, suddenly turned to scowl at him; and shortly afterwards he left England on his self-imposed exile from which he was destined never to return.

After some time spent in Switzerland in company with the Shelleys, he went to Venice, where he spent much of the years 1816–1819. All this time he was busily writing and publishing. *The Prisoner of Chillon*, *Mazeppa*, and the last two cantos of *Childe Harold* belong to this period. In 1818 also he began *Don Juan*, which was published at intervals from 1819 until his death. His dramas, of which *Cain* and *Manfred* are the best-known, appeared between 1821 and 1824.

Of his life in Italy much has been written condemning him. In the eyes of many, he redeemed himself when, a few months before his death, he left Italy for Greece and there took a leading part in the struggle for Grecian independence. His colorful and romantic career came to a close when he succumbed to a fever at Missolonghi on April 19, 1824.

Oh! Snatched Away in Beauty's Bloom

These lines probably refer to a lost love, the mysterious Thyrza, to whom Byron addressed a poem in 1811 (See the Globe Edition, page 299).

She Walks in Beauty

The 1832 edition of Byron's poems has the following note on this poem: "These stanzas were written by Lord Byron on returning from a ballroom, where he had seen Mrs. (now Lady) Wilmot Horton, the wife of his relation, the present governor of Ceylon. On this occasion Mrs. W. H. had appeared, with numerous spangles on her dress."

The Destruction of Sennacherib

For the Biblical account of this story see II Kings XVIII–XIX, especially XVIII, 13 and XIX, 35.

298, l. 21. **The widows of Ashur.** That is, of Assyria (which was the ancient Semitic Kingdom of Ashur).

NOTES

THE PRISONER OF CHILLON

The Castle of Chillon is situated on the eastern side of Lake Geneva. François de Bonnivard, the Swiss patriot whose afflictions are celebrated in the poem, was imprisoned here from 1530 to 1536 for his opposition to the Duke of Savoy. Byron visited the spot with the Shelleys in June, 1816, and shortly afterwards composed the poem. But the Bonnivard of Byron's poem is a romantic idealization, and not a historical figure. In a note Byron says, "When this poem was composed I was not sufficiently aware of the figure of Bonnivard." The three brothers are wholly imaginary.

CHILDE HAROLD'S PILGRIMAGE, CANTO III

In his Preface to the first and second Cantos of *Childe Harold*, Byron says: "The following poem was written, for the most part, amidst the scenes which it attempts to describe.... A fictitious character is introduced for the sake of giving some connection to the piece. ... It has been suggested to me by friends ... that in this fictitious character ... I may incur the suspicion of having intended some real personage; this I beg leave, once for all, to disclaim—Harold is the child of the imagination, for the purpose I have stated."

The first two cantos were published in 1812; the third, in 1816; and the fourth, in 1818. The whole poem has been called a glorified guidebook. But it is valuable not so much for its descriptions as for the thoughts and feelings which the places visited aroused in the mind of the author. The third canto, given here, reveals most of the characteristics of the poet. Permeated with the author's own personality, it is marked by passion, concentration, rapidity of movement, and sharp contrasts in thought and imagination. The influence of Shelley's ideal of love and of Wordsworth's feeling for nature is apparent. The Spenserian stanza, which is used in the poem, is admirably adapted to the beauty and majesty of the thought expressed.

The following outline will show the subjects treated and the places visited in this Canto; the numbers enclosed in parentheses refer to the stanzas of the poem.

I. Introduction (1–16)
    1. Last Leaving of England and Personal Reflections
II. Waterloo and the Duchess of Richmond's Ball (17–35)
III. Reflections on Napoleon (36–45)
IV. Journey on the Rhine (46–61)
    1. The Ruined Castle of Drachenfels (55)
    2. Coblentz and the Tomb of Marceau (56–57)
    3. The Fort of Ehrenbreitstein (58)
V. Switzerland (62–109)
    1. The Alps (62)
    2. The Battlefield of Morat (63–64)
    3. Aventicum and the Story of Julia (65–67)

NOTES

    4. Lake Geneva and the Influence of Nature (68–75)
    5. Rousseau and the Revolution (76–84)
    6. Lake Geneva—Descriptions and Reflections (85–98)
    7. Clarens and Rousseau (99–104)
    8. Lausanne and Gibbon; Ferney and Voltaire (105–109)
VI. Conclusion (110–118)
    1. Prospect of Italy (110)
    2. Final Reflections (111–117)
    3. Farewell to his Daughter (118)

312, ll. 2–3. **Ada.** Byron's daughter, Augusta Ada, was born in 1815, later married the Count of Lovelace, and died in 1852.

    ll. 10–18. This stanza shows Byron's love for the ocean. Compare the famous passage on the ocean in Canto IV (sts. 179–180).

313, l. 19. **I did sing one.** Childe Harold, Cantos I and II.

314, ll. 46–49. **'Tis to create,** etc. These lines, which express the poet's theory of art, are worthy of the most careful study.

317, l. 145. **Empire's Dust.** The Battle of Waterloo, in which Wellington and Blücher overthrew Napoleon and the French empire, was fought on June 18, 1815, a year before this Canto was written.

318, l. 158. **"pride of place,"** etc. A term in falconry, meaning the highest point of flight. The eagle referred to in this line is Napoleon.

    l. 168. **The patched-up idol,** etc. Refers to the "Holy Alliance," toward which Byron was bitterly hostile.

319, l. 180. **Harmodius.** Harmodius and Aristogeiton, with swords hidden in myrtle leaves, slew the Athenian Hipparcus in 514 B. C.

    l. 182. **And Belgium's capital had gathered,** etc. The famous ball was given by the Duchess of Richmond on June 15, 1815, the eve of the battle of Quatre Bras; many British officers, including Wellington, were present. Byron's descriptive power is at its best in this division of the poem.

320, l. 200. **Brunswick.** The Duke of Brunswick, nephew of George III, who was killed early in the battle of Quatre Bras.

321, l. 225. **"Cameron's gathering."** The slogan or battle cry of the Cameron clan.

    l. 226. **Albyn.** Gaelic for Scotland.

    l. 235. **Ardennes.** "The wood of Soignies is supposed to be a remnant of the forest of Ardennes . . . immortal in Shakespeare's *As You Like It*." (Byron)

322, l. 261. **Howard.** Major Howard, son of Byron's unsympathetic guardian, the Earl of Carlisle. Byron satirized the earl in *English Bards and Scotch Reviewers*.

    ll. 262–270. One of the finest stanzas in Byron's poetry.

324, ll. 316 f. **There sunk the greatest,** etc. Byron's estimate of Napoleon expressed in this division of the poem should be compared with estimates given by the author in Canto IV (sts. 89–92) and in the *Ode on Napoleon Buonaparte.*

331, l. 476. **In one fond breast.** Byron's half sister, Augusta. See his *Epistle to Augusta*, where he refers to her faithfulness amid the almost universal slander of the people of his native country.

l. 496. **The castled crags of Drachenfels.** The ruined castle of Drachenfels is on the right bank of the Rhine, opposite Bonn.

333, l. 541. **Marceau.** A general of the French Republic who fell near Coblentz in 1796.

l. 554. **Ehrenbreitstein.** A fortress on the Rhine opposite Coblentz. It was captured by the French in 1799.

335, l. 601. **Morat.** Here the Duke of Burgundy was defeated by the Swiss in 1476.

l. 608. **Cannæ.** Hannibal defeated the Romans at this place in 216 B. C.

l. 609. **Marathon.** The scene of the famous victory of the Greeks over the Persians, 400 B. C.

336, l. 616. **Draconic.** Refers to the strict laws formulated by Draco, earliest of Athenian lawgivers.

l. 625. **Aventicum.** The Roman capital of Helvetia, now known as Avenches.

l. 627. **Julia.** According to Byron, Julia Alpinula was a young Aventian princess who died in a vain endeavor to save her father, who was condemned to death as a traitor.

337, ll. 644 f. Professor Hardin Craig says: "In stanzas LXVIII–LXXV Byron probably shows his greatest resemblance to Wordsworth, and yet there seems to be little enough in them of the spirit of peaceful acquiescence, which is the characteristic mood of Wordsworth."

338, l. 673. **The blue rushing of the arrowy Rhone.** "The color of the Rhone at Geneva is blue, to a depth of tint which I have never seen in water, salt or fresh, except in the Mediterranean and Archipelago." (Byron)

340, l. 719. **One whose dust was once all fire.** Rousseau was born at Geneva and spent his youth there. For Rousseau's influence see the editor's comment in the Introduction, page xx.

341, l. 743. **Julie.** The heroine of Rousseau's novel, *The New Heloise*, the scene of which is laid near Lake Geneva.

l. 746. **The memorable kiss.** "This refers to the account, in his Confessions, of his passion for the Comtesse d' Houdetot, . . . and his long walk every morning, for the sake of a single kiss which was the common salutation of French acquaintance." (Byron)

l. 762. **Pythian's mystic cave.** The oracle of Apollo at Delphi; the prophetess was called Pythia.

NOTES 541

343-4, ll. 797-841. For pure idyllic beauty these stanzas have never been surpassed. Note the imagery and rhythm of these lines.

345, l. 847. **Cytherea's Zone.** The girdle of the Cytherean Aphrodite (Venus), which was supposed to bring love to its wearer.

347, ll. 905-13. "This stanza is the climax toward which the preceding ones, descriptive of the storm, have been mounting. Without much paradox it may be called the most essentially Byronic thing in Byron." (F. I. Carpenter)

l. 923. **Clarens.** A town on Lake Geneva, mentioned in Rousseau.

350, l. 977. **Lausanne! and Ferney!** Gibbon finished his *The Decline and Fall of the Roman Empire* at Lausanne in 1788; Voltaire spent the last nine years of his life at Ferney.

351, l. 1022 f. **Italia!** etc. This imaginary view of Italy prepares us for Byron's itinerary in Canto IV.

l. 1024. **The fierce Carthagenian.** Hannibal.

To Thomas Moore

Thomas Moore (1779-1852) was Byron's intimate friend and authorized biographer.

Don Juan

Don Juan, a long poem of sixteen cantos, is considered by many as Byron's masterpiece. Ostensibly the story of the traditional Spanish hero, Don Juan, it is in fact a satire against all that Byron found hollow in British politics, society, and literature. In verse that flows as easily as conversation, he mocks the morals of his countrymen, and launches his bitterest witticisms against their hypocrisy. The poem recites the intrigues and wanderings of the hero, but is occupied primarily with the author's reflections on life as he saw it. It is flippant, witty, caustic, cynical, and withal not entirely sincere. The libertinism of the hero offended the public of Byron's day, who took the poem as a "eulogy of vice," whereas it was intended, according to Byron, as "the comic epic of the human race."

At the opening of the present selection, Juan is being entertained by Haidee at the home of her father. To enliven the occasion a native poet is asked to sing. His song (*The Isles of Greece*) is followed by Byron's reflections on the theme.

356, l. 674. **"Ça Ira."** "It will speed": The famous Revolutionary song of the French.

l. 677. **If Pindar sang horse-races.** Pindar, the chief lyric poet of Greece, is known especially for his odes, celebrating the victories won in the Greek games; some of his odes celebrate the victors in horse-races.

l. 684. **De Stael.** Madame de Staël (1766-1817) was the author

NOTES

of *De l'Allemagne*, in which Goethe and other German authors are discussed.

l. 685. **Trecentisti.** Italian artists of the fourteenth century.

l. 688. **Sappho.** Famous Greek poetess of love (c. 600 B. C.)

l. 690. **Delos.** According to an ancient fable, the island of Delos, the birthplace of Phoebus Apollo, rose in the Ægean Sea.

357, l. 693. **Scian and the Teian Muse.** The Scian muse is Homer, from the island of Scio, which claimed to be his birthplace. The Teian muse is Anacreon, who was born at Teios in Asia Minor.

l. 698. **"Islands of the Blest."** "The Μακάρων νῆσοι of the Greek poets were supposed to have been the Cape de Verd Islands, or the Canaries." (Byron)

ll. 705–6. **A king**, etc. Xerxes, King of Persia, who in 480 B. C. was defeated by the Greek navy at Salamis.

358, l. 728. **Thermopylæ.** Memorable as the scene of the heroic death of Leonidas and his three hundred Spartans in their attempt to stem the tide of the Persian invasion (480 B. C.)

359, l. 741. **Pyrrhic dance.** Grecian war dance, in quick time.

l. 742. **Pyrrhic phalanx.** Mode of warfare used by King Pyrrhus of Epirus (318–272 B. C.)

l. 745. **Cadmus.** Legendary King of Thebes, who is supposed to have invented the Greek alphabet.

ll. 749–50. **Anacreon . . . Polycrates.** Anacreon, who sang of love and wine, was entertained at Samos by the tyrant Polycrates (d. 522 B. C.)

ll. 753–55. **Chersonese . . . Miltiades.** For several years before the Battle of Marathon, Miltiades reigned as a tyrant over the Chersonese in Crete.

l. 760. **Suli. . . . Parga.** Sulla is a fortress on the River Suli southwest of Janina; "Parga" is in Albania.

360, l. 764. **Heracleidan blood.** The blood of Heracles, from whom the Heracleidæ are fabled to have descended.

l. 777. **Sunium's marbled steep.** Cape Colona.

362, l. 813. **Marlborough's skill.** Famous general at the Battle of Blenheim, 1704.

l. 819. **Johnson's way.** Refers to Samuel Johnson's life of Milton in *Lives of the English Poets* (1779–80).

l. 834. **peddler poems.** This refers to the humble characters in Wordsworth's poems.

363, l. 838. **Espoused two partners.** Edith and Sarah Fricker.

l. 850. **Joanna Southcote's Shiloh.** "The fanatic founder of a sect of religious enthusiasts. She proclaimed that she was to become the mother of a second Shiloh." (F. I. Carpenter)

366, ll. 932–33. Refers to events told by tales of Boccaccio and Dryden.

368, l. 973. **Cantabs.** Cambridge University students or graduates.
l. 982. Ποιητικής. The *Poetics* of Aristotle.

On This Day I Complete My Thirty-Sixth Year

This was Byron's last poem; it was written in Greece a few weeks before his death.

PERCY BYSSHE SHELLEY

Shelley was born in Field Place, Sussex, in 1792. He was the oldest son of a wealthy country squire whose inability to understand his strange child became an important factor in his son's later career. At the age of ten, young Shelley was sent to Sion House Academy, near London. Two years later he went to Eton, where he was called by the older boys "mad Shelley" because of his determined and desperate attempts to resist the system of "fagging" then in force.

At the age of eighteen he went to Oxford, only to be expelled, in March, 1811, for writing and circulating a pamphlet of rebellious and atheistical content, *The Necessity of Atheism*. This affair brought upon him the disapprobation of his father; and when, during the summer of the same year, he eloped with Harriet Westbrook, a London schoolgirl of sixteen, his father's displeasure was increased. But he continued his son's allowance, and the Shelleys set out for Ireland. For two or three years Shelley read extensively in philosophy and literature, and made himself generally obnoxious by the expression of his radical views.

In 1814 Shelley met William Godwin (author of *Political Justice*), and shortly afterward he eloped with Godwin's daughter, Mary, to France. In 1816 Harriet, who in the meantime had formed other attachments, ended her life by drowning in the Serpentine. Shelley now married Mary Godwin and set out for Italy in search of better health and to avoid any legal action that might be taken against him in England.

In Italy he did his greatest work, and between 1818 and 1822 appeared *Prometheus Unbound*, *The Cenci*, *Adonais*, and *Hellas*, besides a considerable number of fine lyrics. His life came to a sudden close on July 8, 1822, when he was drowned in a squall on the bay of Spezzia. His body, which was later found, was cremated in the presence of his friends—Byron, Leigh Hunt, and Trelawny; his ashes were buried in the Protestant Cemetery at Rome, near the grave of Keats.

Like Byron, Shelley was the poet of revolt. Profoundly stirred by the events of the Revolution and greatly influenced by the teachings of William Godwin, Shelley set out to reform the world. He was opposed to custom, intolerance, and force; and he believed that society could be transformed through the power of love. As Professor Woodberry points out, he represents "the ideal of personal and social aspiration, of the love of beauty and virtue equally, and of the hope of eradicating misery from the world." Shelley is best

NOTES

known to modern readers by his lyrics; he has been called the greatest lyrical poet in the English language.

Ozymandias

The thought of this sonnet may be summarized as follows: The passions stamped in lifeless stone (on the statue of Ozymandias in Egypt) survive the hand of the sculptor that produced them and the mind of man that conceived them. Compare Keats's *Ode on a Grecian Urn*, written two years later.

Stanzas Written in Dejection, Near Naples

In a letter to Peacock, Shelley says: "The scenery which surrounds this city is more delightful than any within the reach of civilized man." In a note, Mrs. Shelley tells us that when the poem was composed, Shelley was exhausted by "constant and poignant physical suffering."

Prometheus Unbound: Transformation of Asia

Prometheus Unbound, suggested by the *Prometheus Bound* of Æschylus, is Shelley's greatest poem, both in content and in form. In Shelley's version, the Titan, Prometheus, who offended Jupiter by his gift of fire and the arts to man, is chained on the mountain top and subjected to physical torture. He revokes the curse which he has pronounced upon Jupiter, but refuses to reveal the secret upon which the fate of the god depends. Jupiter weds Thetis, and a child (Demogorgon) is born, who is to slay his father. This was the secret which Prometheus so persistently withheld. After the fall of Jupiter, Prometheus is released by Hercules and reunited to Asia, who typifies the generative spirit of Nature. The poem is said to be "the supreme expression in imaginative form of the new spirit of democracy."

The selection in the text reveals the transformation of Asia, which forecasts the reign of Love and Liberty and the end of tyranny. Professor Vida D. Scudder vividly describes the scene: "Her being glows with a strange radiance, so intense that it hides her from the view. A voice—the voice of Prometheus—is heard chanting to her a worshipful lyric, the highest expression alike of Shelley's genius and of his faith; and with her responsive song of almost equal beauty, and of profound meaning, the act concludes."

Ode to the West Wind

"The poem is the finest union of all the elements of Shelley's inspiration in one song—nature, liberty, and personal pathos, held through sorrow on a triumphal note of hope for the world." (Woodberry)

381, l. 21. **Mænad.** Mænads were women in Bacchic ecstasy, who formed part of the train of Dionysius.

l. 32. **pumice isle**, etc. The island was covered with lava;

NOTES

hence the name. Baiae's Bay is part of the Gulf of Pozzuoli, west of Naples.

THE INDIAN SERENADE

384, l. 11. **Champak.** An Indian tree somewhat like the magnolia, with orange-colored flowers.

THE CLOUD

This is a pure nature poem without any reference to the Divine or the human spirit.

387, l. 81. **cenotaph.** Literally, an empty tomb; here, a monument to a person buried in some other place.

TO A SKYLARK

In this poem Shelley reaches the high-water mark of his lyrical genius. The verse-form, the beautiful images, the rhythm and melody, the human interest, and the intense emotional appeal—all these make the poem one of the supremely great lyrics in the language.

ADONAIS

This poem, one of the most sublime of English elegies, is modelled upon the Greek pastorals of Theocritus, Bion, and Moschus. It is written in the Spenserian stanza.

399, l. 12. **Urania.** Not the muse of astronomy, but the heavenly goddess described by Plato in the *Symposium*.
400, l. 30-31. **Sire,** etc. John Milton.
  l. 36. **The third,** etc. Probably an echo of Dryden's lines on Homer, Dante, and Milton: "Three poets in three distant ages born."
  l. 42. **Struck by the envious wrath,** etc. For example, Chatterton and Burns.
  l. 44. **And some yet live.** Such as Byron, Wordsworth, and Shelley himself.
401, l. 55. **That high Capitol.** Rome, where Keats came in 1820.
  l. 63. **liquid.** Serene.
403, l. 107. **clips.** Embraces.
404, l. 133. **She pined away.** Narcissus, for whose love the nymph, Echo, pined away and became merely a voice.
  l. 140. **To Phœbus was not Hyacinth so dear.** Hyacinth, greatly loved by Phœbus Apollo, was turned into a flower that bears his name.
  l. 141. **Narcissus.** Narcissus scorned Echo's love and became infatuated with his own reflection in a pool of water; after his death he was changed into a flower whose name he bears.

546 NOTES

l. 151. **the curse of Cain.** Refers to the literary critics who were thought to have been responsible for Keats's death. See the preface to this poem.

408, l. 238. **the unpastured dragon.** The critic looking for fresh prey.

244 f. **The herded wolves,** etc. The critics who were subservient to political parties.

l. 250. **Pythian of the age.** A compliment to Byron, whose *English Bards and Scotch Reviewers* first won him fame.

409, l. 264. **Pilgrim of Eternity.** Byron, the author of *Childe Harold's Pilgrimage*.

l. 268. **Ierne.** Ireland.

l. 271. **one frail form.** Shelley himself.

l. 276. **Acteon-like.** Acteon was a young hunter who saw Diana bathing with her nymphs; for his transgression he was turned into a stag and killed by his own hounds.

411, l. 307. **What softer voice.** Leigh Hunt.

414, l. 399. **Chatterton.** Chatterton, to whose memory Keats dedicated Endymion, committed suicide at the age of eighteen.

l. 401. **Sidney.** Sir Philip Sidney died at thirty-two.

l. 404. **Lucan.** Latin poet, who was forced by Nero to commit suicide at thirty-six.

416, l. 439. **a slope of green recess.** Protestant cemetery at Rome.

l. 444. **one keen pyramid.** The tomb of Caius Cestus.

Final Chorus from Hellas

Hellas, a Lyrical Drama was written at Pisa. It was inspired by the revolution in southern Greece, which developed into the Greek War of Independence. The poem, like *Prometheus Unbound*, is full of beautiful lyrics, celebrating the downfall of tyranny and the advent of a golden age of freedom.

418, l. 9. **Peneus.** River in Thessaly.

l. 11. **Tempes.** The vale of Tempe, which the River Peneus traverses, is noted for its beauty.

l. 12. **Cyclads.** Islands in the Ægean Sea.

l. 13. **Argo.** The ship in which Jason sought the golden fleece.

419, l. 18. **Calypso.** The nymph who detained Odysseus for seven years.

l. 21. **Laian.** Laius, King of Thebes, was the father of Œdipus, whose family suffered strange misfortunes.

l. 24. **a subtler Sphinx.** Œdipus, who solved the riddle of the Sphinx, became king, but brought blindness and banishment upon his own head.

ll. 31–36. **Saturn and Love . . . gold.** The age of gold, which existed before the overthrow of Saturn by Jupiter, was thought of as one of love and happiness.

JOHN KEATS

In a short period of twenty-six years John Keats produced a body of poetry of such extraordinary beauty and power that, irrespective of what he might have accomplished had he lived longer, he has an unchallenged place among the immortals. Born in 1795 in London, the son of a livery-stable keeper, Keats was brought up in surroundings little calculated to develop poetic genius. At the age of eight he was sent to a private school at Enfield, where he met James Cowden Clarke, who lent him books and aroused his interest in Spenser's *Faerie Queen*. Left an orphan at fifteen he was placed under the guardianship of two successful but unsympathetic merchants who withdrew him from school and apprenticed him to a surgeon at Edmonton. During this period Keats employed his leisure moments in reading, in translating the *Æneid*, and in writing poems in imitation of Spenser. In 1814 he went to London, where he met Leigh Hunt, Wordsworth, Shelley, Hazlitt, and the artist Haydon. In 1816 he gave up medicine to devote all his energies to poetry, and in the following year his first volume of poems appeared, including, along with many juvenile pieces, some of his finest sonnets. At this time his failing health began to alarm his friends, and he was induced to go to the Isle of Wight for recuperation. Here he began the composition of *Endymion*, which was published, along with other poems, in 1818. The publication of this volume was followed by a torrent of criticism from *Blackwood's Magazine* and *The Quarterly Review*, which for many years was thought to have hastened the poet's death. The real causes of Keats's depression at this time were his illness, his love affair with Fanny Brawne, and the death of his brother Thomas. But notwithstanding his despondency, Keats wrote, during the next year, his greatest poems, which were published, in 1820, under the title *Lamia, Isabella, The Eve of St. Agnes, and Other Poems*. By this time Keats's health was such that the doctors told him that another winter in England would be fatal; and so in November, accompanied by his friend Severn, he set out for Rome. After a brief rally he rapidly sank, and died in Severn's arms, on February 23, 1821. He was buried in the Protestant Cemetery in Rome near the tomb of Caius Cestius.

As a poet Keats's fame rests primarily on his beautiful sonnets, his immortal odes (the best in the English language), and the fragment *Hyperion*. He has been called the poet of sensuous beauty. To him truth finds its fullest expression in idealized beauty, and idealized beauty leads to joy. An artist to his finger tips he turned to Greek myth and to external nature as the best material for expressing his high conception of truth and beauty.

Keen Fitful Gusts

This sonnet, written shortly after a visit to Leigh Hunt's cottage at Hampstead, is Keats's tribute to Hunt's kindness, which is compared to Milton's friendship for Edward King in *Lycidas* (ll. 11–12), and to

Petrarch's love for "Laura" (11. 13–14) embodied in his immortal sonnets.

On First Looking into Chapman's Homer

Chapman's translation of the *Iliad* and the *Odyssey* appeared, in complete form, in 1616. Two hundred years later, Keats spent a memorable night with his friend, Cowden Clarke, in reading Homer, and recorded the feelings set forth in this immortal sonnet.

423, l. 6. **demesne.** domain.
    l. 11. **Cortez.** Mistake for Balboa. Whether the error was made deliberately or unconsciously is not known.

Proem to Endymion

These lines are noteworthy for their expression of Keats's love of beauty as manifested in nature and in art. Compare *Ode on a Grecian Urn*, lines 49–50.

When I Have Fears

Critics have pointed out that this sonnet is the most Shakespearean, both in form and phrasing, of all Keats's sonnets. The content is personal, revealing the tragic foresight of the author's death.

426, l. 3. **charactery.** writing.
    l. 8. **the magic hand of chance.** Refers to the uncertainty of poetic inspiration.

Lines on Mermaid Tavern

The Mermaid Tavern was the literary club frequented by Shakespeare, Ben Jonson, Beaumont and Fletcher, Herrick, Carew, and others. Jonson was the ruling spirit of the club.

Robin Hood

In 1818 John Hamilton Reynolds sent Keats two sonnets on Robin Hood. To show his appreciation of the favor, Keats wrote the present poem and sent it to his friend with these words: "In return for your dish of Filberts, I have gathered a few Catkins; I hope they'll look pretty."

428, l. 33. **morris din.** A popular outdoor dance in which the performers wore fantastic costumes and bells.
    l. 34. **song of Gamelyn.** The pseudo-Chaucerian *Tale of Gamelyn* is a story of outlawry. Keats here applies the term to the tales of Robin Hood.
    l. 36. **"green shawe."** Green wood.

THE EVE OF ST. AGNES

This is one of the most Romantic of all the poems of the period. Its mediæval setting and spirit, its beautiful imagery of words and phrases, and its richness in color and music suggest Coleridge. "St. Agnes" was a Roman maiden who was beheaded about 300 A.D. The story of the poem, which is Keats's own invention, is based on the facts set forth in stanza VI. Several situations in the poem might be compared to situations in Shakespeare's *Romeo and Juliet*.

429, l. 1. **St. Agnes Eve.** January 20 (St. Agnes Day was the 21st).

432, l. 71. **and her lambs unshorn.** When St. Agnes Day was celebrated, two lambs were sacrificed at the church; the lambs were then shorn and the wool was made into cloth by nuns (see lines 115–17).

436, l. 171. **Since Merlin paid his Demon all the monstrous debt.** The story of Merlin, an ancient British prophet and magician, forms the subject of one of the Arthurian romances; the story is later told by Tennyson in *The Idylls of the King*. "The monstrous debt" was paid to the Devil for the use of magic.

438, l. 241. **missal.** A prayer book with pictures of converted heathen in the attitude of prayer.

439–40, ll. 262–70. This stanza is often quoted as an example of Keats's appeal to the sense of taste. "Fez" is a district in Northern Morocco; "Sarmarcand" is a city in Turkestan; "Lebanon" is a mountain range in Syria, famed for its cedars.

LA BELLE DAME SANS MERCI

This is the title of a poem by Alain Chartier, a French poet of the fifteenth century. The romantic suggestiveness of the title appealed to Keats, and he wrote this poem, which owes nothing in content or form to the original French story.

BARDS OF PASSION AND OF MIRTH

This poem was written in Keats's personal copy of Beaumont and Fletcher, and therefore probably refers to these two dramatic poets.

ODE TO A NIGHTINGALE

The following odes, written in the same year, have the same general theme—the worship of beauty. The *Ode to a Nightingale* was written on some scraps of paper one morning while Keats sat under a tree at the home of his friend Brown at Wentworth Place in Hampstead. He was deeply moved by the song of a nightingale that was building her nest in the garden. This fact, together with the recent death of his brother Tom and his fear of the disease of consumption, formed the inspiration of the poem. Kipling says it is one of the five great odes in the English language.

447, l. 4. **Lethe-wards.** Lethe, the river of forgetfulness, in Hades.
 l. 7. **Dryad.** Tree nymph.
448, l. 13. **Flora.** Goddess of spring and flowers.
 l. 14. **Provençal song.** Provence, the home of the mediæval troubadours.
 l. 16. **Hippocrene.** Fountain of the muse on Mount Helicon.
450, ll. 65–67. See Ruth II.

Ode on a Grecian Urn

The theme of this poem is the permanence of beauty. The figures on the urn lack reality, but they are not subject to sorrow, change, or death. Keats's theory of beauty as the expression of truth is plainly set forth in the last two lines. The poem was inspired not by any actual vase, but by many Greek sculptures which he may have seen in the British Museum and elsewhere.

452, l. 41. **Attic.** Greek.
 l. 41. **brede.** Braid or ornament.

Ode to Psyche

Keats wrote his brother George, May, 1819: "The following poem [Ode to Psyche] ... is the first and the only one with which I have taken even moderate pains." Psyche is supposed to symbolize the human soul, made perfect and beautiful through immortal love.

453, l. 14. **budded Tyrian.** Purple color, from a dye made at Tyre.
 l. 20. **aurorean love.** Aurora is the goddess of dawn.
 l. 27. **Vesper.** The evening star.

Ode on Melancholy

This poem goes back to the thought expressed in the *Ode to a Nightingale*. There the poet found beauty the source of his deepest despondency. In the *Ode on Melancholy* he treats the same theme emphasizing the idea that our despondency is increased by dwelling upon the transitoriness of earthly beauty.

To Autumn

In his beautiful description of an autumn day Keats asserts, with the faith of Tennyson in a Divine Being, that the principle of eternal beauty, once grasped by the mind of man, is his possession forever.

Bright Star

This sonnet, written at sea, was Keats's last poem.

NOTES

WALTER SAVAGE LANDOR

WALTER SAVAGE LANDOR lived to be nearly ninety years of age, surviving all of his contemporary Romanticists and becoming the friend of Robert Browning and Swinburne of the Victorian era. The son of a wealthy physician, he was born in 1775 at Warwick, and was educated at Rugby and Oxford, where he was noted for his skill in turning verses in English and Latin and for his defiance of authority. Leaving Oxford after one year he went to London and published, in 1795, his first collection of poems. In 1798 he published *Gebir*, a fantastic story of a Moorish invader of Spain, which some critics contend might have rivaled the *Lyrical Ballads* (1798) as the first landmark of the Romantic Triumph, if Landor had had at this time "greater artistic poise and sureness." On his father's death, in 1805, Landor came into the possession of a large fortune. Three years later he joined the British Army in Spain, and equipped, at his own expense, a thousand volunteers in the uprising against Napoleon. In the same year, after an impulsive marriage to the daughter of a Swiss banker, he settled first at Bath, then at Llanthony Abbey in Wales. In 1814 he moved to France, where he remained for seven years; then he took up his residence at a beautiful villa on the slope of the Fiesole, near Florence. On his separation from his wife, in 1835, he returned to Bath, where he spent the next twenty years. In 1857 he returned to Italy and remained there until his death in 1864.

Landor was neither a Romanticist nor a Victorian. His works show some of the imaginative awakening of the Romanticists, but his clearness of outline, his compression of thought, and his precision in diction can best be described by the term Greek. As a prose writer his enduring fame rests chiefly on *Imaginary Conversations* (1824–1846), which reveals, in the classical form of dialogue, the innermost life and character of the great personages in ancient and modern history. His most ambitious poems are *Hellenics* (1847) and *Heroic Idyls* (1863). But as a poet he is best known as the author of a few love poems, including *Rose Aylmer* and the *Lyrics to Ianthe*, which show deep feeling and the classical perfection of form.

ROSE AYLMER

Rose Aylmer was a beautiful girl whom Landor met during his residence in Wales. Her father was Henry (Baron) Aylmer.

PAST RUINED ILION

458, l. 1. **Ilion.** Troy.
l. 2. **Alcestis.** The heroine of a Greek drama of that name written by Euripides.

ARTEMIDORA

This statuesque picture of husband and wife should be compared to Keats's *Ode on a Grecian Urn*.

552 NOTES

459, l. 5. **other rivers.** That is, of the lower world.
l. 11. **Iris stood over her dark hair.** Iris, the messenger of the gods, was supposed to loosen the hair of dying persons; otherwise their spirits could not depart.

THOMAS HOOD

ANOTHER transitional writer who belongs quite as much to the Victorian as to the Romantic period is Thomas Hood, who was born in London in 1799 and who died in Hampstead in 1845. In his own day he was known as a magazine editor, as an illustrator, and as a writer of comic verse. His literary life began in 1821 as subeditor of the *London Magazine;* later he conducted two magazines of his own. In his capacity as editor he came in contact with some of the leading writers of the day, including Lamb and De Quincey. His humorous productions, best represented in the *Comic Annuals* (1830–1838), took a strong hold on the public and led him to believe that nature intended him to be a professional jester. Fortunately he later changed his mind and wrote the poems which show the real sympathy and tenderness of the man. The best known of these are *The Song of the Shirt, The Bridge of Sighs,* and *The Haunted House.*

CHARLES LAMB

CHARLES LAMB was born in London in 1775 in an attic of the Inner Temple, where his father, the clerk of a barrister, had his residence. He grew up "among the somber old-world gardens and courts," and throughout his life loved the city more than the country. At seven years of age he entered Christ's Hospital as a student, where he met Coleridge and Leigh Hunt. Unable to go to college he became, at fourteen, a clerk in the East India Office; and at seventeen he moved to a desk in the East India House, where he remained until his superannuation thirty years later. (See *The Superannuated Man* for an account of this period of his life.) An early disappointment in love (probably with the "fair Alice" of *Dream Children*) brought on what he termed "a temporary unhinging of his reason." He had barely recovered when his sister Mary, in a fit of insanity, killed her mother. After his sister's release from the asylum, Lamb undertook the responsibility of her care. They took up lodgings in various quarters of London, where Mary, except for brief intervals when the old malady returned, proved to be a stimulating and helpful companion. His first important literary work, *The Tales from Shakespeare* (1807), was in collaboration with his sister. During their residence in London, Charles and Mary Lamb received frequent visits from Wordsworth, Coleridge, Leigh Hunt, and other distinguished literary men of England. In 1825, after his retirement from the East India House, Lamb moved with his sister to Enfield, where he died in 1834.

Most of Lamb's literary work was done during his moments of leisure while he was a clerk in the East India House. After the success of his *Tales from Shakespeare* he was invited to edit a volume

NOTES

of *Specimens of English Dramatists Contemporary with Shakespeare* (1807). In this work he restored an interest in the neglected Elizabethan drama just as Scott had restored an interest in the ballad a few years earlier. The *Specimens* became at once popular, and established Lamb's position as a literary critic. His place in literature, however, chiefly rests on his *Essays of Elia*, which appeared in the *London Magazine* from 1820 to 1826. These essays, which reveal the author's charming personality, his whimsical humor, his tender pathos, and his interest in the oddities of people, are written in a manner which shows the author's intimate relationship with his reader. Lamb is the best representative of the type of the familiar or personal essay in English literature.

Dream-Children: A Reverie

This essay is a kind of reverie, not unusual with Lamb, who was wont to sit and dream of what might be.

Page 471. **great-grandmother Field.** Lamb's grandmother, Mary Field, was housekeeper for a Hertfordshire family, by the name of Plumer, for over fifty years.

472. **apparition of two infants.** Two children of the Plumer family were said to have disappeared during the seventeenth century.

474. **John L.** Lamb's brother John died in 1821, shortly before this essay was written.

475. **when the doctor took off his limb.** This incident is probably imaginary.
the fair Alice W-n. Ann Simmons, whom Lamb met while visiting his grandmother in Hertfordshire. (See the life of Lamb above.)
Bridget. In the *Essays of Elia*, Lamb is James Elia, and Mary Lamb is Bridget.

The Superannuated Man

476. **Sera tamen,** etc. "Freedom, though late, has taken thought of me."

479. **Esto perpetua!** "Be thou perpetual."
Boldero, etc. Fictitious names for officials of the East India House.

482. **Gresham.** A wealthy English merchant, who in 1566 founded the Royal Exchange in London.
Whittington. Lord Mayor of London in 1419.
Aquinas. Italian teacher and writer of theology; he was sainted by the Catholic Church.
Carthusian. A strict brotherhood of monks.

483. **Elgin Marbles.** Lord Elgin bought these famous relics of the Parthenon in Athens for the British Museum.

354 NOTES

484. **Lucretian pleasure.** Pleasure derived from the comparison of our own comfort with another's hardship.
cum dignitate. "Ease with dignity."
Opus operatum est. "The labor has been performed."

WILLIAM HAZLITT

WILLIAM HAZLITT, the son of a Unitarian minister, was born at Maidstone, in Kent, in 1778. In 1783 his father moved with his family to America in a vain search for religious liberty, but returned to England three years later and settled at Wem, in Shropshire. After studying for several years under the tutorship of his father, Hazlitt entered, at fifteen, a theological school at Hackney. His lack of sympathy for dissenting theological views led him to give up the ministry at the end of a year and return home, where he entered upon a course of extensive reading in literature and philosophy. In 1798 Coleridge, on the point of leaving the ministry, visited the elder Hazlitt at Wem and there delivered his last sermon. Young Hazlitt was profoundly impressed by the sermon, and received encouragement from the poet to continue his investigation in philosophy. However, he found it necessary to make a living; and, influenced by his brother's success as a miniature painter, he decided to study art. He spent the winter of 1802–1803 in Paris, copying some of the famous paintings in the Louvre. Shortly after this he met Lamb and Hunt, who encouraged him to take up writing as a profession. He did considerable hack-work for a time, and in 1812 went to London to begin work on the *Morning Chronicle*, first as a reporter and later as a dramatic critic. Presently he found himself and began pouring forth his literary criticisms, which first appeared in the form of lectures. The best known of these are *Lectures on the English Poets* (1818) and *Lectures on Dramatic Literature of the Age of Elizabeth* (1821). In 1825 he published a series of criticisms on contemporary writers entitled *The Spirit of the Age*. In addition to his literary criticism he wrote a number of delightful essays for *The Examiner* and the *London Magazine*, which were later published as *The Round Table*, *Table Talk*, and *The Plain Speaker*. He died in 1830.

Hazlitt's unfortunate disposition and quarrelsome nature estranged him from many of his friends; even Lamb had difficulty in getting along with him. Furthermore he made enemies by his espousal of the cause of the French Revolution and Napoleon Bonaparte.

As a writer of clear, unadorned, effective English, Hazlitt had no equal until Macaulay appeared.

ON POETRY IN GENERAL

485. **"spreads its sweet leaves,"** etc. *Romeo and Juliet*, I, 1, 158.
486. **"the stuff of which our life is made."** *The Tempest*, IV, 1, 156.
"man's life," etc. *King Lear*, II, 4, 276.

NOTES 555

487. Ariosto. Italian poet of the sixteenth century.
    Angela and Medoro. Characters in *Orlando Furioso*.
    "which ecstasy is very cunning in." *Hamlet*, III, 4, 138.

On Familiar Style

491. cum grano salis. With a grain of salt.
492. Mr. Cobbett. William Cobbett (1766–1835) was a radical English journalist of the Romantic Period.
493. "A well of native English undefiled." See Spenser's *Faerie Queen*, IV, II, 32. Spenser refers to Chaucer.
494. Erasmus. Great European scholar.
    Florilegium. The word as used here means a collection of big words.
    tulipomania. A craze for tulips.
    Sermo humi abrepens. Speech which creeps on the ground.
495. Ancient Pistol. Character in Shakespeare's *Henry IV* and *Henry V*.
    fantoccini beings. Puppets.
    "That strut and fret," etc. *Macbeth* V, 5, 25

LEIGH HUNT

Leigh Hunt was born at Southgate, near Edmonton, on October 19, 1784, the youngest son of an unenterprising and roving Unitarian preacher. After being educated at Christ's Hospital, he tried reading law under one of his brothers, but soon abandoned this work and obtained a clerkship in the War Office. Already two predominating traits of his character were observable in young Hunt—his lack of steadiness and his hankering for writing and getting in print. At twenty-one he began his long career of journalism by contributing theatrical critiques to his brother's paper, the *News*. In 1808 the two started the *Examiner*, which attained to notoriety from the first by its advanced liberalism. This journal Leigh Hunt edited for fourteen years. For a scurrilous reference to the Prince Regent in the *Examiner* (1812) he was fined 500 pounds and sentenced to two years of imprisonment. He was now made a political martyr and hero by his Liberal friends, and as a consequence really enjoyed his detention.

Upon being released, he published *The Story of Rimini* (1816), a daring expansion of the great Francisco scene in the *Inferno*, and was gratified to see that his martyrdom had helped his popularity. During 1819–1820 he conducted another periodical, the *Indicator*, in which he published many of his best essays.

His journey to Italy in 1821 to edit the *Liberal*, for which Byron and Shelley had projected the plans and the money, was the beginning of misfortune for Hunt. The *Liberal* failed dismally after four numbers, when Shelley was drowned and Byron withdrew his assistance. Hunt, mortified by his failure, and humiliated by his dependence upon Byron's contemptuous generosity, returned to England and settled down to a gruelling life of journalism and hack-work. He lived through another generation, struggling for some years with actual want. In 1843 he received a pension of £1000, and was mentioned as a possible candidate for the poet-laureateship, only to see Wordsworth appointed. He died in 1859.

Although Leigh Hunt published a considerable body of poetry, most of it proved ephemeral; a few short poems remain well known. He lives by virtue of his rich and genial relationship with literary figures like Lamb, Moore, Shelley, Coleridge, and Carlyle; by his felicitous personal essays; and by his critical sketches, most of which may be better described as delightful gossip about books than as literary criticisms.

Getting Up on Cold Mornings

500. **the degenerate King.** Francis I of France.
Cardinal Bembo. Italian Cardinal and author.
Haroun Al Rascid. Caliph of Bagdad. See *Arabian Nights*.
Bedridden Hassan. Probably Hassan-ben-Sabah, the founder of the Moslem sect of the Assassins.
501. **Wortley Montague.** Son of Lady Mary Wortley Montague, famous for her social and literary talents.
"Sweetly recommends itself," etc. *Macbeth*, I, 6, 2.
503. **Vis inertiæ.** Power of inertia.

THOMAS DE QUINCEY

Thomas De Quincey, born in 1785 in the manufacturing city of Manchester, was the son of a prosperous merchant of good descent. After the death of his father, in 1791, his mother moved to Bath, where the boy was sent to school. At fifteen he entered the Manchester Grammar School, but ran away two years later, wandering in Wales and leading a vagabond existence in the slums of London. Finally reclaimed by his family, he was sent up to Oxford in 1802, and remained at the University until 1808. Although his career at Oxford was brilliant, he left without taking a degree, apparently having been offended because he was not permitted to answer the questions in Greek. He began the study of law, but in 1809 gave it up, leased Wordsworth's old home at Grasmere, and began, under the influence of the Lake poets, his career as a man of letters. In 1820 he went to London and began writing for the *London Magazine*. The opium habit, which was begun at Oxford, had now taken a lasting hold on him. He himself tells the whole story in *The Confessions of an English Opium Eater*, published in the *London Magazine* in 1821. In 1839 he moved to Edinburgh, where he lived until his death in 1839.

De Quincey's writings in the field of autobiography, philosophy, history, and literary criticism are dominated by the spirit of romanticism. Many of his prose passages have almost the imagination and the emotional appeal of the greatest poetry of the period. The

Suspiria de Profundis, which pictures the phantasmagoric creation of his dreams, suggests Coleridge.

Levana and Our Ladies of Sorrow

The title *Suspiria de Profundis*, meaning *Sighs from the Depths*, was given to three magazine articles. *Levana and Our Ladies of Sorrow* is the subtitle of the third article. All three form part of the *Confessions of on Opium Eater*.

- 506. **Parcae.** The Fates.
- 507. **Rama.** The name of a place in Palestine near Jerusalem. Cf. Matt. 11, 18.
- 508. **within the bedchamber of the Czar.** Czar Nicholas I.
- 510. **the tents of Shem.** Shem was the eldest son of Noah. His descendants are a nomadic people.
  Cybele. The mother of the gods.

INDEX OF AUTHORS

Blake, William, 83
Burns, Robert, 44
Byron, George Gordon, Lord, 295
Campbell, Thomas, 288
Coleridge, Samuel Taylor, 191
Cowper, William, 1
Crabbe, George, 34
De Quincey, Thomas, 504
Hazlitt, William, 485
Hood, Thomas, 464
Hunt, Leigh, 497
Keats, John, 422
Lamb, Charles, 471
Landor, Walter Savage, 457
Moore, Thomas, 293
Scott, Sir Walter, 273
Shelley, Percy Bysshe, 371
Southey, Robert, 267
Wordsworth, William, 97

INDEX OF TITLES

Abou Ben Adhem (Hunt) 497
Address to the Unco Guid (Burns) 60
Admiral Blake and Humphrey Blake, *from* "Imaginary Conversations" (Landor) 460
Adonais (Shelley) 396
Ae Fond Kiss (Burns) 77
After-Thought (Wordsworth) 161
A Man's a Man for A' That (Burns) 82
Auld Lang Syne (Burns) 66

Battle of Blenheim, The (Southey) 267
Biographia Literaria (Coleridge) 258
Bishop Bruno (Southey) 269
Blossom, The (Blake) 88
Bridge of Sighs, The (Hood) 464
Bright Star (Keats) 457
Brignall Banks, *from* "Rokeby" (Scott) 280

Caledonia, *from* "The Lay of the Last Minstrel" (Scott) 273
Castaway, The (Cowper) 31
Cavalier, The, *from* "Rokeby" (Scott) 282
Character of a Happy Warrior, The (Wordsworth) 151
Childe Harold's Pilgrimage: Canto III, (Byron) 312
Chorus from Hellas (Shelley) 418
Christabel (Coleridge) 227
Clod and the Pebble, The (Blake) 94
Cloud, The (Shelley) 384
Composed Upon Westminster Bridge (Wordsworth) 134
Coronach (Scott) 279
Cotter's Saturday Night, The (Burns) 53
County Guy, *from* "Quentin Durward" (Scott) 286
Cradle Song, A (Blake) 95

Death of Artemidora (Landor) 459
Dejection: an Ode (Coleridge) 250
Destruction of Sennacherib, The (Byron) 297
Dirge, A (Shelley) 422
Divine Image, The (Blake) 88
Don Juan: From Canto III (Byron) 356
Dream, A (Blake) 91
Dream Children (Lamb) 471
Duncan Gray (Burns) 79

INDEX OF TITLES

Elegiac Stanzas (Wordsworth) 147
Epistle to John Lapraik (Burns) 46
Epitaph (Coleridge) 258
Eve of St. Agnes, The (Keats) 429
Expostulation and Reply (Wordsworth) 106

France: An Ode (Coleridge) 223
Frost at Midnight (Coleridge) 221

Green Grow the Rashes (Burns) 45

Harp that Once Through Tara's Halls, The (Moore) 293
Here's a Health to King Charles, *from* "Woodstock" (Scott) 287
Highland Mary (Burns) 78
Hohenlinden (Campbell) 289
How Sweet I Roamed (Blake) 83
Hunting Song (Scott) 276
Hymn Before Sunrise (Coleridge) 255
Hymn to Intellectual Beauty (Shelley) 371

Indian Serenade, The (Shelley) 383
Infant Joy (Blake) 91
It is a Beauteous Evening (Wordsworth) 135
It is not to be Thought of (Wordsworth) 137
I Travelled among Unknown Men (Wordsworth) 109
I Wandered Lonely as a Cloud (Wordsworth) 139

Jock of Hazeldean (Scott) 283
John Anderson, My Jo (Burns) 67

Keen, Fitful Gusts (Keats) 422
Kubla Khan (Coleridge) 193

La Belle Dame Sans Merci (Keats) 444
Lamb, The (Blake) 87
Lament, A (Shelley) 396
Light Shining out of Darkness (Cowper) 2
Lines Composed a Few Miles above Tintern Abbey (Wordsworth) 103
Lines on the Mermaid Tavern (Keats) 426
Lines: When the Lamp is Shattered (Shelley) 420
Lines Written in Early Spring (Wordsworth) 99
Lochinvar (Scott) 274
London (Wordsworth) 136
Lord Ullin's Daughter (Campbell) 291

Mad Song (Blake) 85
Mary Morison (Burns) 44
Michael (Wordsworth) 112
Mild is the Parting Year (Landor) 458

INDEX OF TITLES

Milton: From the Prophetic Book (Blake) 96
Mutability (Shelley) 395
My Days among the Dead Are Past (Southey) 272
My Heart Leaps Up (Wordsworth) 127
My Heart's in the Highlands (Burns) 65
My Silks and Fine Array (Blake) 84

Night (Blake) 89

Ode: Bards of Passion and of Mirth (Keats) 446
Ode: Intimations of Immortality (Wordsworth) 154
Ode on a Grecian Urn (Keats) 450
Ode on Melancholy (Keats) 454
Ode to a Nightingale (Keats) 447
Ode to Duty (Wordsworth) 149
Ode to Psyche (Keats) 452
Ode to the West Wind (Shelley) 380
Of a' the Airts (Burns) 64
Oft in the Stilly Night (Moore) 294
On Another's Sorrow (Blake) 92
On Familiar Style (Hazlitt) 488
On First Looking into Chapman's Homer (Keats) 423
On Getting Up on Cold Mornings (Hunt) 498
On His Seventy-Fifth Birthday (Landor) 464
On Poetry in General (Hazlitt) 485
On the Extinction of the Venetian Republic (Wordsworth) 138
On the Loss of the Royal George (Cowper) 3
On the Receipt of My Mother's Picture (Cowper) 27
On this Day I Complete My Thirty-Sixth Year (Byron) 369
Oh! Snatched Away in Beauty's Bloom (Byron) 295
Ozymandias (Shelley) 374

Past Ruined Ilion (Landor) 458
Pibroch of Donuil Dhu (Scott) 284
Piping Down the Valleys (Blake) 86
Poison Tree, A (Blake) 94
Preface to the Lyrical Ballads (Wordsworth) 162
Prelude, The: From Book I (Wordsworth) 140
Prelude, The: From Book III (Wordsworth) 142
Prelude, The: From Book XI (Wordsworth) 145
Prisoner of Chillon, The (Byron) 299
Proem to Endymion: From Book I (Keats) 424
Prometheus Unbound: Act II, Scene 5 (Shelley) 376
Proud Maisie, *from* "The Heart of Midlothian" (Scott) 286

Rarely, Rarely, Comest Thou (Shelley) 393
Red, Red Rose, A (Burns) 65
Resolution and Independence (Wordsworth) 128
Rime of the Ancient Mariner, The (Coleridge) 196

INDEX OF TITLES

Robin Hood (Keats) 427
Rose Aylmer (Landor) 457

Scorn Not the Sonnet (Wordsworth) 162
Scots, Wha Hae (Burns) 81
She Dwelt among Untrodden Ways (Wordsworth) 109
Shepherd, The (Blake) 87
She Walks in Beauty (Byron) 296
She Was a Phantom of Delight (Wordsworth) 137
Slumber Did My Spirit Seal, A (Wordsworth) 112
Soldier Rest, *from* "The Lady of the Lake" (Scott) 277
Solitary Reaper, The (Wordsworth) 138
Song of the Shirt, The (Hood) 468
Sonnet on Chillon (Byron) 298
Sonnet to Mrs. Unwin (Cowper) 31
Stanzas for Music (Byron) 298
Stanzas Written in Dejection Near Naples (Shelley) 375
Stanzas Written on the Road Between Florence and Pisa (Byron) 369
Strange Fits of Passion (Wordsworth) 108
Superannuated Man, The (Lamb) 476
Suspiria de Profundis: Levana and our Ladies of Sorrow (De Quincey) 504
Sweet Afton (Burns) 76

Tables Turned, The (Wordsworth) 102
Tam o' Shanter (Burns) 68
Task, The. Book IV. (Cowper) 4
The World is too Much with Us (Wordsworth) 161
This Lime-Tree Bower My Prison (Coleridge) 191
Three Years She Grew (Wordsworth) 110
Tiger, The (Blake) 95
Time (Shelley) 392
'T is the Last Rose of Summer (Moore) 298
To a Mountain Daisy (Burns) 62
To a Mouse (Burns) 51
To a Skylark (Shelley) 387
To Autumn (Keats) 456
To My Ninth Decade (Landor) 464
To Night (Shelley) 391
To One Who Has Been Long in City Pent (Keats) 423
To—: One Word is too often Profaned (Shelley) 420
To Robert Browning (Landor) 459
To the Cuckoo (Wordsworth) 126
To the Daisy: With Little Here to Do (Wordsworth) 132
To the Muses (Blake) 85
To Thomas Moore: My Boat is on the Shore (Byron) 355

Village, The (Crabbe) 34

INDEX OF TITLES

Walking with God (Cowper) 1
We Are Seven (Wordsworth) 97
When I Have Fears that I May Cease to Be (**Keats**) **426**
Work Without Hope (Coleridge) 257
Written in London (Wordsworth) 136

Ye Flowery Banks (Burns) 75
Ye Mariners of England (Campbell) 288

INDEX OF TITLES

Walking with God (Cowper) 4
We Are Seven (Wordsworth) 97
When I Have Fears that I May Cease to Be (Keats) 198
Work Without Hope (Coleridge) 237
Written in London (Wordsworth) 130

Ye Flowery Banks (Burns) 75
Ye Mariners of England (Campbell) 225

INDEX OF FIRST LINES OF POEMS

A chieftain to the Highlands bound, 291
A simple child, 97
A slumber did my spirit seal, 112
A thing of beauty is a joy forever, 424
Abou Ben Adhem (may his tribe increase!), 497
Ae fond kiss, and then we sever! 77
Ah! County Guy, the hour is nigh, 286
Ah what avails the sceptered race, 457
Ah what can ail thee, wretched wight, 444
All nature seems at work. Slugs leave their lair, 257
And did those feet in ancient time, 96
And in the frosty season, when the sun, 140
Artemidora! Gods invisible, 459

Bards of Passion and of Mirth, 446
Behold her, single in the field, 138
Bishop Bruno awoke in the dead midnight, 269
Breathes there a man with soul so dead, 273
Bright star, would I were steadfast as thou art, 457
Bring the bowl which you boast, 287

Can I see another's woe, 92

Duncan Gray came here to woo, 79

Earth has not anything to show more fair, 134
Eternal Spirit of the chainless Mind! 298

Five years have past; five summers, with the length, 106
Flow gently sweet Afton, among thy green braes! 76
From that time forth, Authority in France, 145

God moves in a mysterious way, 2
Green grow the rashes, O! 45

Hail to thee, blithe Spirit! 387
Hark! 't is the twanging horn! O'er yonder bridge, 4
Hast thou a charm to stay the morning-star, 255
He is gone on the mountain, 279
How sweet I roamed from field to field, 83
How sweet is the shepherd's sweet lot! 87

567

INDEX OF FIRST LINES OF POEMS

I arise from dreams of thee, 383
I bring fresh showers for the thirsting flowers, 384
If from the public way you turn your steps, 112
I have no name, 91
I heard a thousand blended notes, 99
I met a traveller from an antique land, 374
In Xanadu did Kubla Khan, 195
Is there for honest poverty, 82
Is thy face like thy mother's, my fair child! 312
I strove with none, for none was worth my strife, 464
I thought of Thee, my partner and my guide, 161
It is a beauteous evening, calm and free, 135
It is an ancient Mariner, 197
It is not to be thought of that the flood, 137
I travelled among unknown men, 109
It was a dreary morning when the wheels, 142
It was a summer evening, 267
I wandered lonely as a cloud, 139
I was angry with my friend, 94
I was thy neighbor once, thou rugged Pile! 147
I weep for Adonais—he is dead! 399

John Anderson my jo, John, 67

Keen, fitful gusts are whisp'ring here and there, 422

Little Lamb, who made thee? 87
Love seeketh not itself to please, 94

Mary! I want a lyre with other strings, 31
Merry, merry sparrow! 88
Mild is the parting year, and sweet, 458
Milton! thou shouldst be living at this hour, 136
Much have I travelled in the realms of gold, 423
My boat is on the shore, 355
My days among the Dead are past, 272
My hair is grey, but not with years, 299
My heart aches, and a drowsy numbness pains, 447
My heart leaps up when I behold, 127
My heart's in the Highlands, my heart is not here, 66
My loved, my honoured, much respected friend! 53
My love is like a red, red rose, 65
My silks and fine array, 84

No, no, go not to Lethe, neither twist, 454
No! those days are gone away, 427

O blithe New-comer! I have heard, 126
O, Brignall banks are wild and fair, 280

INDEX OF FIRST LINES OF POEMS 569

Obscurest night involved the sky, 31
Of a' the airts the wind can blaw, 64
O friend I know not which way I must look, 136
Oft in the stilly night, 294
O Goddess! hear these tuneless numbers, wrung, 452
Oh! for a closer walk with God, 1
Oh! Snatched away in beauty's bloom, 295
Oh, talk not to me of a name great in story, 369
Oh that those lips had language! Life has passed, 27
O Mary, at thy window be, 44
Once a dream did weave a shade, 91
Once did She hold the gorgeous east in fee, 135
One more word unfortunate, 464
One word is too often profaned, 420
On Linden, when the sun was low, 289
On the brink of the night and the morning, 376
O wild West Wind, thou breath of Autumn's being, 380
O world! O life! O time! 396
O ye wha are sae guid yoursel, 60
O, Young Lochinvar is come out of the west, 274

Past ruined Ilion Helen lives, 458
Pibroch of Donuil Dhu, 284
Piping down the valleys wild, 86
Proud Maisie is in the wood, 286

Rarely, rarely, comest thou, 393
Rough wind, that moanest loud, 422

Scorn not the Sonnet; Critic you have frowned, 162
Scots, wha hae wi' Wallace bled, 81
Season of mists and mellow fruitfulness, 456
She dwelt among the untrodden ways, 109
She walks in beauty, like the night, 296
She was a Phantom of delight, 137
Should auld acquaintance be forgot, 66
Sleep, sleep, beauty bright, 95
Soldier, rest! thy warfare o'er, 277
Souls of poets dead and gone, 426
St. Agnes' Eve—Ah, bitter chill it was! 429
Stern Daughter of the Voice of God! 149
Stop, Christian passer-by!—Stop, child of God, 258
Strange fits of passion have I known, 108
Swiftly walk o'er the western wave, 391

The Assyrian came down like a wolf on the fold, 297
The awful Shadow of some unseen Power, 371
The flower that smiles to-day, 395
The Frost performs its secret ministry, 221

INDEX OF FIRST LINES OF POEMS

The harp that once through Tara's halls, 293
The sun descended in the west, 89
The sun is warm, the sky is clear, 375
The Village Life, and every care that reigns, 34
The wild winds weep, 85
The world is too much with us; late and soon, 161
The world's great age begins anew, 418
There be none of Beauty's daughters, 298
There is delight in singing, though none hear, 459
There was a roaring in the wind all night, 128
There was a time when meadow, grove, and stream, 154
Thou still unravished bride of quietness, 450
Three years she grew in sun and shower, 110
Thus, usually, when he was asked to sing, 356
Tiger, Tiger, burning bright, 95
'T is the last rose of summer, 293
'T is the middle of the night by the castle clock, 226
'T is time this heart should be unmoved, 369
Toll for the brave! 3
To Mercy, Pity, Peace, and Love, 88
To my ninth decade I have tottered on, 464
To one who has been long in city pent, 423

Unfathomable sea! whose waves are years, 392
Up! Up! my Friend, and quit your books, 102

Waken, lords and ladies gay, 276
Wee, modest, crimson tipped flow'r, 62
Wee, sleekit, cowrin, tim'rous beastie, 51
Well! If the Bard was weather-wise who made, 250
Well, they are gone, and here must I remain, 191
When chapman billies leave the street, 68
When I have fears that I may cease to be, 426
When the lamp is shattered, 420
Whether on Ida's shady brow, 85
While briers, an' woodbines budding green, 46
While the dawn on the mountains was misty and gray, 282
Who is the Happy Warrior? who is he, 151
Why weep ye by the tide, ladie? 283
Why, William on that old grey stone, 100
With fingers weary and worn, 468
With little here to do or see, 132

Ye banks, and braes, and streams around, 78
Ye Clouds! that far above me float and pause, 226
Ye flowery banks o' bonie Doon, 75
Ye mariners of England, 288

St. Mary's Seminary-Junior College